The Complete Book of
WATERCOLOUR

KESHAW KUMAR

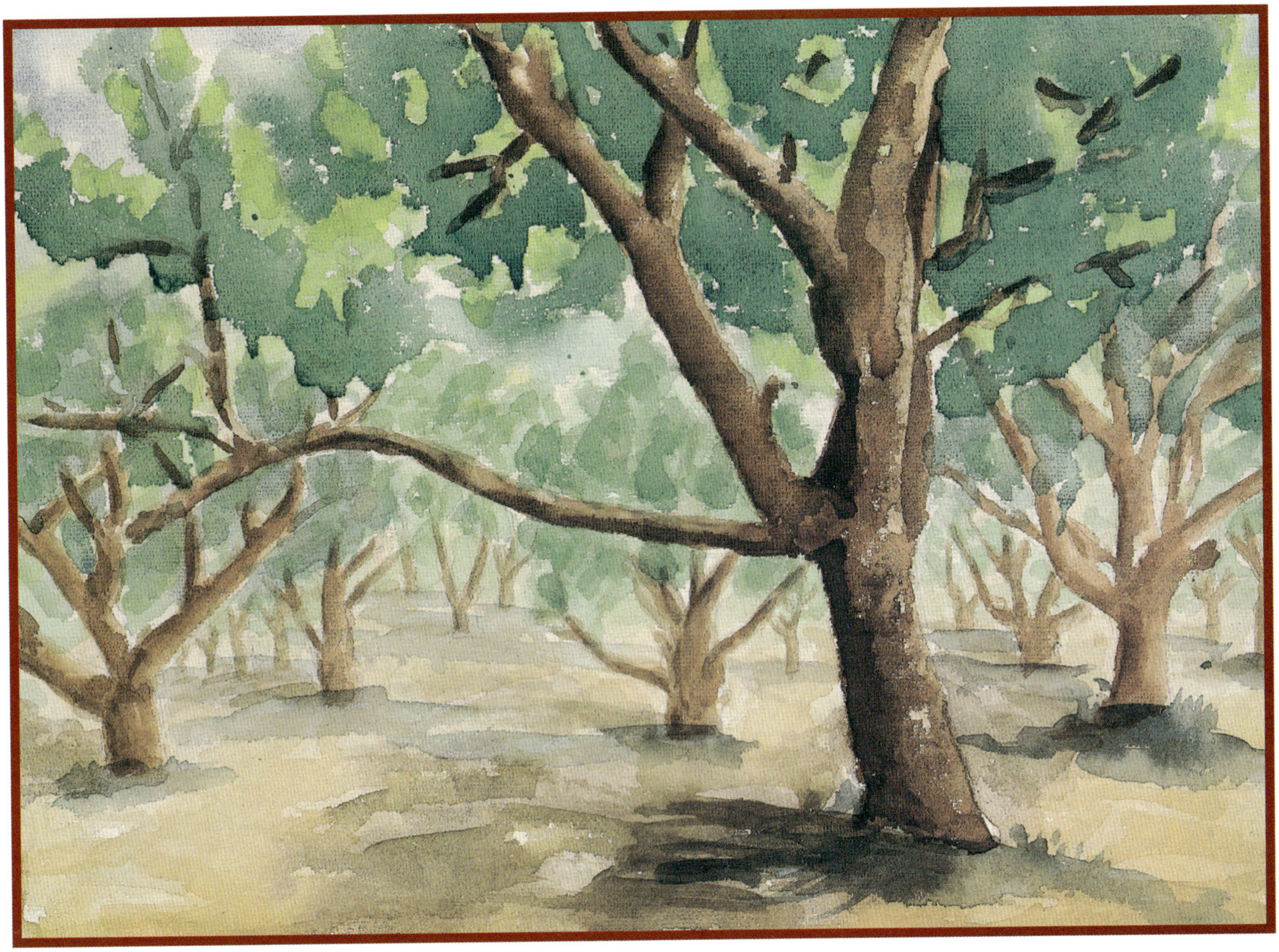

ADARSH
BOOKS

Forth Reprint -2012

THE COMPLETE BOOK OF WATERCOLOUR

By : Keshaw Kumar

ISBN 10 : 8187138793
ISBN 13 : 9788187138792 | **Hard Cover**

ISBN 10 : 8183630936
ISBN 13 : 9788183630931 | **Paper Back**

Published by :
Adarsh Books
New Delhi

Distributed by :
Adarsh Enterprises
4396/4,Tulsidas Street, Ansari Road,
Daryaganj, New Delhi - 110 002
Phone : 23246131, 23246132
Fax : 0091 1123246130
e-mail : adarshbooks@vsnl.com
website : adarshbooks.com

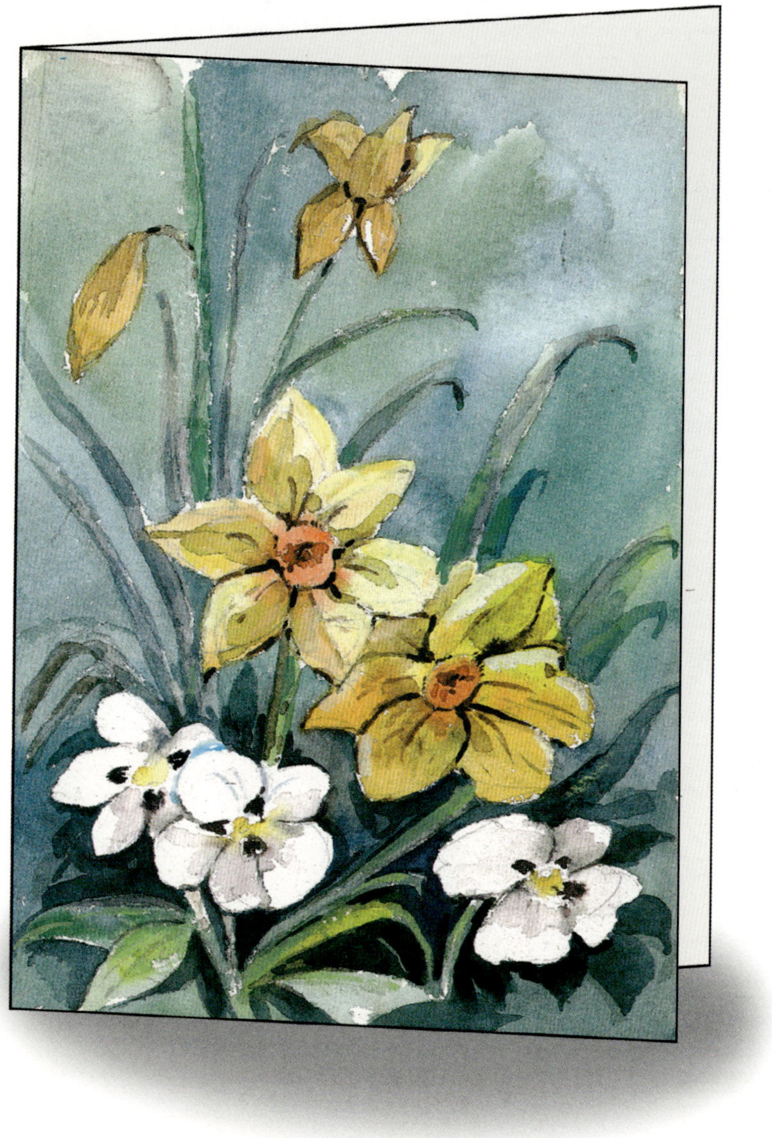

Printed at :
Swan Press, New Delhi

To My Brother
"Because I Inspired to him
and he is my Inspiration"

Contents

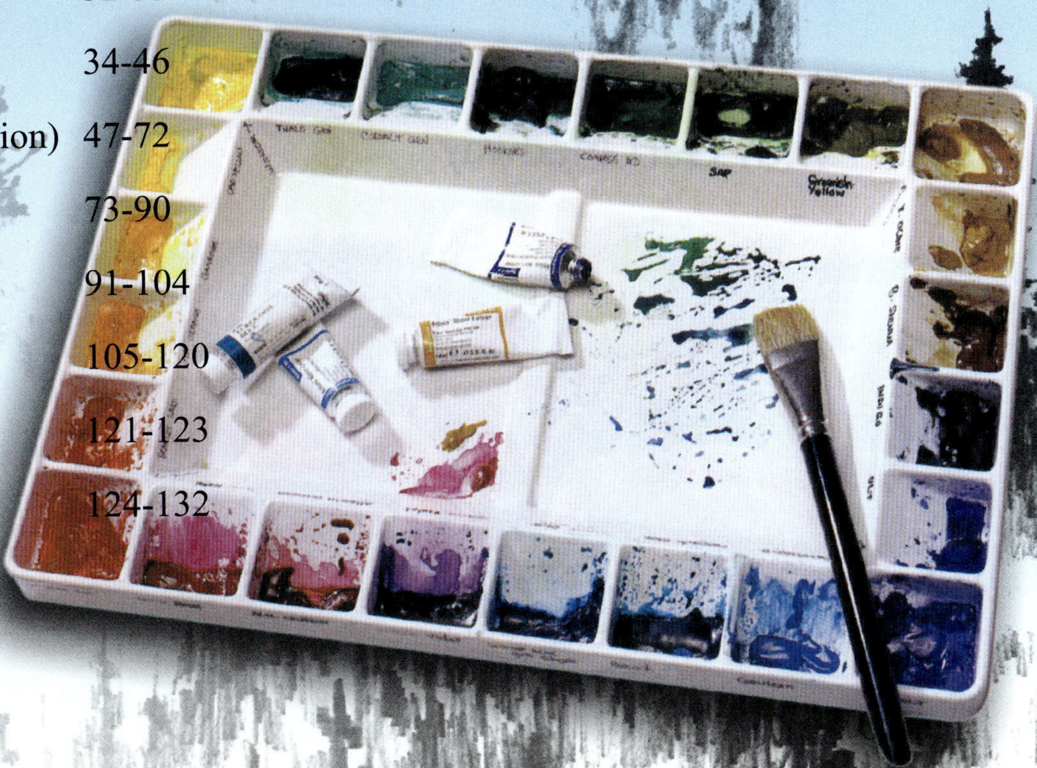

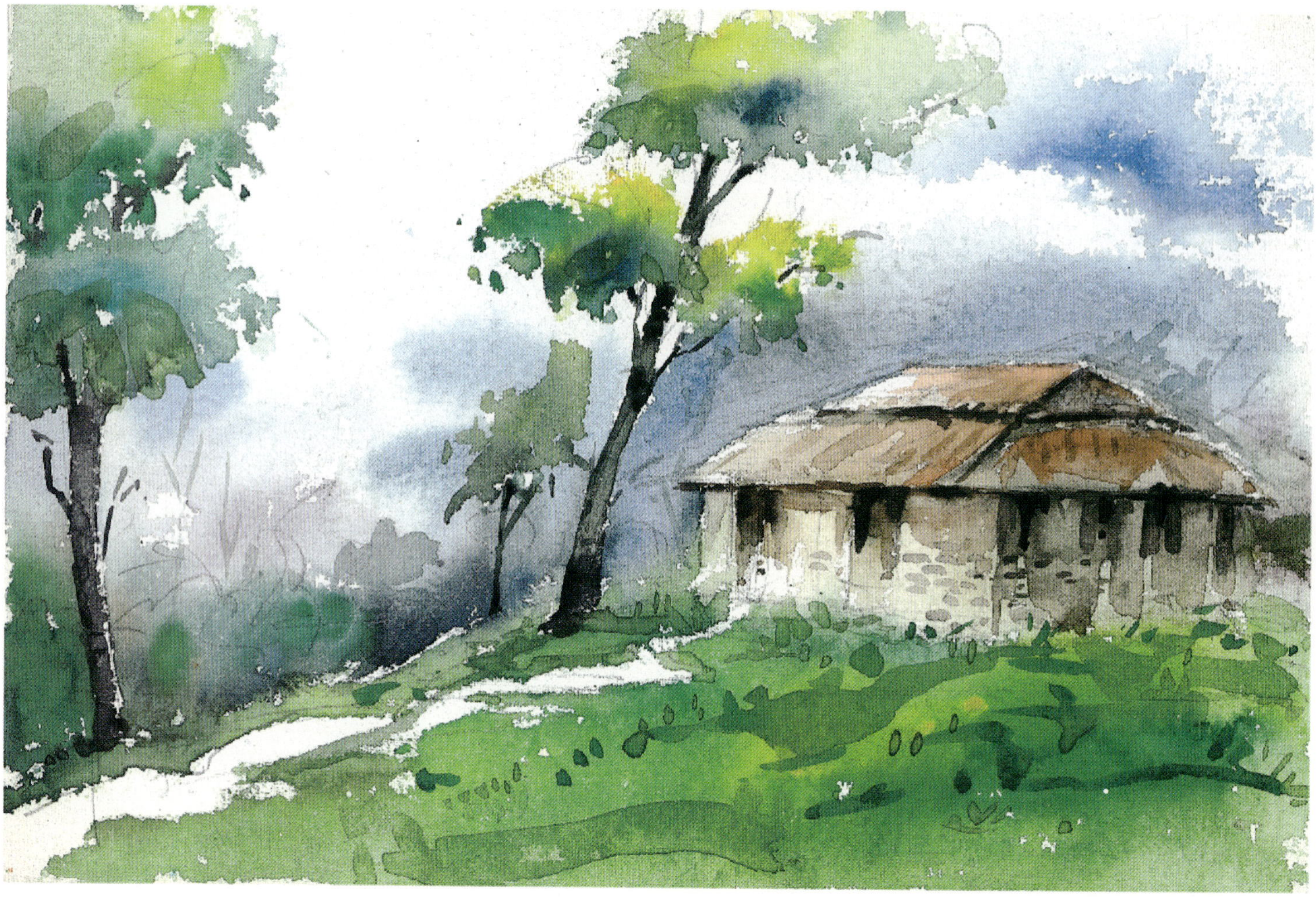

Introduction

Watercolour is the most popular painting medium, just as its name indicates, it is based on water. To get started with watercolour does not require a lot of materials. A little paint box, a brush and paper are enough. These items should be selected with great care. The secret of success with watercolour painting is to work with confidence. Once you learn to paint you will be delighted to find that very often the paint does much to the work for you. Sometimes the most interesting and beautiful effects are being achieved through an unexpected combination of colours and designs.

Doing watercolour is quite different from oil painting. Oils being an opaque medium, the applied colours form layers upon layers. If any colour scheme goes wrong, it is possible to correct it by recolouring just that particular patch. But there is absolutely no such chance in watercolours. If the previous colour is wrong and again applying another colour over it, both of them should mix giving a different colour. Quite unexpectedly, every colour is affected by the previously applied colour.

Materials and Equipment

The watercolourist does not require much in the way of materials. One requires only a few items – paper, burush and paint. It is only then that make use of to get desired and best possible results.

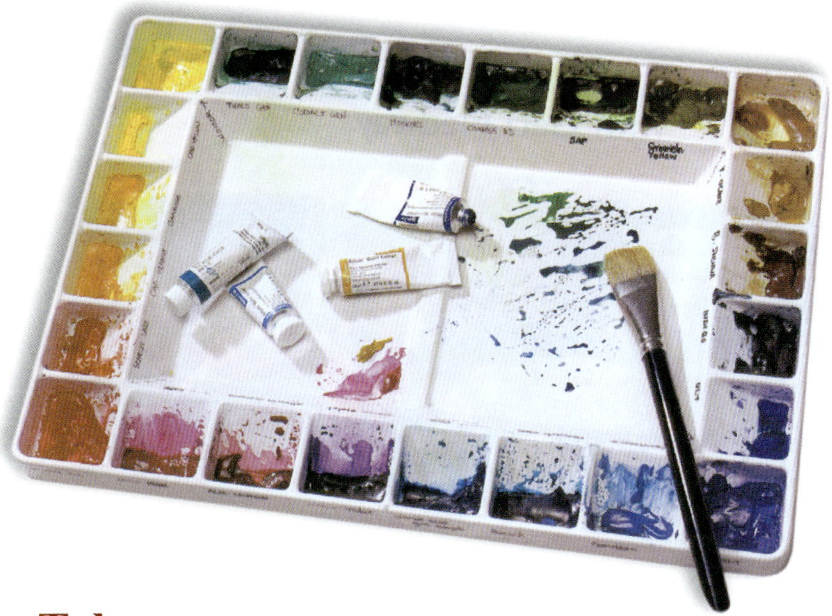

The Medium

Colours

Watercolour painting, just as its name indicates is based on water. Watercolour paints are sold in solid and liquid form.

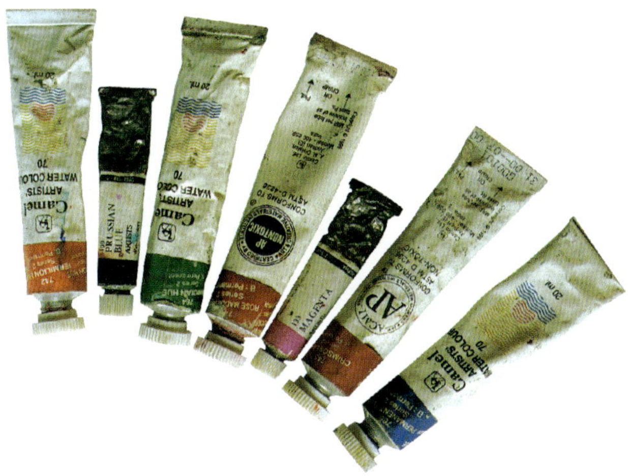

Tubes

Tube colour is richer than cake colour and is useful for creating large areas of wash quickly; simply squeeze the paint on to a palette and mix it with water. It is best to squeeze out only a few colour at a time, keeping them well apart so that there would have no unexpected mixing of colours if you use more water to mixing.

Cakes

These small blocks of semi-colours can be bought individually as well as in special paint boxes with slots to hold the cakes in the place and a lid that opens out to form a convenient mixing palette. But as this process yields colour in a small quantity, cakes are unsuitable for works requiring large washes. However, it is useful for outdoor work, as they are easily portable.

Brushes

With watercolour brushes it pays to buy the best one can afford. The better the brush, the better it performs and the longer it lasts. Cheap brushes do not perform well and wear out quickly.

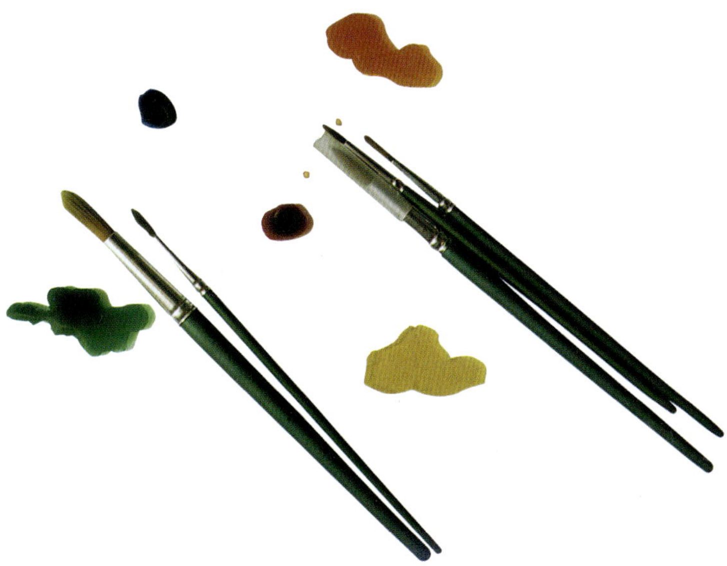

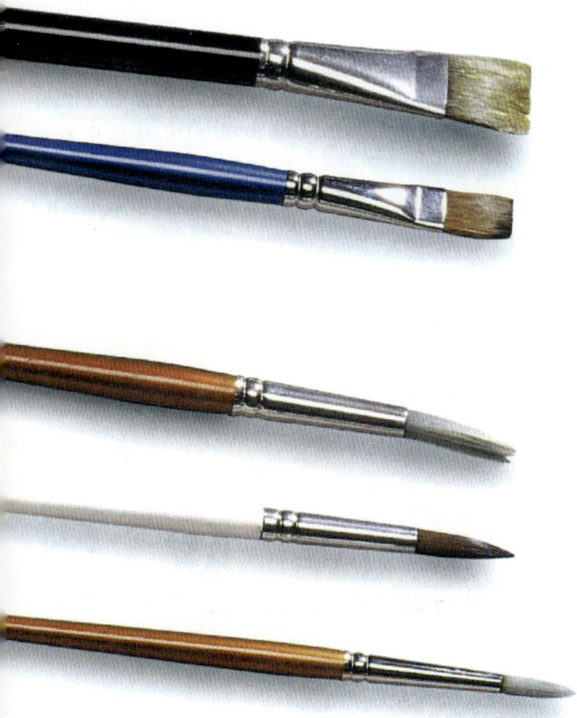

Sable Hair Brushes

These are the best choice for watercolour painting. They are expensive, but a pleasure to use and if they are properly cared for they will last a long time.

Synthetic Fibre Brushes

Synthetic fibre brushes are a popular alternative to sable because they cost a lot less and are still quite springy and responsive. However they don't hold the paint or last nearly as long. Also available are mixtures of synthetic and sable, which have good colour holding and pointing properties.

Round Brushes

These are bullet-shaped brushes that come to a fine point. This brush has slightly longer bristles, while the rest of the bristle part is roundish and with the tip you can paint fine details. The brushes are generally available from No. 000 to as large as No. 16.

Flat Brushes

Flat brushes are wide and square ended. They are ideal for spreading water rapidly over the paper to create a wash. The flat edge is useful for making clean-cut lines.

Paper

There is a wide selection of watercolour papers in the market, varying in texture, weight and quality — perhaps the most important in achieving the best results, as the results of these paints change with paper quality. Which type one would have to choose is depending on the personal painting style and how much one can afford.

Watercolour paper can be either handmade or machine made and this difference is reflected in the price. Handmade paper is the most suitable paper for watercolour. The best quality handmade paper is made from cotton rag instead of the usual wood pulp. Handmade papers are generally recognisable by their irregular surface and ragged edges. Machine made papers are the cheapest but some have a rather mechanical surface grain.

Paper Texture

The surface texture of paper is known as its grain or 'tooth'. There are three kinds of surface.

Hot-Pressed (HP) is smooth, with almost no 'tooth'. It is suitable for finely detailed work but most artists find its surface too slippery for watercolour.

Note : (Meaning is not hot pressed, and sometimes referred to as 'cold- pressed') H.P. has a semi rough surface equally good for vigorous wash and fine brush detail. This is the most popular type of surface for beginners.

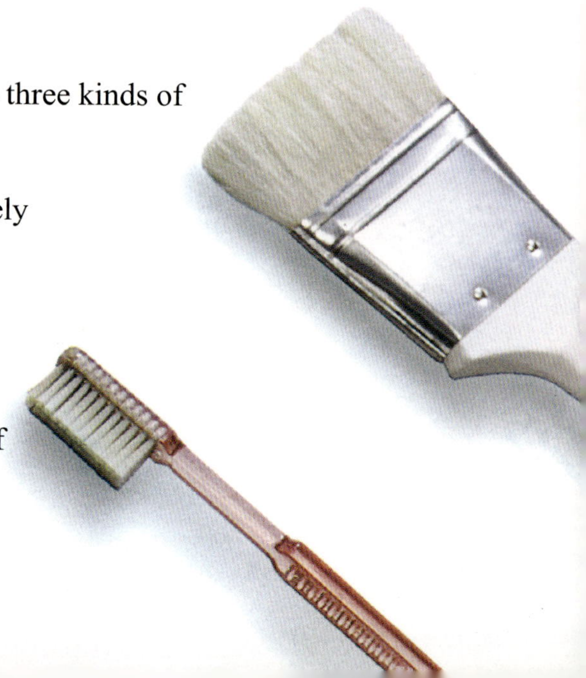

Watercolour Process

Wet-in-wet is one of the most beautiful and expressive techniques in watercolour painting. When colours are applied to a wet or damp surface they merge gently into each other and dry with soft, hazy quality. This is particularly effective in painting skies and water, producing it gentle gradations of tone that evoke the ever-changing quality of the light.

When painting in watercolour, it should have maintained that a brush stroke must be allowed to dry before applying another colour of tone.

In this topic deseribed the possibilities offered by applying or removing paint while the background is still wet. Make sure to mix plenty of paint. There is nothing more frustrating than running out of colour halfway through and having to stop to mix more.

Flat Wash

Watercolour paint is extremely sensitive to any alteration in the wetness of the surface. In order to paint this area, it is not necessary to wet the paper beforehand, but it is important that it be painted in a continuous manner to avoid possible break between the brush strokes.

Graded Wash

When the background is still wet, a clean and dry brush may be moved across the paper to remove some of the colour. The paper must be quite wet, but not to the extent that the paint itself runs. The procedure to remove paint is as follows:

With a dry brush, first remove all the colours. Then wash the brush in clean water, squeeze it out, and repeat the process. The more often a brush is passed across an area of the paper, the more the wet background it becomes, like the white of the paper.

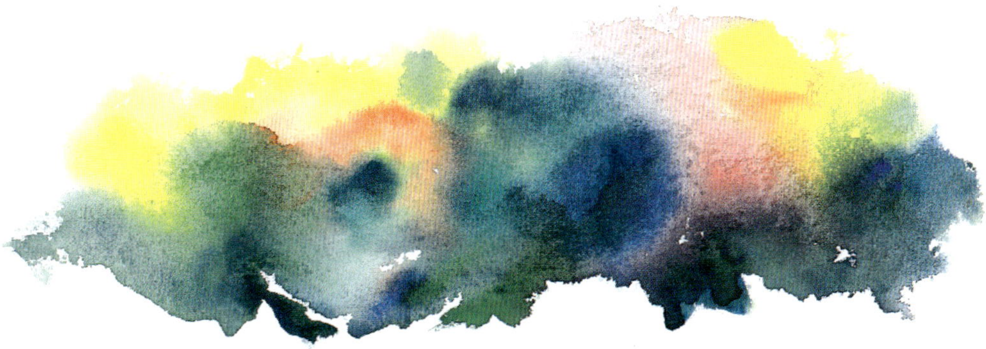

Wet-in-Wet Wash

This means that the second wash is added while the first one is still wet. To catch the wetness of the earlier wash in time, a lot of experience is needed. This exercise is very simple but opens up many options for the work you have seen in previous sessions.

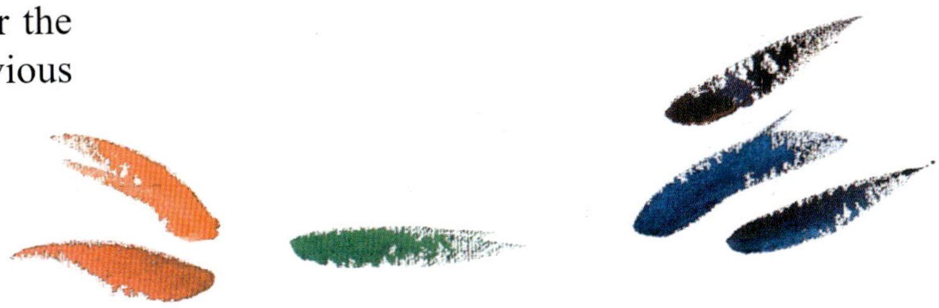

Stretching Watercolour Paper

Except the 300 lbs weight paper, all other papers crumple up with the nearest touch of water, which makes painting on them difficult. So the following methods are used to stretch paper and get a plain surface:

1. Place the paper on a wooden support and wet with a sponge.

2. Once the paper is soaked, apply the waterproof adhesive tape round the edges. Once the paper has dried, it is stretched as if it were the skin of a drum. Once you have finished painting, cut round it with a knife. Leave the gummed paper stripe in place until the painting is completed and dry.

Palettes

Watercolour palettes come in a range of shapes and sizes, and are made of either ceramic, enamelled metal or plastic. They are always white, which allows one to see the true colour of a wash with minimum distortion and they all have recesses or wells that allow you to mix the paint with generous amounts of water.

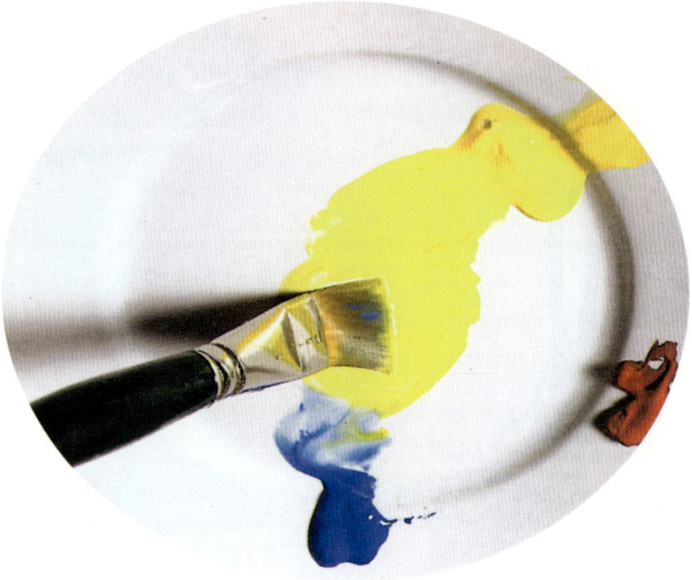

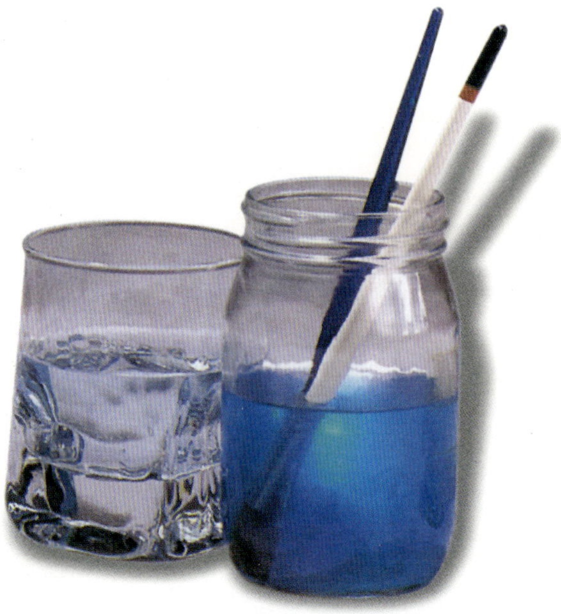

Colour Range

The Colour Wheel

The arrangement of colours on the colour wheel helps the artist understand the relationship between the colours and the effect they have on one another when used together. The various classifications such as secondary colours obtained by mixing primary colours. Complementary colours as well as warm and cool colours can be appreciated by just a glance.

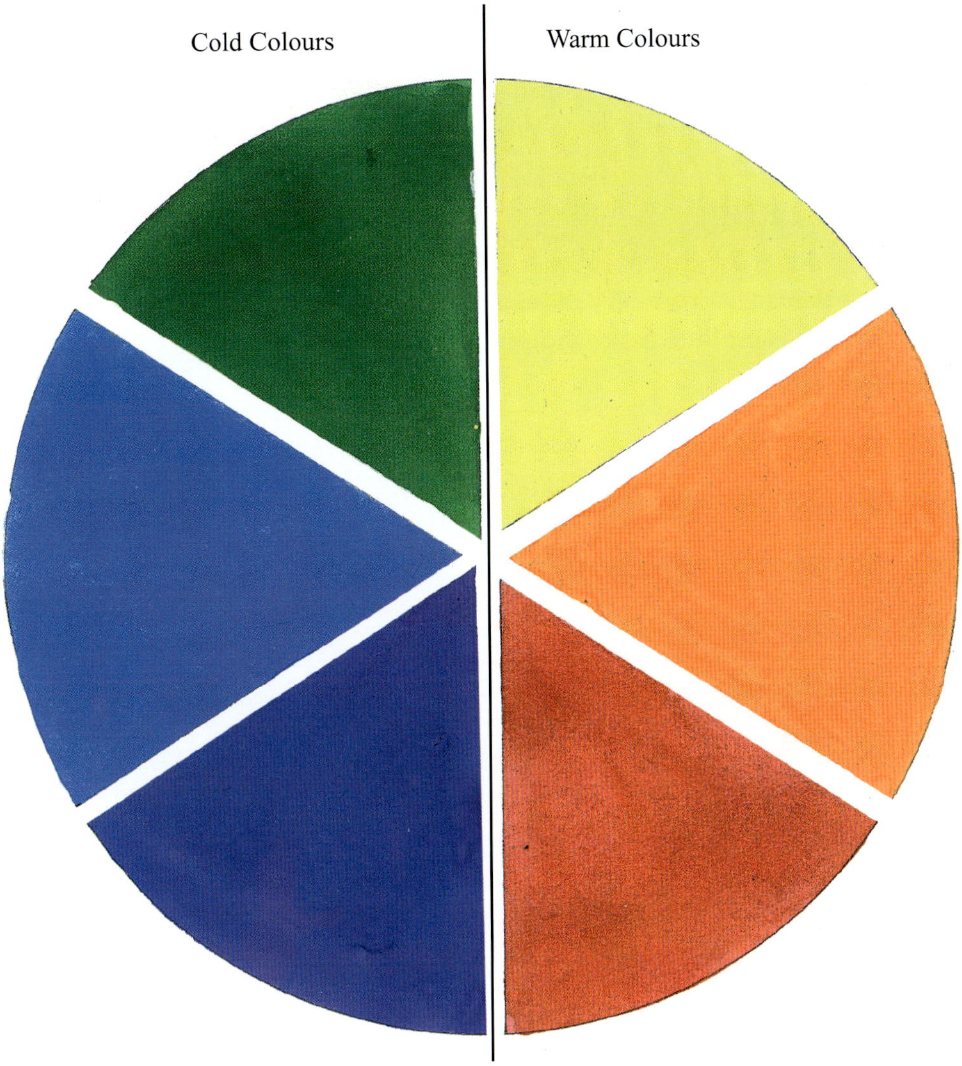

The Primary Colours

Whatever other colours are being decided to include in a paintbox, there should have three essential colours. These are the primary colours — Red, Yellow and Blue because they cannot be produced from mixtures of other colours.

The Secondary Colours

The secondary colours are produced by mixing primary colours.

1. Red and yellow make orange.
2. Blue and yellow make green.
3. Red and blue make purple.

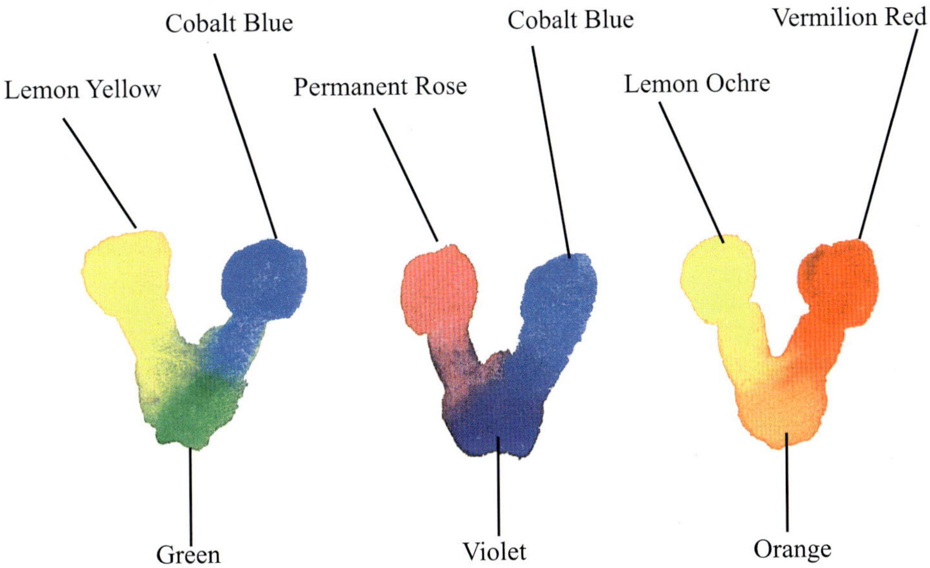

The Complementary Colours

Any two colours diagonally opposite each other on the colour wheel are called complementary colours. For example, blue is the complementary of orange, red of green and yellow of violet. When placed side by side, two complementary colours have a powerful effect on each other. A small patch of red in a large area of green can make both the red and green look that much brighter. Similarly blue appears more vibrant with orange nearby. These complementary colours, when used carefully in paintings, some dramatic results can be achieved.

The cool range

Blue, green and violet are cool colours. The cool range of colours begins as a mix of yellow and cyan makes green, while red and blue make violet.

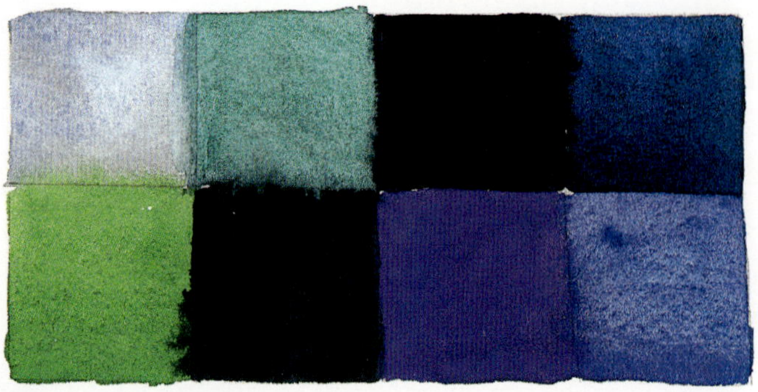

Ideas for cool colour schemes

- Snowy winter scenes
- Dew kissed morning landscapes
- Cloudy scenes
- Happy playful scenes
- Peaceful night

The warm range

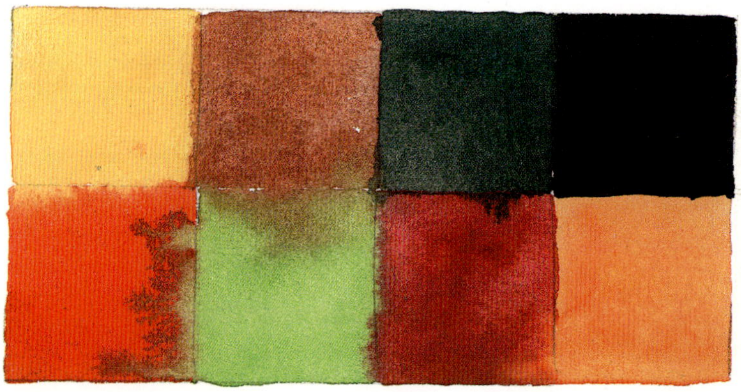

Red, yellow and orange are warm colours. The colours excite the mind. The two primary colours red and yellow make warm orange colour.

Subtle tones once you have tried mixing paint in different quantities, you can create a rainbow of subtle shade. Start with the primary and secondary colours, try them in various amounts and with more or less water depending on how light you want your washes to be. A drop of blue added to yellow with a drop of red to make a lovely autumn brown.

- Hot and sunny landscapes
- Sunrise scenes
- Passionate, fiery sunset
- Bustling marketplaces
- Bold advertisements and signs

Ideas for Warm colour schemes

Landscape's Composition

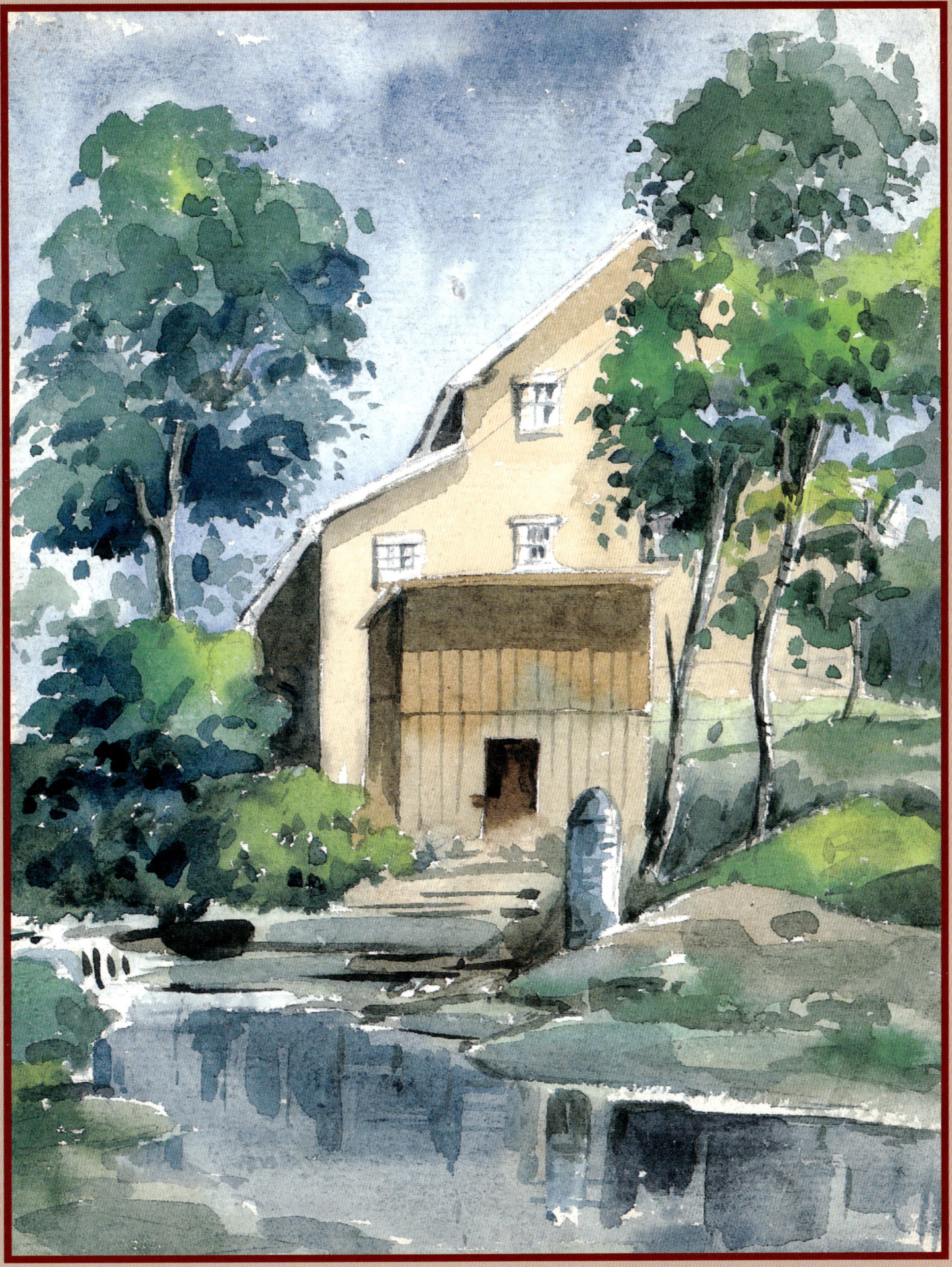

Landscape

When the surface is wet, the paint spreads. On a dry surface, the brushstroke can be controlled. The two techniques facilitate the realisation of all kinds of landscape. Although what is important is to use the correct technique at the right time and place. If the two techniques are used together with certain ability, this can pay dividends for the landscape painted, or trees reflections and atmosphere in the background of the picture.

Watercolour on Dry and Wet Backgrounds

Trees seem such complicated subjects with branches, thousands of leaves, different bark and so on. But using the broad impressionistic approach is quick and effective right way to start with yellow and little blue for a spring green. More blue will give the darker, softer green of midsummer, add a little red for the brown of autumn foliage.

Dry the brush with a bit of cloth or the fingers of your hand. Take thick colour on the brush, if you find you are too slow and paint has dried give a stroke on the background.

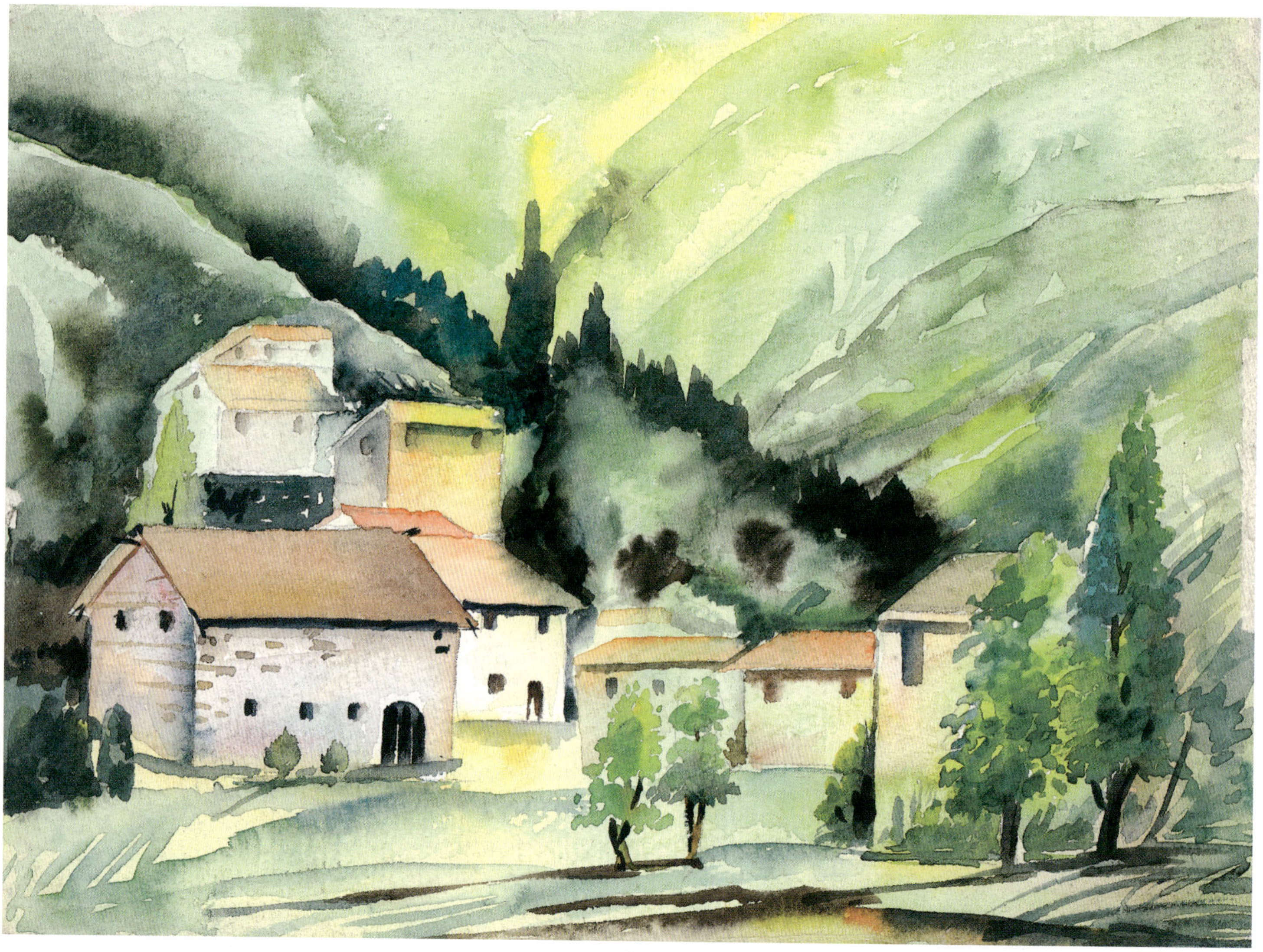

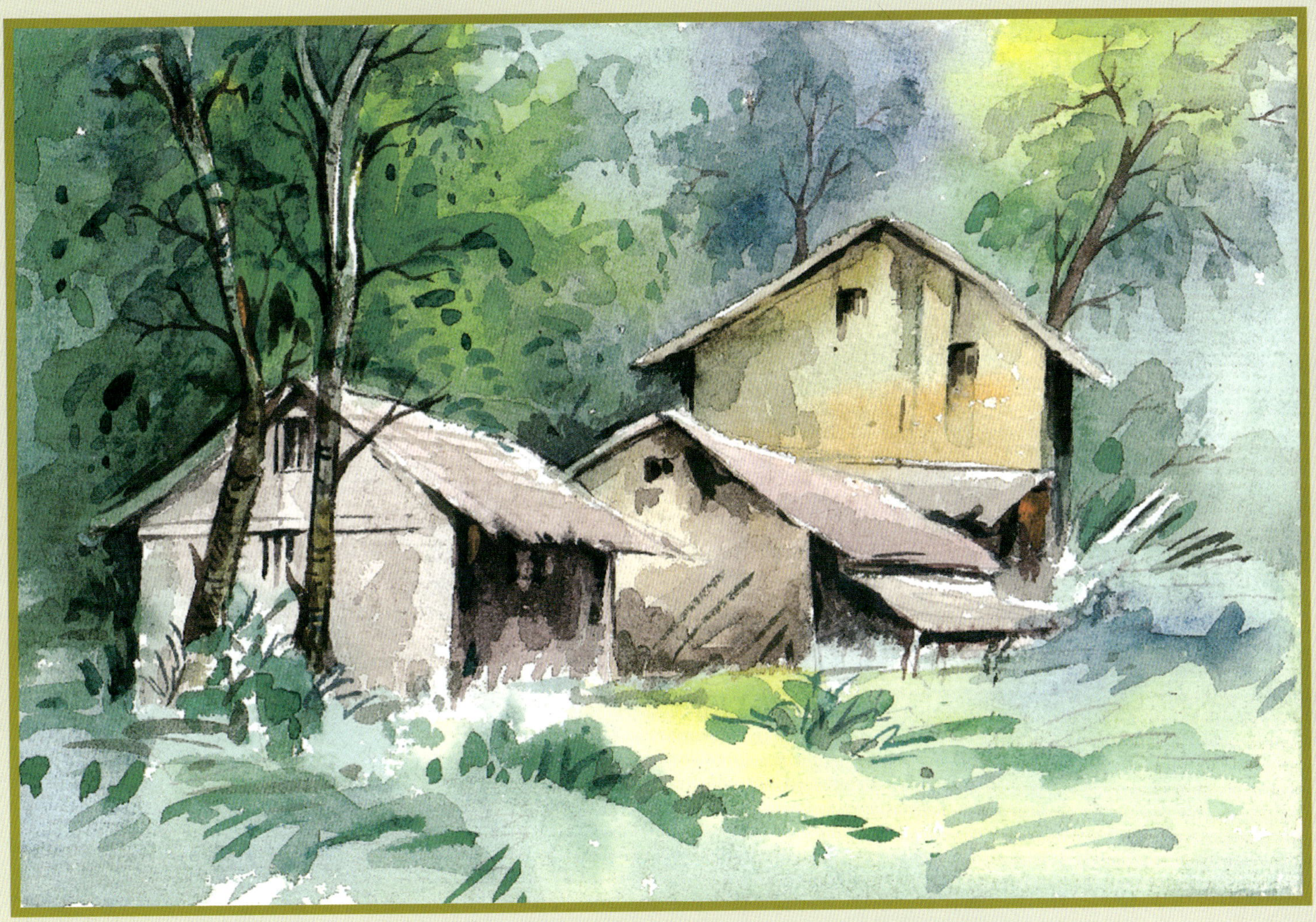

Harmony of Colours (Step by Step)

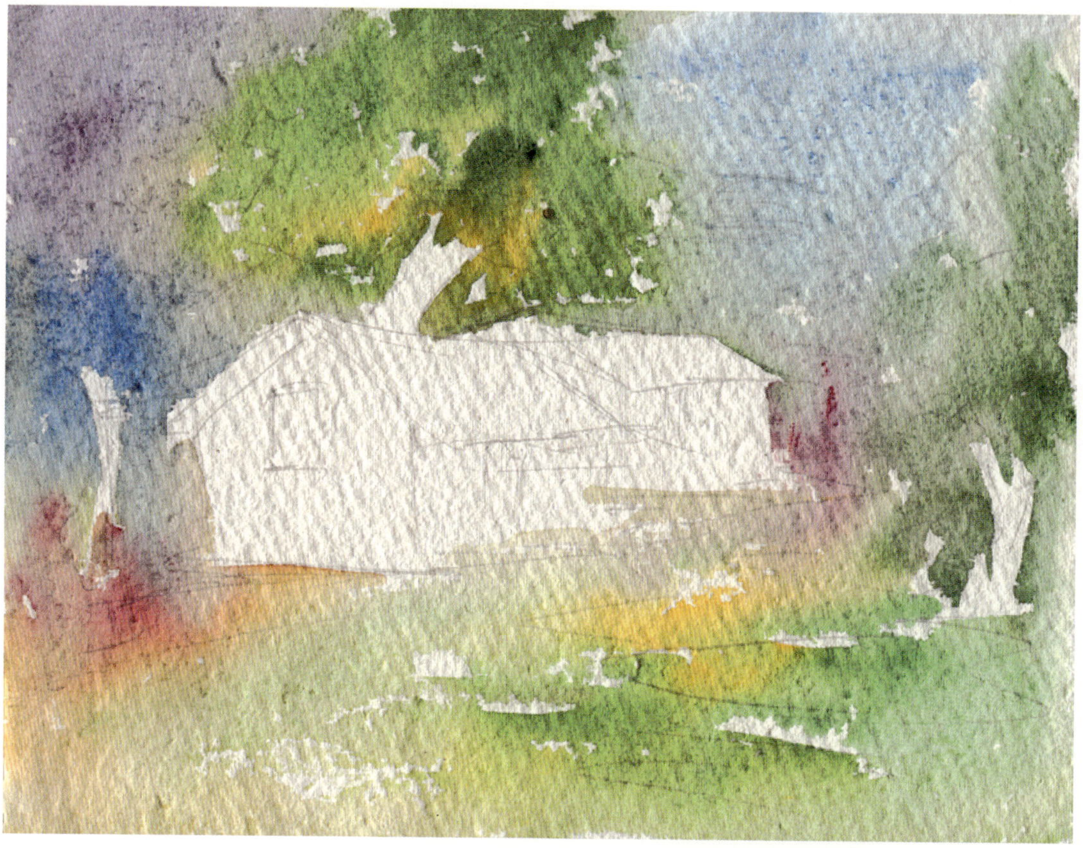

After completing a light and sharp line drawing, wet the paper. While the paper was damp, we can release Sap Green and Gamboge on the trees, Cobalt Blue and a little touch of Crimson on the sky. Wherever appropriate, it should be released Yellow and a tinge of light Sap Green on the ground.

Care was however taken to keep the identity of trees while applying a little touch of Sap Green on it. Distant trees were coloured dull with Cobalt Blue patches, whereas the houses' roofs were depicted by Scarlet and a tinge of Orange. Few shades of Burnt Umber to identify the doors and windows clearly were used. Sap Green was used for the ground to give it a more realistic look.

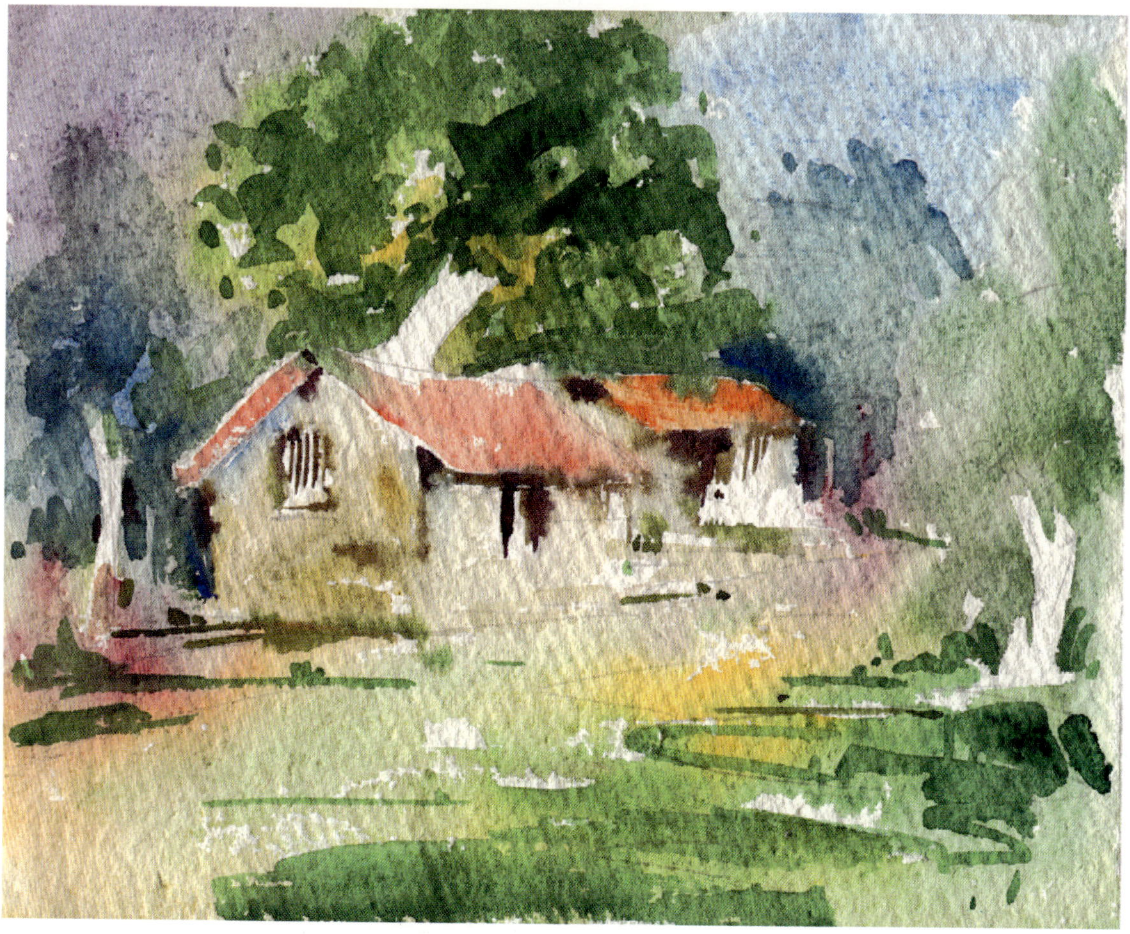

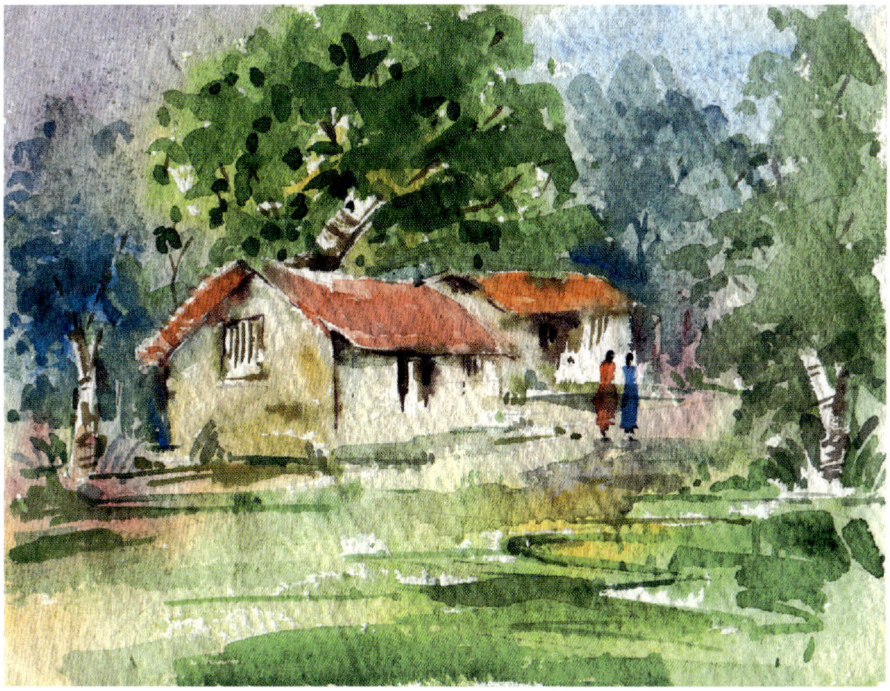

Some small patches of Sap Green indicate the trees clearly and give it a new look. A shade of Cobalt Blue was used for the small trees. The use of Cobalt Blue gave a surprise effect to the painting. Sap Green strokes depict the distant trees. Few strokes of Burnt Sienna are flown on the tree's stems. Scarlet has been used and fainter tinges of Orange on the houses' roofs. A little darkened shade of Sap Green prevails on the ground. Continuous small details with Scarlet were too added to it which gave it an appropriate look. The human figures were highlighted by Scarlet and Cobalt Blue, and their heads with black.

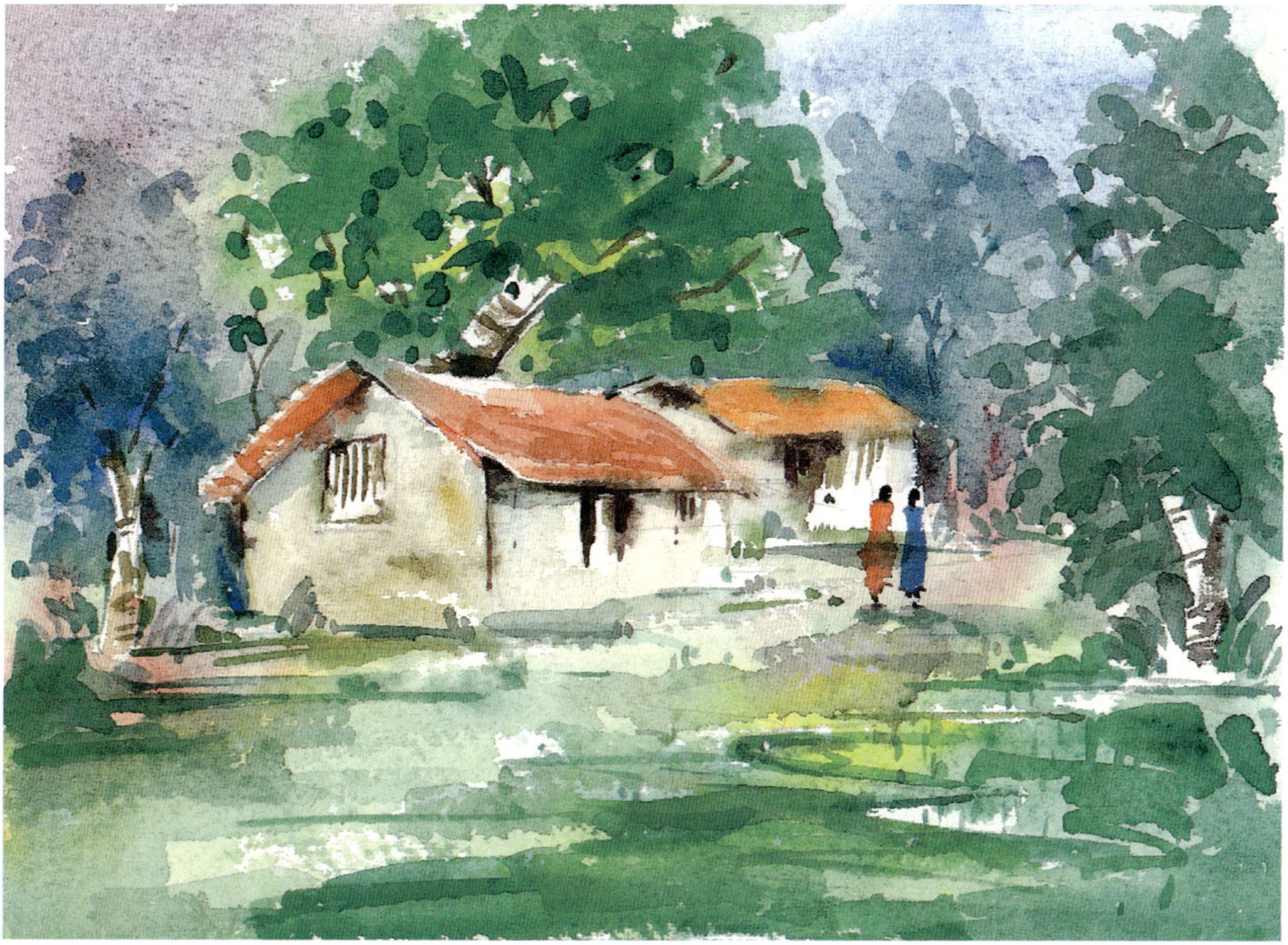

Some shimmed shades of Scarlet were released around the left tree but at the lower part. The Sap Green tones not only create a visual impact of distance of the ground, but also of lightly wet grass.

Picturesque

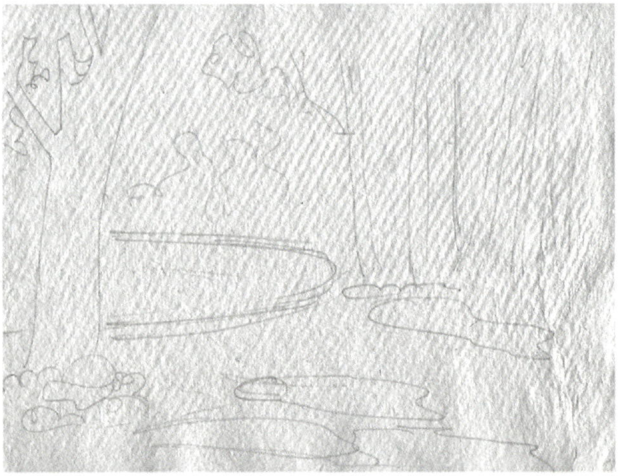

Here as it is depicted, a raw sketch of a natural scenery on handmade paper giving a typical expression.

After sketching, slightly wet the paper with brush and released a thick mixture of Burnt Umber and Sap Green on the bigger tree. Vermilion with little Sap Green was mixed to represent the tree's leaves.

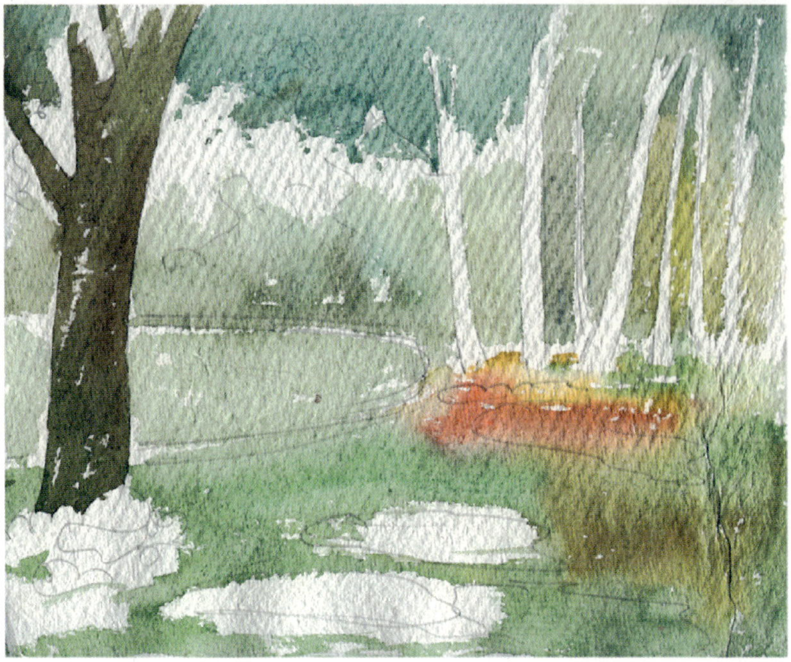

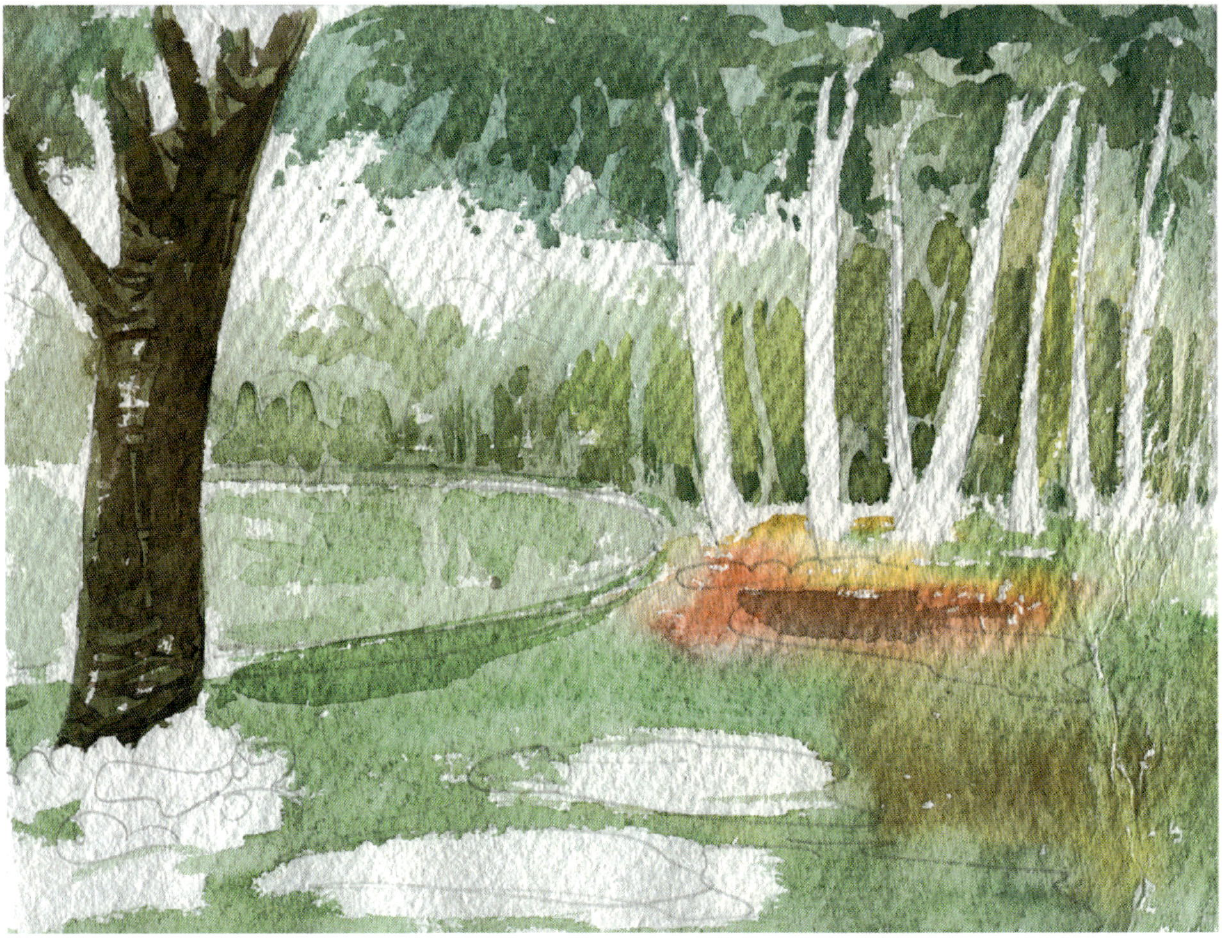

For minute details, Burnt Umber patches were applied on the tree's stem. To depict the copious of trees, light shades of Sap Green have used to give an effect of distance of trees. and applied various shades of Sap Green on the ground and topped it with little Scarlet.

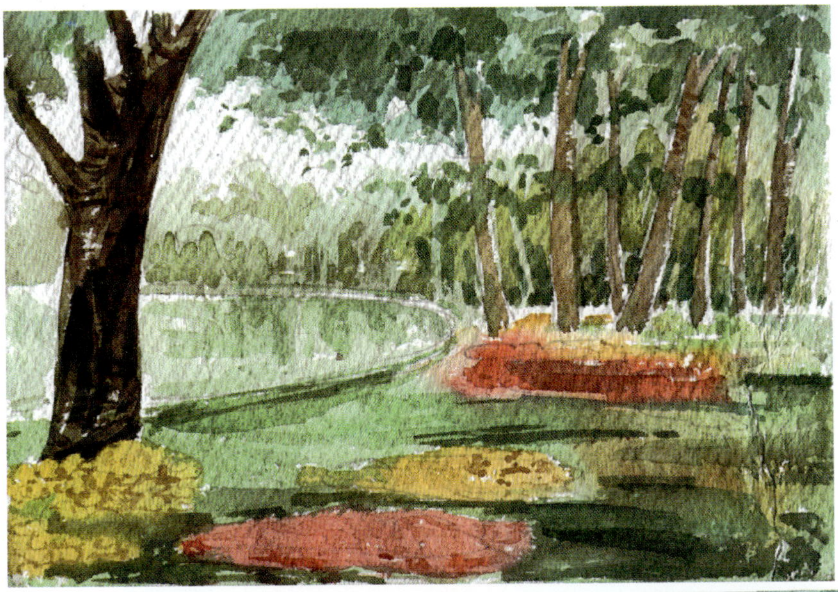

The distant tree's stems were coloured with Burnt Umber and a tinge of Sap Green. To give the natural effect of flowers on the lighter portions of the ground, Gamboge with a slight touch of Scarlet was flown on it. Sap Green patches applied behind the bigger tree bring out the reflection of water.

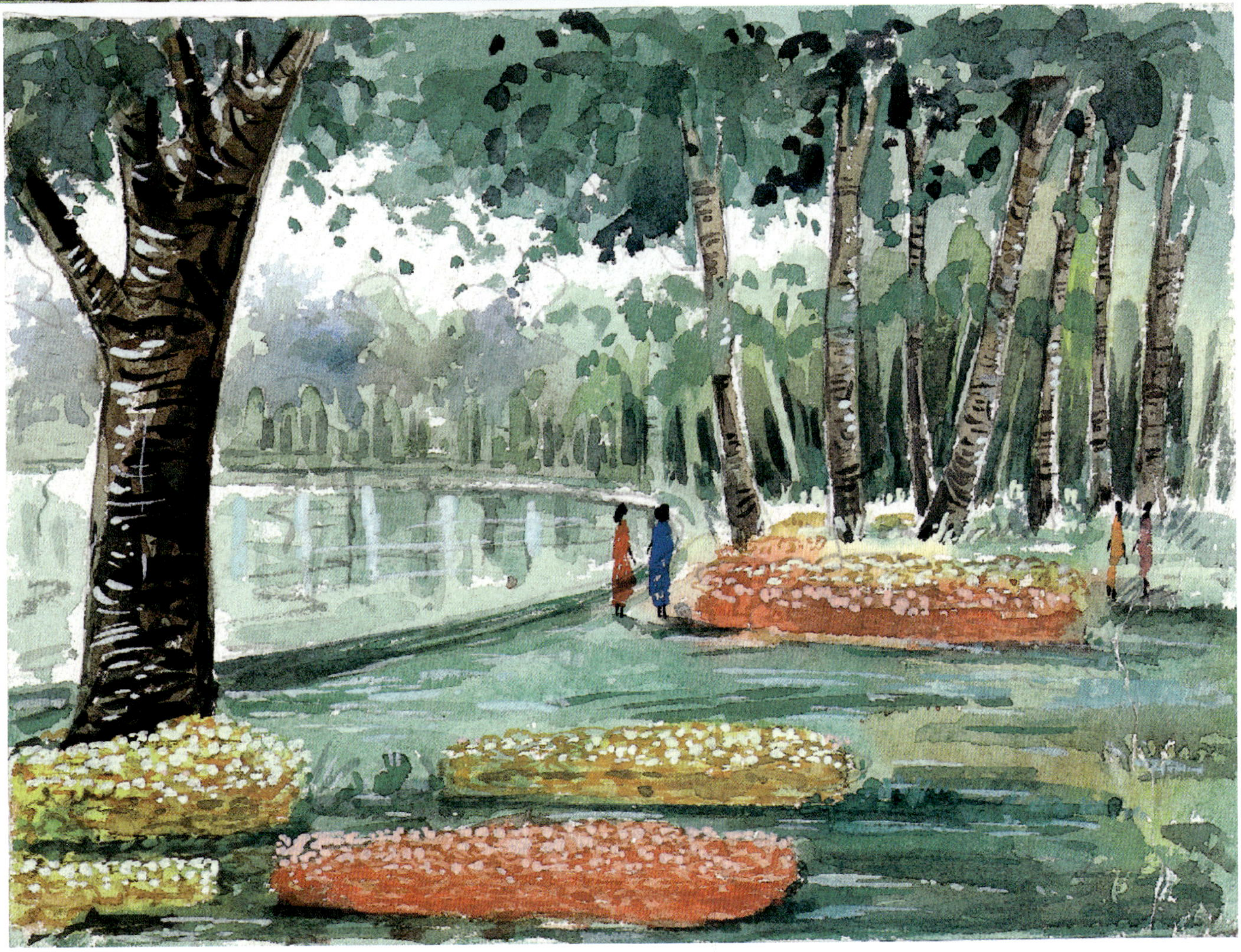

A final touch of Sap Green and Vermilion brings out the effect of the tree leaves as if from a distance. In comparison to these trees, the other more distant trees were given prominence by Cobalt Blue and a slight touch of Sap Green. Dark tones were applied on the trees near the more distant trees. Some minute patches of Burnt Umber and White applied on the stems create a wonderful scene. Small patches of Scarlet and White were added to give the effect of scattered flowers. A proportionate mixture of Sap Green and White highlights the ground. A fainter tinge of Burnt Umber and little White were spread on the stem of the bigger tree. Sap Green flown on the leaves and a mixture of Yellow-Scarlet tinged with a touch of White make the flowers look more attractive and beautiful. Few strokes of Scarlet and Cobalt Blue give the clear effect of one man, whereas Orange and little touch of Crimson identify the second man.

Waterfall

As sketches are the foremost part in paintings, it should be drawn in such a way, that each and every sketch should look identical. After a light line drawing, and damp the paper the excess water was dripped.

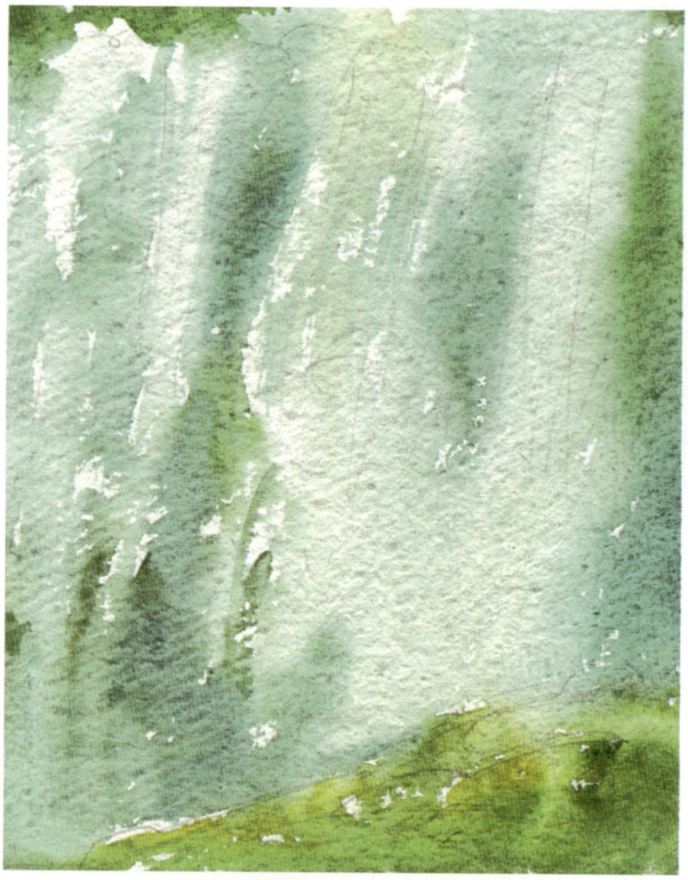

Leaving the ground white, flew a Sap Green and little touch of Gamboge on the damp paper. Light touches of Cobalt Blue were flown at some places where they looked appropriate.

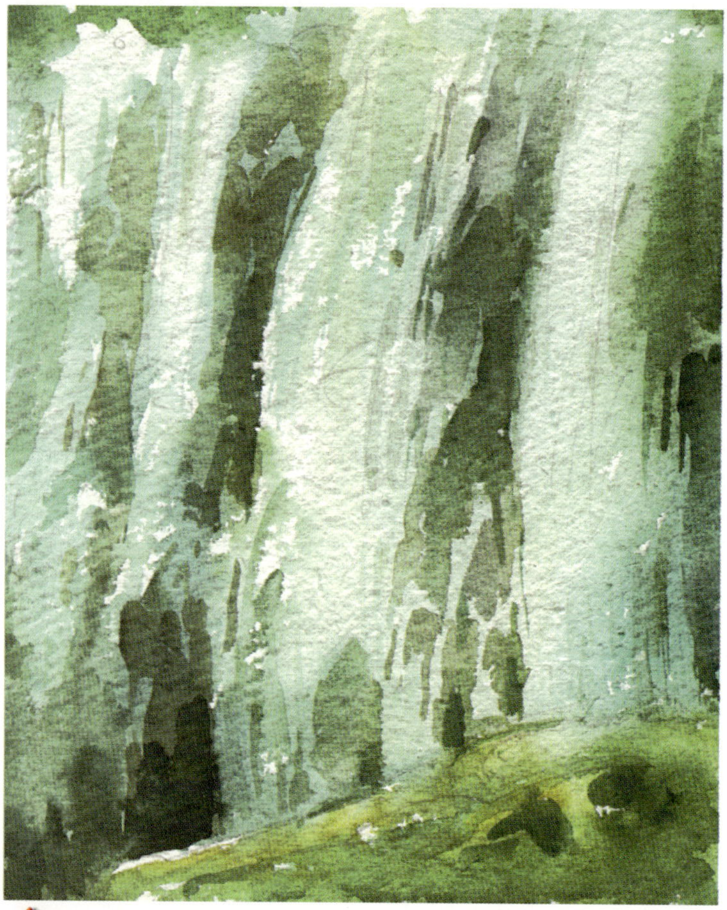

The Sap Green patches not only highlights the waterfall but also gives it a stupendous and attractive view. Wherever needed, darker tone was applied.

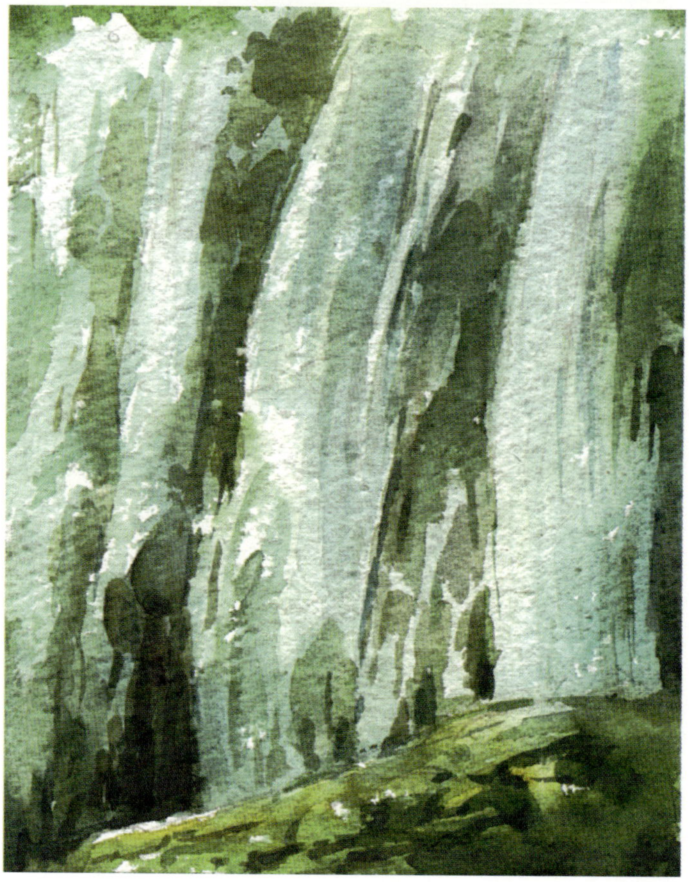

A dark tone of Sap Green was applied in such a way, that it gave the clear effect of falling water. Gamboge, Sap Green and little touch of Vermilion were used to highlight the ground.

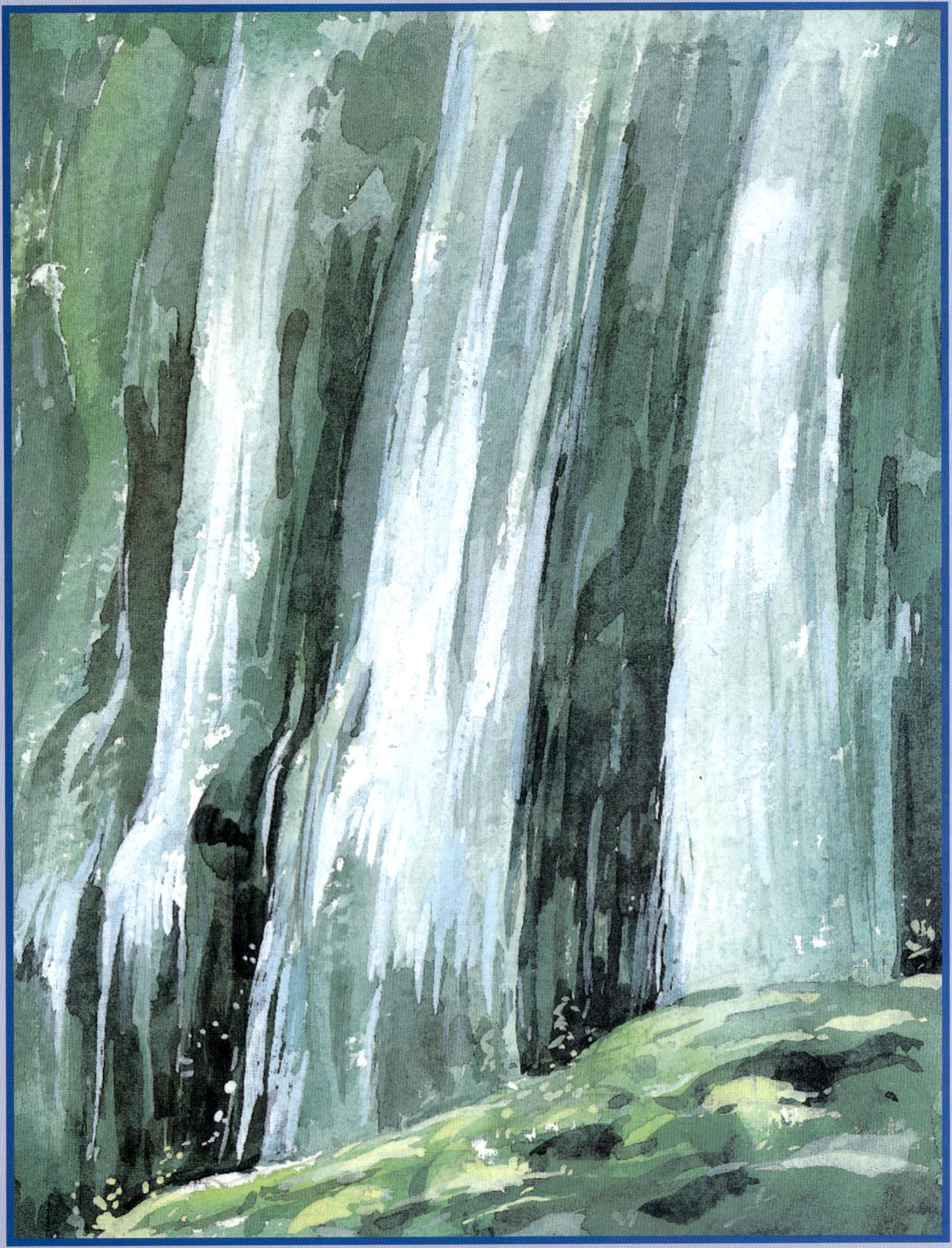

Leaving the water untouched, a dark tone of Sap Green has been released. Sap Green used with some dull patches of Vermilion for the ground. To give the proper effect of falling water, Poster White colour has been used wherever required. While depicting the natural ethereal quality of the ground, Gamboge and Poster White have been applied. A mixture of Sap Green and Poster White gave a distant and splendid look.

Poise Light and Shade

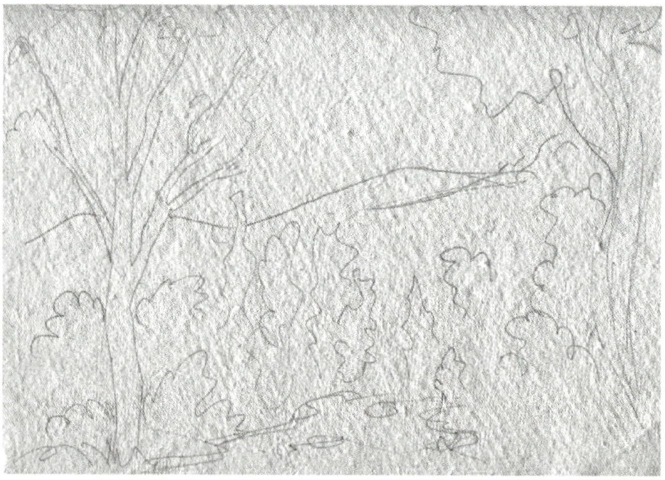

Special care should always be taken while drawing a sharp and light line for any painting. After completing the sketch, a first wash was applied on the cloudless sky.

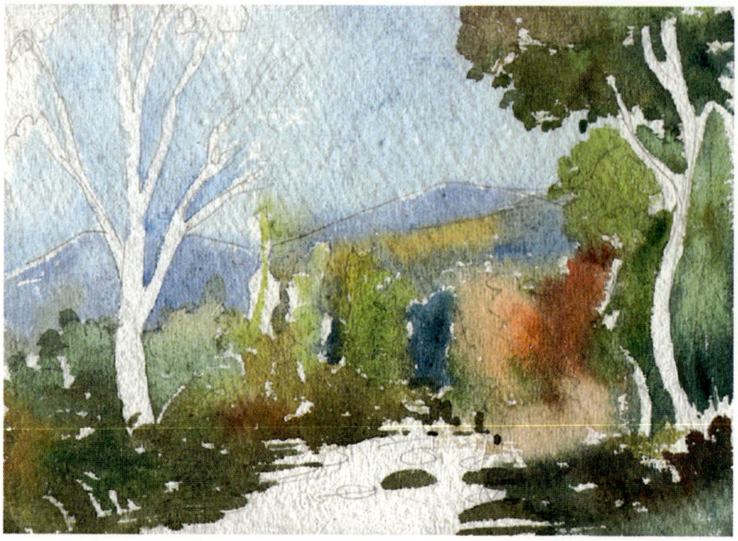

Cobalt Blue was released on the sky as well as on the mountains. To bring out the difference between the two, a slightly dark tone was released on the upper portions of the mountains and light patches of Gamboge was flown at the lower portions. Sap Green and Scarlet were flown with water to give it a natural look. Leaving the first tree untouched, the artist could release Sap Green hue on the second tree. Retaining some portion of ground White, the artist flew a mixture of Burnt Umber and Sap Green wherever required.

One prevailed Yellow Ochre and a light touch of Sap Green on the first tree, whereas a proper combination of Burnt Umber and Sap Green for the second tree.

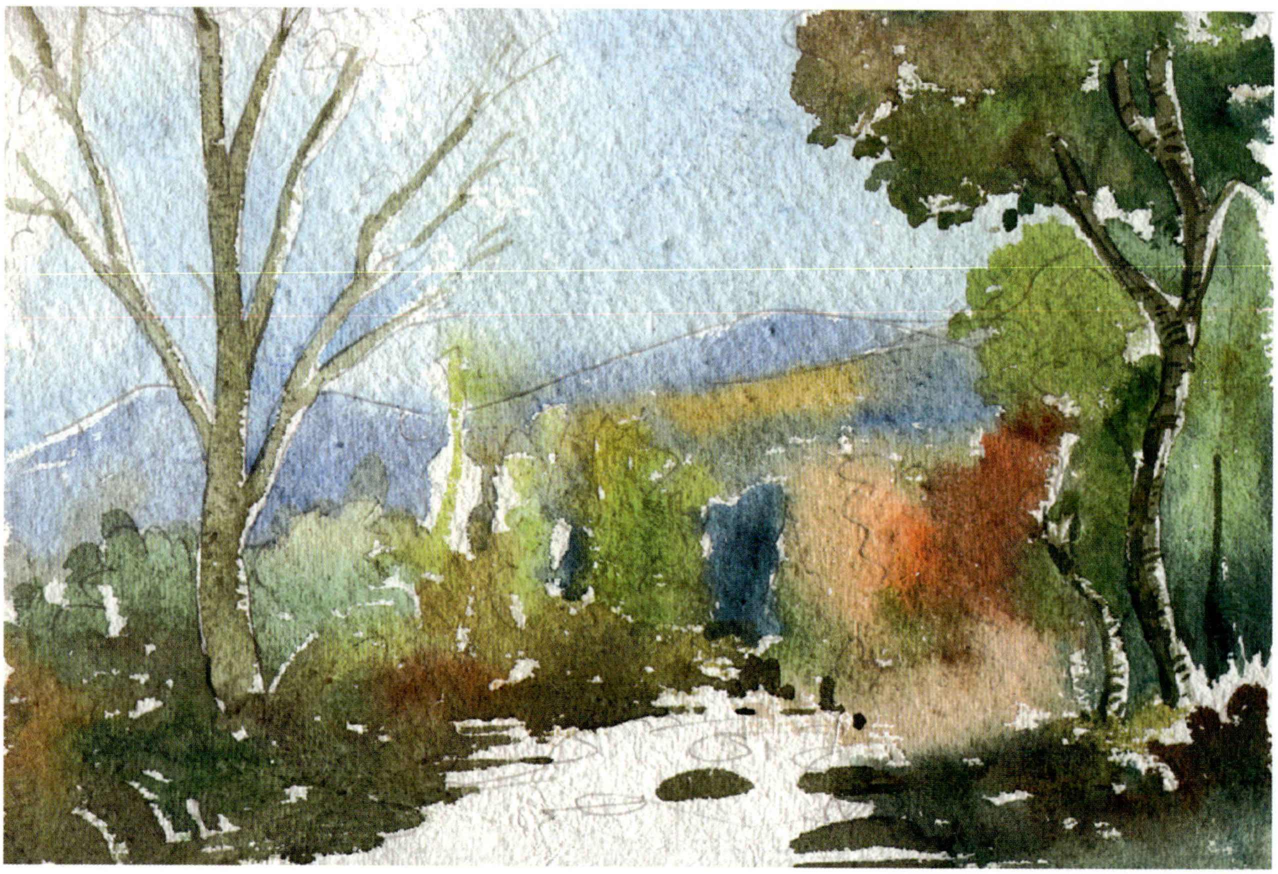

While colouring the first tree, Sap Green patches were mixed with Cobalt Blue whereas for the stem the artist used Burnt Umber. Smaller trees were treated with Sap Green and a dimmed patch of Prussian Blue. The combination of Sap Green and white strokes in between on the ground created an attractive background. The choice of Sap Green and Prussian Blue for the second tree highlighted the landscape.

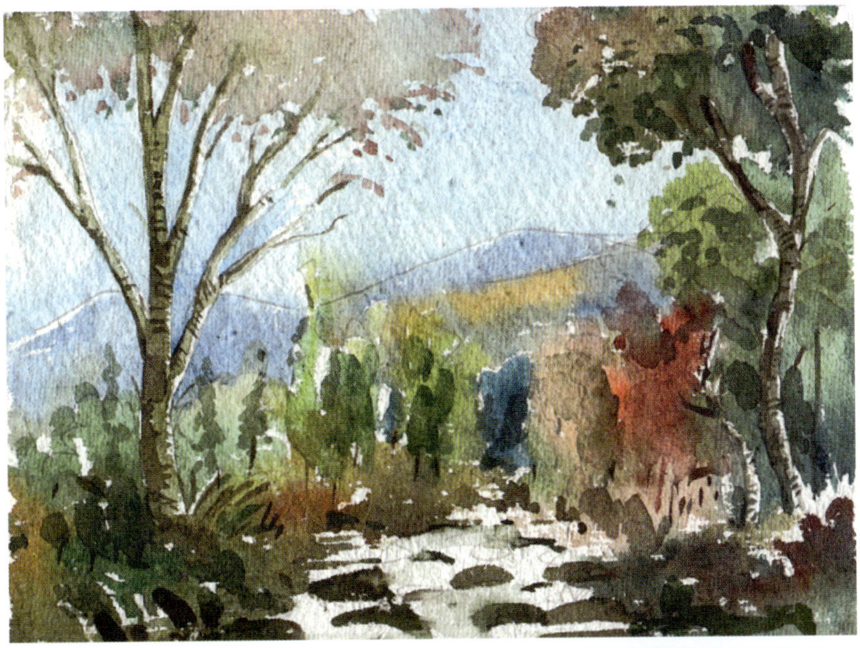

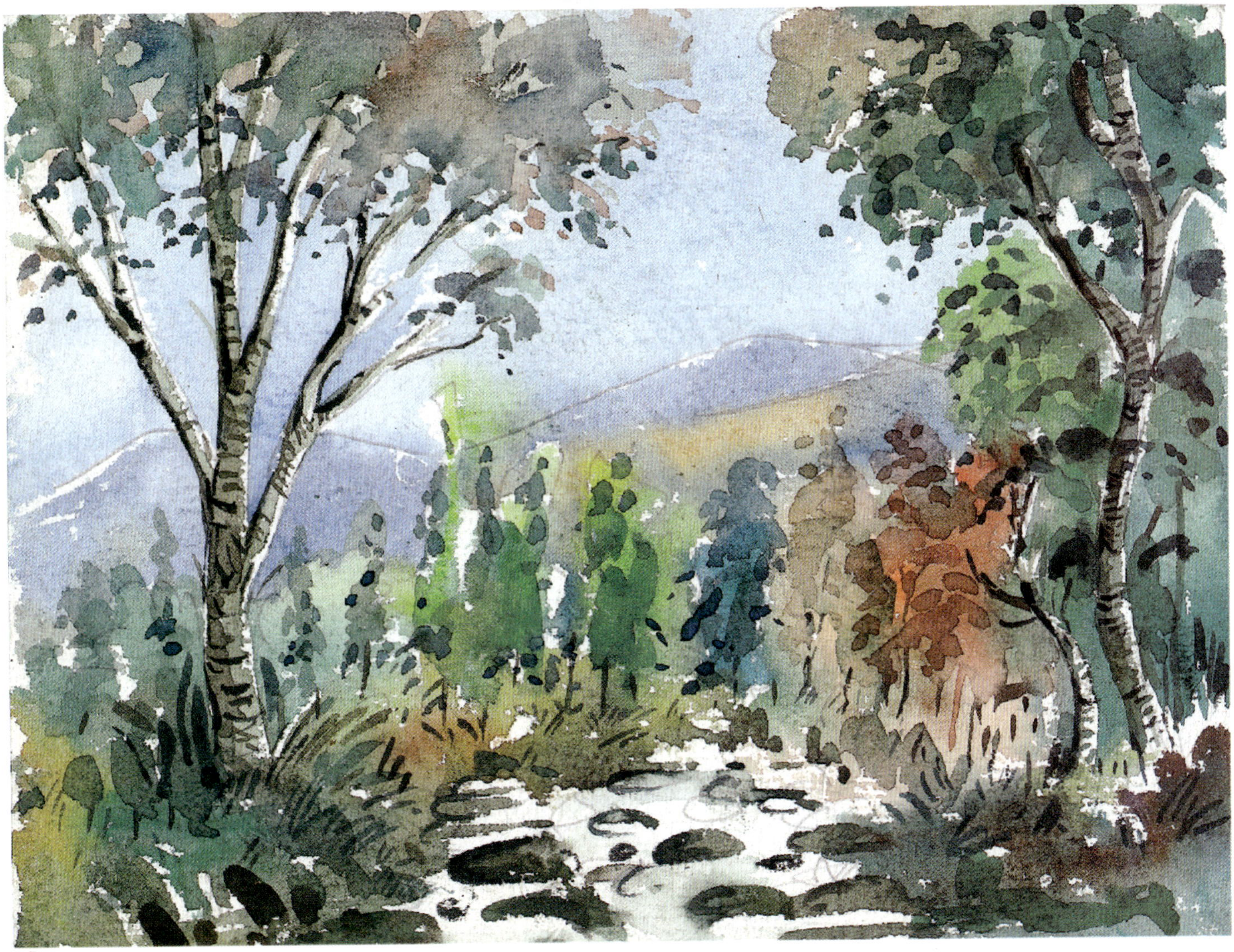

Suggestive strokes of Sap Green hue was applied on the right tree. To bring out the peculiar textures on the stem, the artist released Burnt Sienna patches. Small detailed patches of Sap Green were added with a slight touch of Vermilion on the grasses around the lower trees. The dark tone of previously used colours were used for the stems and grasses. For the smaller trees, the artist used the same colours as before, but little darker shades.

Touching Natural Beauty

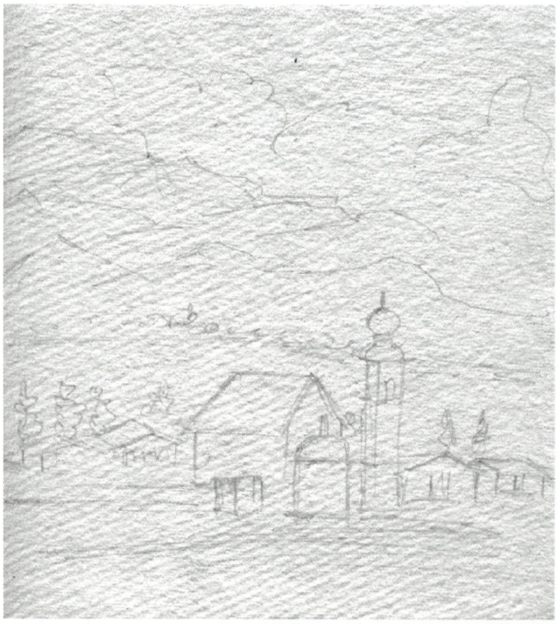

The paper was washed in the portion where the cloudless sky has been drawn, after the line drawing was completed.

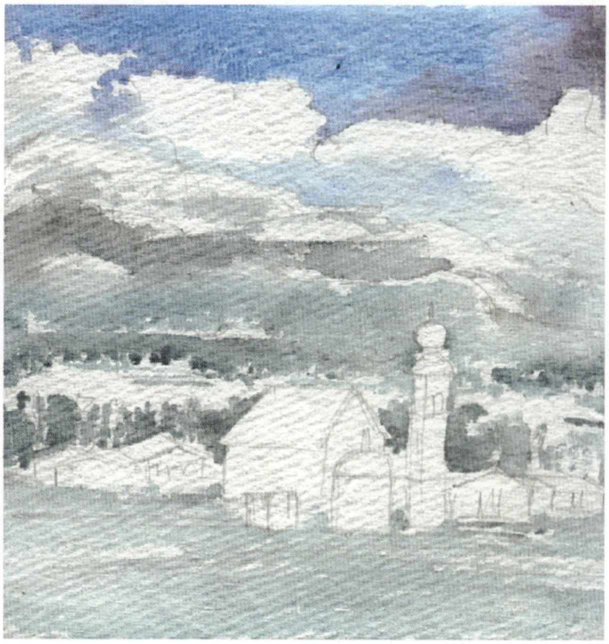

With the bursh the artist used light patches of Cobalt Blue and a touch of Crimson at some places to achieve a proper balance for the sky. While colouring the mountains, the flew tinted Blushed and Black, leaving it white where required.

A dark patch of Sap Green was freely released behind the houses. The trees drawn behind the houses giving a distant look was coloured with Sap Green. He let the white portion behind the trees untouched. A fainter tint of Sap Green prevailed on roofs of houses whereas Burnt Sienna with a little touch of Yellow Ochre on the tomb. Dark tones were applied on some doors and windows.

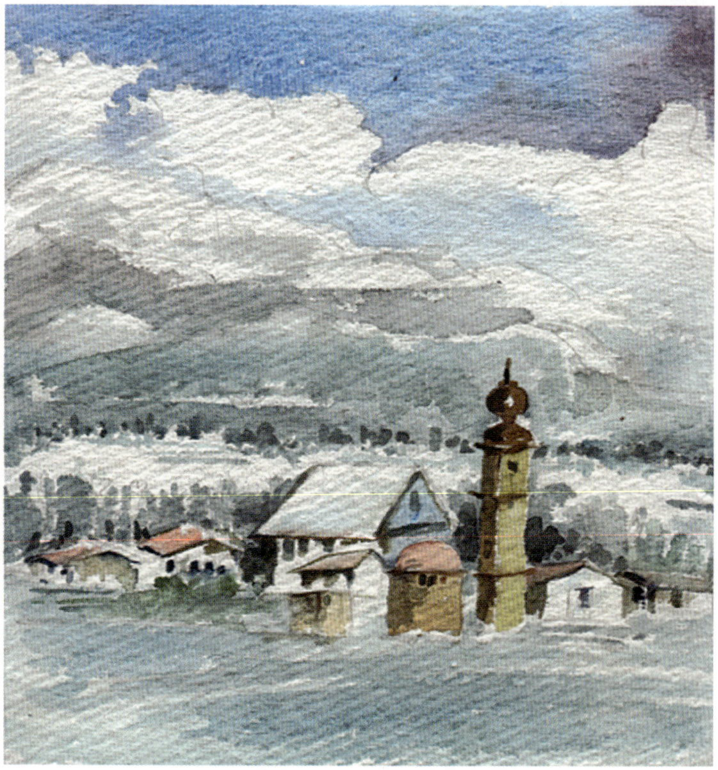

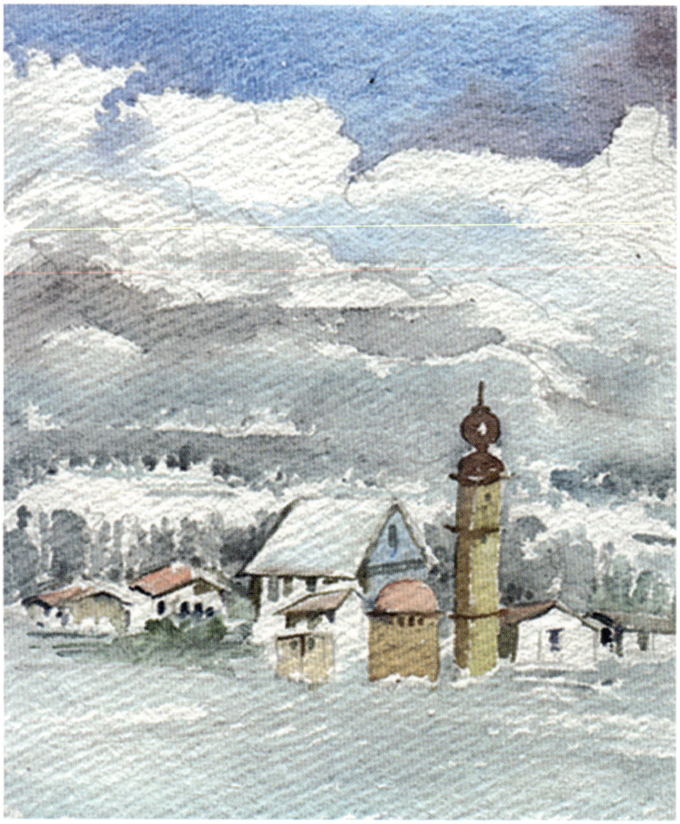

The artist released a dark tone of Sap Green on the distant trees drawn at the nether portion of the mountains. Previously used patches were flown freely on the houses and the dome. The ground was coloured with Cobalt Blue which made a pleasant scene.

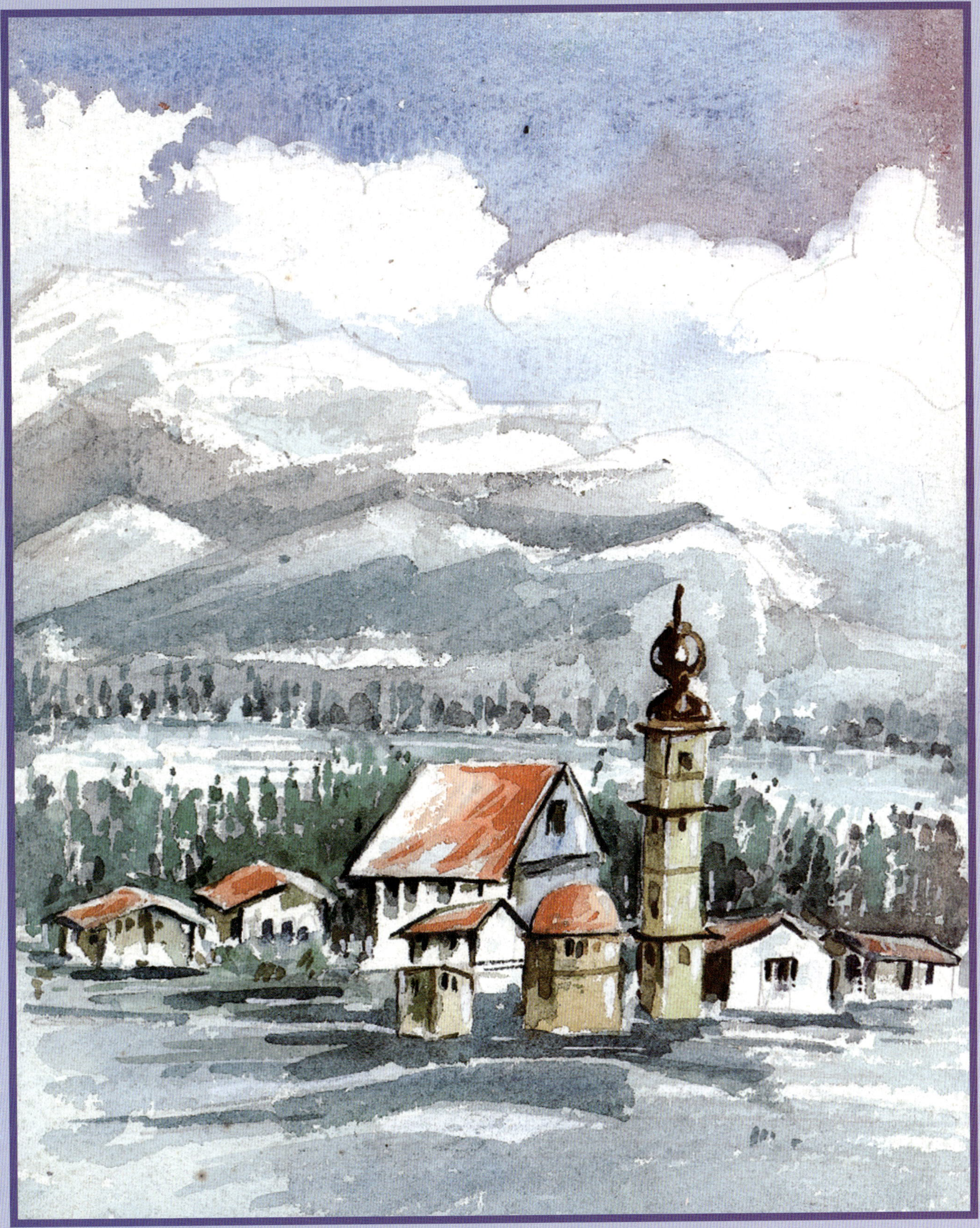

To maintain the balance, artist used a thick flow of previously used colours on the mountains wherever required. The natural effect of water was achieved by adding a few strokes of Cobalt Blue and Sap Green. The final tones applied on the trees behind the house were balanced with Sap Green. To depict the houses, roofs, he used a slight touch of Scarlet, the roofs with Burnt Umber and ground with Cobalt Blue, and give them an attractive natural look with White poster colour. This creates adjacent and cohesiveness in the painted landscape.

Natural Ethereal Quality

When the landscape drawing was complete, artist wet the paper and dripped out the excess water.

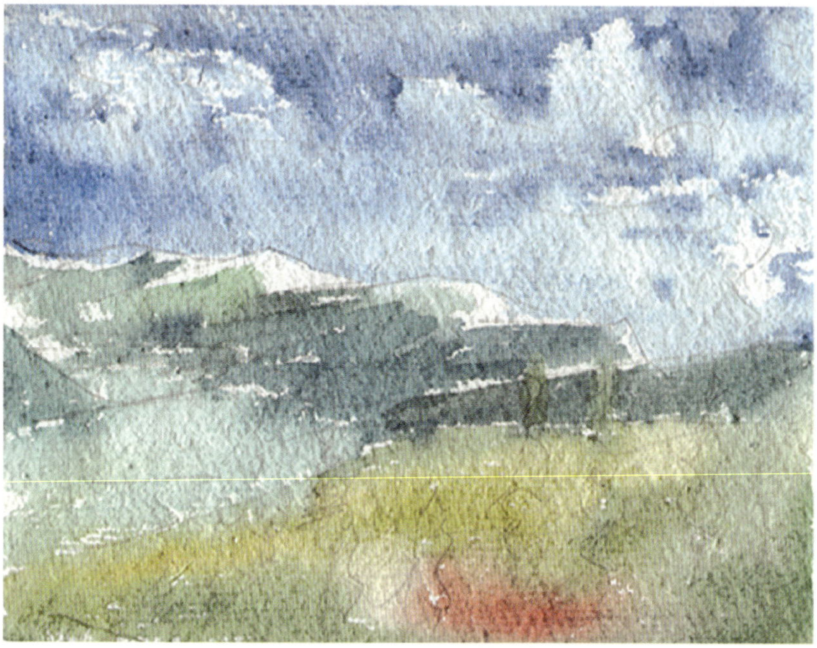

In appropriate dimensions, Cobalt Blue patches were released, keeping a proper poise between light and dark. Leaving the paper white, he freely released dull Sap Green with a slight touch of Prussian Blue and Cobalt Blue. To depict the ground, Yellow Ochre, fainter tinge of Scarlet and some Greenish hue were released.

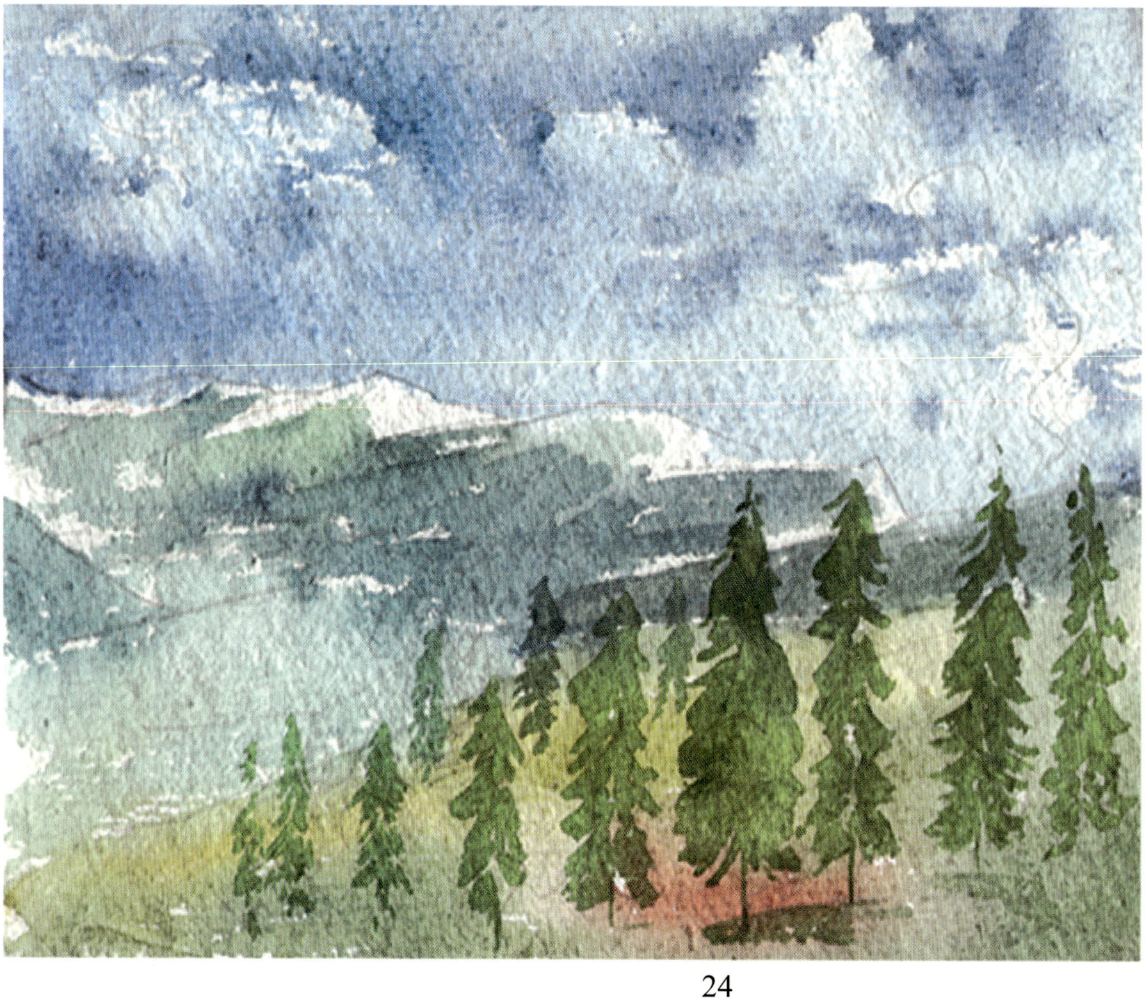

He later started colouring the trees. Right choice of Sap Green colour brought out the trees clearly.

Basing on the previous tone applied on the mountains, the artist released not only some dimmed patches of Sap Green but applied some Minutiae too.

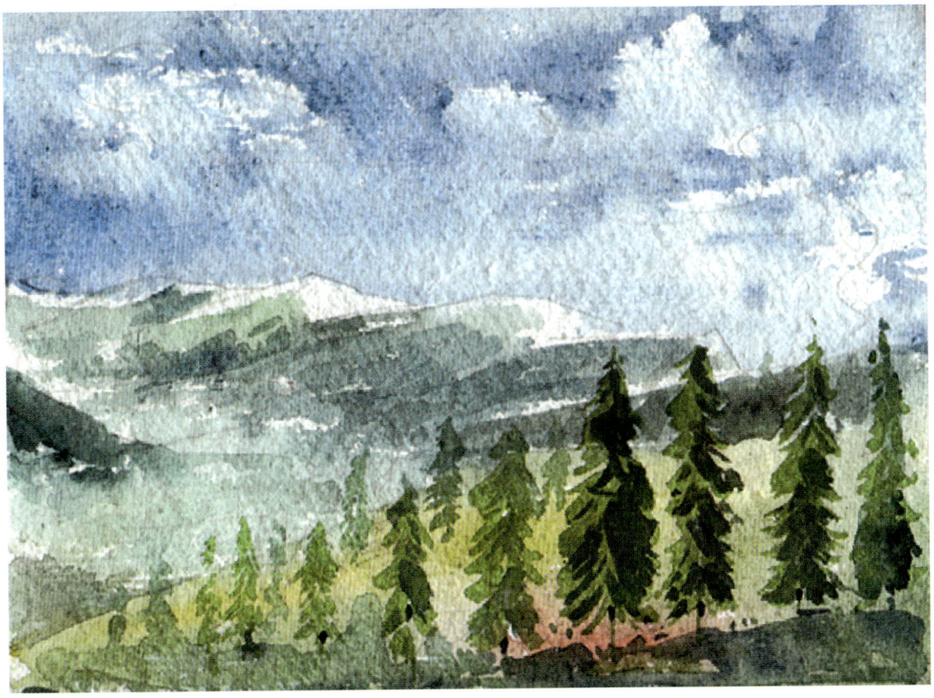

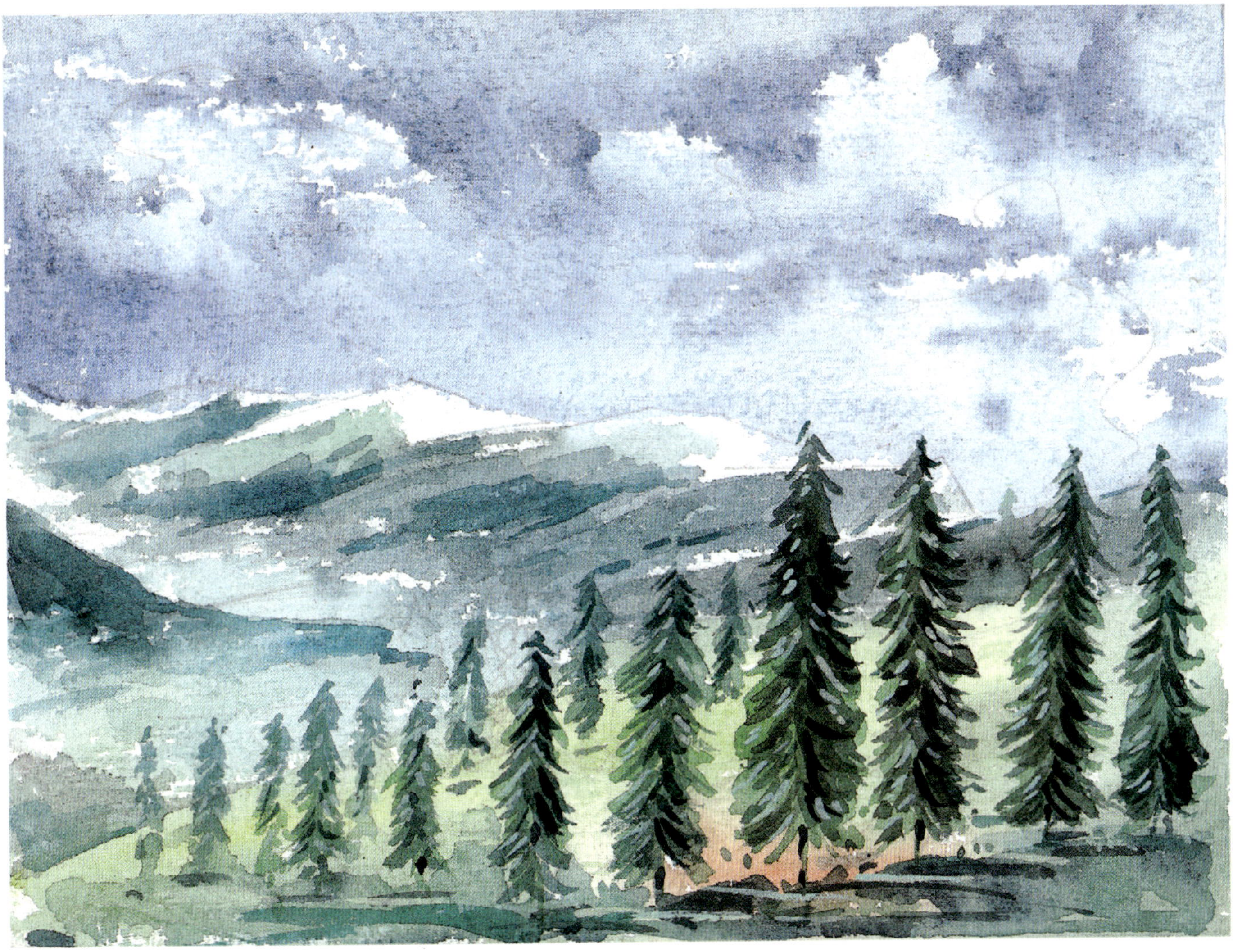

Small patches of Scarlet and a slight mixture of Poster White was used to highlight the trees, whereas dark and suggestive strokes obtained by mixing Sap Green with Vermilion to highlight the leaves. A proportionate mixture of Sap Green and White colour was released on the ground at some places which adds liveliness to the painting. Thus, this maintained balance and gives a splendid appearance.

A Perspective Look

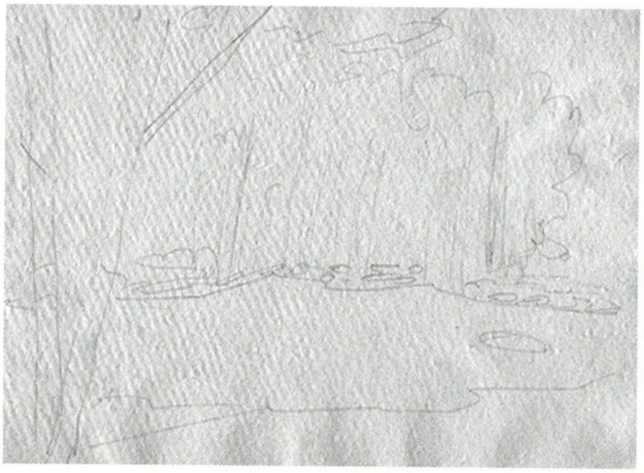

After drawing, wet the paper in the area where the cloudless sky is depicted, and flew colours while the paper was still wet.

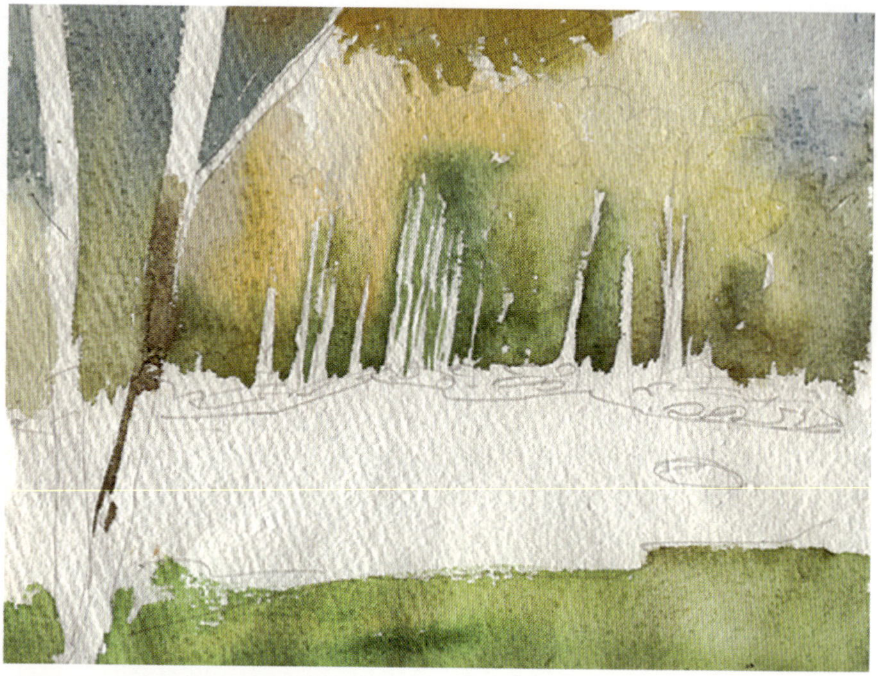

When paper was damp, artist began flowing a gamboge tinge obtained by mixing sap green with a little cobalt blue in distant trees. Some light stroke of burnt umber was prevailing in a front tree. The ground comprises mainly of sap green with a slight touch of gamboge.

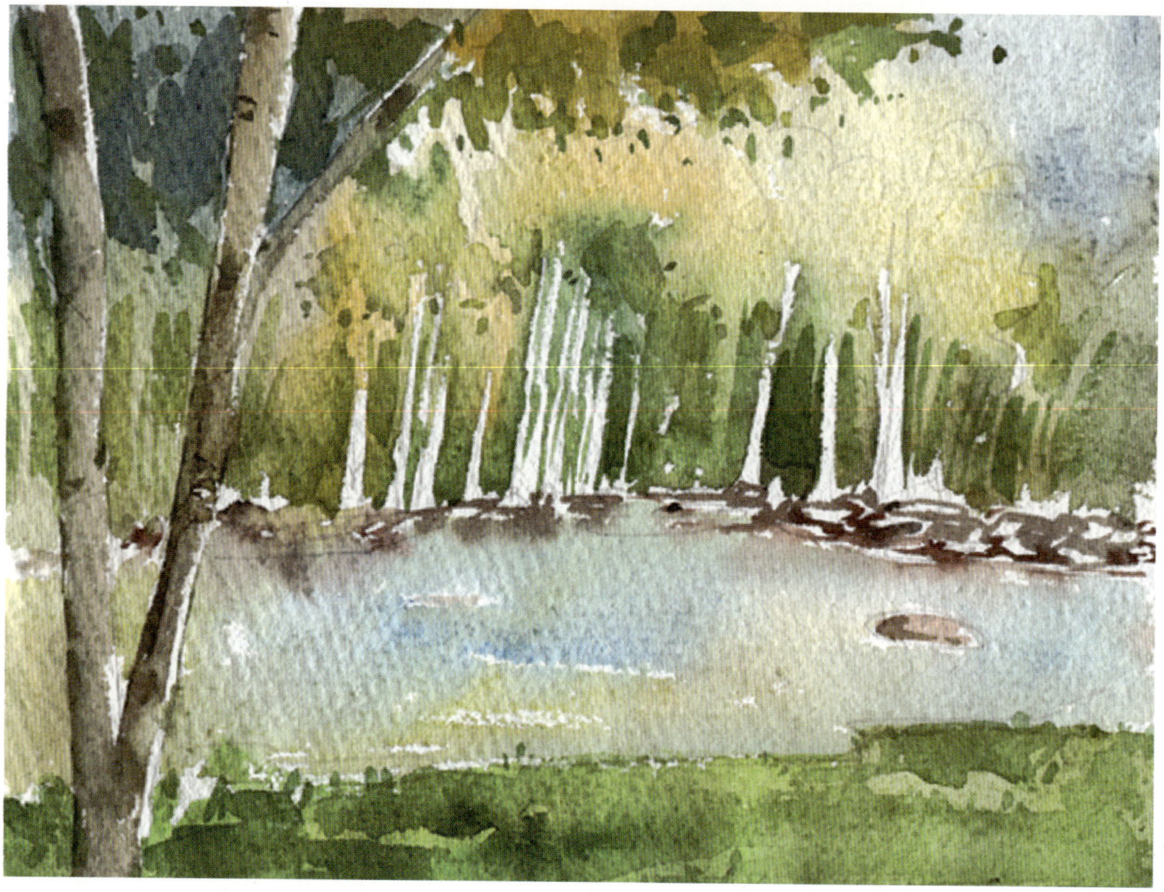

A fainter tint of Cobalt Blue with slightly mix of Yellow Ochre was used to give an effect of water. Special care was taken while highlighting the rocks between the water with Burnt Sienna patches. Not only on the trees, but Burnt Umber and a little Yellow Ochre was released on the stem too. Further to the previous colours already flown on the ground, darker patches were applied. Light strokes were used on the trees to give it a perspective look.

A dark stroke of Sap Green flown on the trees give a proper perspective look. Some minutiae did on the dark patches make the rocks look prominent. Detailing was done with tinted Cobalt Blue-Sap Green and a fainter tinge of Burnt Umber was used on the front tree. As per the previous coluors applied on the ground, some dark colours were used to give an effect of grass.

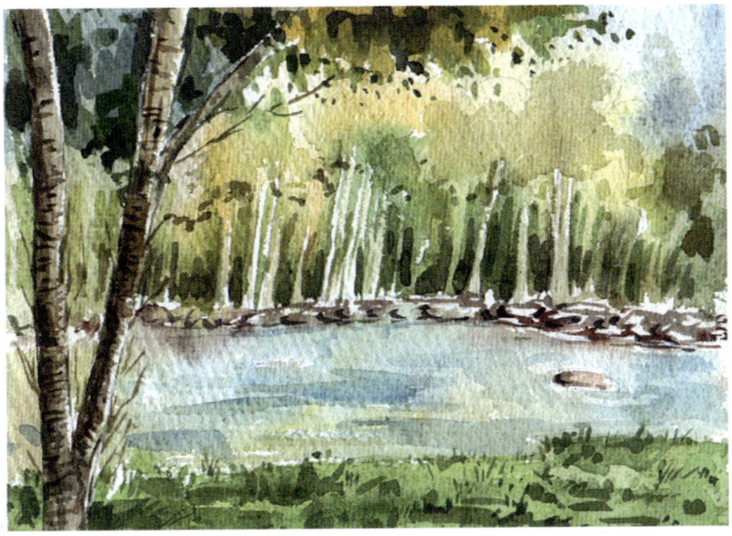

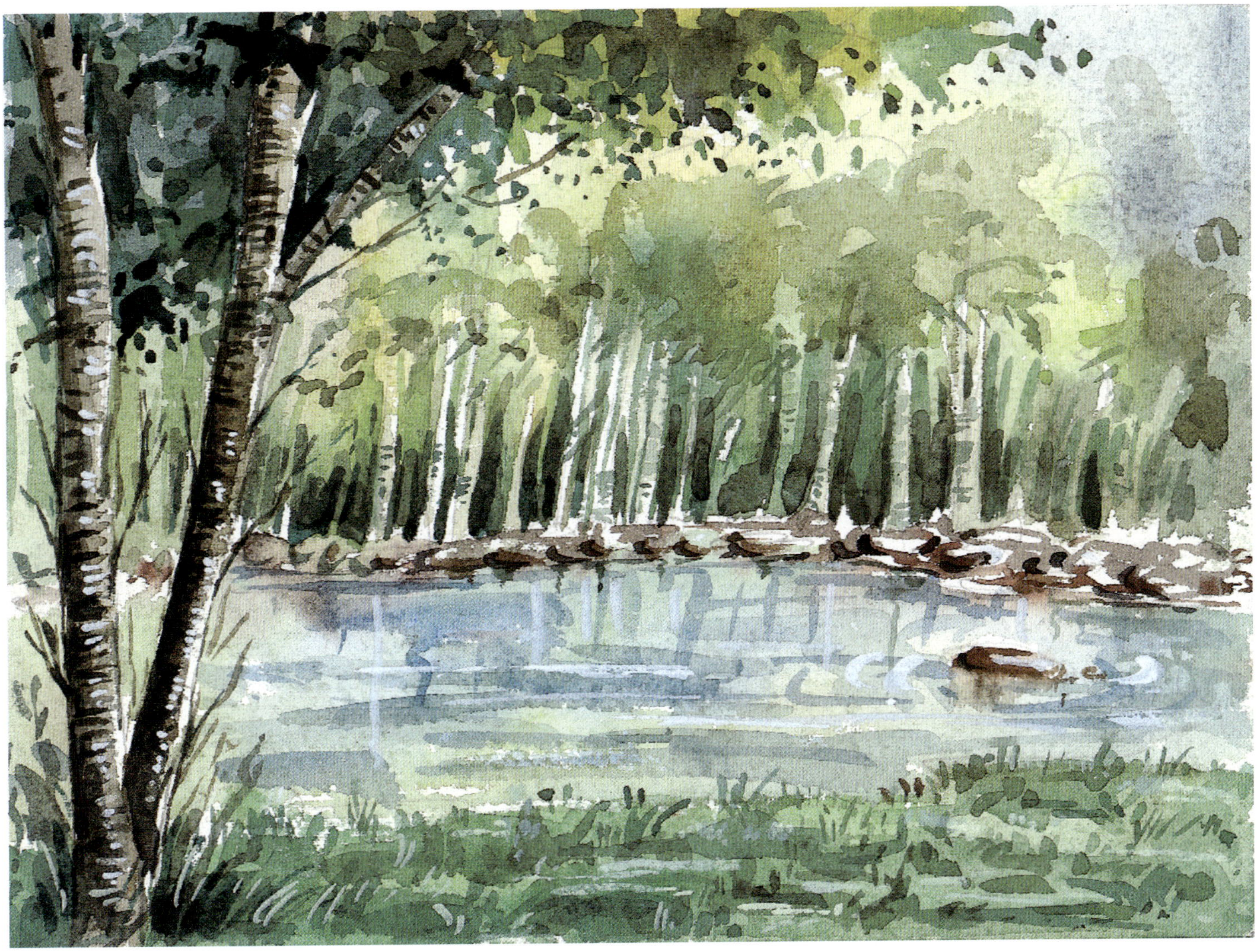

Some minute details were done with Sap Green and a little mixture of Vermilion. Burnt Umber adds depth to the stems and highlights the same. White poster colour was also released. With careful consideration of colours and values, an irregular patch of colours was released on the trees and drawn at distant place wherever required. A few dull strokes were released on the leaves. This thick mixture of Cobalt Blue and a touch of White gave a distinct look to water. A touch of Sap Green and Vermilion give a splendrous look to the grass. White and a Greenish tinge was used to highlight it.

Stupendrous Scene in Red

After the paper was made damp in water, the artist dried it completely, and made a light, sharp and accurate pencil drawing depicting natural beauty.

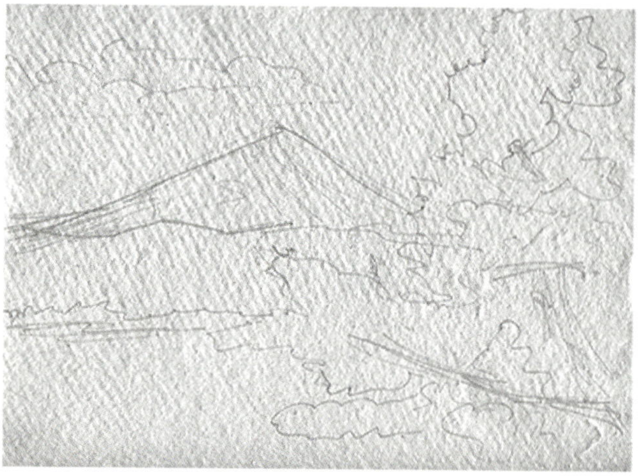

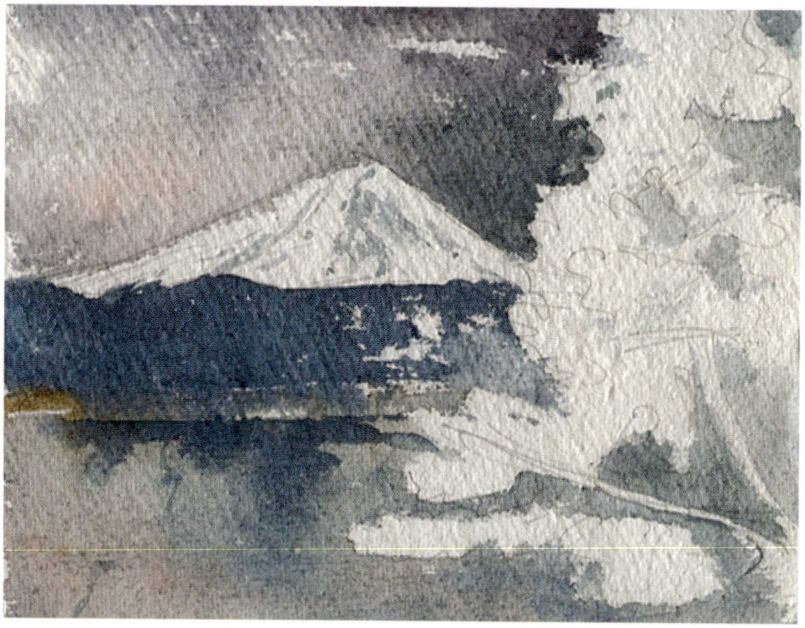

Cobalt Blue and a light mixture of Prussian Blue depict the sky. Some dull shades of Cobalt Blue indicate the mountains clearly. A few strokes of Prussian Blue with Cobalt Blue were applied on the mountains. He retained white for the trees, and released previously used colours on the water to show the reflection of the mountains.

To give the intrinsic effect of water, light Cobalt Blue shades were applied. Scarlet was used on the trees which not only highlights the scene but makes it eye-catching.

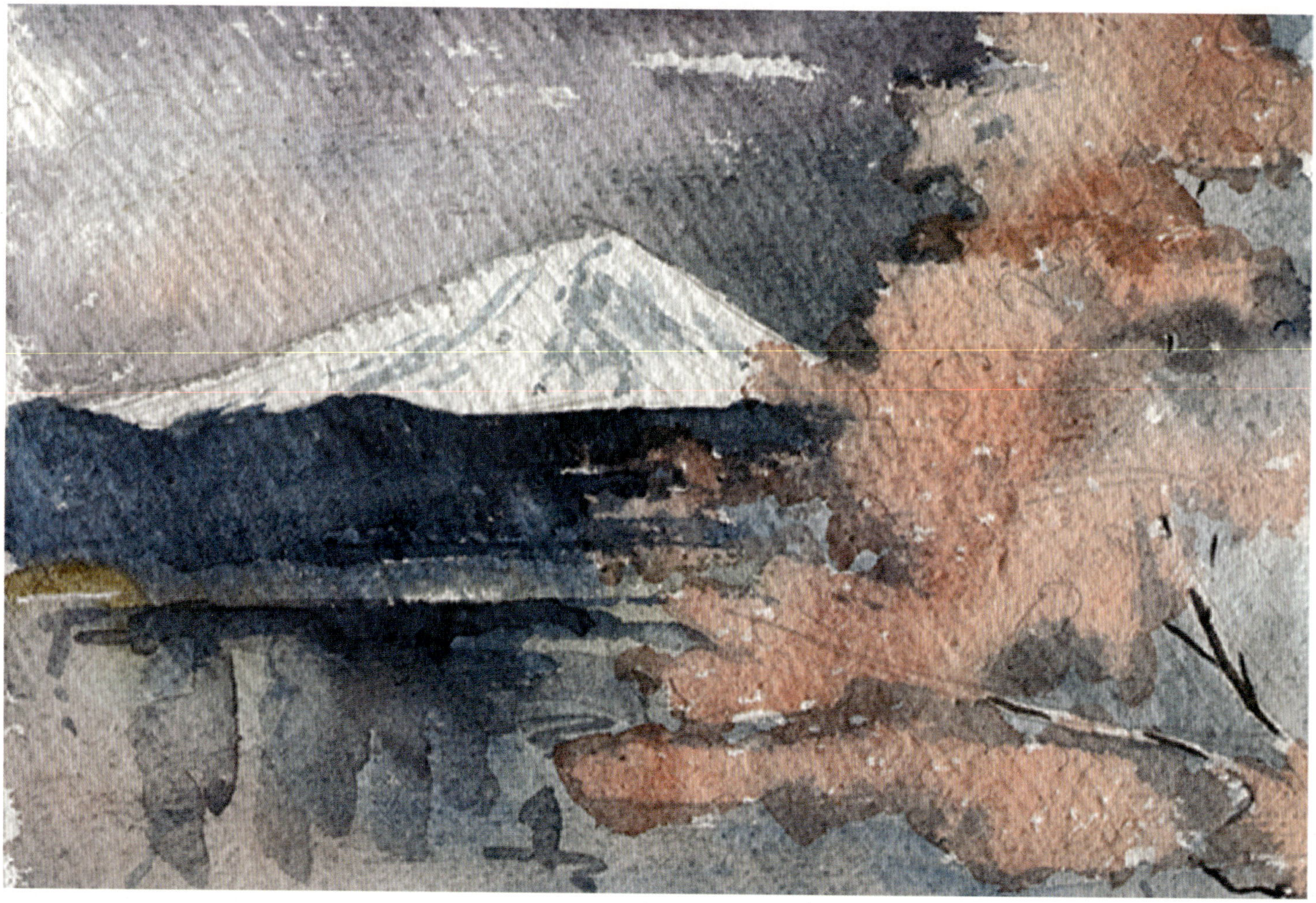

In conjunction with the colours used previously, some dark patches were used for the mountain. Little Scarlet Hue was released on the tree leaves. This highlights each and every leaf sharply. Burnt Sienna depicts the stem clearly.

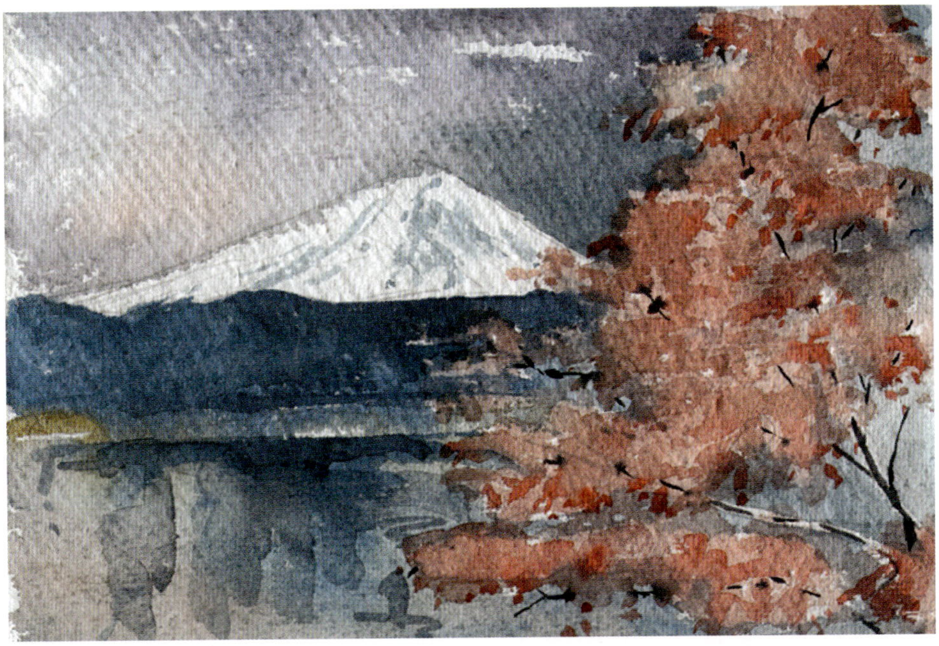

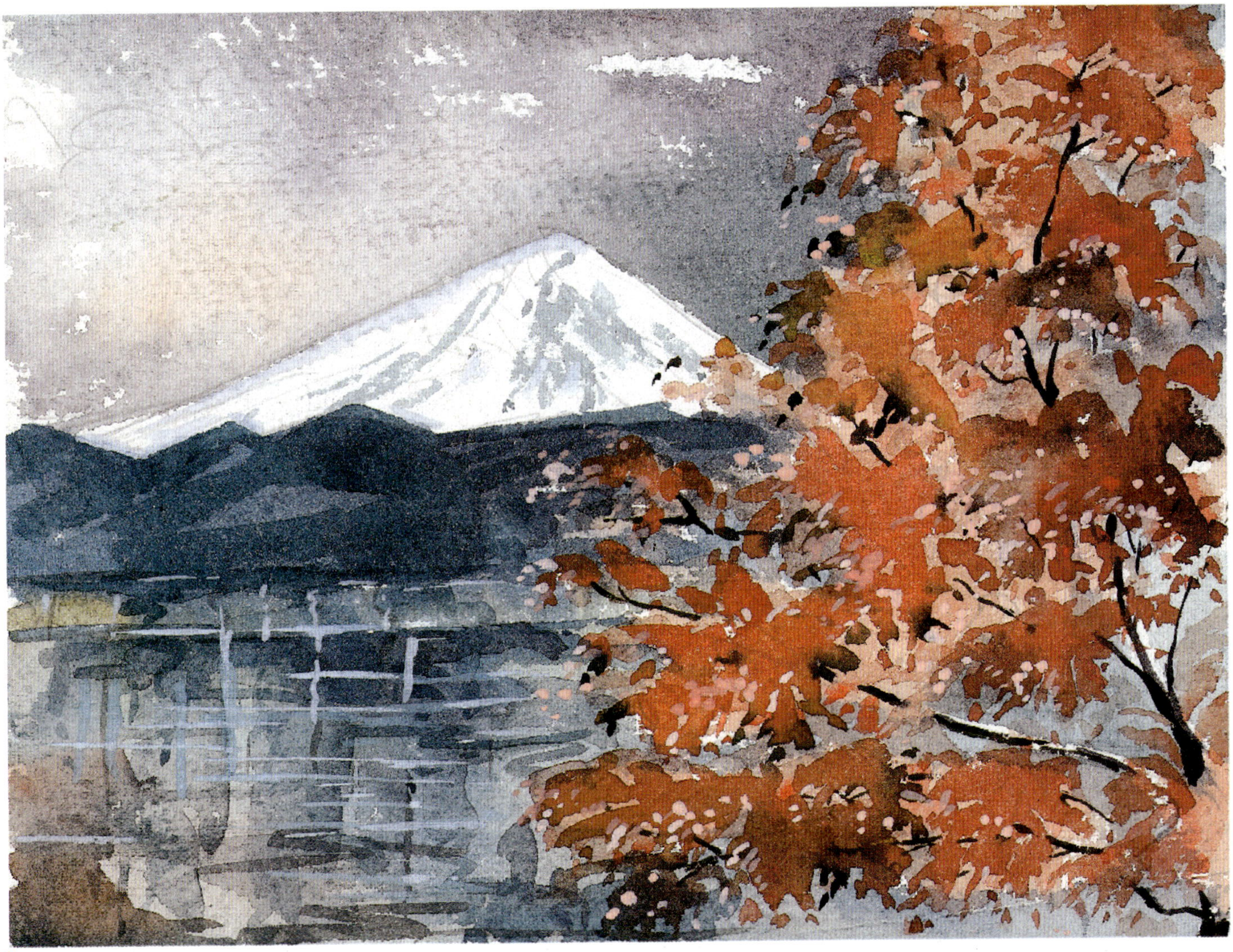

To bring out the natural beauty, Prussian Blue patches were flown on the mountains and little shades to highlight the water. Irregular patches of Scarlet were flown on the tree. White poster colour was used to give an effect of water. The use of faint tinted Scarlet with a touch of Poster White at some places, highlight the tree. Wherever required, the stem was made dark with Burnt Umber Hues. The perspective use of colours, light and shades create the ethereal quality on the landscape.

Highlight Copiousness of Tree

The artist slightly wet the paper first and dripped off excess water. After the paper dried, he drew a light, accurate and sharp line drawing on handmade paper.

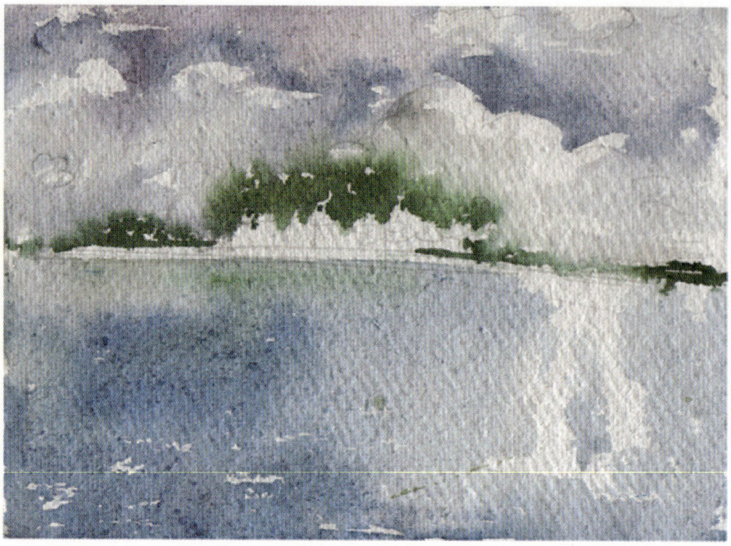

Lightened stroke of Sap Green was released on the trees. Leaving some places untouched, he flew little Cobalt Blue patches to depict the water. Thick layers of Sap Green was used for the reflective images, whereas some light patches of Cobalt Blue gave a clear effect of the water.

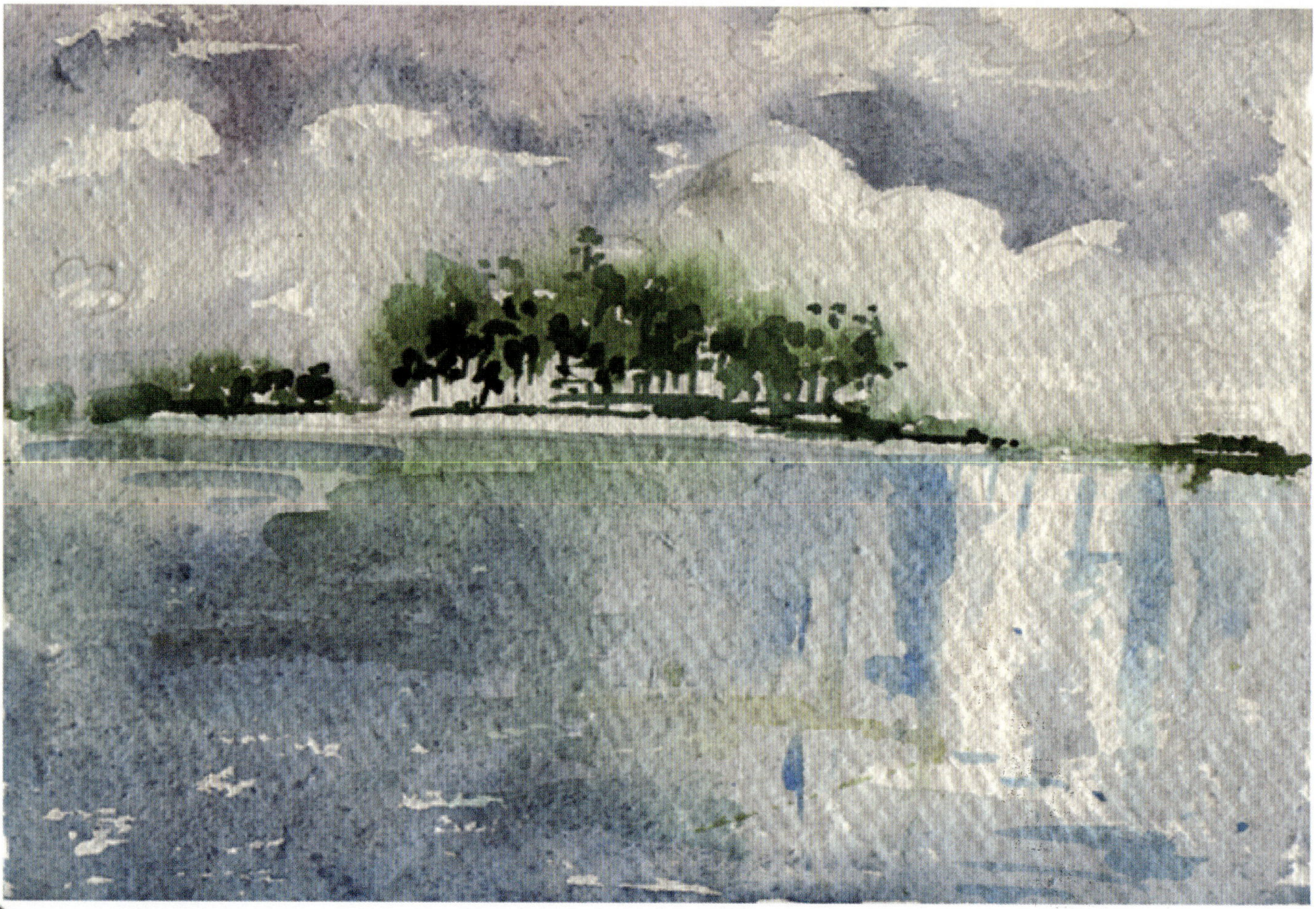

Leaving the clouds untouched, the artist released some light shades of Prussian Blue and Crimson to identify the crude sky. To give the effect of the distant trees he used Sap Green. Retaining the lower portion as white, he released some dull strokes of Sap Green and Cobalt Blue.

Keeping in mind the colours previously used, the artist flew some tiny patches to make the distant trees. The reflective images of the trees in water was ahieved with light patches of Sap Green. At a nether portion the water effect was with a light touch of Sap Green and Cobalt Blue. Dark tones of Sap Green highlights the copiousness of the tree.

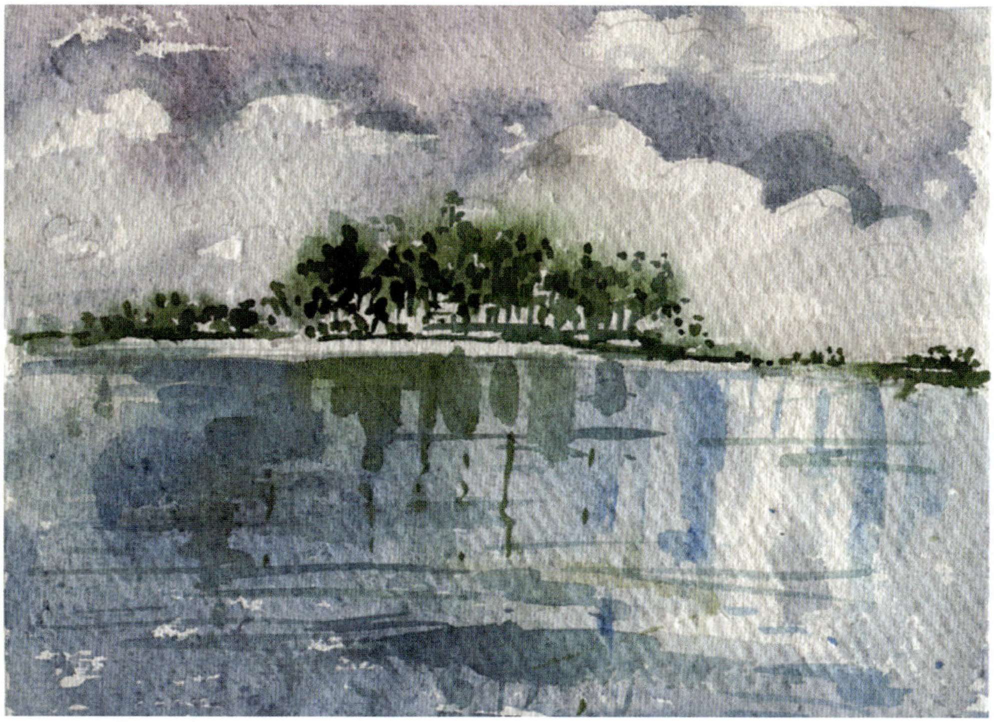

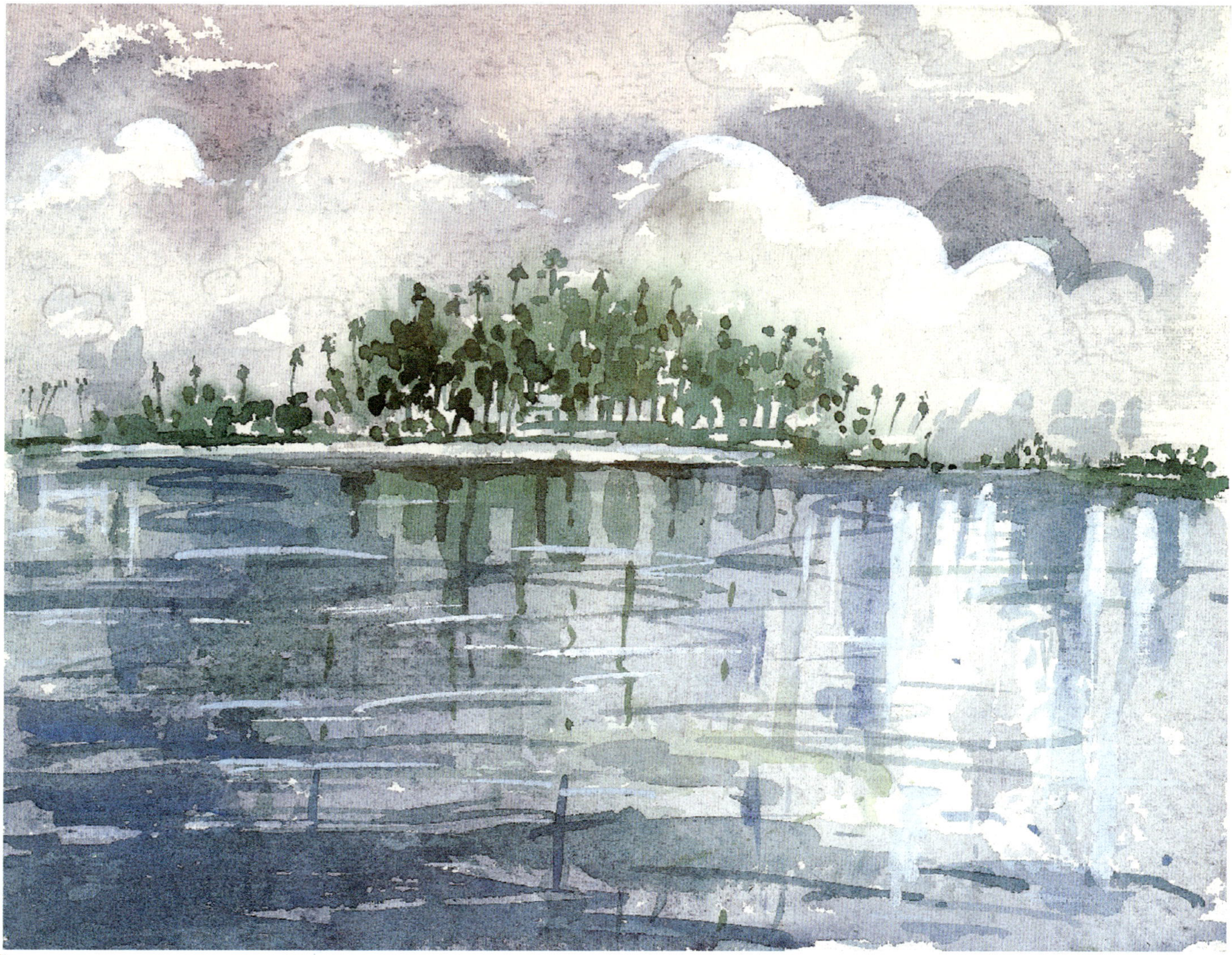

Care was however taken while highlighting the clouds with poster White. Dark patches of Cobalt Blue and a touch of poster White colour not only give a realistic view of the water but highlighted it clearly.

Crude Composition

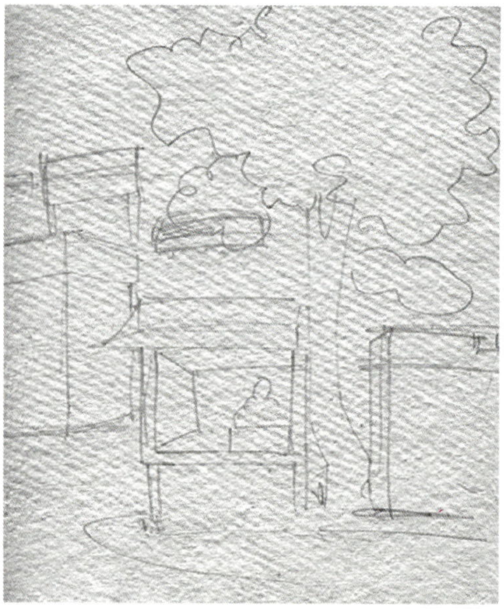

Sketches are the base of the painting. So it should be drawn with utmost care. So we can make a landscape on handmade paper on sketch-board.

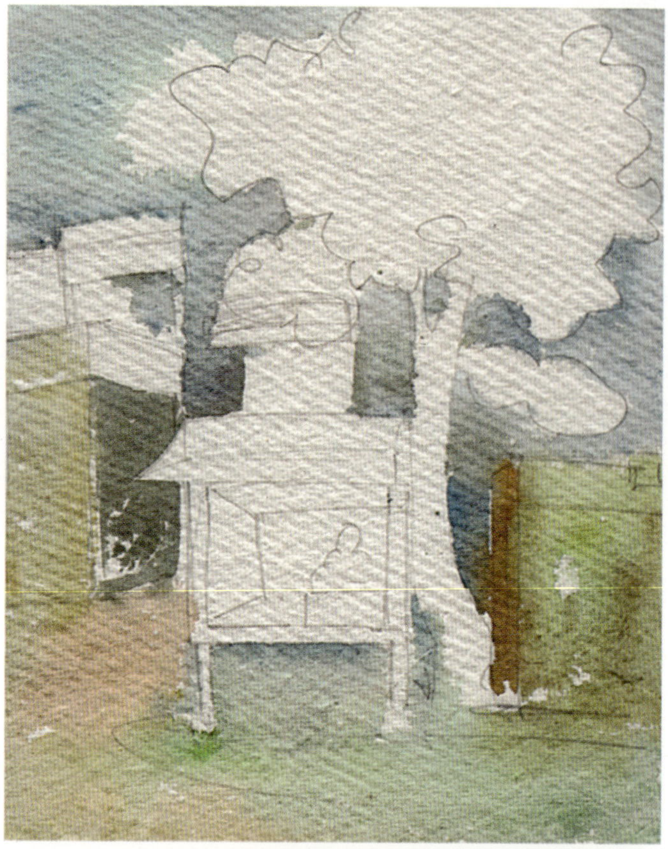

Beginning with Cobalt Blue and a slight touch of Black for the sky, we can fly a fainter tinge of Yellow Ochre, Sap Green and Scarlet not only on the houses but on the ground too. Appropriate colours were freely flown using 8 no. Brush.

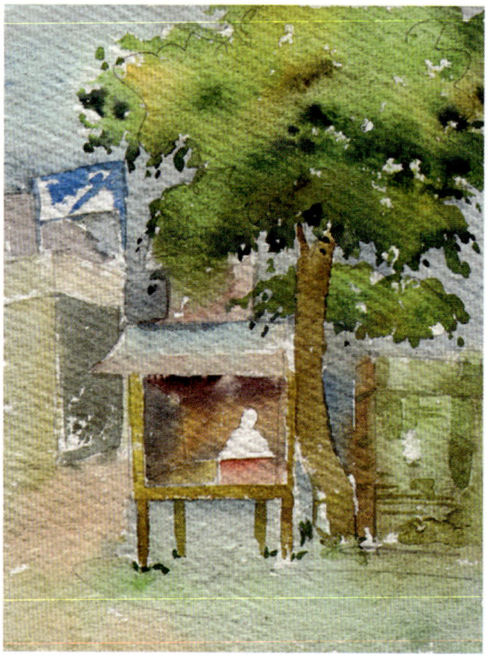

In continuation of the already used colours for the trees, we would use slightly dark tones to create an attractive look. Later, for the pan shop some darker patches were applied. Man sitting in the shop was coloured with Scarlet whereas, some minute details were done using dark colours on the tree's stem. Using the previous colours, some light patches were flown to highlight the trees.

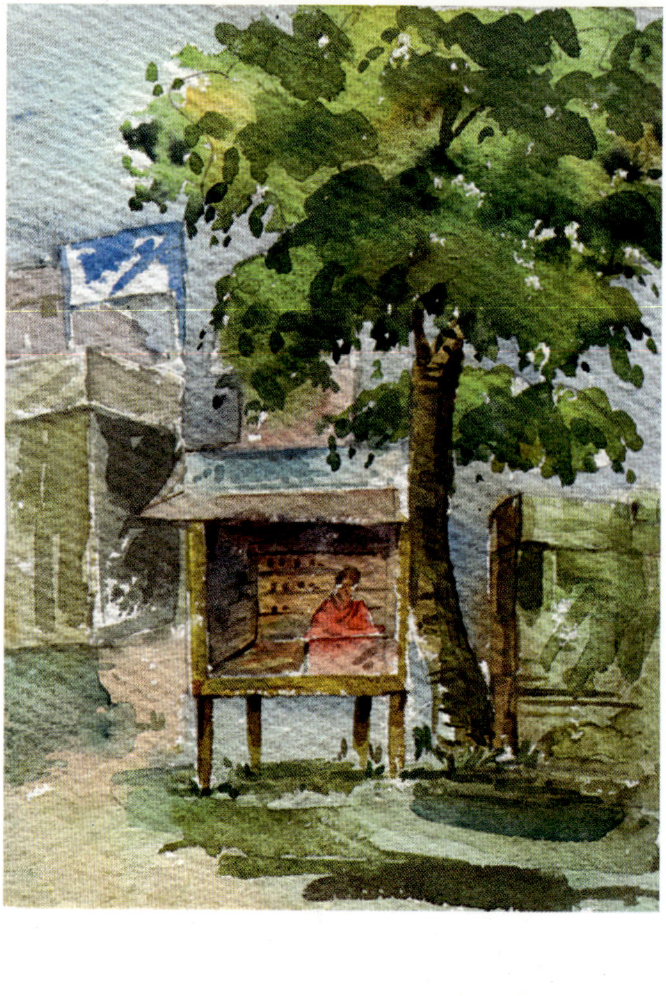

Darker tones of Sap Green, Gamboge was released on the trees, and wherever required, Prussian Blue was flown at some places. While colouring the tree's stem, we have applied a mixture of Yellow Ochre and Burnt Sienna. Yellowish tint mixed with Cobalt Blue and a slight touch of Scarlet colour was used to indicate the pan shop clearly, whereas Cobalt Blue patch was used for the name board.

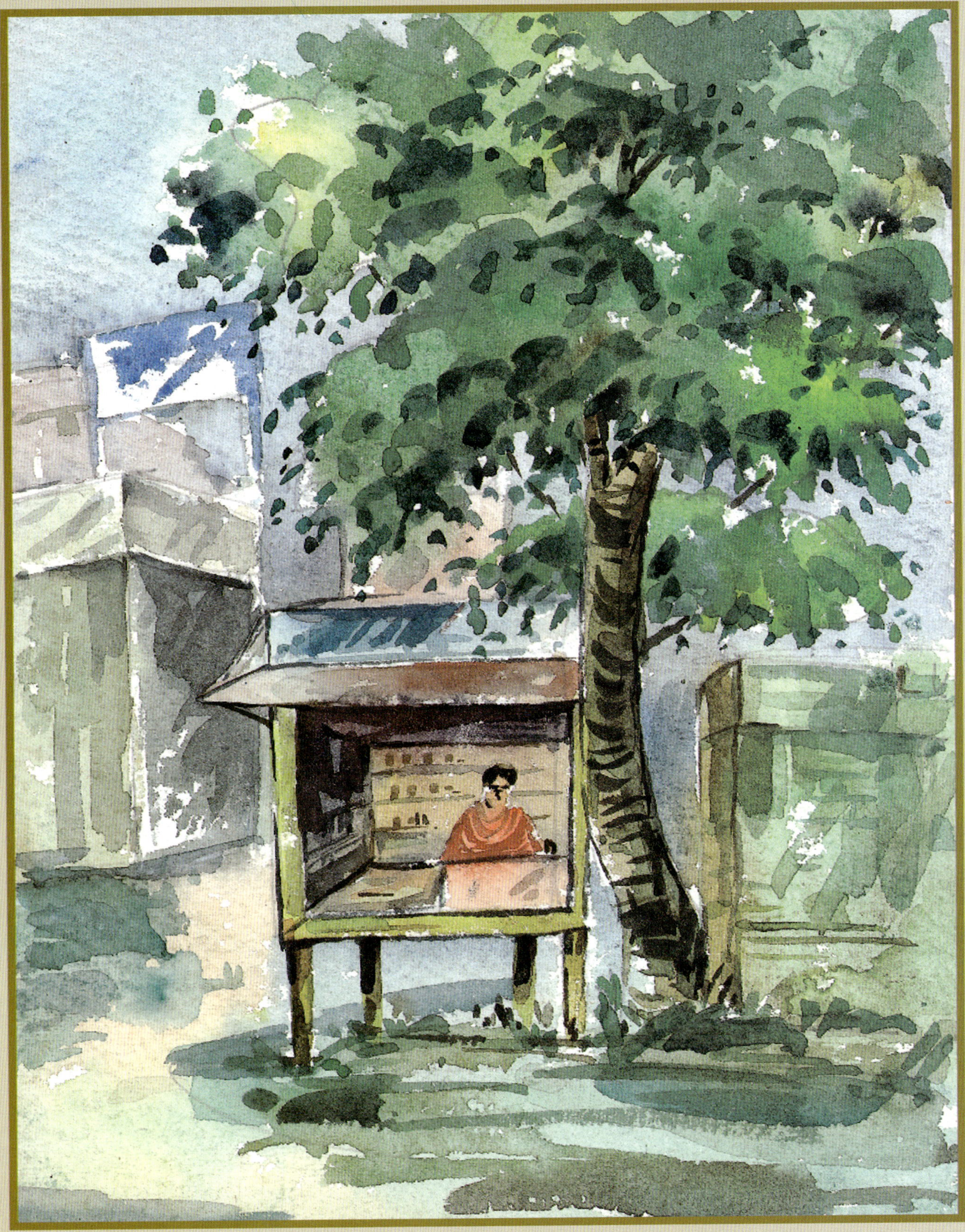

tFor giving minutiae on the trees, dark Sap Green and Vermilion were released wherever required. With Burnt Umber colour some lightened patches was added to depict the finer details of the stem. Bright patches of Cobalt Blue highlighted the pan's name board. Deep strokes of Prussian Blue with Crimson was applied inside the shop. Care was however taken while giving prominence to the man's cloth with Scarlet and some dark shades for the hairs. Darkshades of Burnt Umber was used to indicate the pan stand. Few dark Sap Green's strokes were flown on the ground.

Landscape (Rural Scenery)

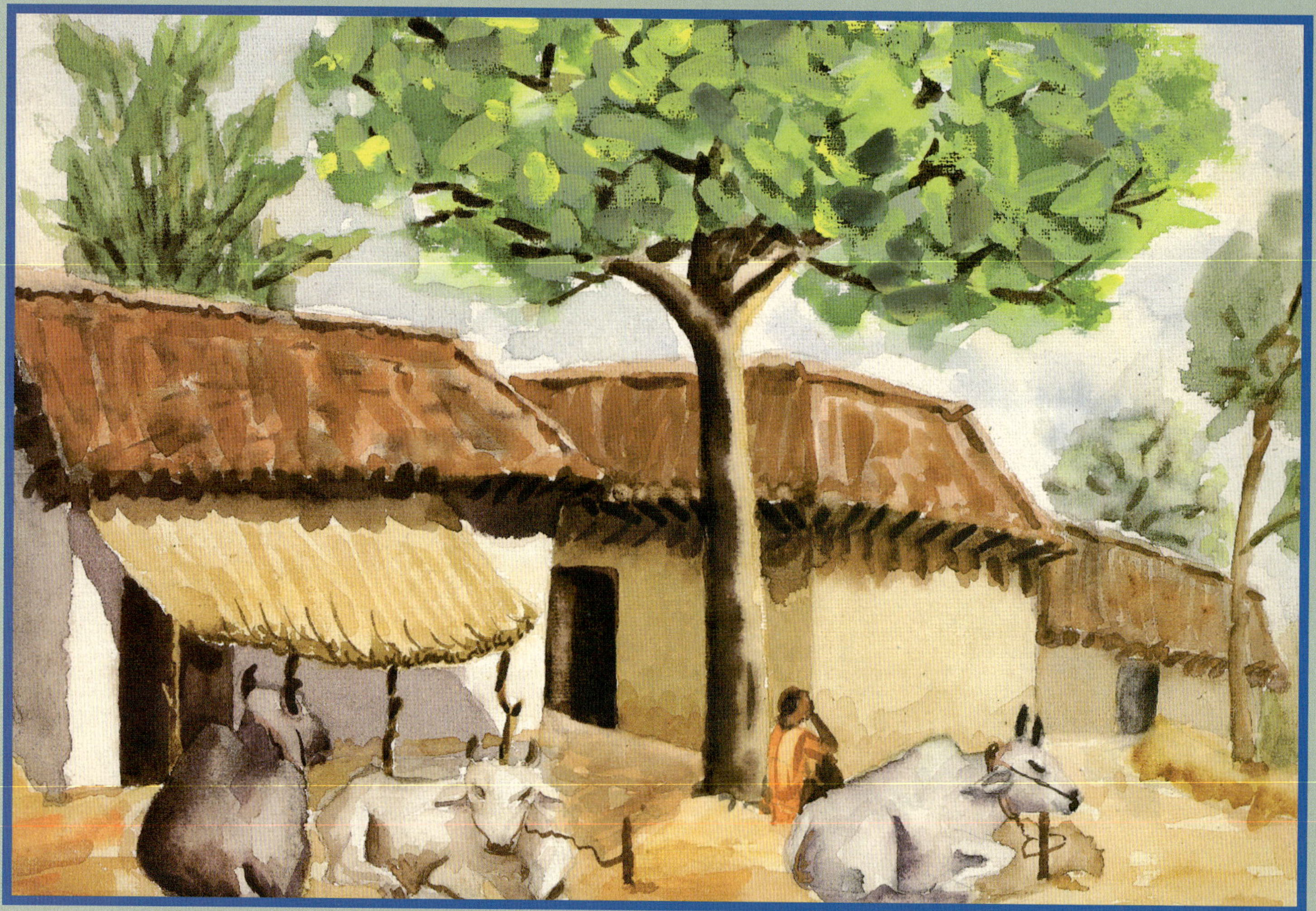

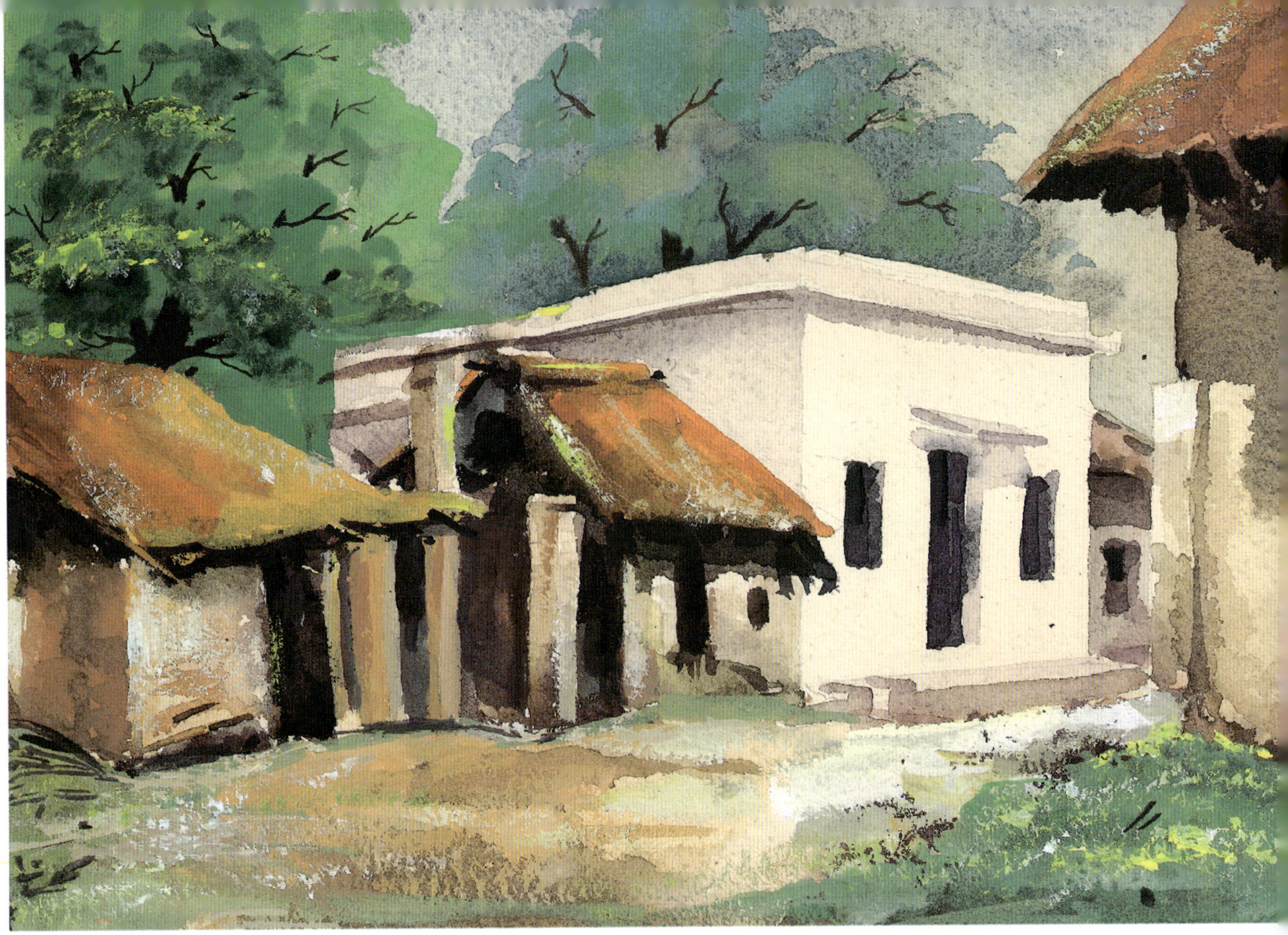

Rural Scenery

Painting a rural scene can bring out the best out of you. Someone or something rural is simple, so your painting should also be simple. It is important to highlight the essentials, but that too with the least number of strokes. The less the number of strokes, the better your painting. And the better your painting, the fresher its appeal and quality.

In this picture, the artist has painted a tree in the foreground, but at the same time he depicted it with a few careless strokes of Sap Green only to create the illusion of a tree. He has taken the pains to draw the individual leaves of the trees for the sake of originality.

The thatched roofs of the houses throw a shadow. A few strokes of Burnt Sienna and some strokes of Black are enough to depict the thatched roofs. The roofs throw a shadow on the mud walls. Yellow walls and a zigzag stroke of Burnt Sienna to complete it.

Not much to be done for the brick house. The pathway is depicted with the help of Burnt Sienna and using a dry brush, he applied Black to give the illusion of a partly lit pathway.
Painting is a process of colouring a surface with paints. We are covering the white surface with strokes and patches

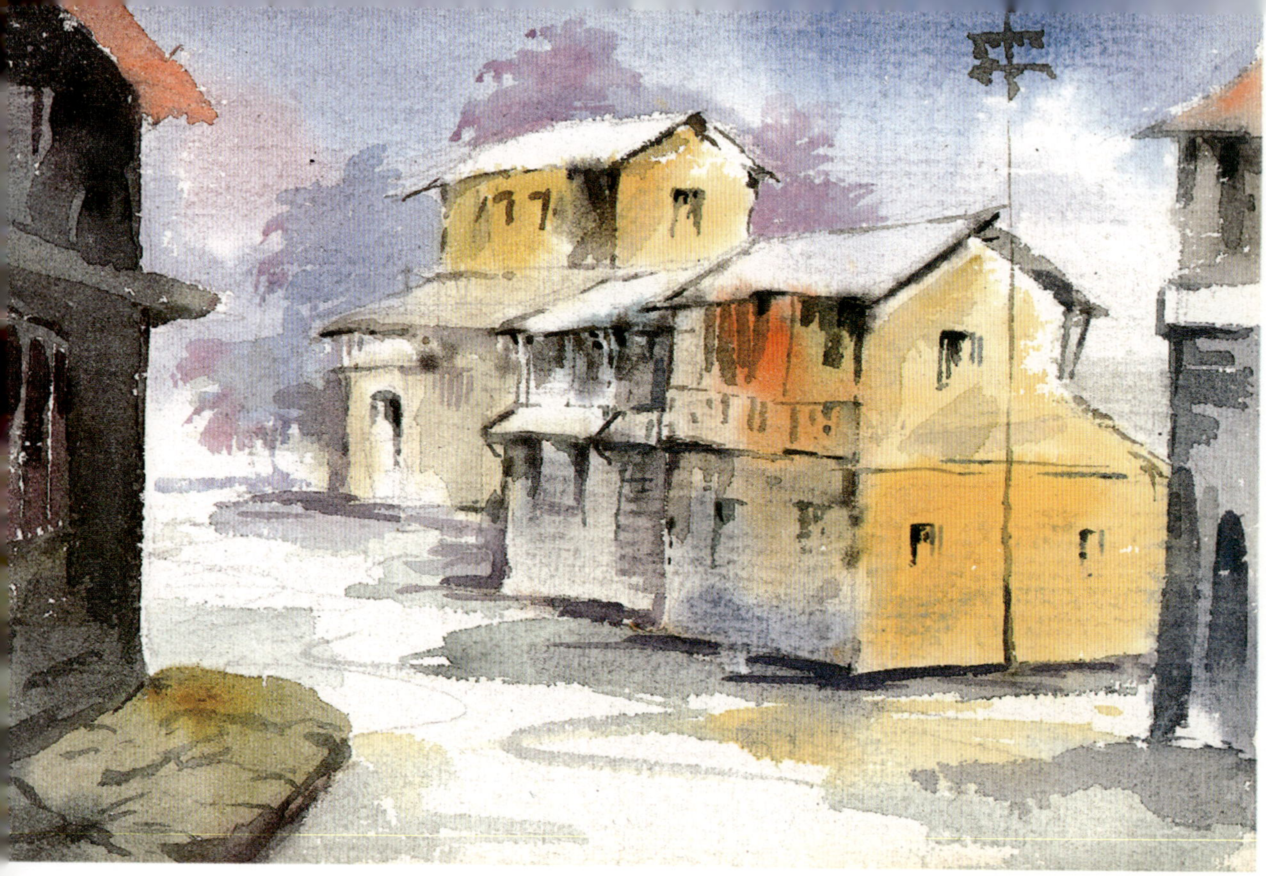

of paints. But the right shade of paint is necessary to achieve the desired result.

In almost every painting there is a centre of attraction which is depicted in light and the unwanted portions are in the dark. In the painting on the left, light floods the building in the centre and the roofs cast some shadows on the walls. However the shack depicted in the painting is in the shade, yet the object under the shade arouse your curiosity. You fail to notice the portion under light.

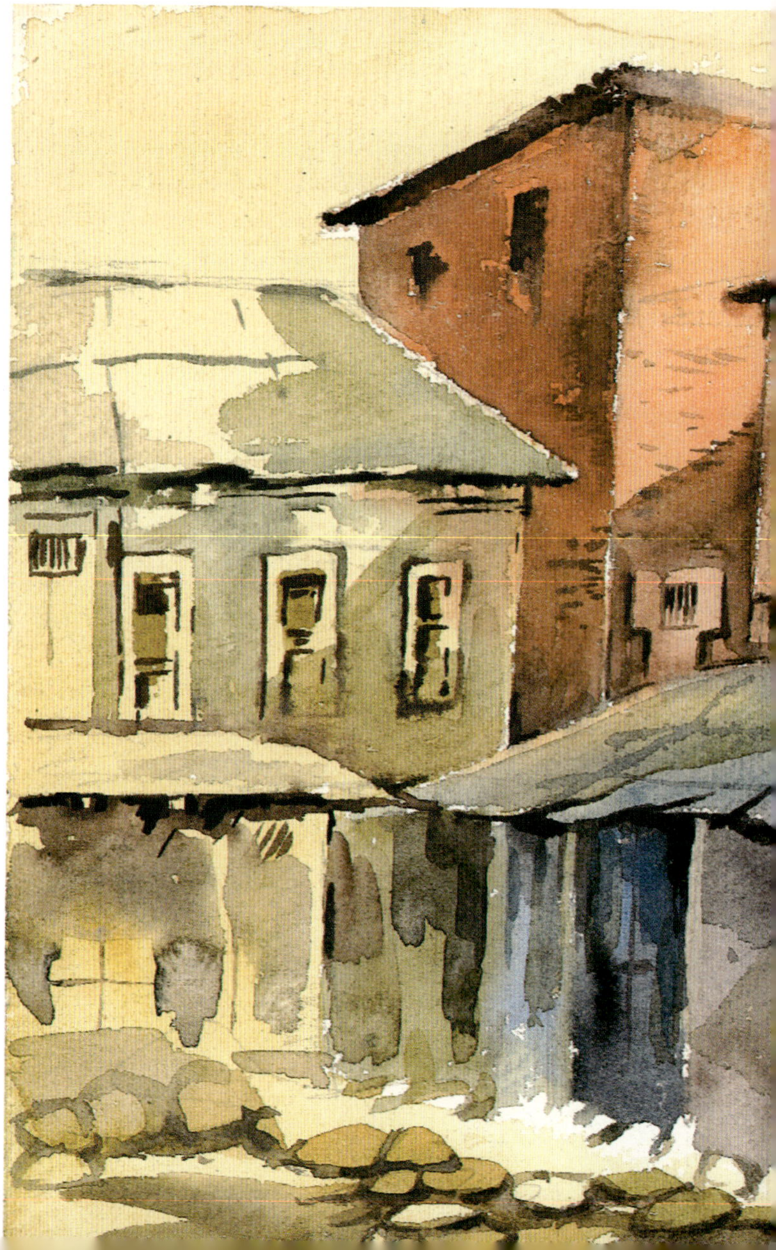

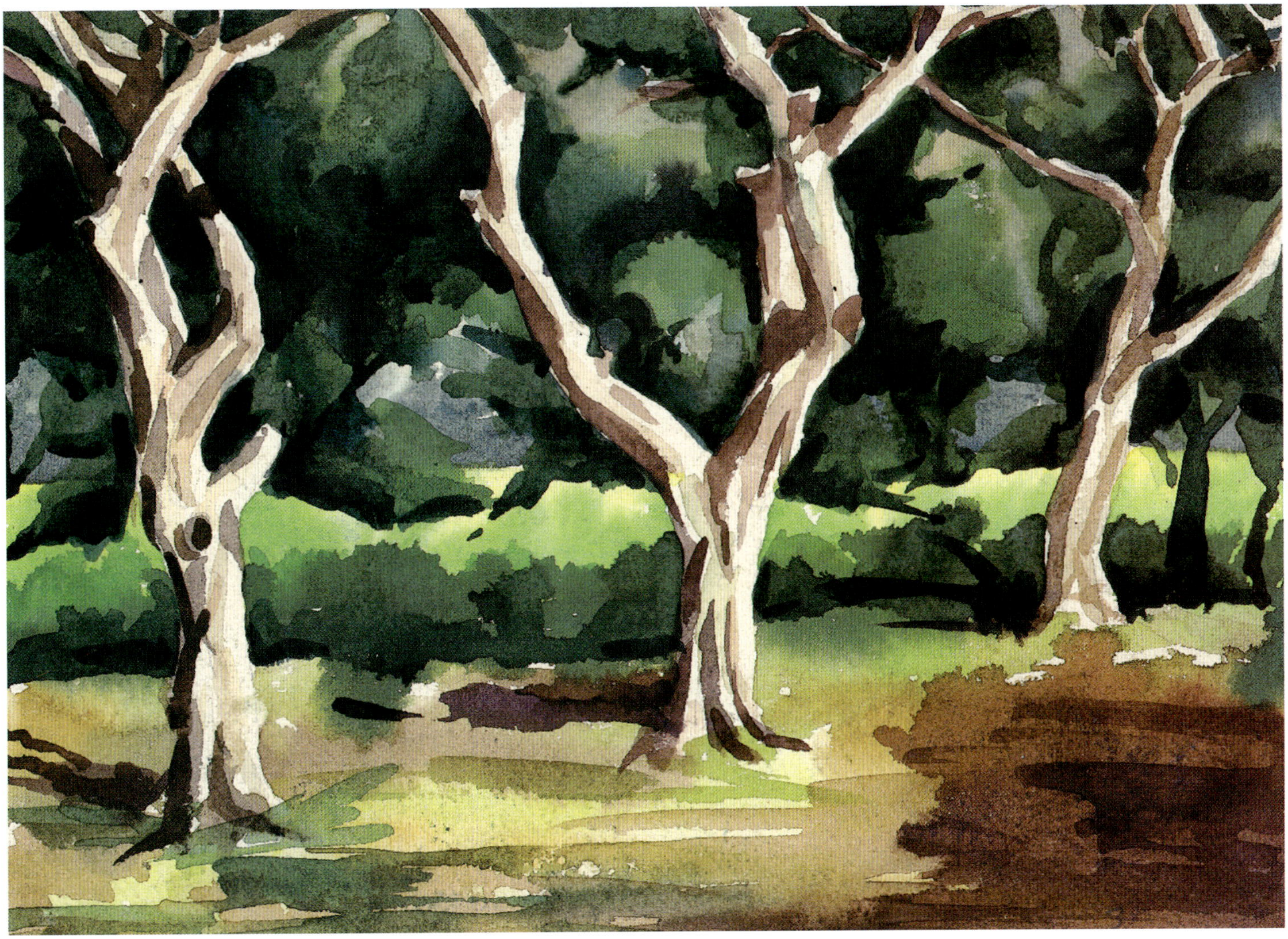

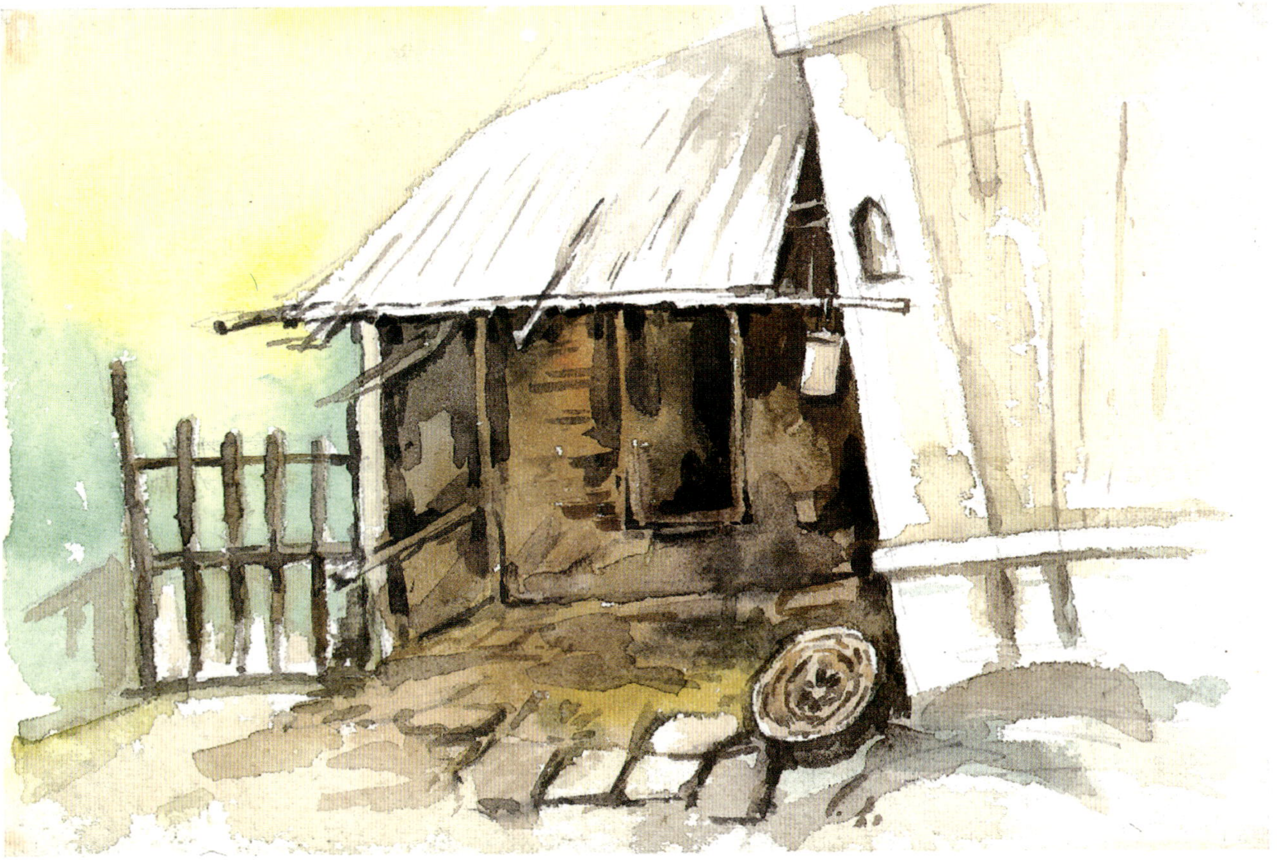

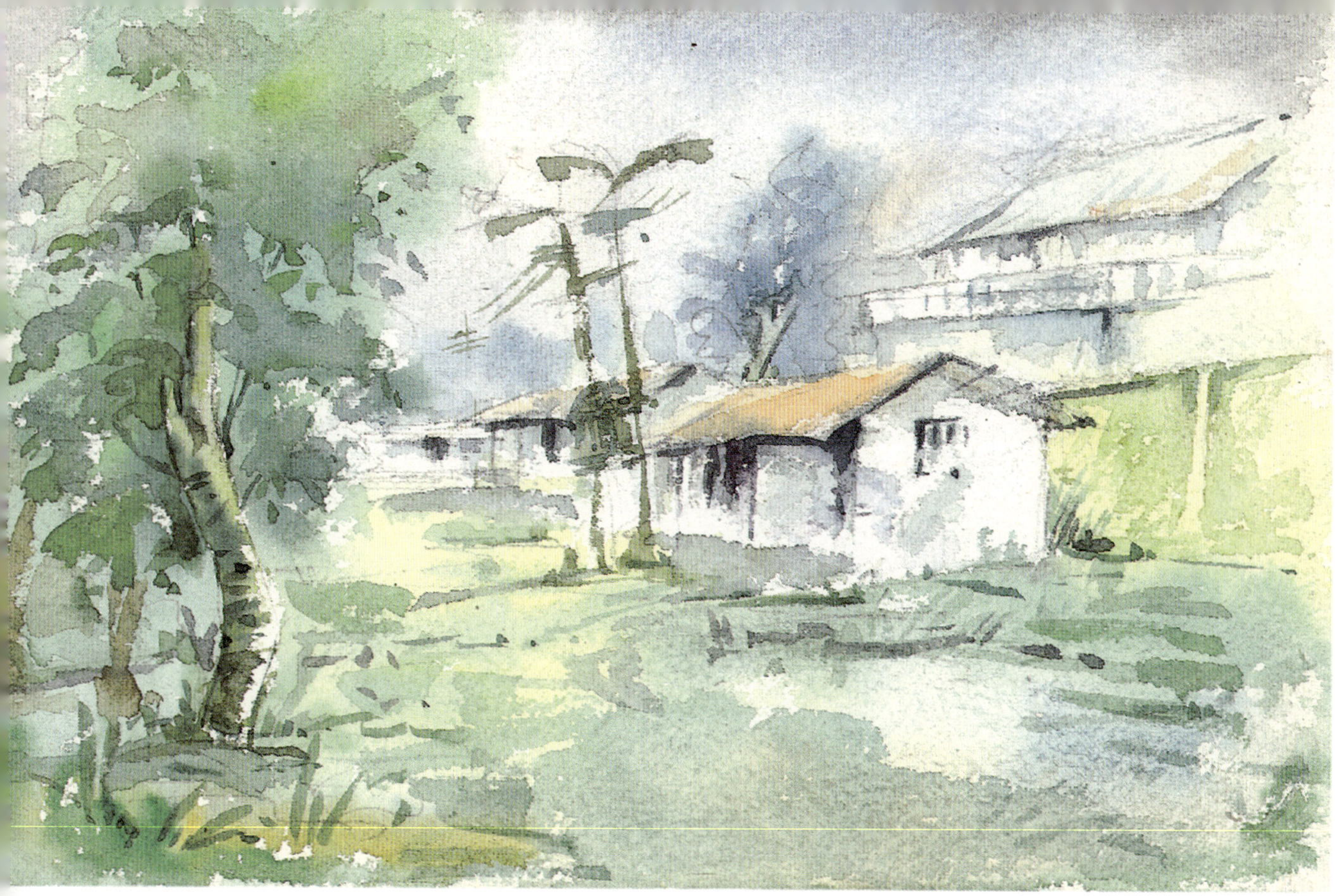

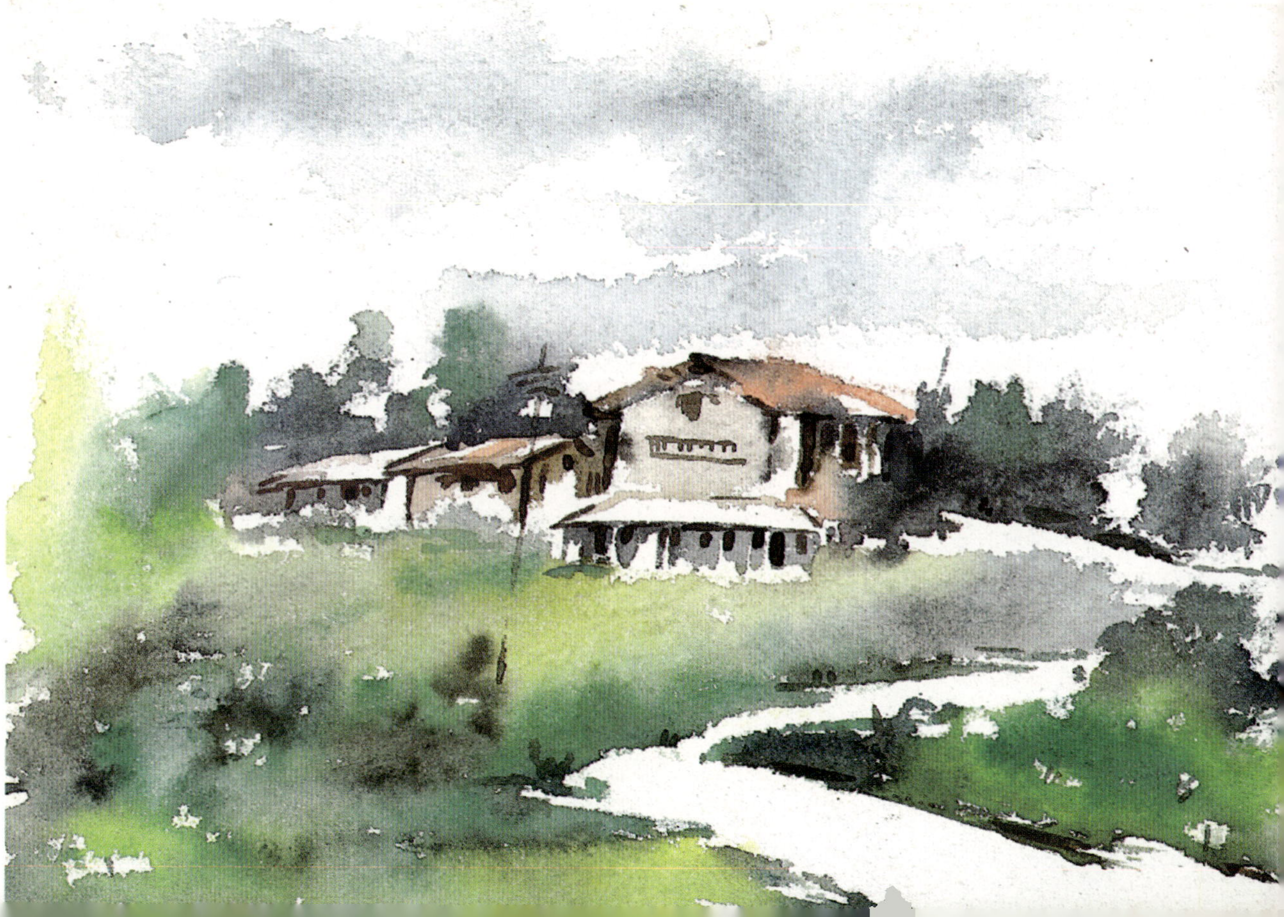

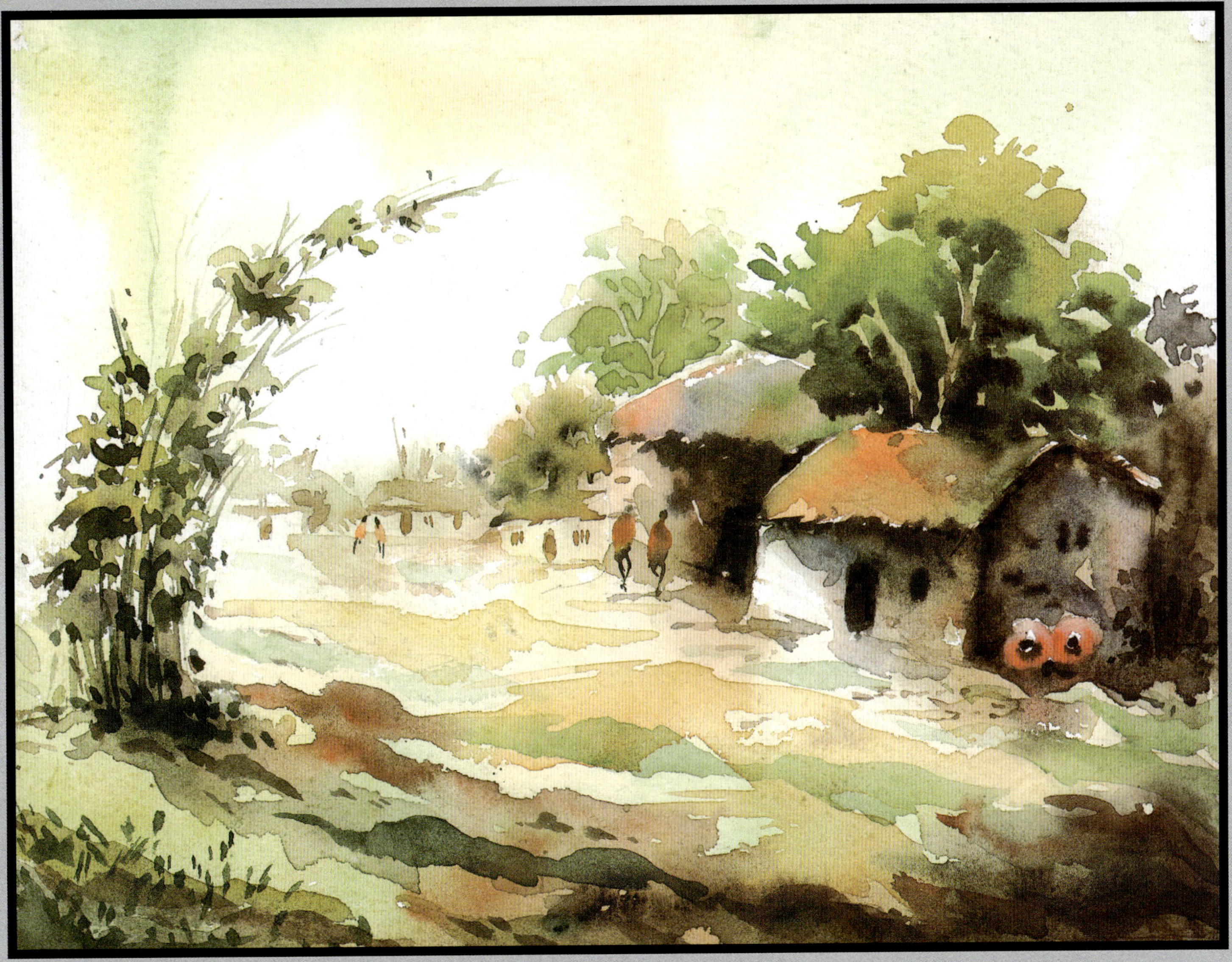

In this painting, the artist has taken the pathway and the vegetation around as the foreground, the houses as the middle ground and trees and the skyline as the background. To keep the painting soft and loose, he has avoided giving outlines to the trees. The clouds have been given three-dimensional shapes for giving it the air of reality. He has not given any solid outlines anywhere in the painting because then they destroy the illusion of form.

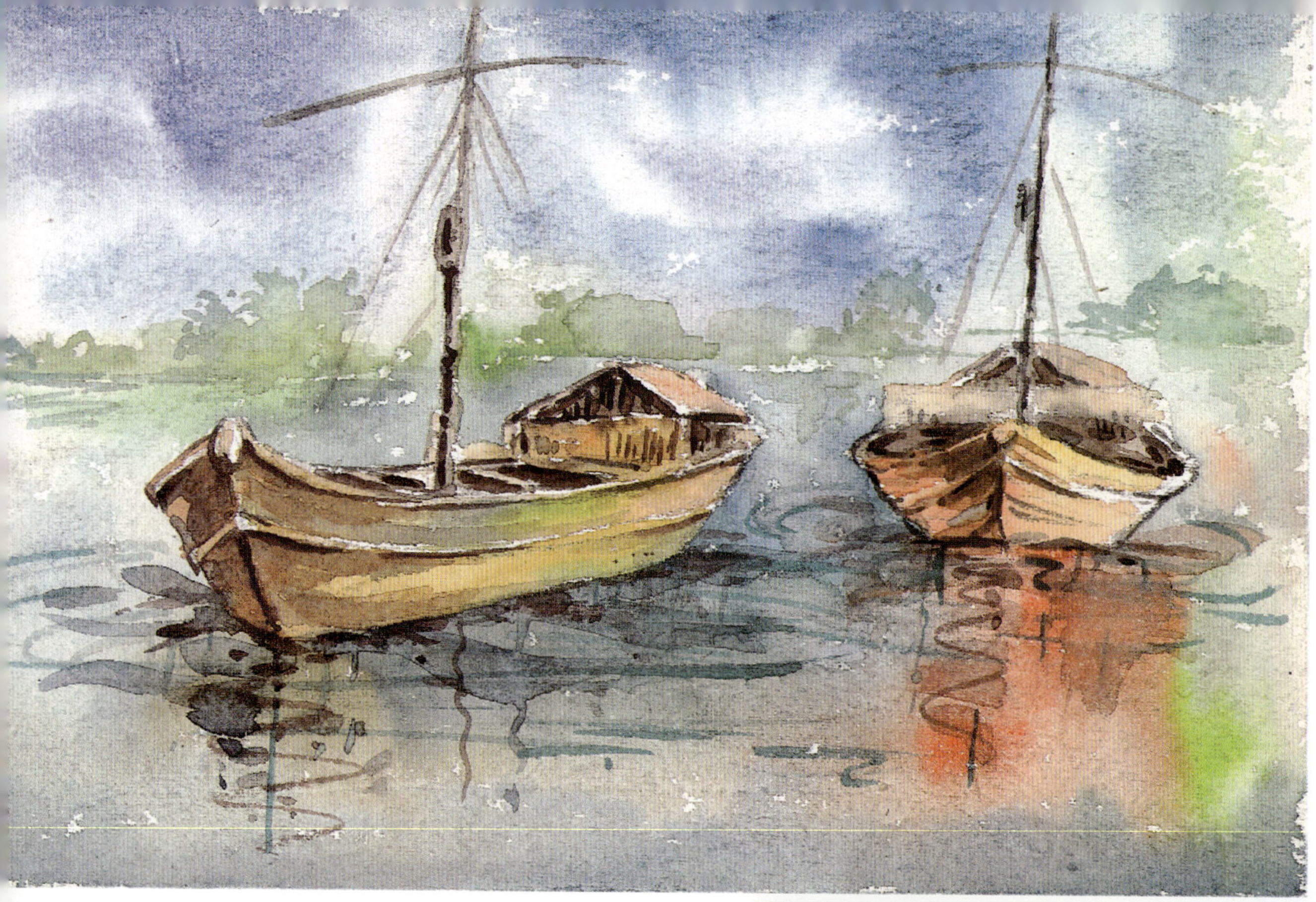

Wet-in-wet wash technique is used while doing watercolours. And for this you need a lot of practice. To achieve the desired effect, the colours have to be blended the right way. Watercolours, as you know by now, are a transparent medium. Every coat of watercolour that you apply on a surface is affected by the colour you have previously applied. So do not overwork with any other colour. Retain the transparency to achieve the desired effect. Here the artist has applied darker patches of the previously applied shade only where the artist wanted to portray the region in the shade. This also brings out a dramatic effect.

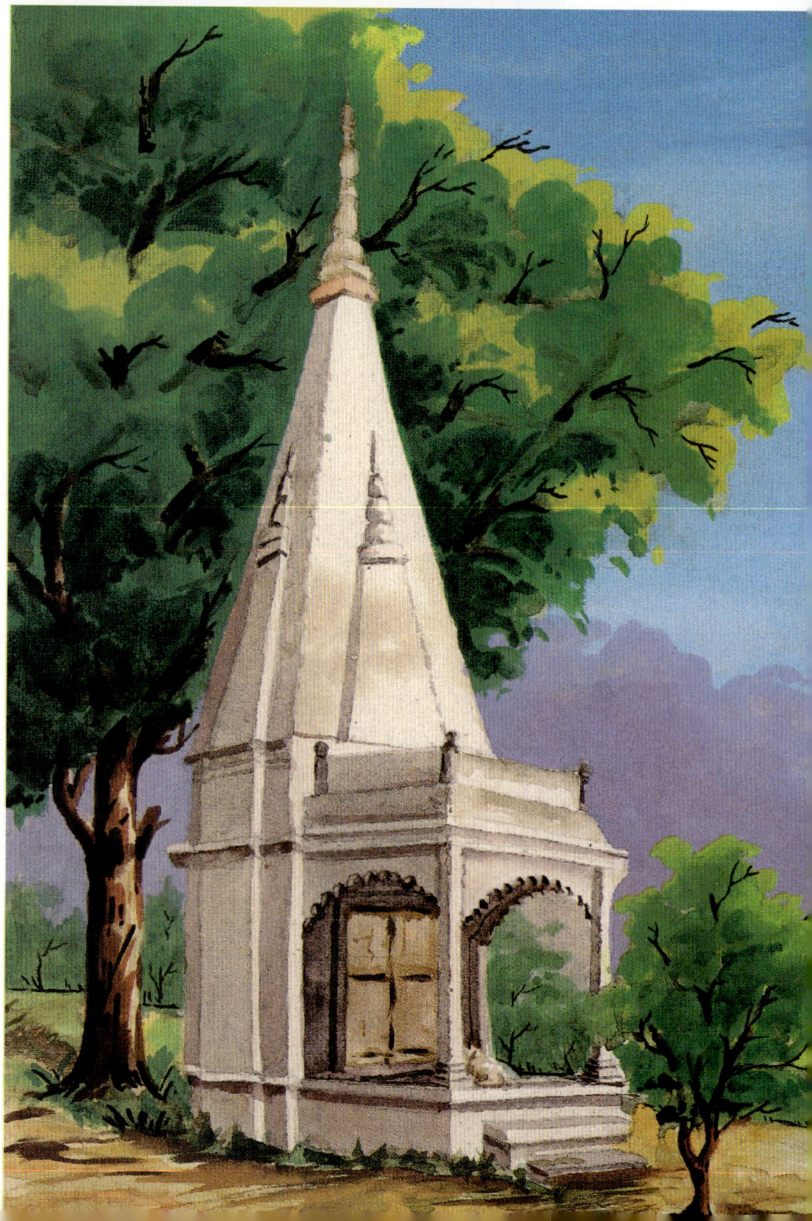

Again after the initial wash, he has applied a very light tone of Blue for the effect of the sky. He used Sap Green strokes to depict the tree and a light tone of Burnt Umber for the house. Darker patches of Sap Green were used to show the thick foliage on the tree and the grass in the foreground, while dark tones of Burnt Sienna for the trunk.

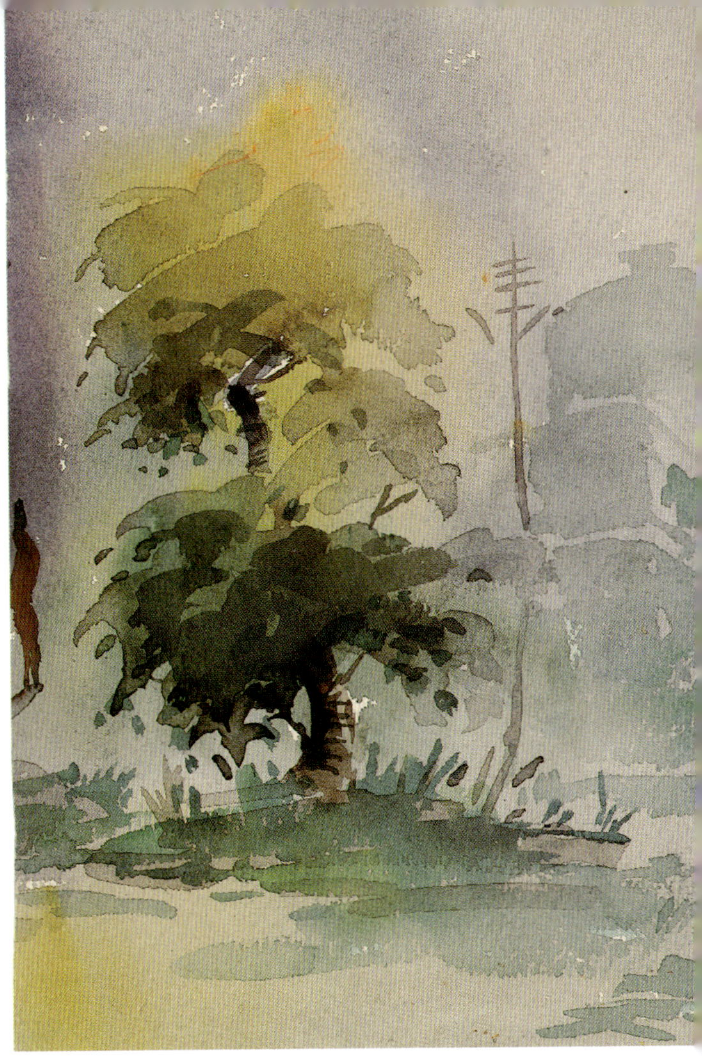

Here the toned ground harmonises with house in the background and the tree in the foreground. The artist has applied darker shades on the trunk because the source of light is somewhere behind the houses in the background. So the region under the tree is also given a dark tone.

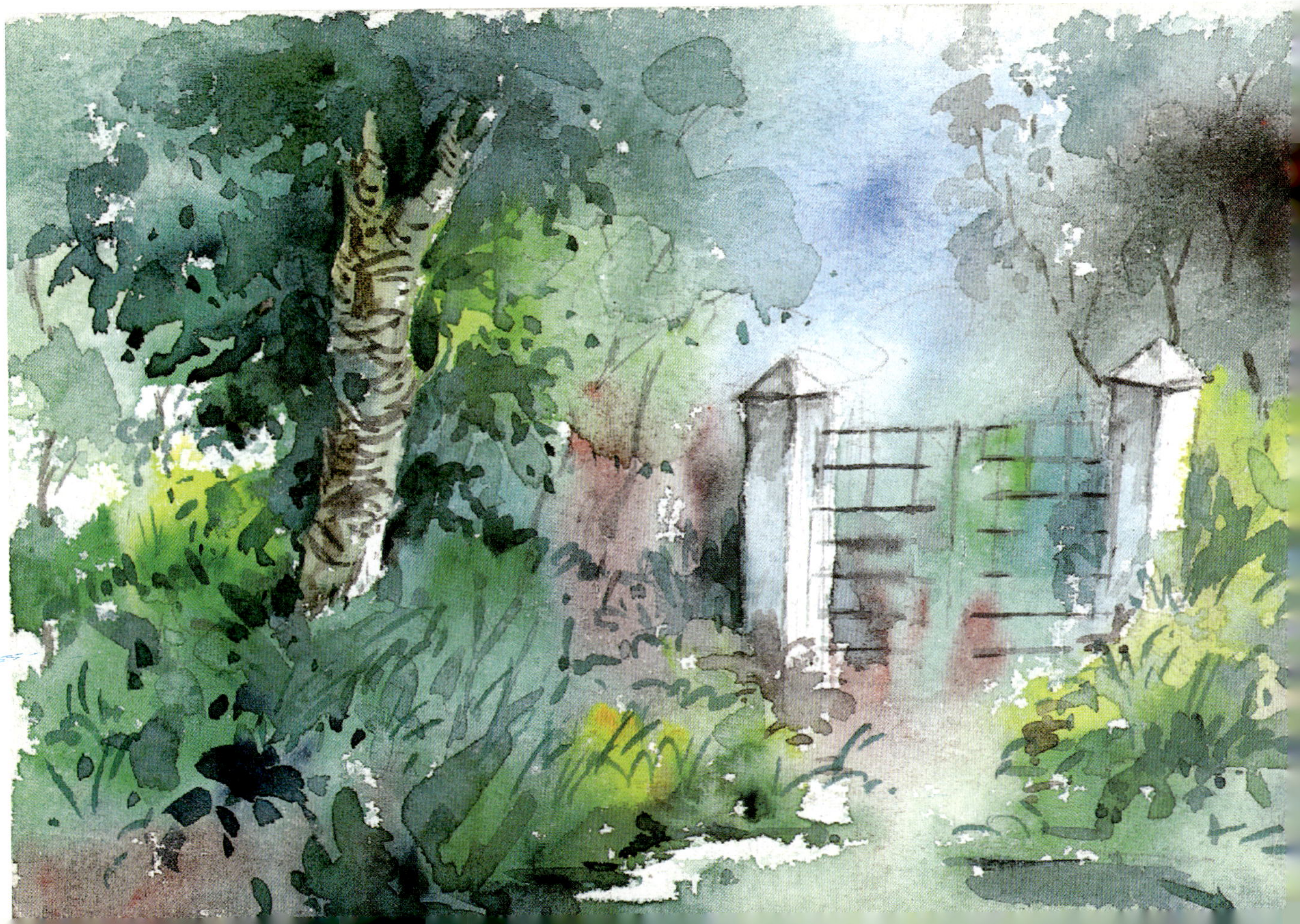

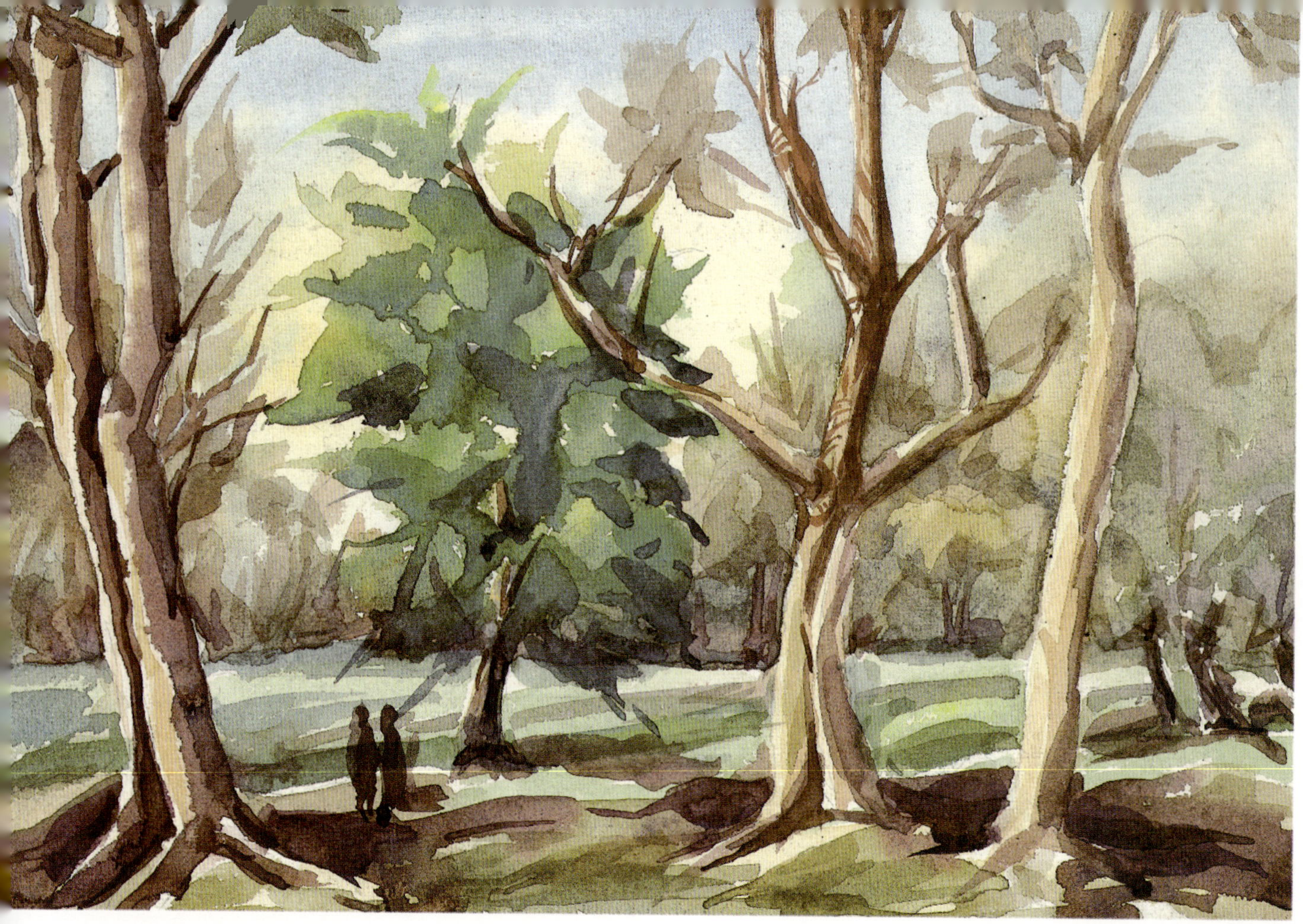

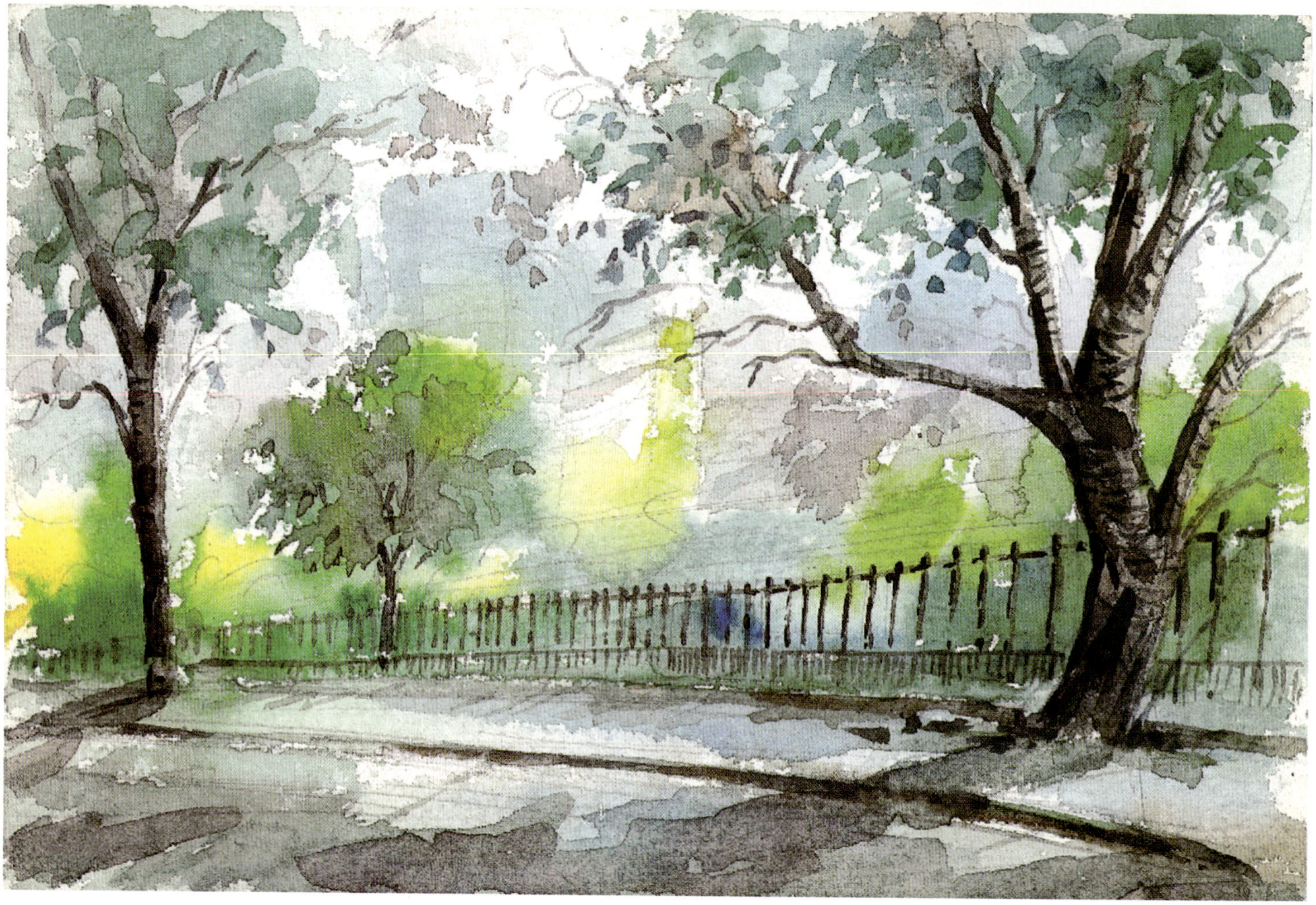

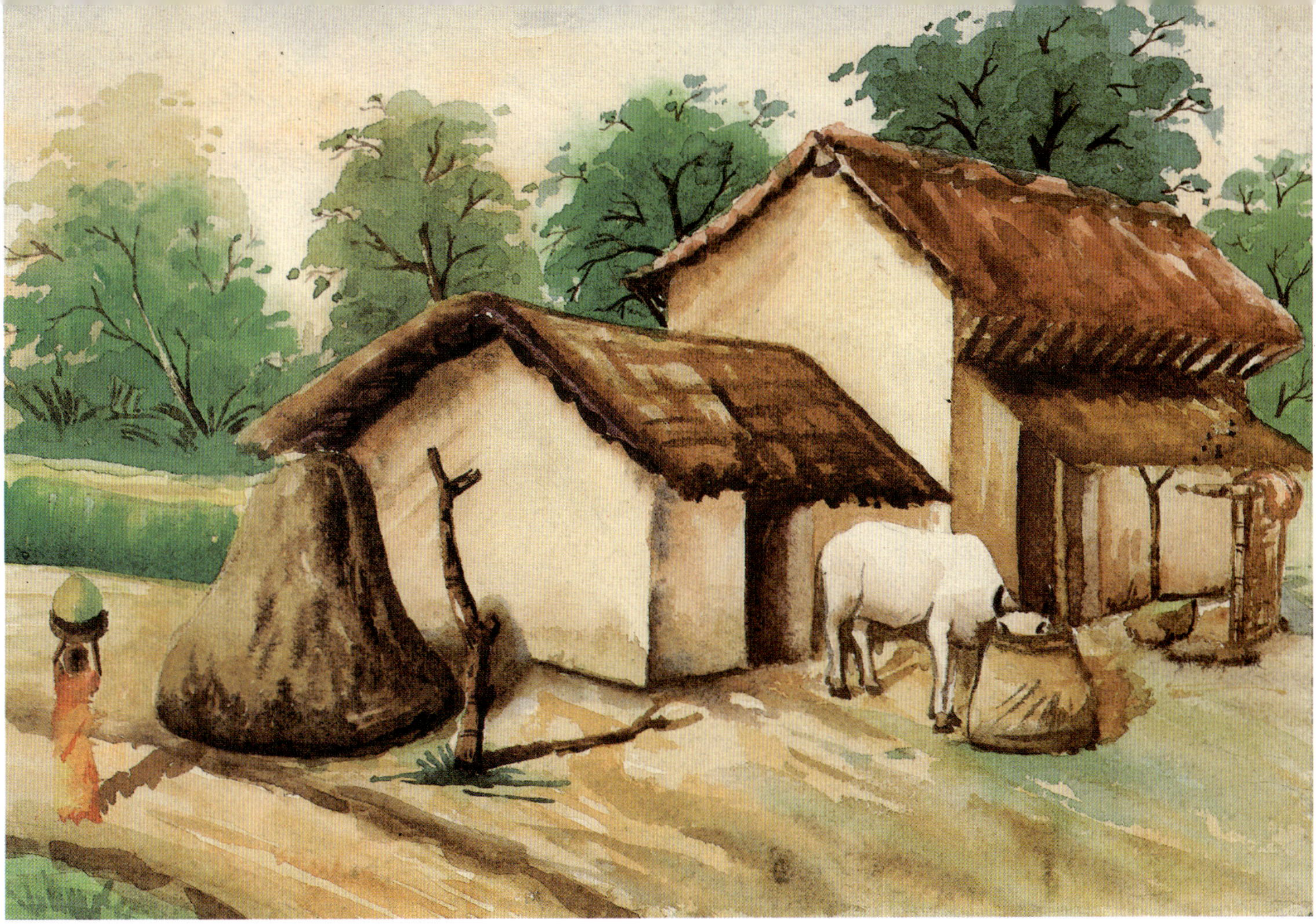

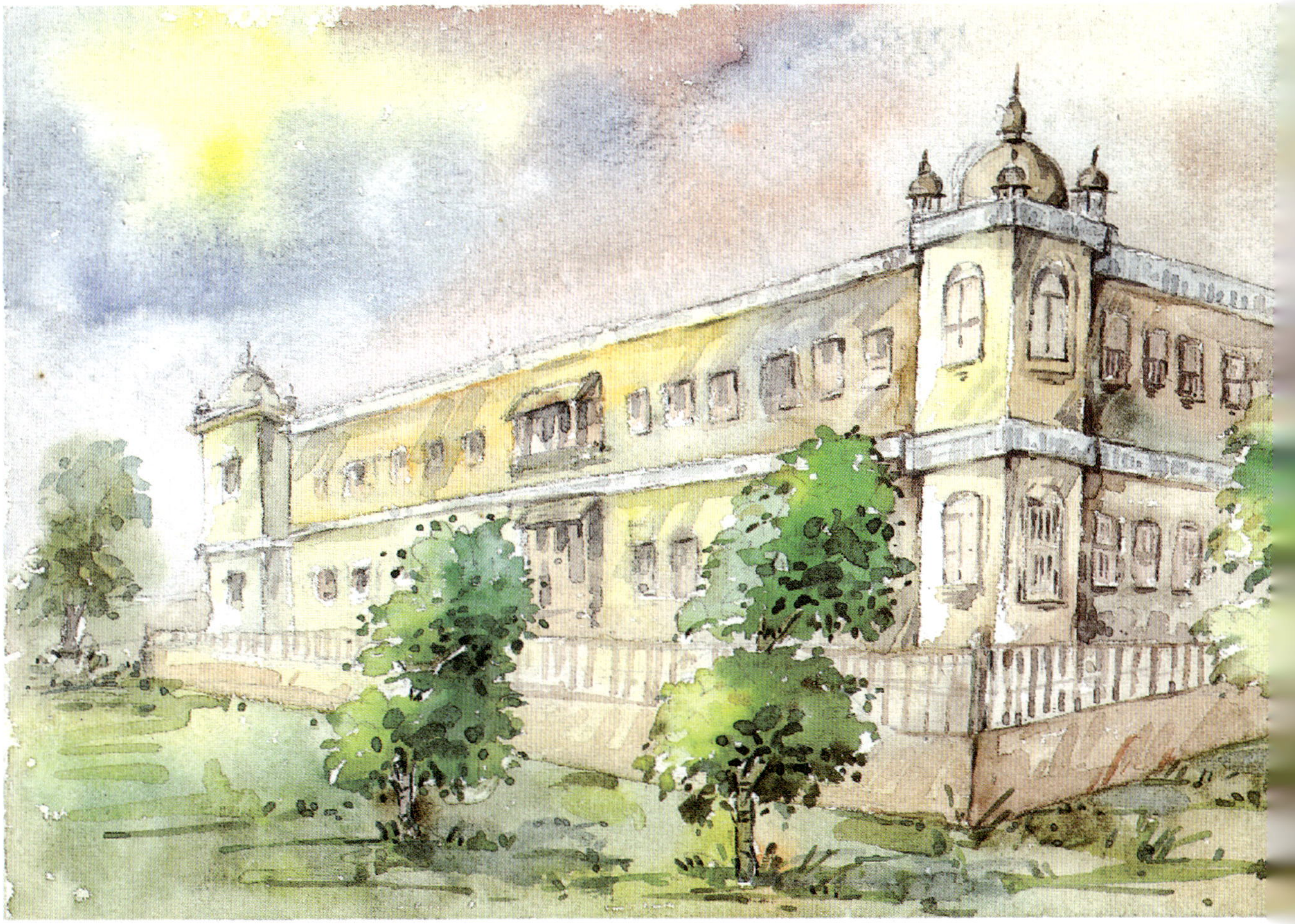

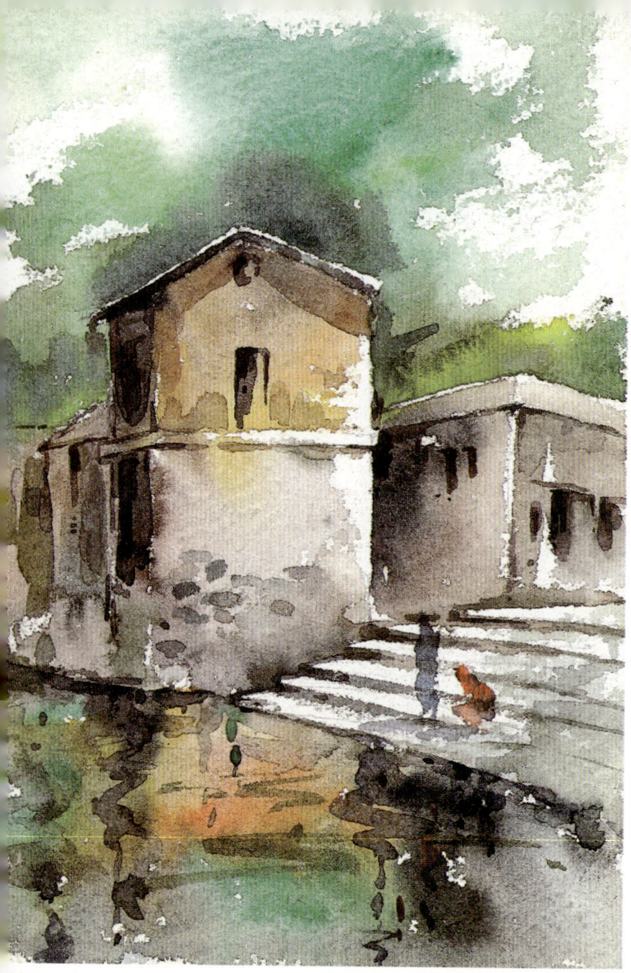

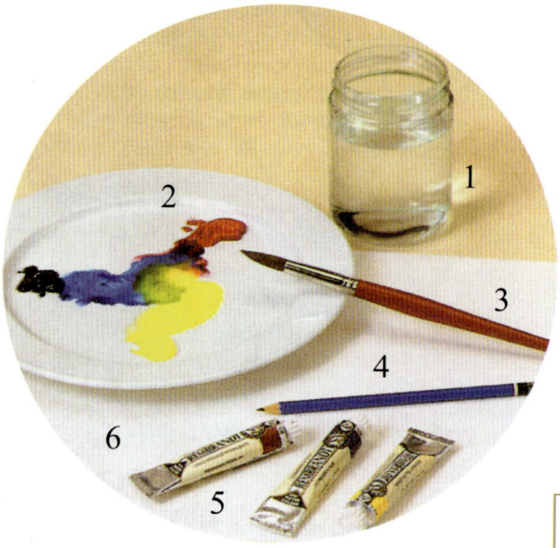

Materials

1. Water Jar
2. Plate
3. Brushes
4. Pencil
5. Tube Colours
6. Paper

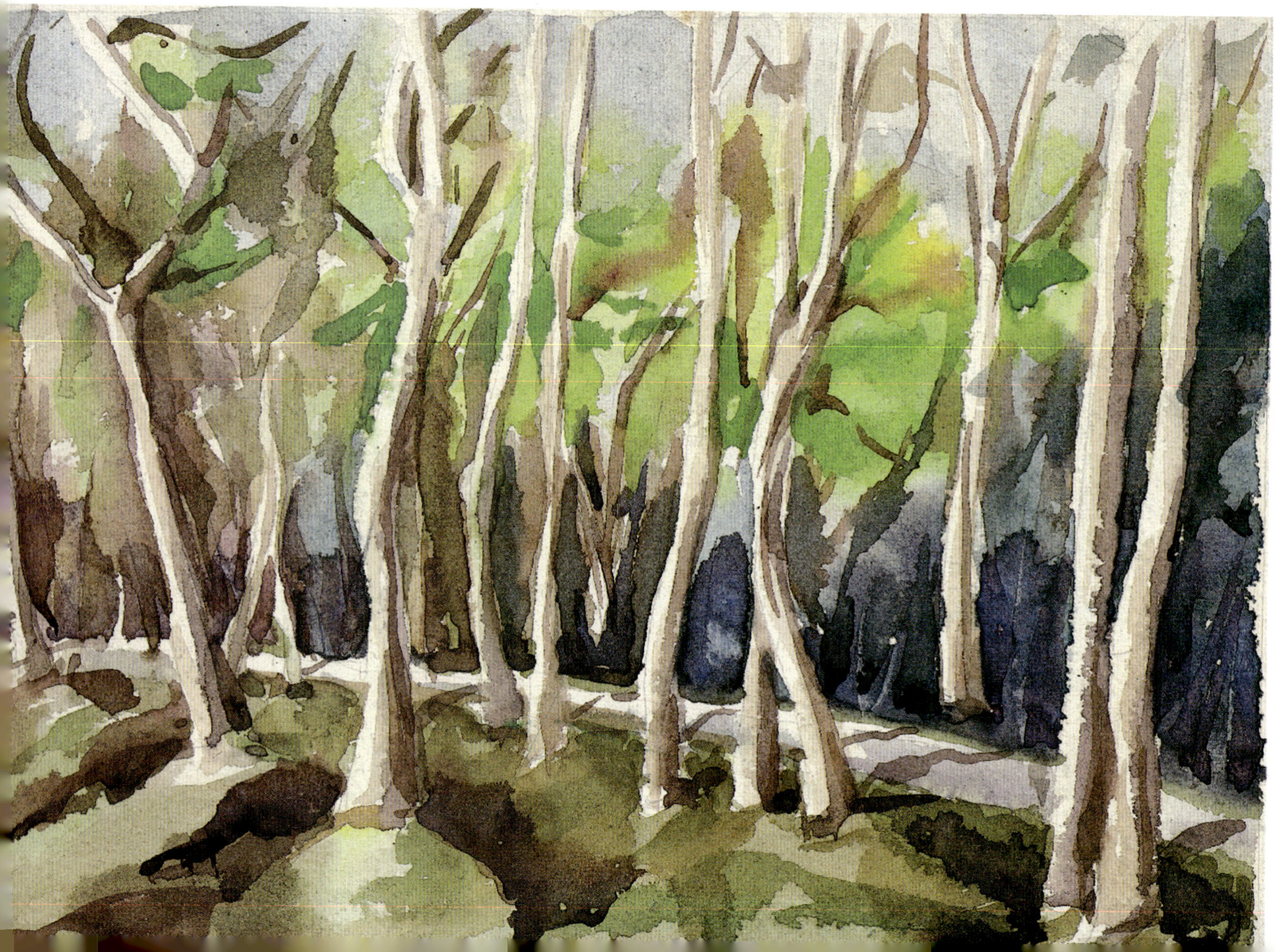

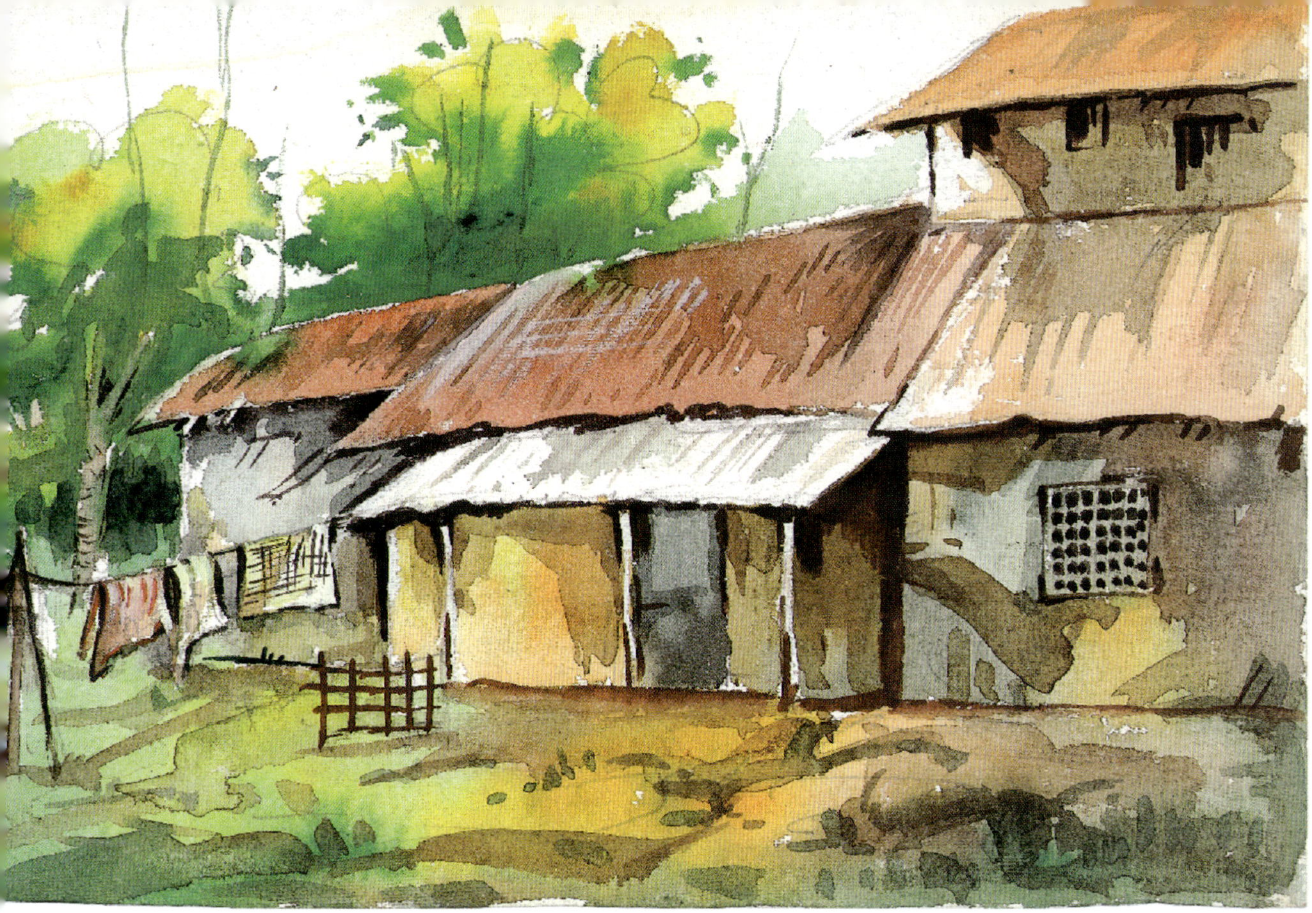

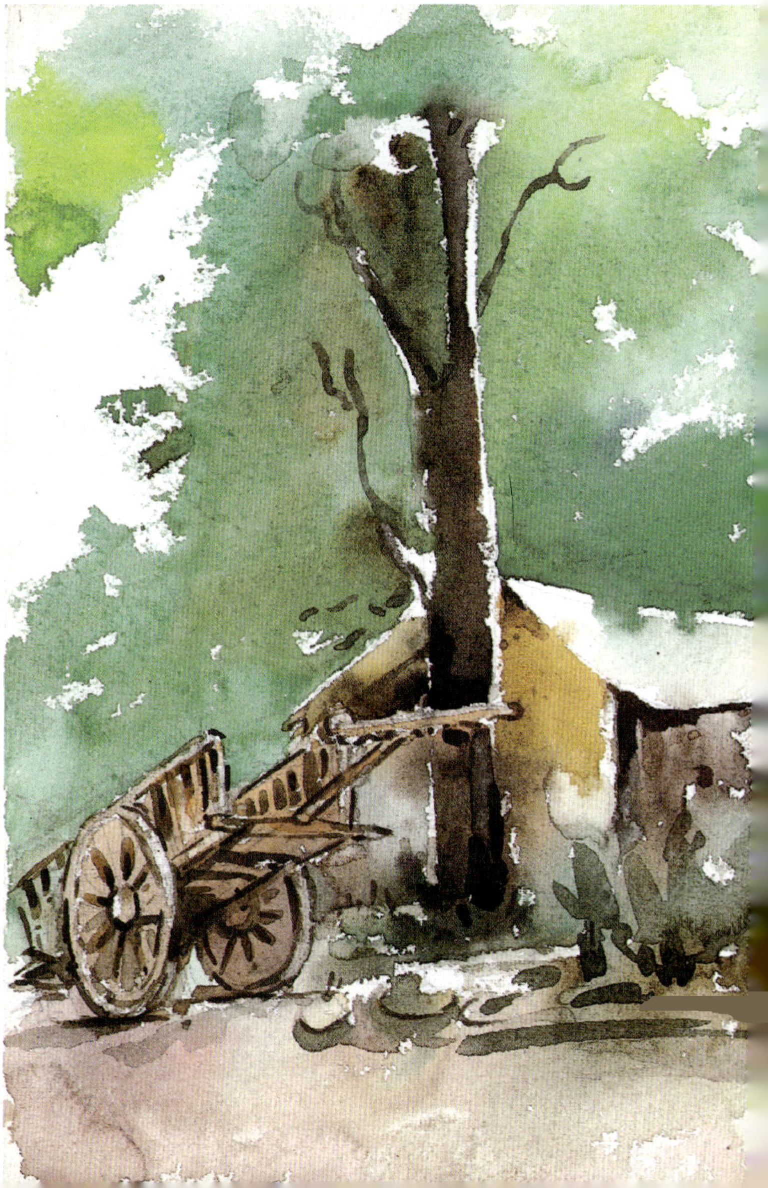

Here the toned ground harmonises with house in the background and the tree in the foreground. Darker shades have been applied on the trunk because the source of light was somewhere behind the houses in the background. So the region under the tree is also given a dark tone.

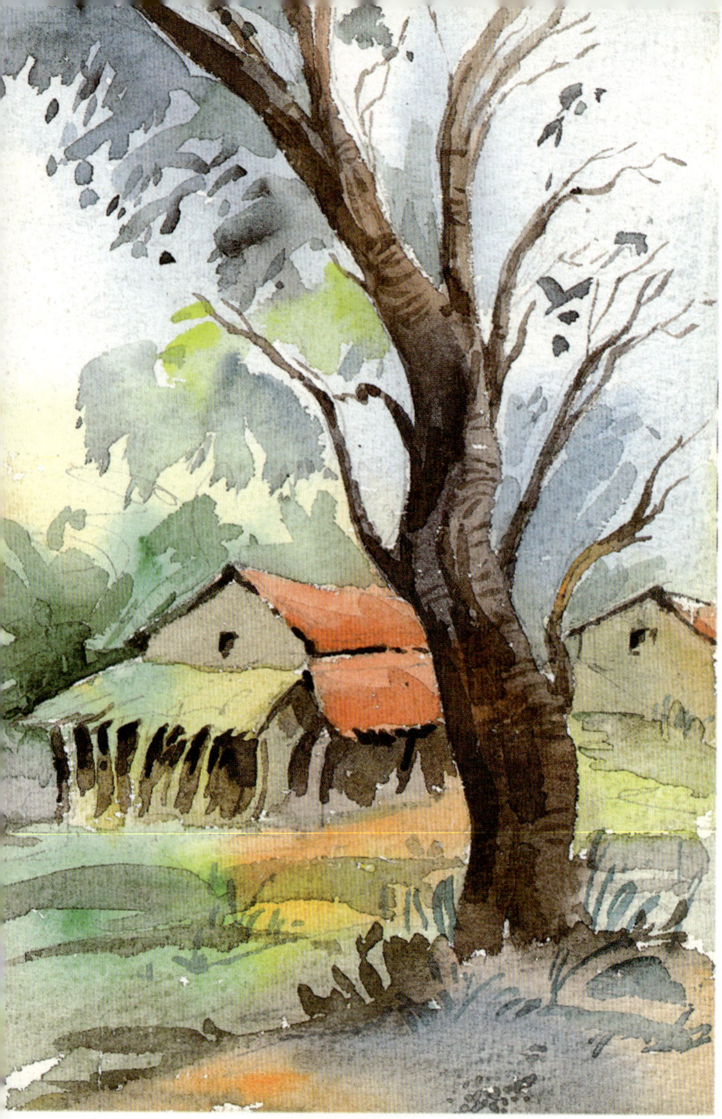

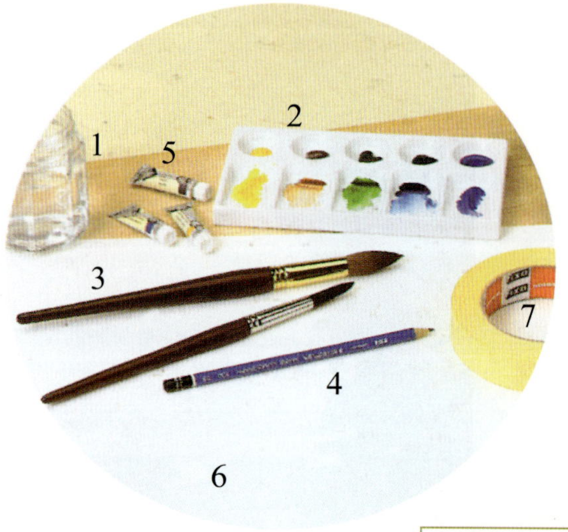

Materials

1. Water Jar
2. Colour Plate
3. Brushes
4. Pencil
5. Tube Colours
6. Paper
7. Tape

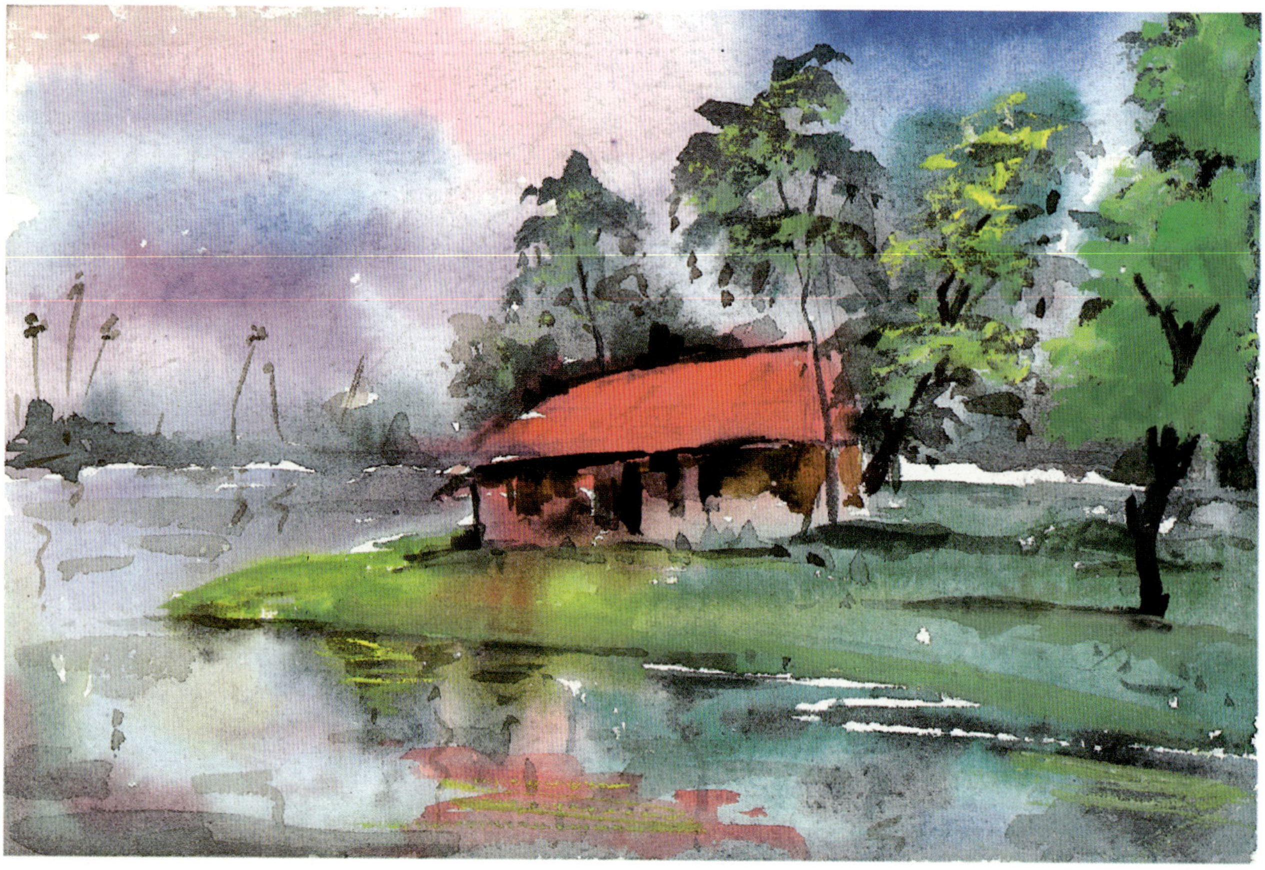

Painting the Skies (Composition)

Most artists use a technique called atmosphere perspective when painting a landscape. This technique helps to create the illusion of depth. A canvas or paper is two-dimensional, but you want the onlookers to believe that your painting is true-to-life or three-dimensional. And to create the illusion you have to work on three planes, that is to say dividing the painting into foreground, middle ground and background.

Always remember that sky tends to set the mood of a landscape. This is because it is the source of light. So it is necessary that you consider the sky as an integral part of your landscape rather than just as a backdrop. Don't try to treat the sky and the land as two separate entities. Try to blend the colour of the sky and the land when you are working on a landscape.

And while painting clouds, give it a three-dimensional form with the help of light and shadow.

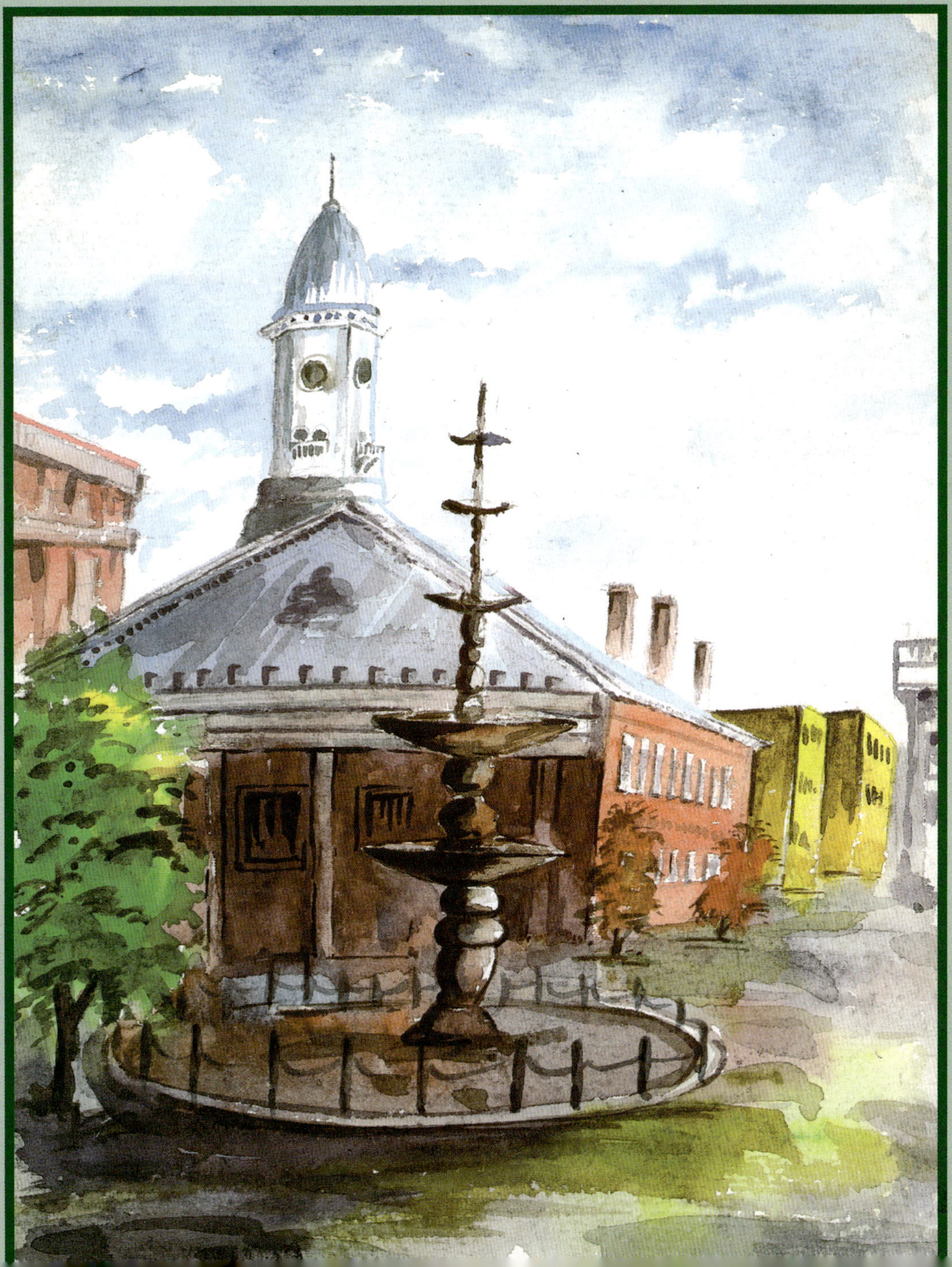

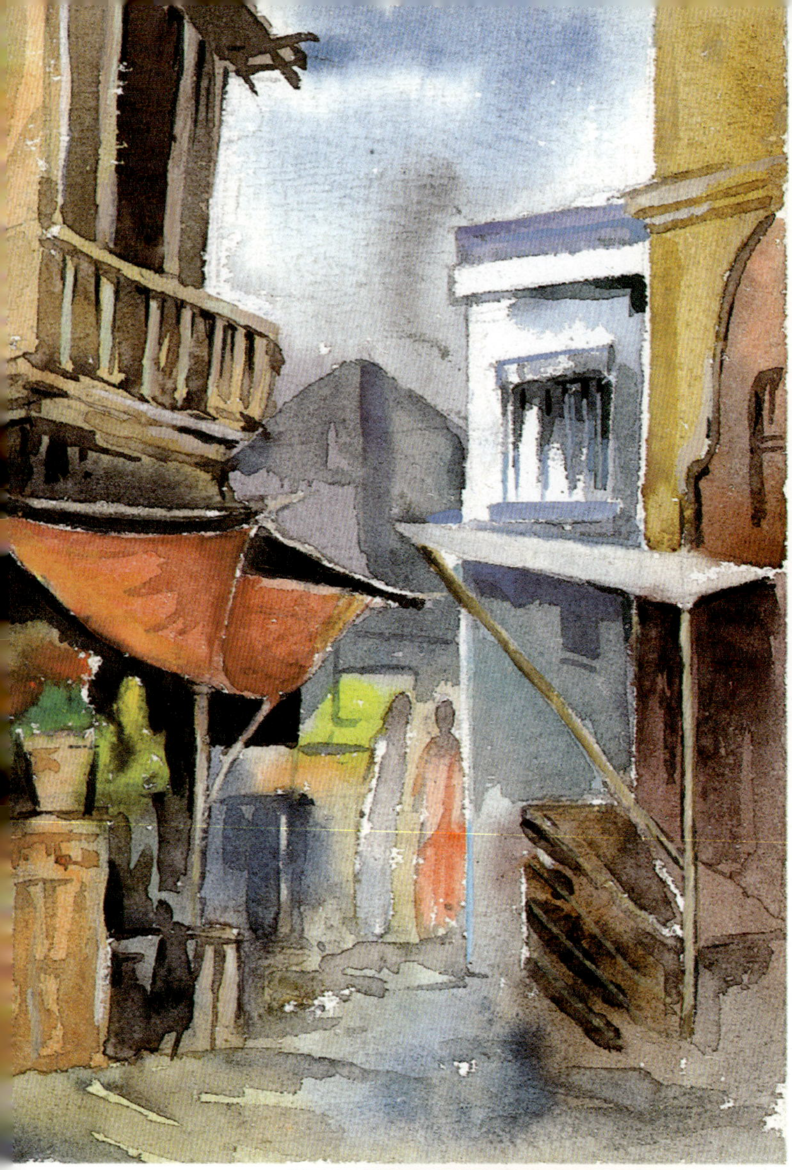

Your painting should have an atmosphere. The onlooker should be able to identify with your painting. And how do you create the right ambience? By using the right colour and playing with light and shade in this painting, the source of light is from the top. To the top of the building and the tent are done in a lighter shade. The portions under the tents are done in a darker hue.

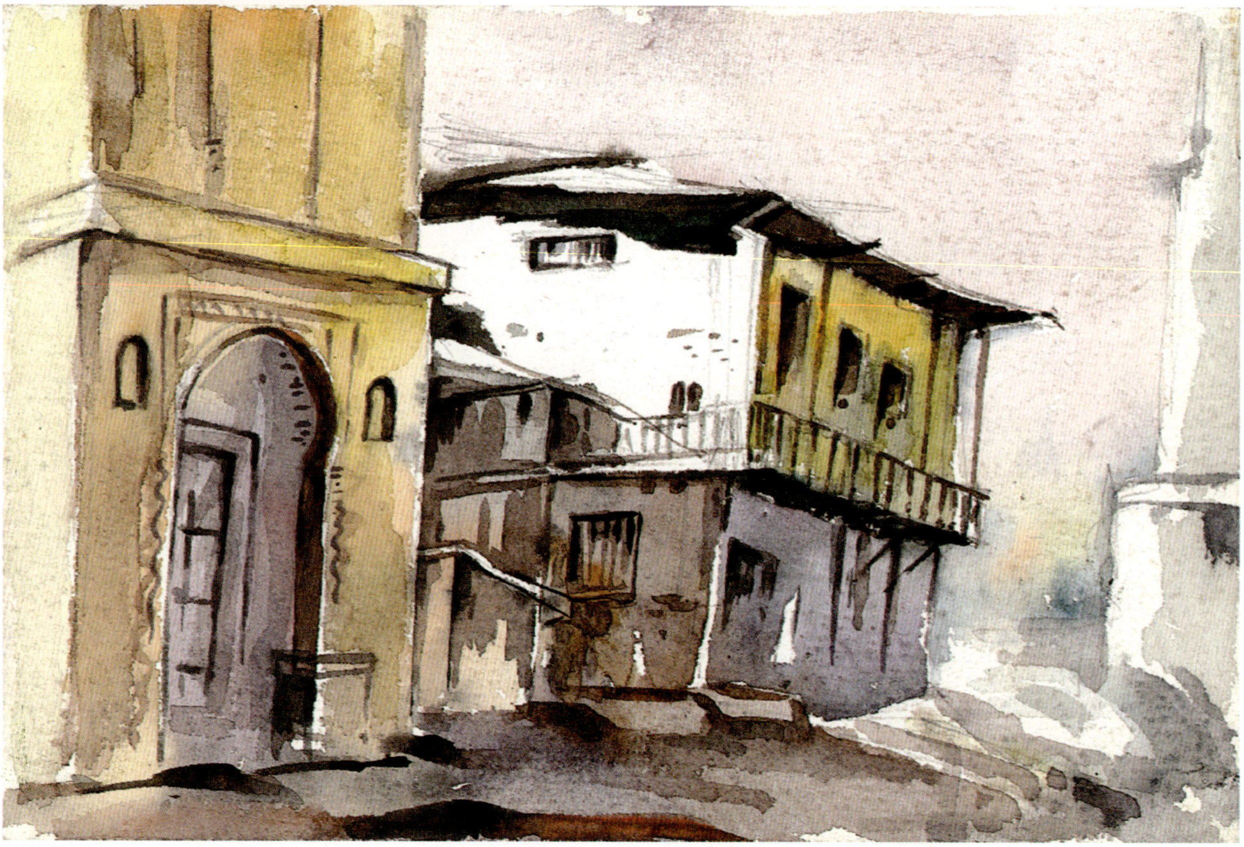

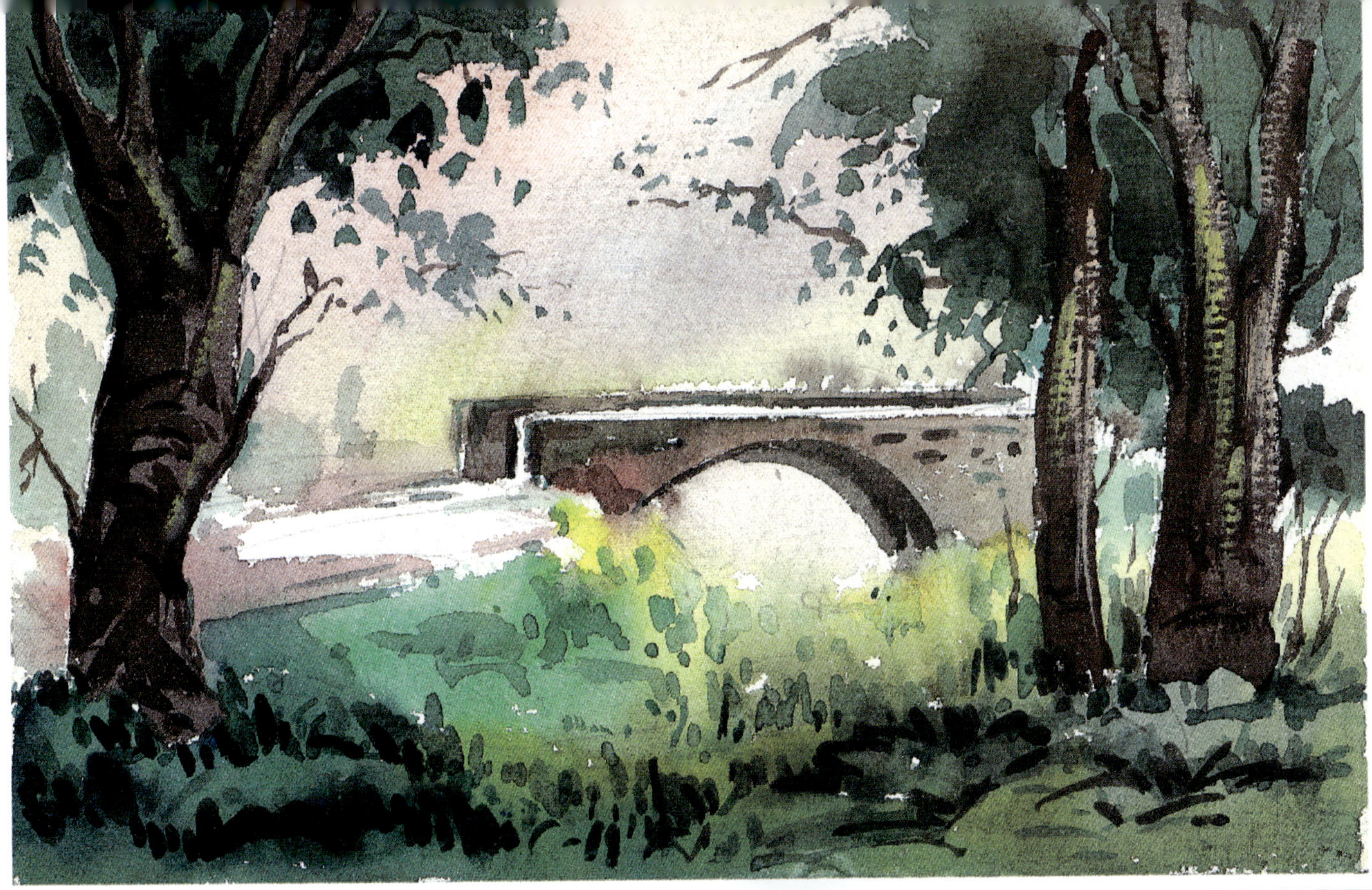

Helpful Hint

Remember that wet watercolour looks deceptively strong and will dry lighter. If you use too little pigment with too much water, your painting will look insipid.

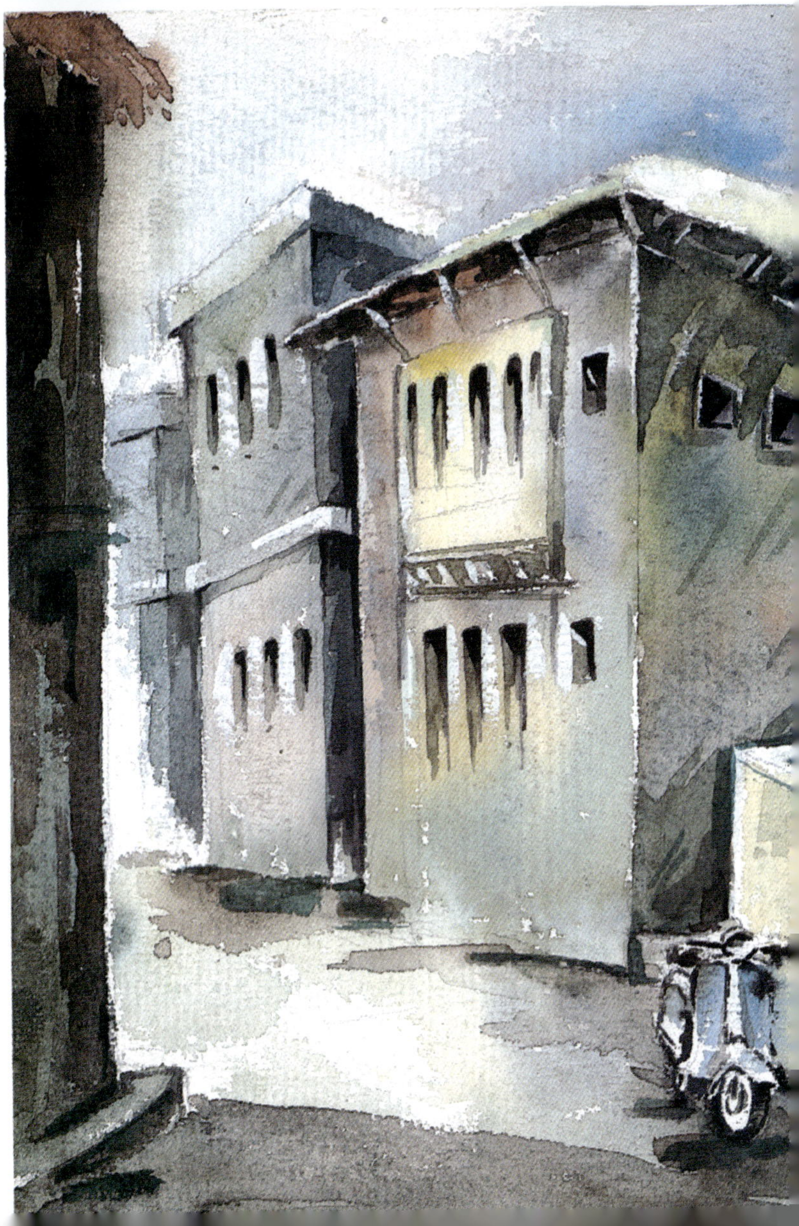

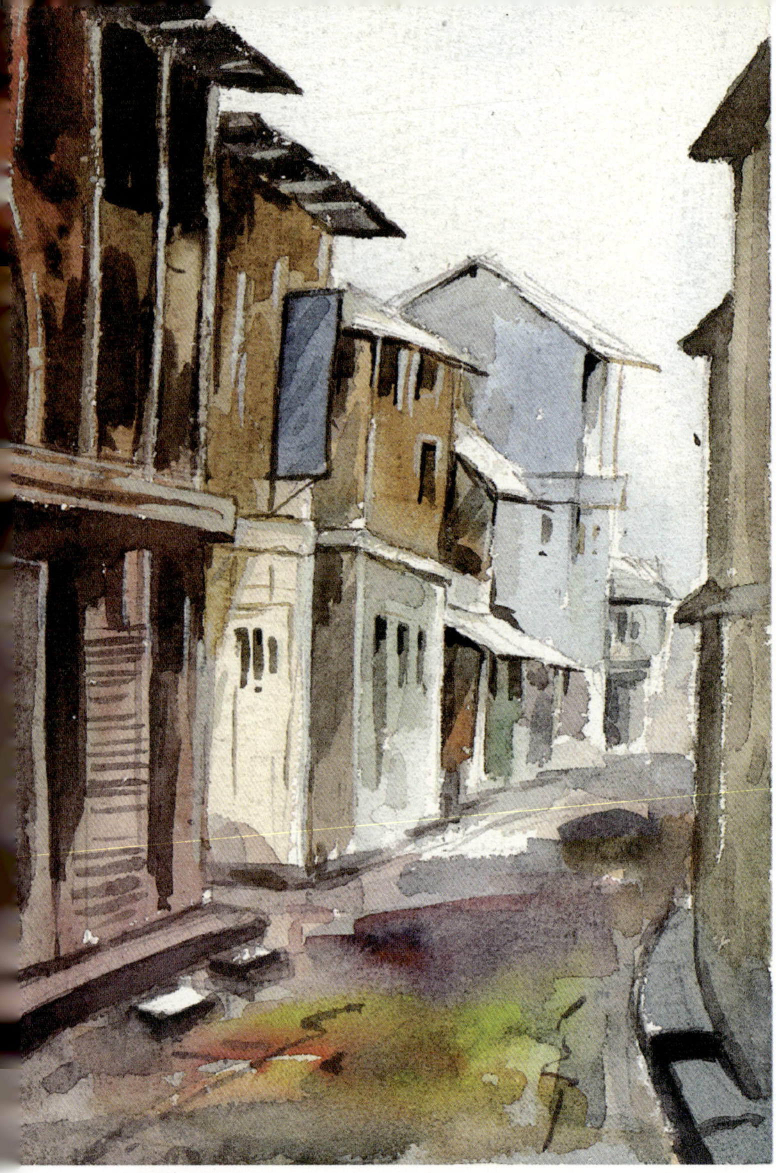

The source of light in this painting is somewhere in the background beyond the painting. It has also been tried to give perspective to the painting. The houses in the background are done in light shades of Burnt Umber and not depicted in great details. The houses in the middle ground have been depicted in a mix of light and dark shades whereas the houses in the foreground are in the darker shade. Likewise light and dark shades of Burnt Sienna are used to depict the pathway.

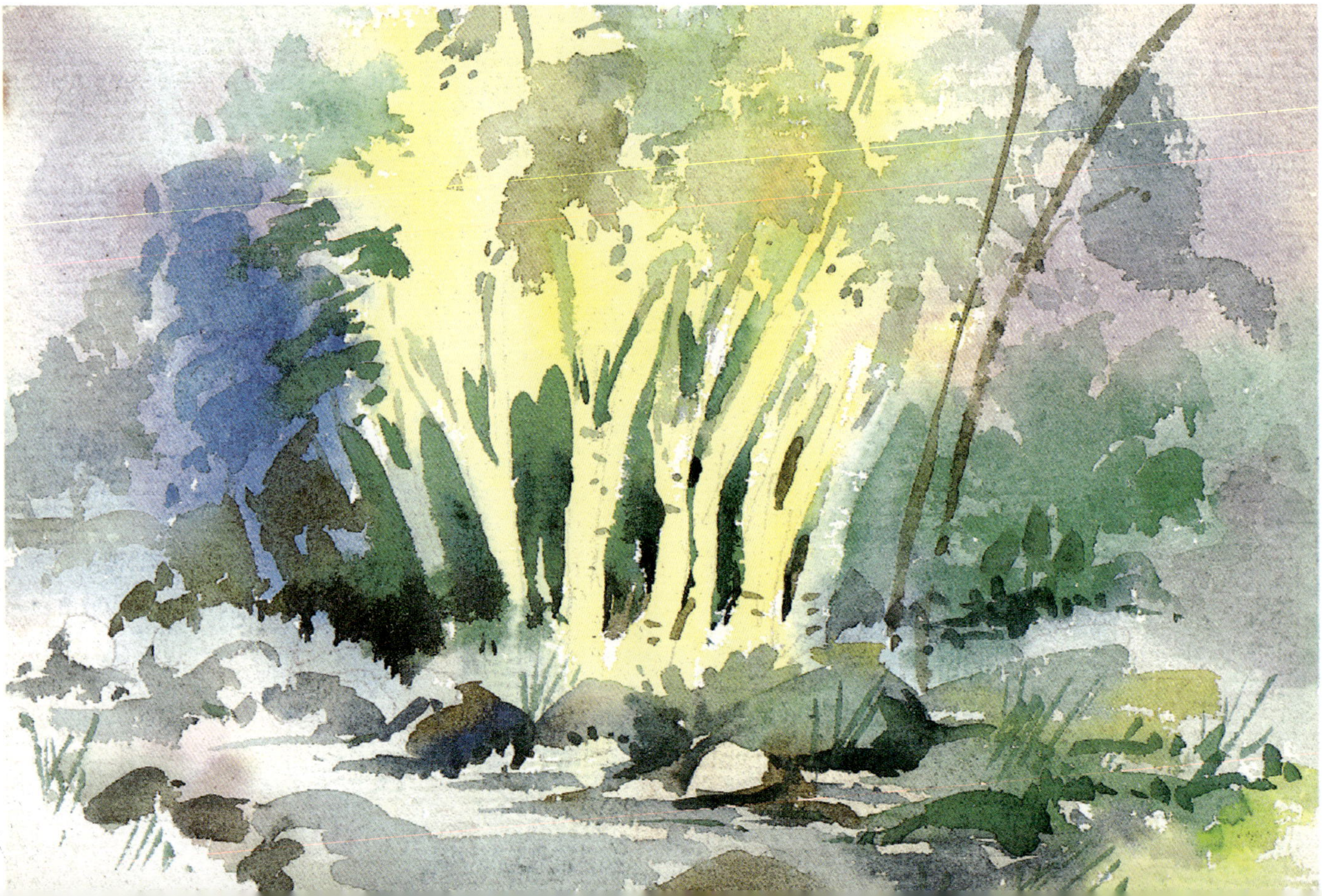

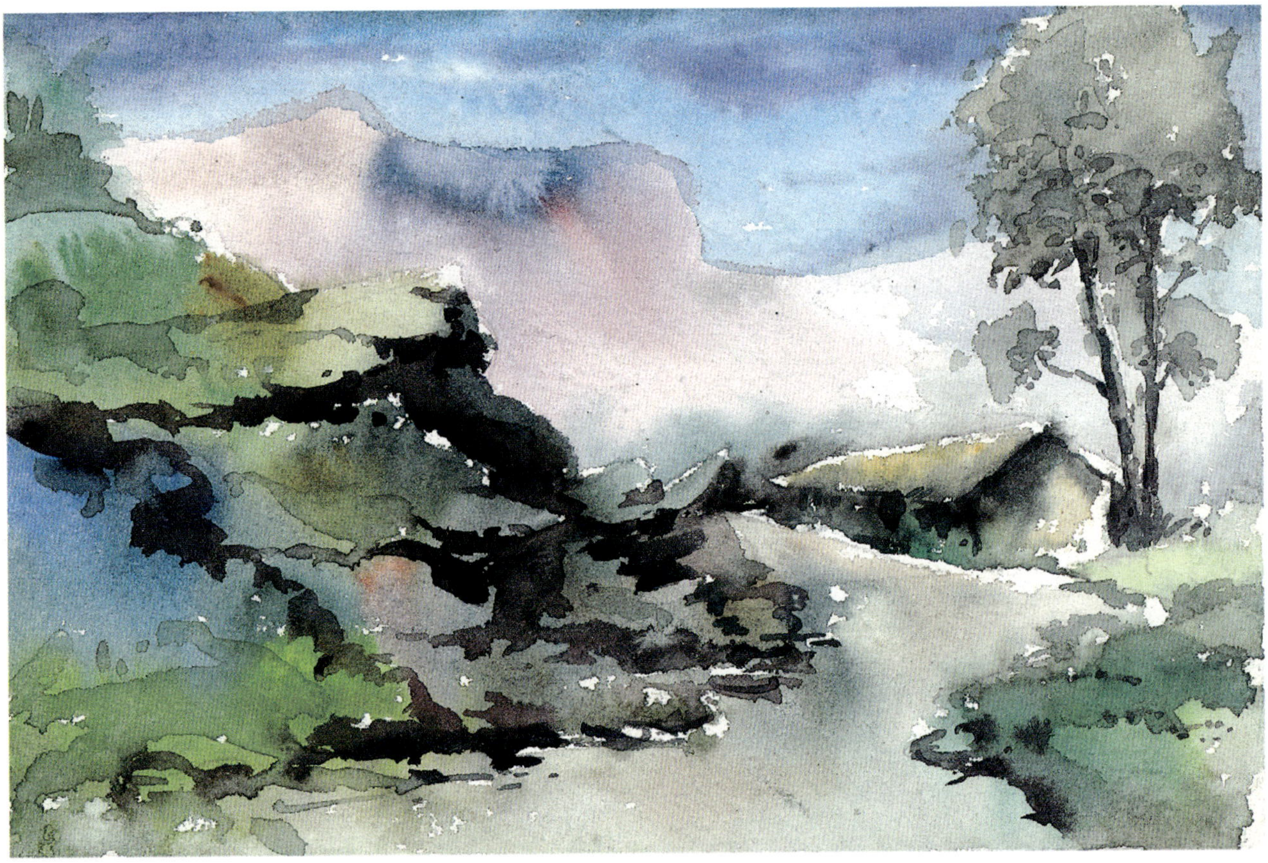

This picture creates a feeling of quiet and solitude. And this has been achieved by using brunt senna colours. After the initial light wash, Blue has been released in the background. On the left, released light tone of Burnt Umber. To depict the tree, Sap Green used. Then added middle tone of Burnt Umber and Sap Green on the mountain and the tree. The artist has depicted the pathway with Yellow. Finally, a few strokes of Burnt Sienna have been used to show light and shade of the mountain and Dark Green on the tree. Burnt Sienna has applied for the tree trunk.

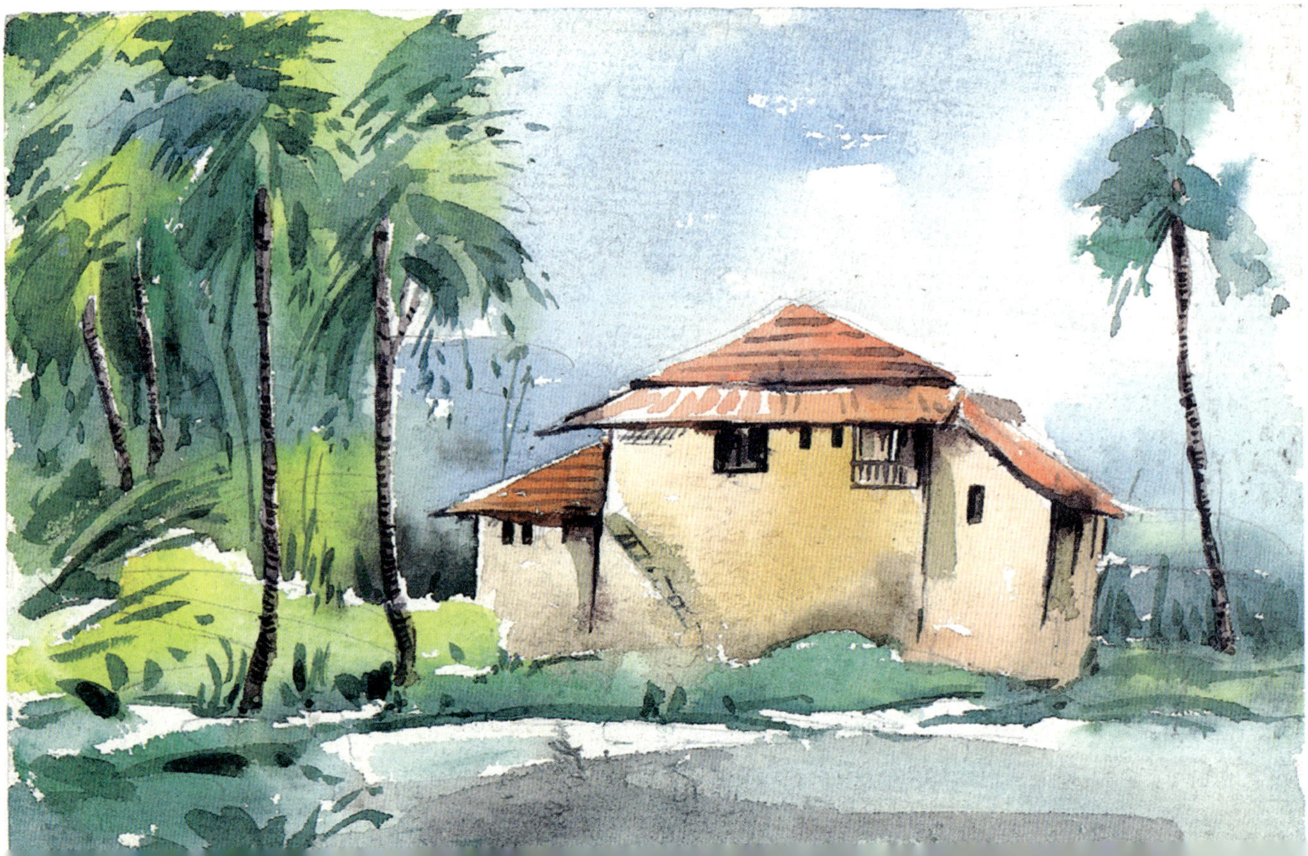

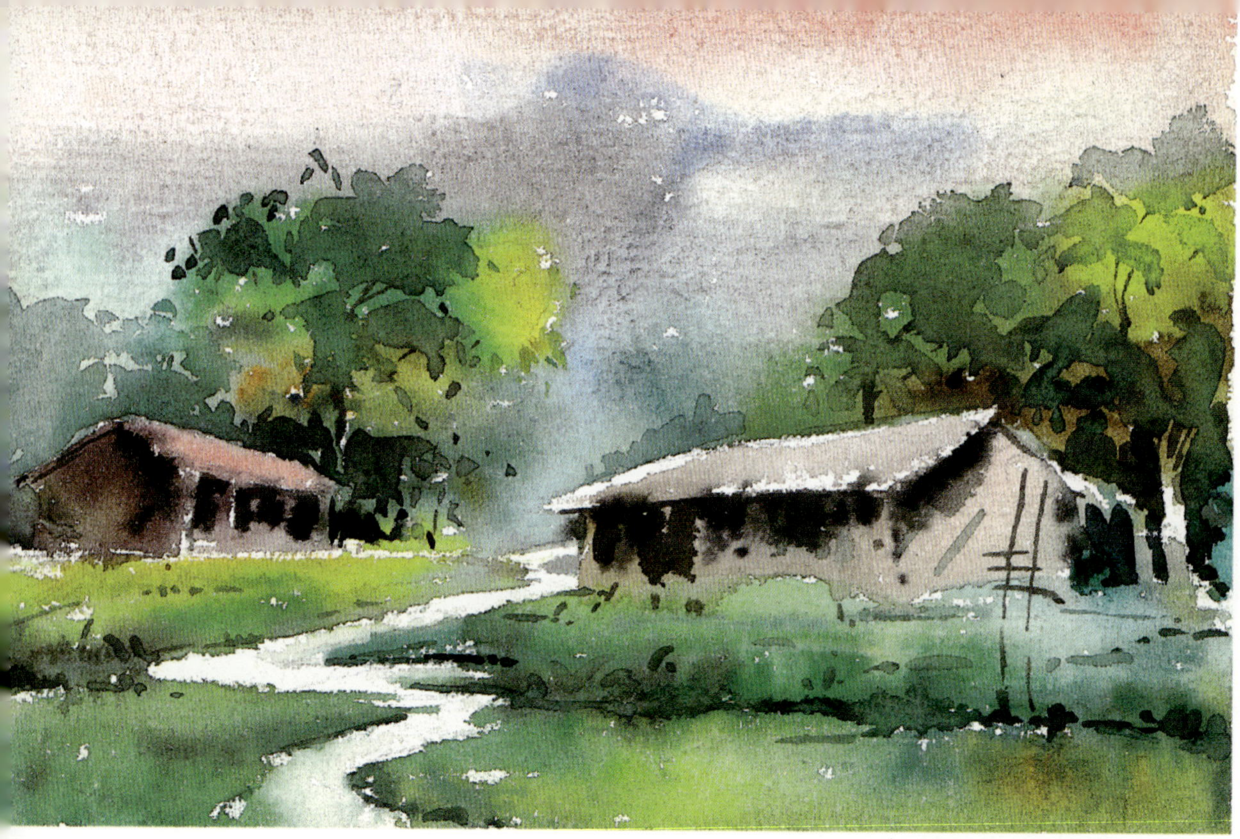

There are many components in this particular painting. In fact, there is a lot of foliage both in the foreground and in the background. In the middle ground are the houses. Further I have played with light and shade.

After the initial wash, the artist has released Viridian in the background. When still wet, he released sap green on the left and right. Simultaneously, he also released yellow in the middle to depict the pathway. The house on the right is in the shade while that on the left is in the light. Again he worked by using light, middle and dark tones of all shades and balanced them with soft shades. In this way the artist has tried to show the perspective in this painting.

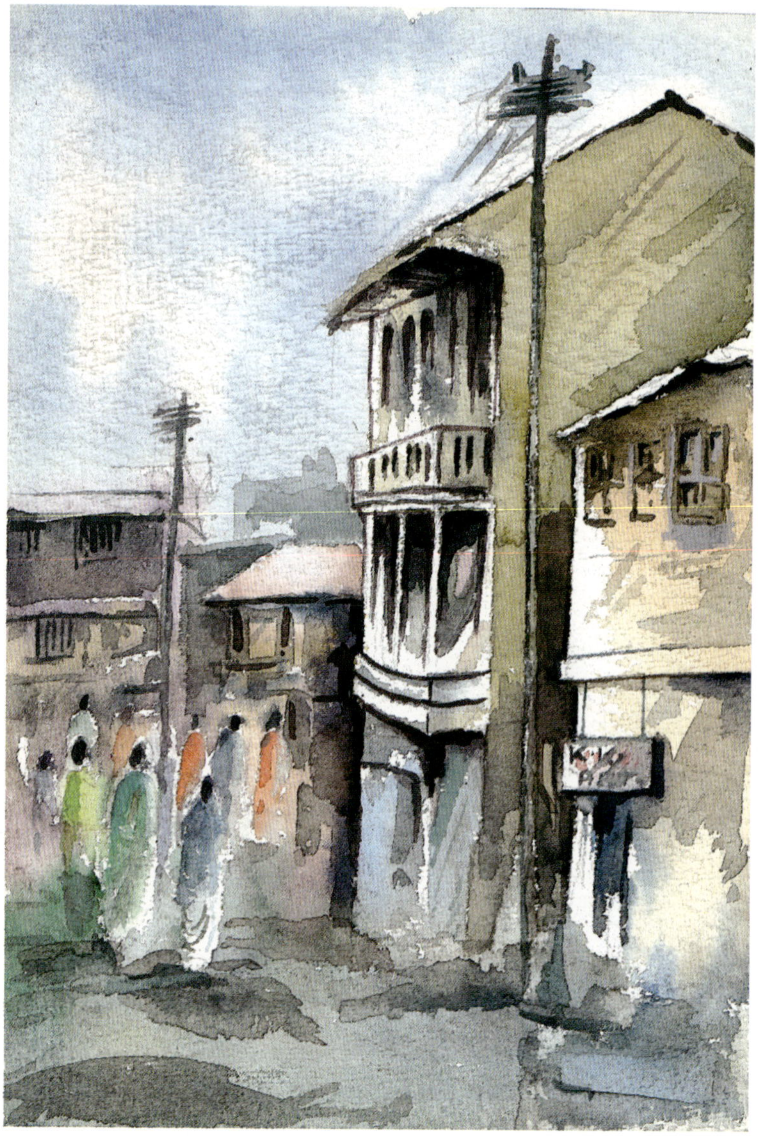

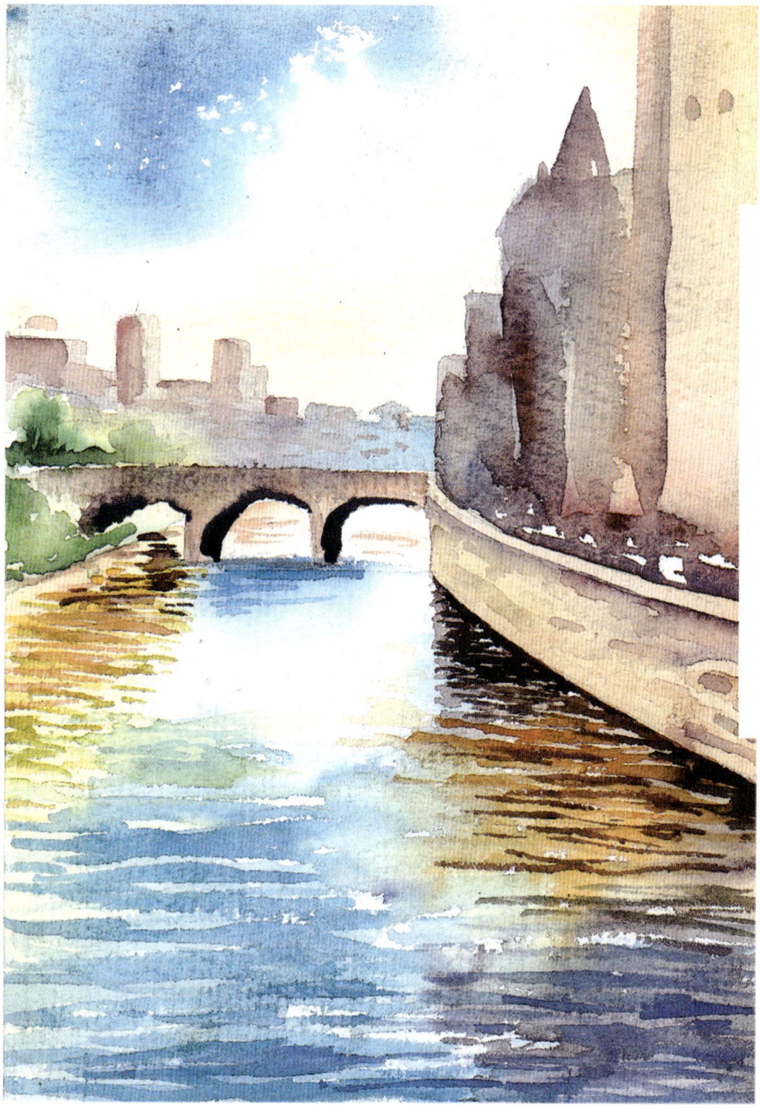

Helpful Hints

If you make a mistake, flood the area with water and then blot off the offending paint with tissue paper or a clean brush.

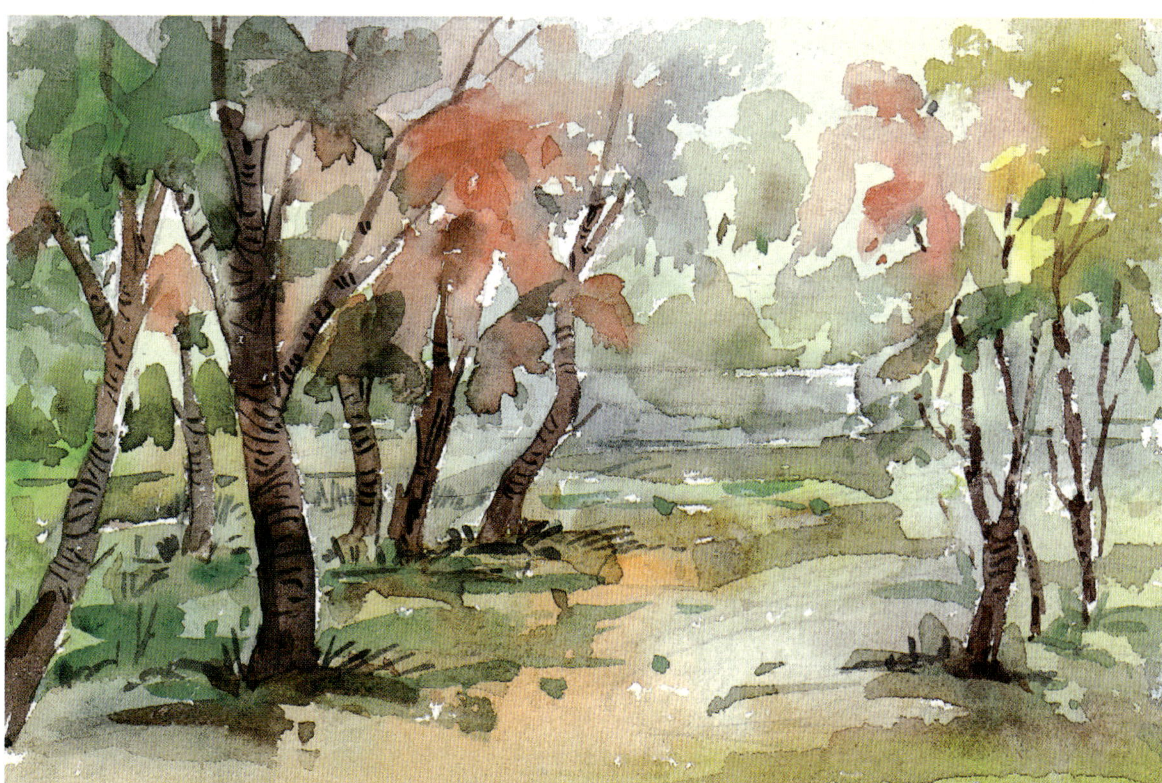

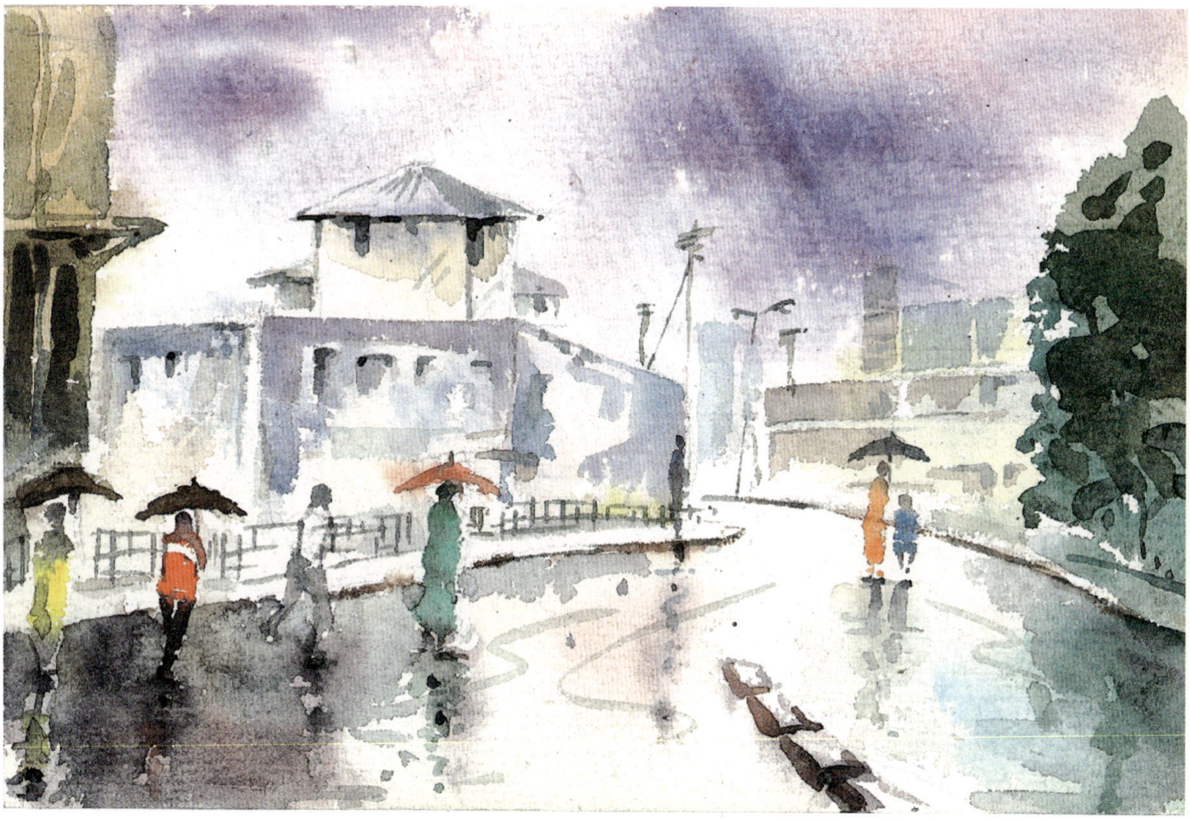

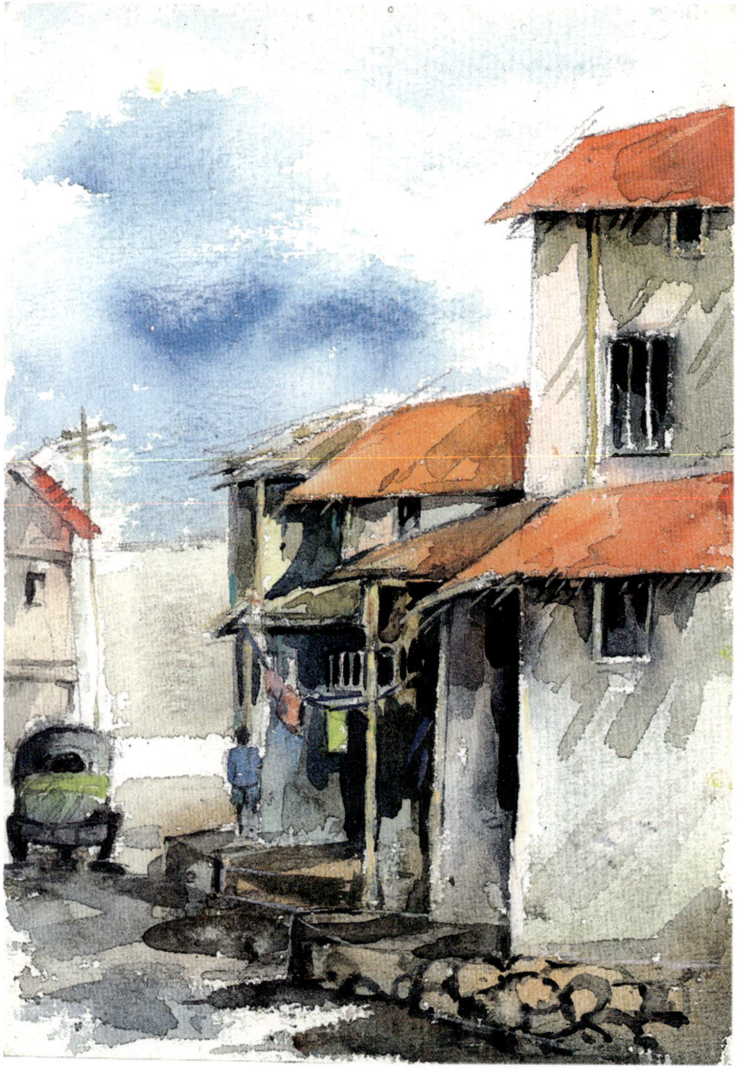

Stormy Skies

Depicting a storm is one of the most challenging weather conditions for an artist.

You get the best results when you are out there among the elements. You can recreate the stormy weather when you are out there among the elements. You can recreate the stormy weather when you experience it with the help of all your senses. Though you can recreate it with the help of photographs, but you may not be able to depict the sheer power and drama of a storm.

When you draw the painting based on your own experience, after you have heard, felt and seen the storm, the tension of the storm will be transferred into the paper without you even realising it.

To depict rain and swirling clouds, apply heavy washes and let them merge wet-in-wet on damp paper. Try tilting the board at an angle so that the colour drifts down towards the horizon, giving an effect of veils of rain in the distance. Let your washes settle unevenly at places. The blotches and blooms suggest stormy clouds and crashing waves.

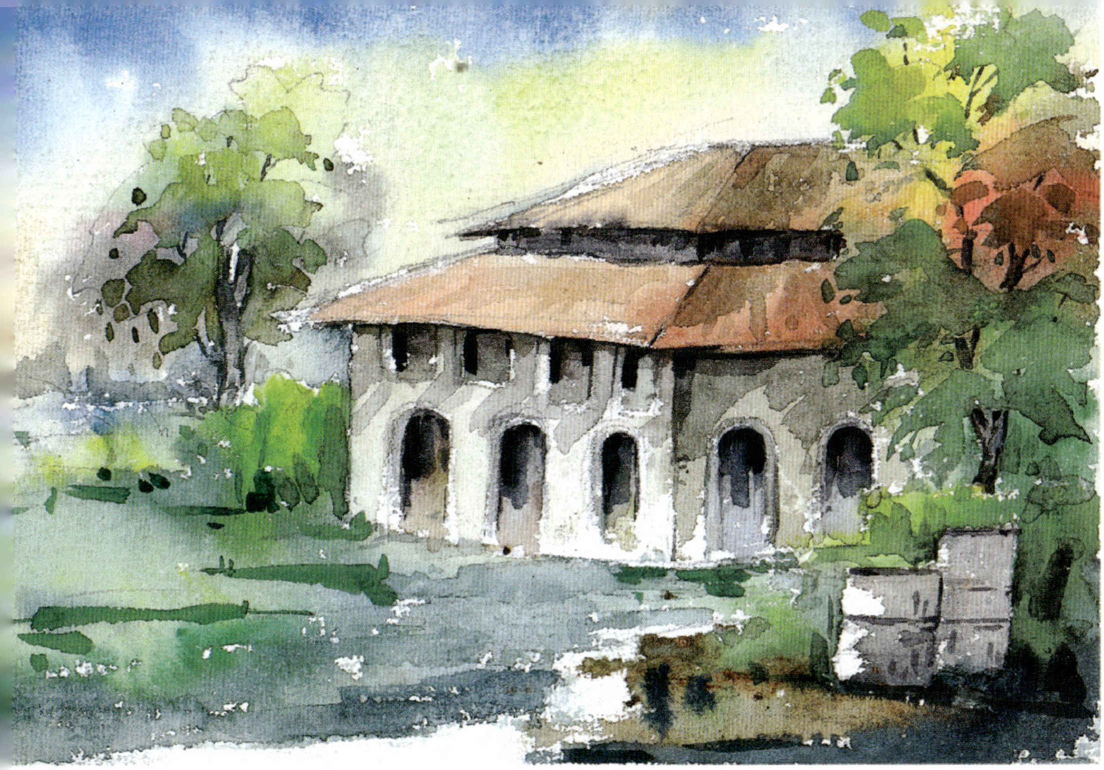

With the wet-in-wet technique it is possible to give an ambience to your painting. With the minimal of strokes and details, and playing with shades the artist created a lasting effect.

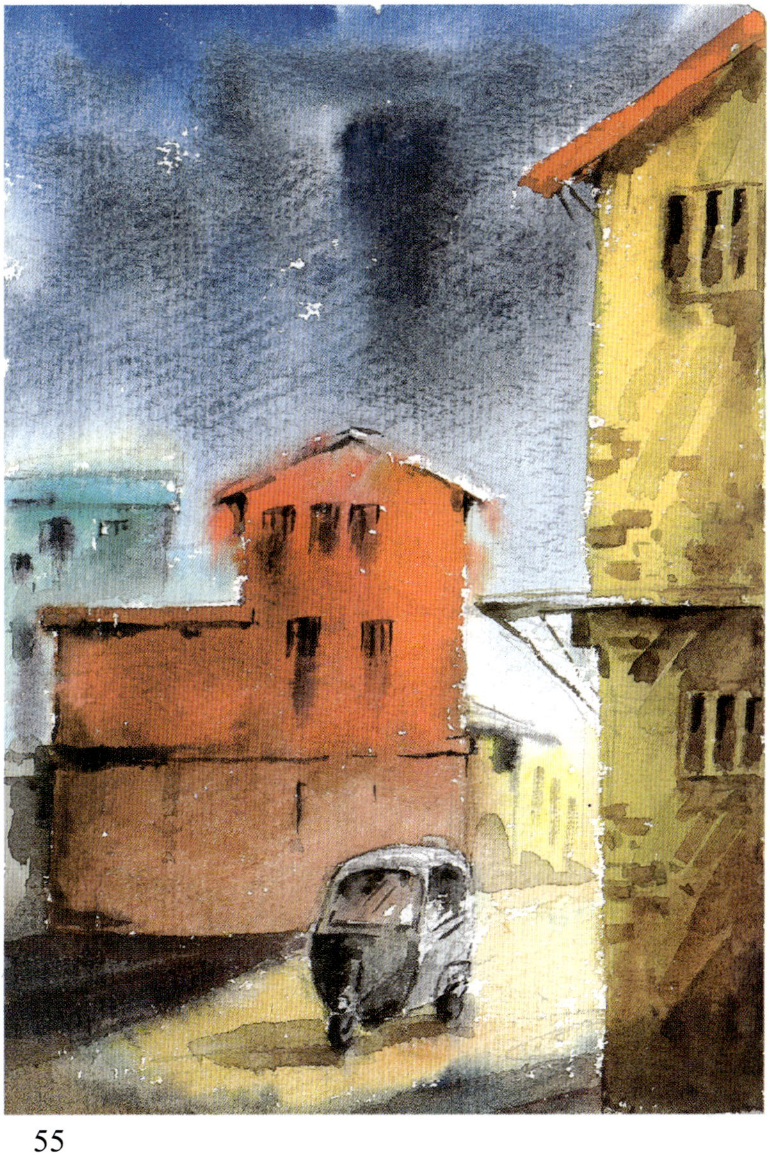

Cityscapes and Townscapes

India presents life in its myriads of forms. This is because almost 70 per cent of the population resides in villages. The rest make up the population in towns and cities. So you get to see life in all its colours.

It is not necessary to pay attention to the content of the painting, but to the beauty of forms, the textures and the essence of what you want to depict. It is not important to draw a painting as the original. You can experiment with colours and shades because experimentation sometimes helps you to get some of the most interesting and beautiful effects.

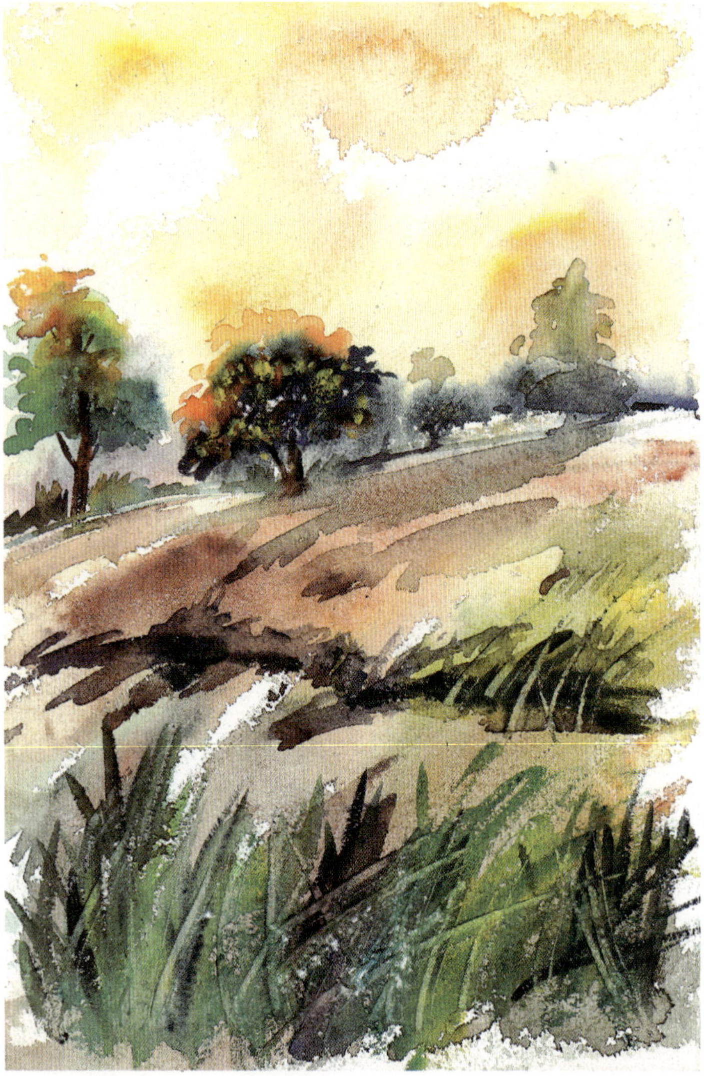

Helpful Hint

When you're waiting for washes to dry, use the back of your hand to test for dryness. It is a more sensitive receptor than the figures and won't leave grease marks on the paper.

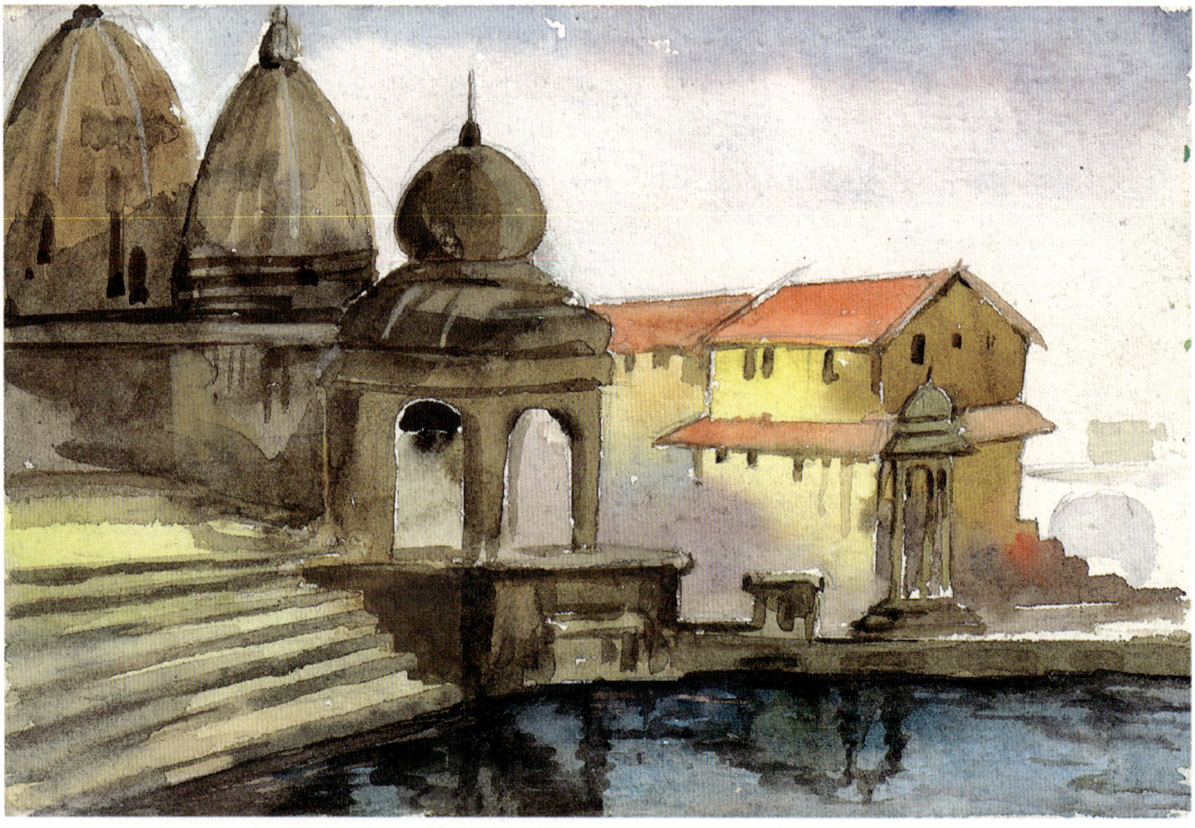

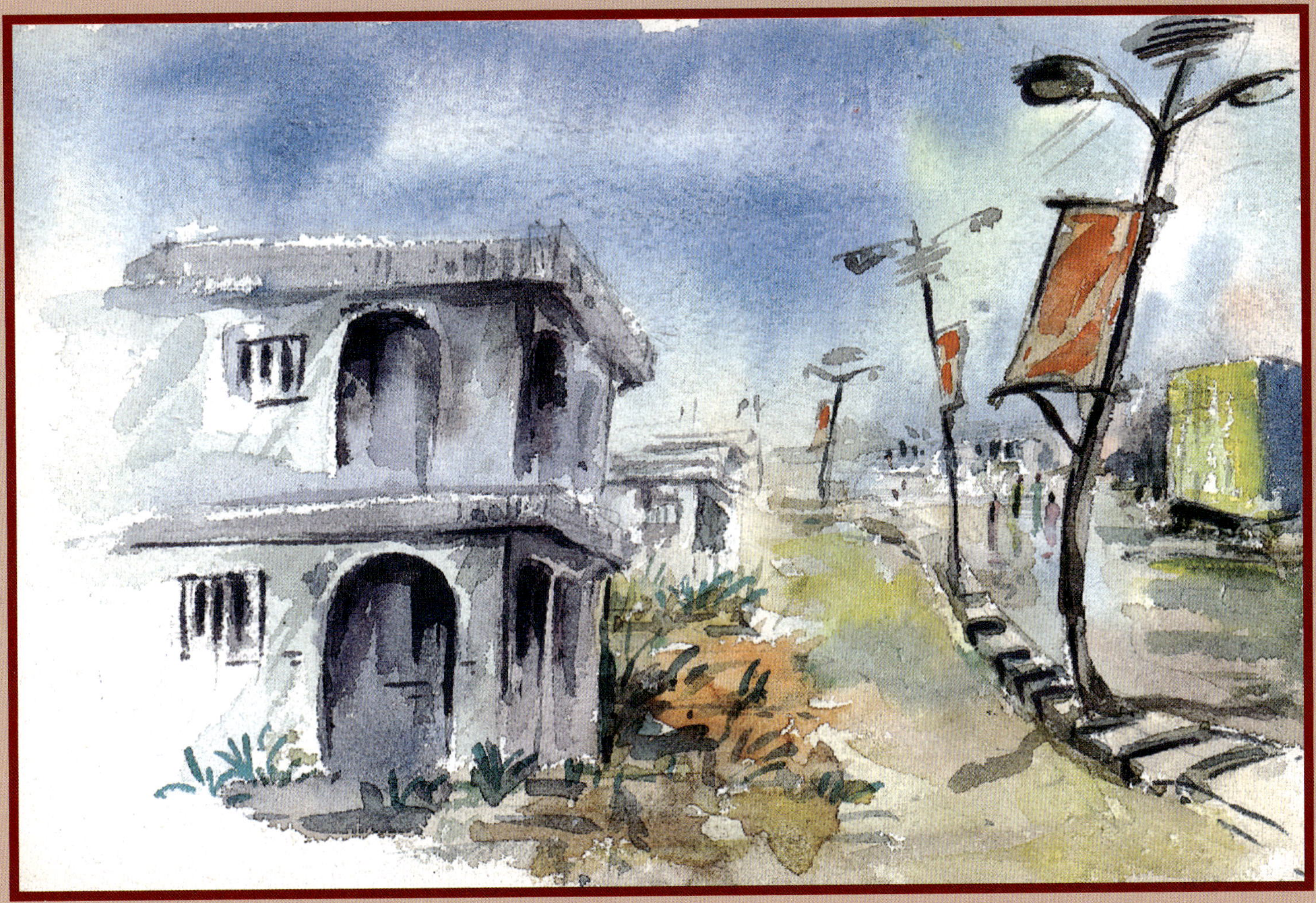

Here the source of light is in the foreground, somewhere beyond the range of the painting. This he has tried to show by using a light tone of Yellow and Burnt Sienna for the house in the foreground. It has been deliberately avoided the details of the mud walls. The houses beyond the house in the foreground are in darker shade of Burnt Sienna. In this way, he played with shade and light.

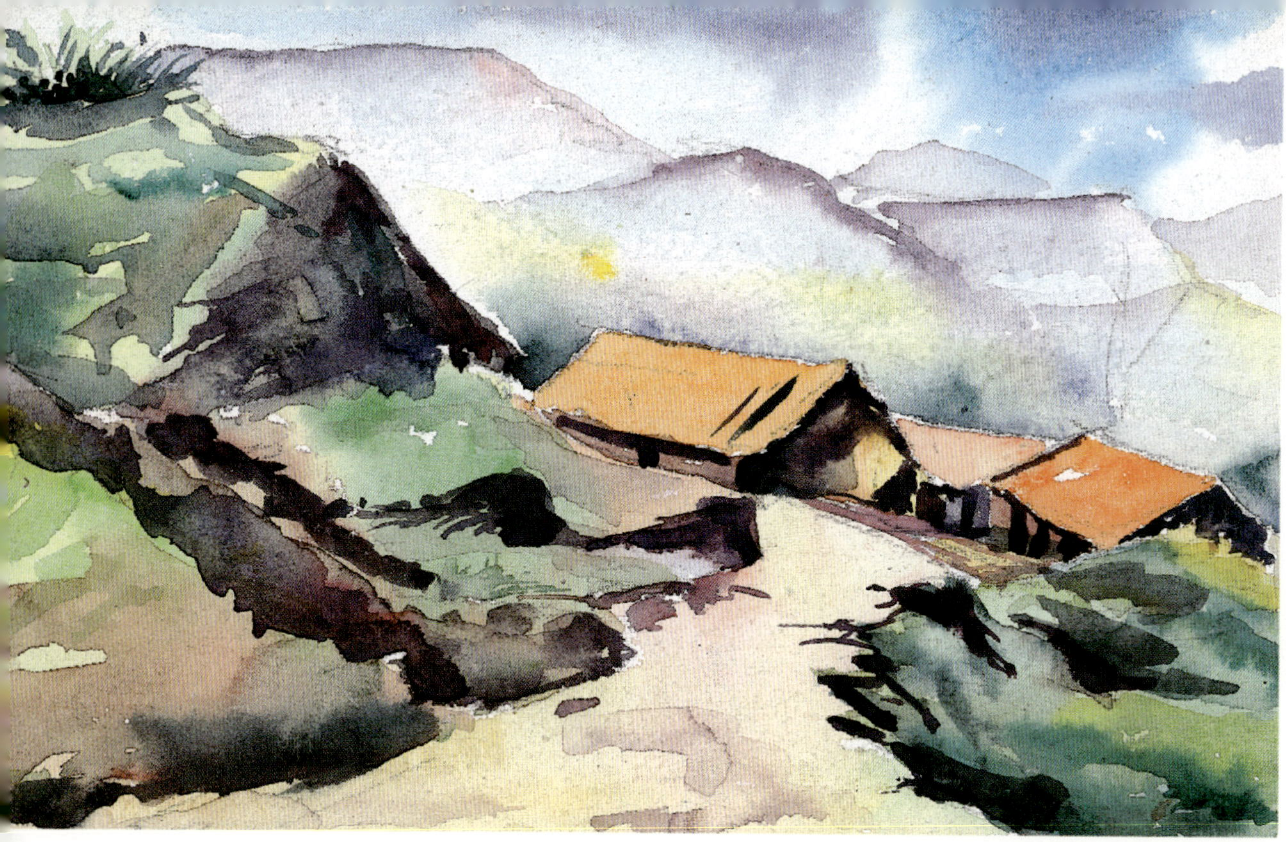

What draws you towards a landscape is the atmosphere it creates. In this particular painting, he has again played with light and dark shades of Burnt Sienna. The roofs of the houses are in the light. Playing with shades of Blue has created a three-dimensional effect and also the depth required to capture the attention of the onlooker.

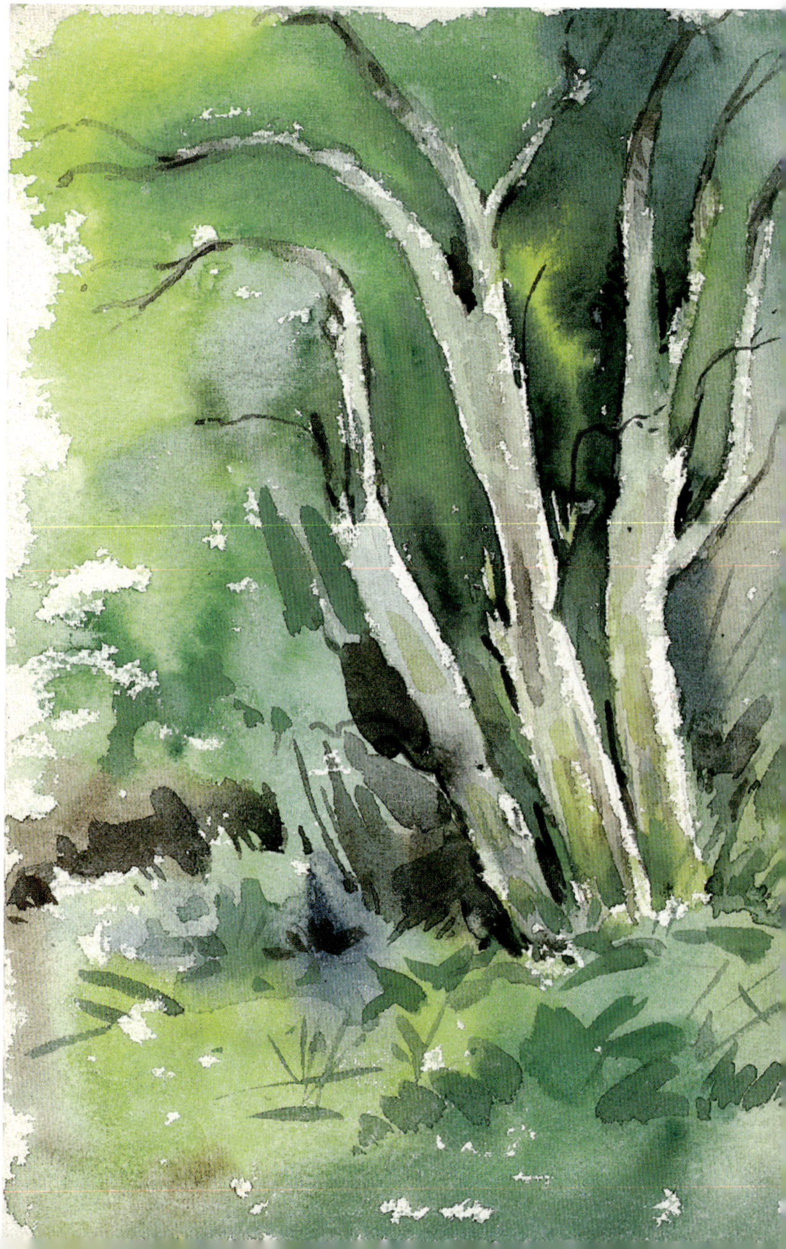

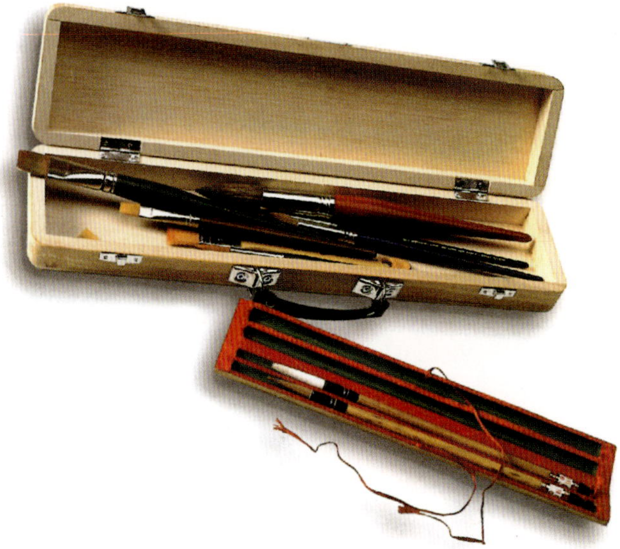

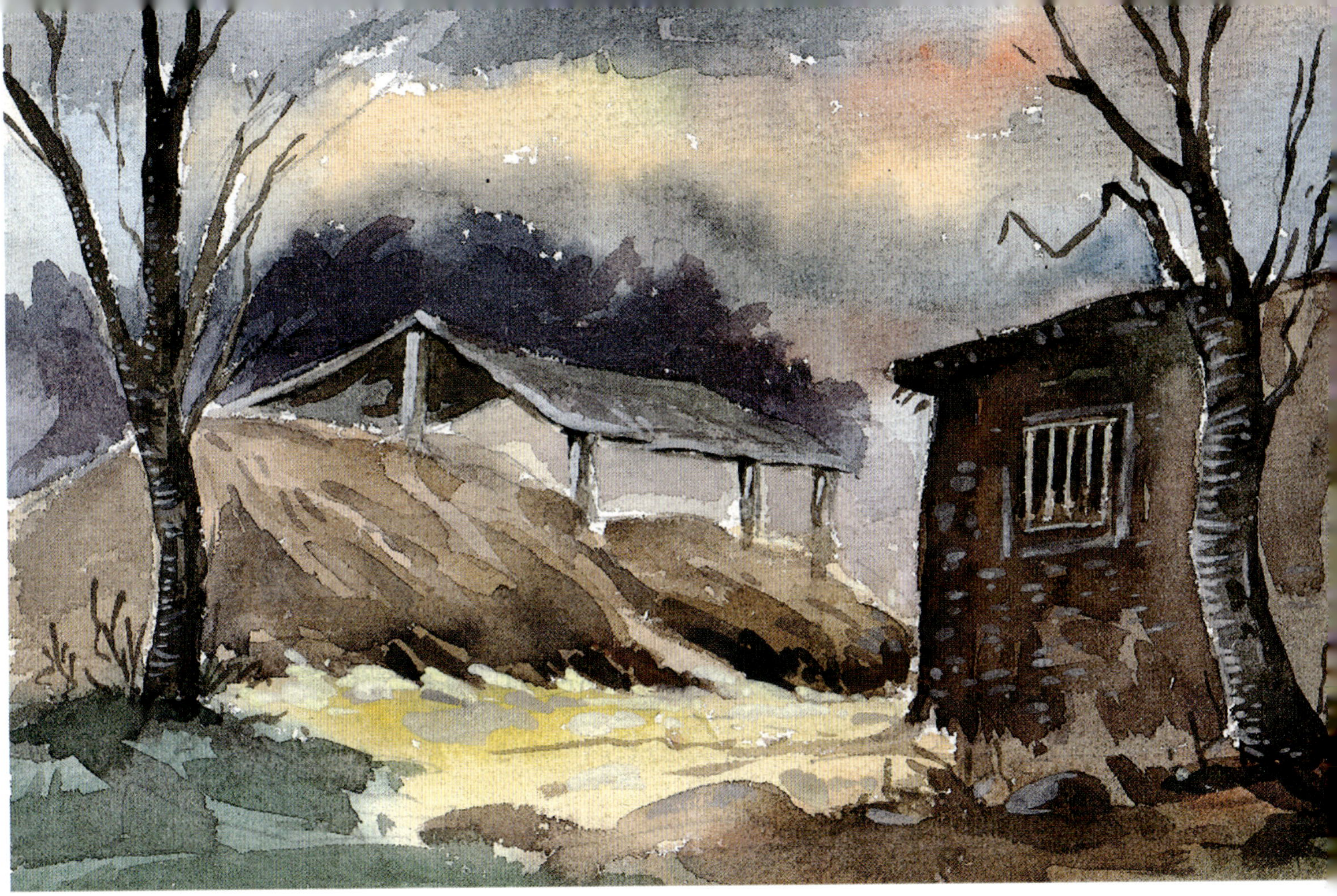

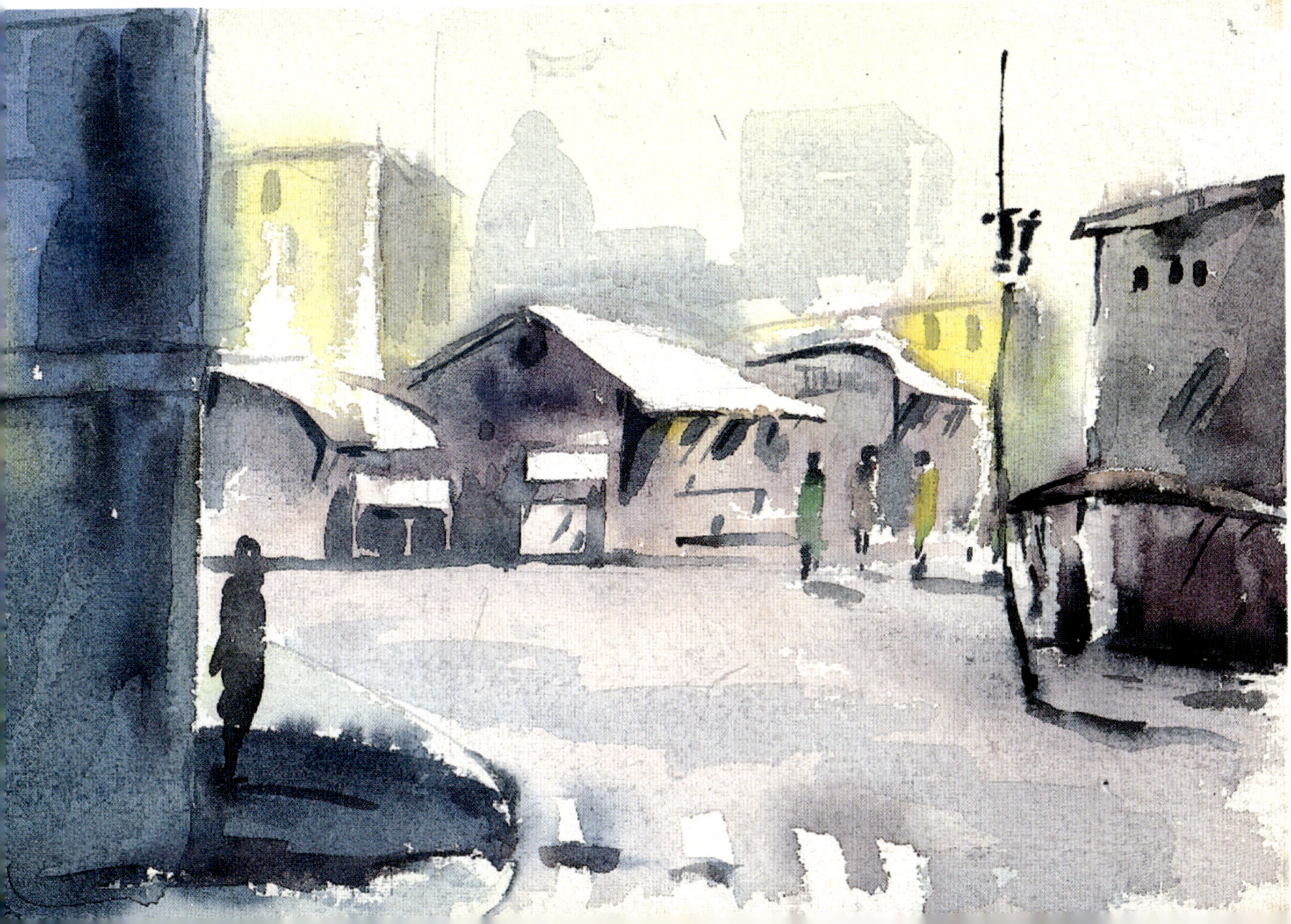

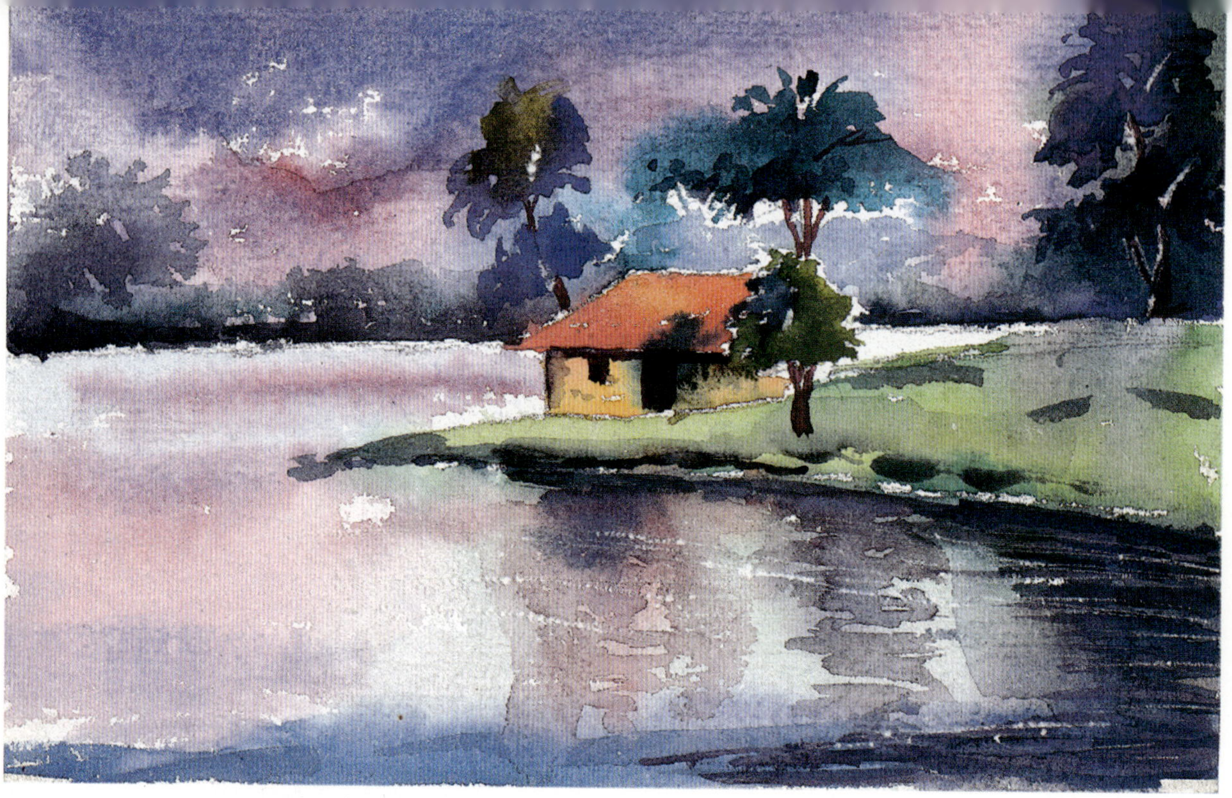

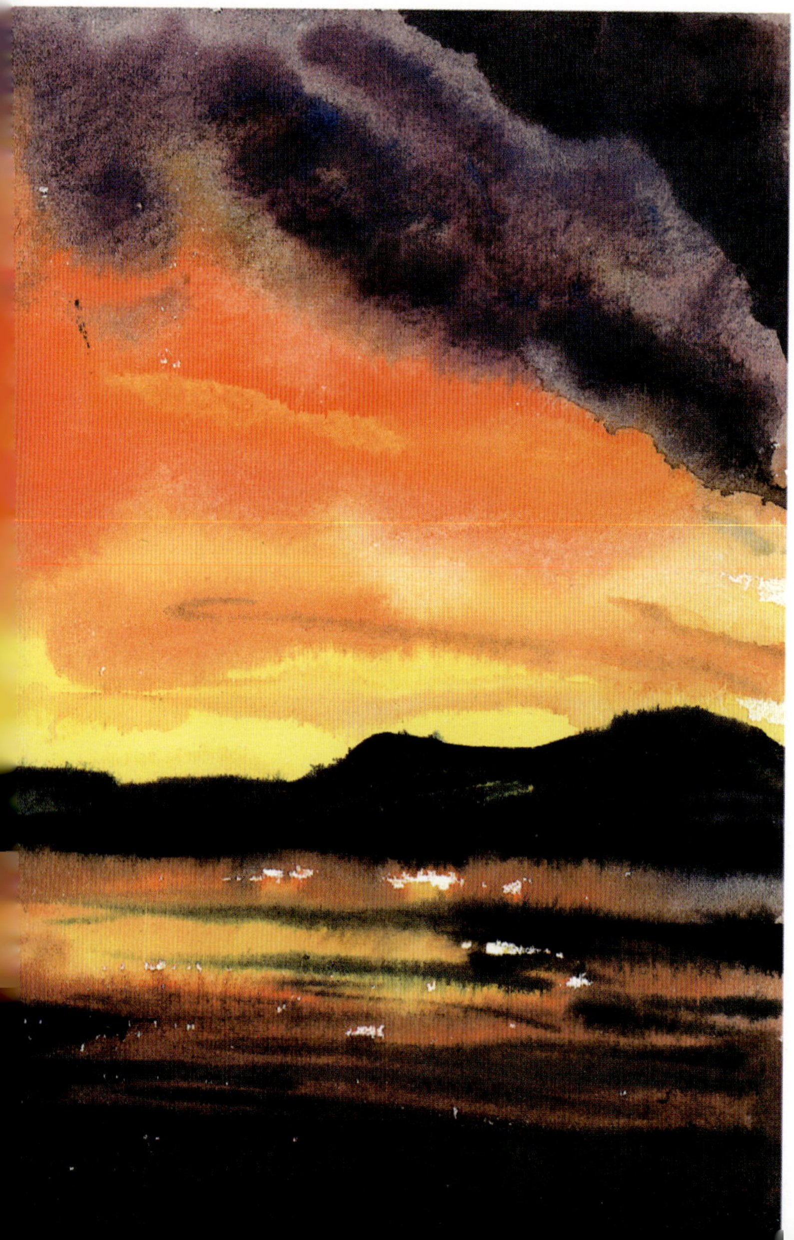

Sunset and the evening skies are a favourite subject with many artists. The subject is a challenge because the period between sunset and nightfall is very short.

To capture the glowing effects of the evening sky, you must be very deft with your fingers. You do not have time to lose in painting elaborately. You have to capture the fading of light by working quickly.

Painting the evening sky is a challenge because you have to capture the mood and atmosphere with the minimum use of strokes and colours.

Never be tempted to use "hot" colours like strong pinks, oranges and reds to depict the sunset. Be selective with colours.

An evening light is depicted in reddish yellow tinge, remember — no strong reds. Pale, soft colours are better than garishly, bright colours. And an evening shadow is in a red-violet shade. And another thing to remember is that morning and evening shadows are longer than those in the noon.

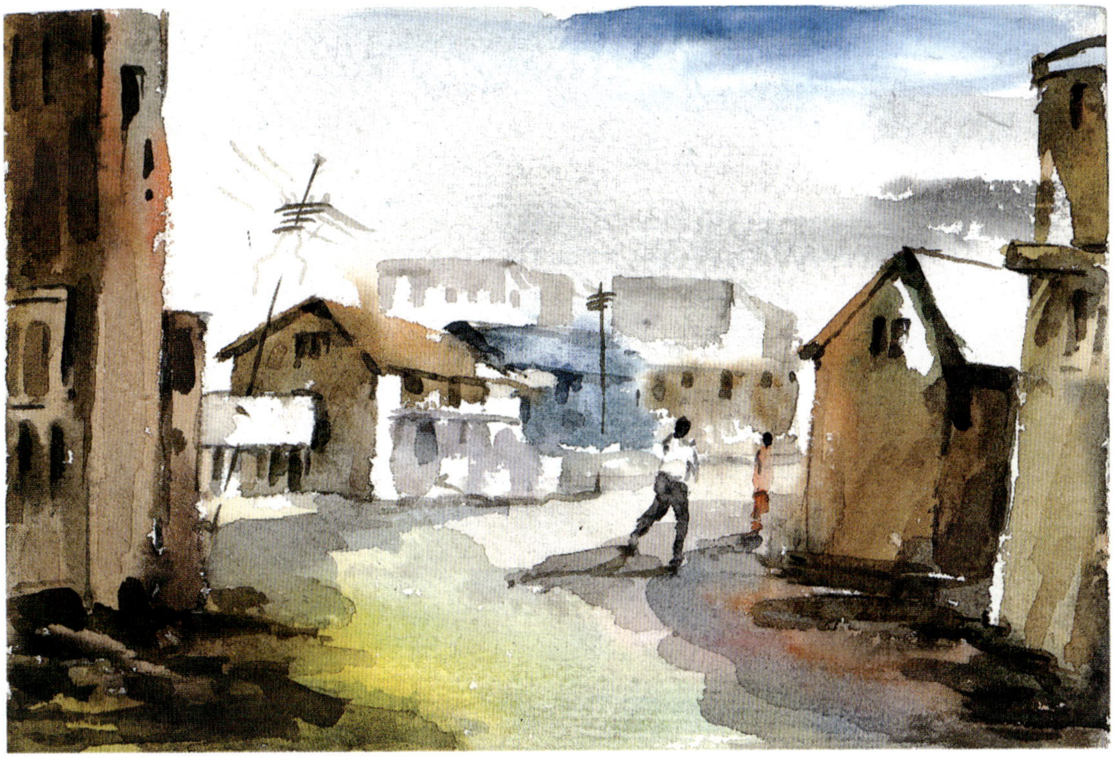

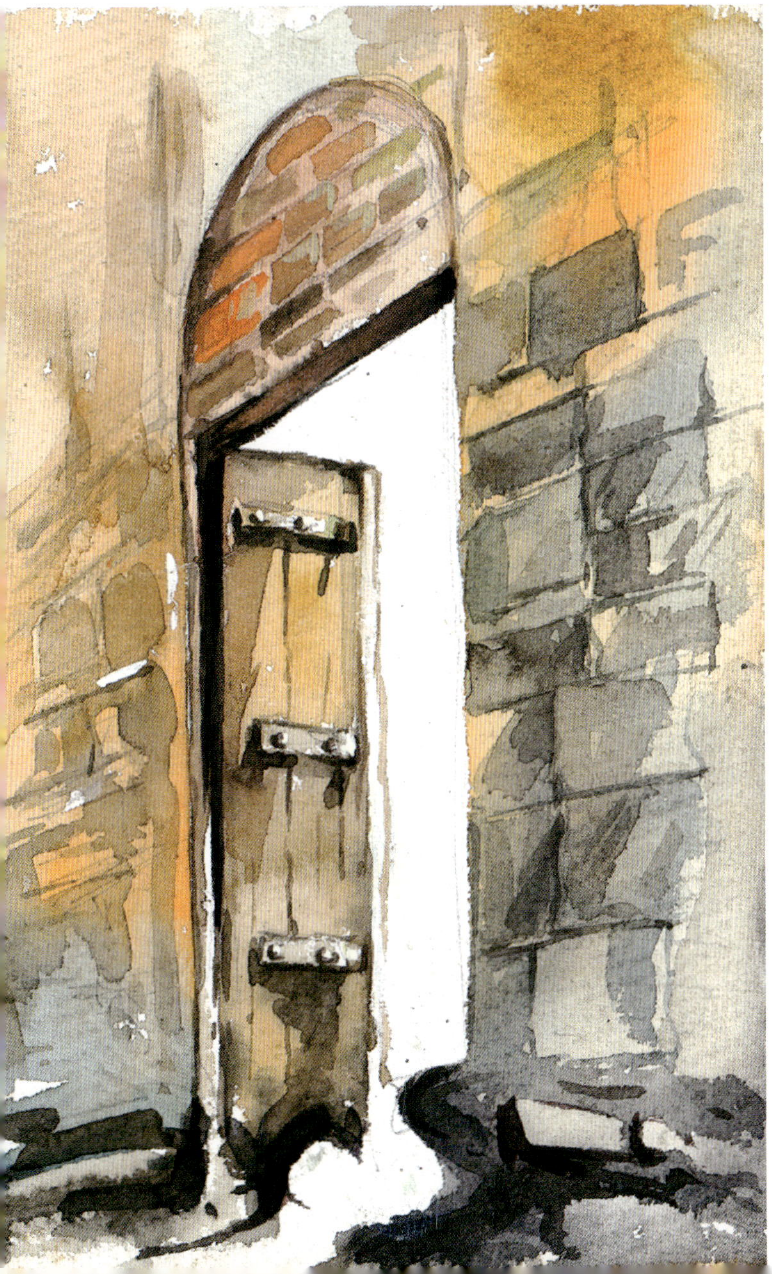

With the wet-in-wet technique it is possible to give an ambience to your painting. With the minimal of strokes and details, and playing with shades the artist has created a lasting effect.

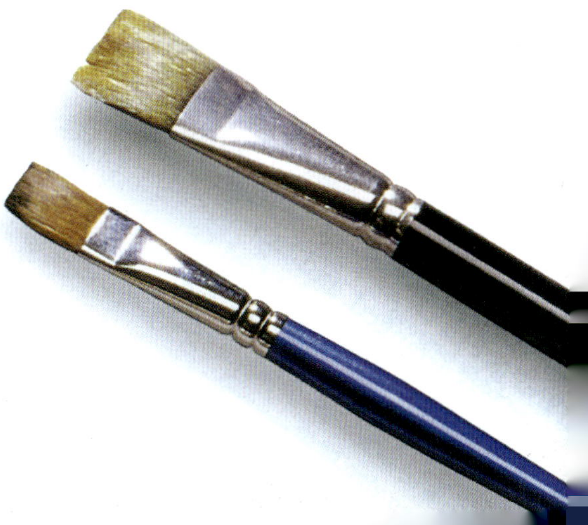

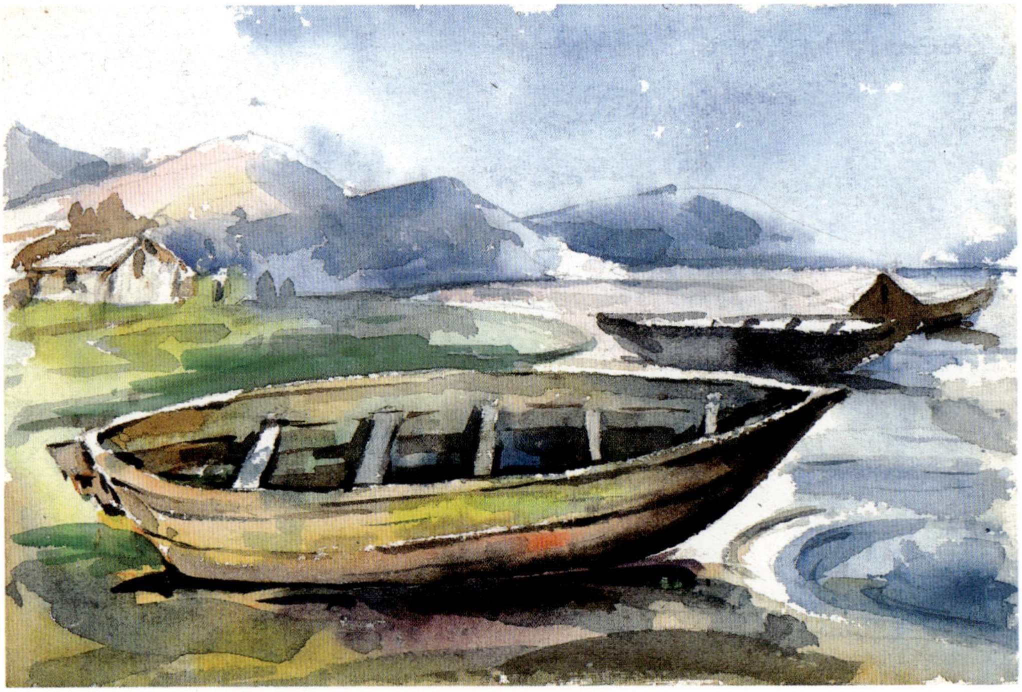

Helpful Hint

Speed is crucial when working wet-in-wet. So have your washes ready mixes in deep-welled palettes or saucers. Before you start painting, remember to mix up plenty of paint so you don't run out at an inconvenient moment.

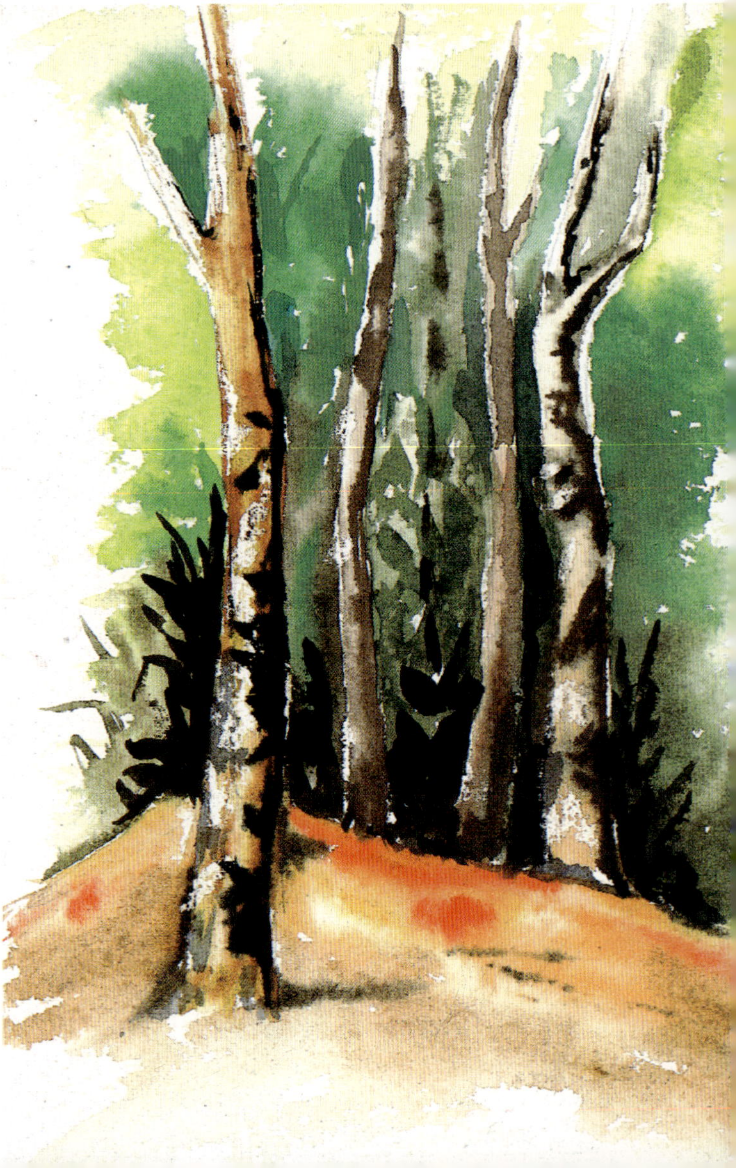

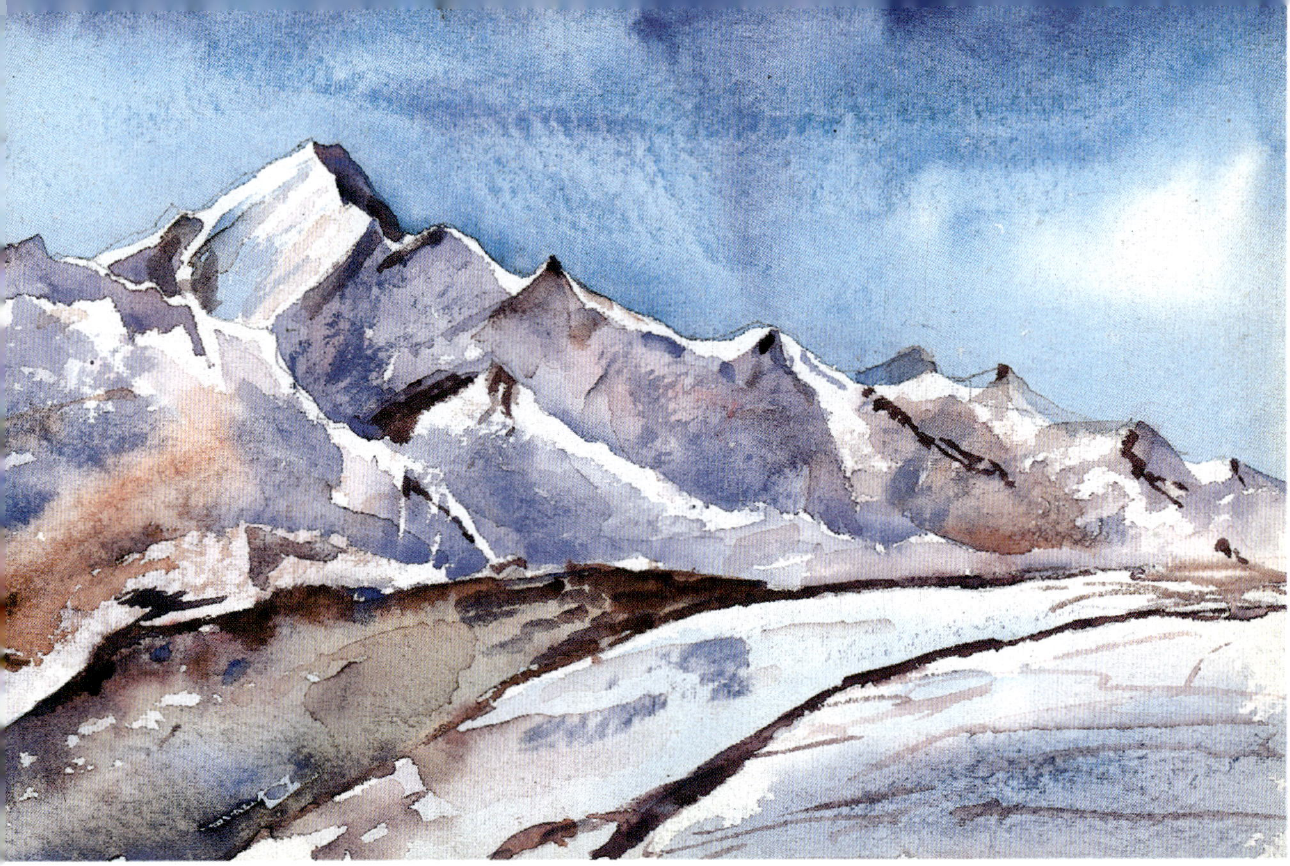

A divine experience! Snow-capped mountains are truly majestic. Now the onlooker has to experience the same while seeing your painting. Again he made the attempt with light and shade then used light and dark shades of Cobalt Blue.

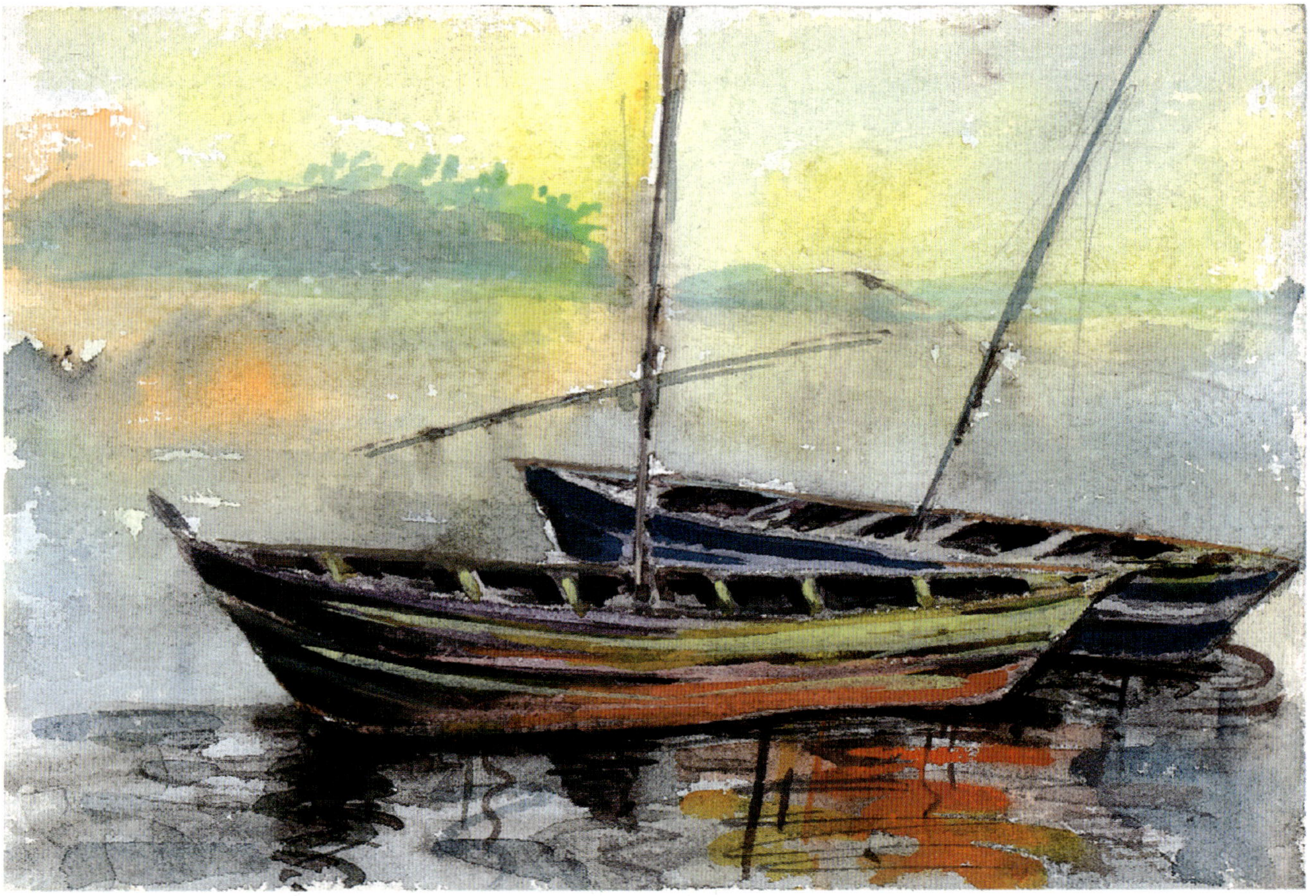

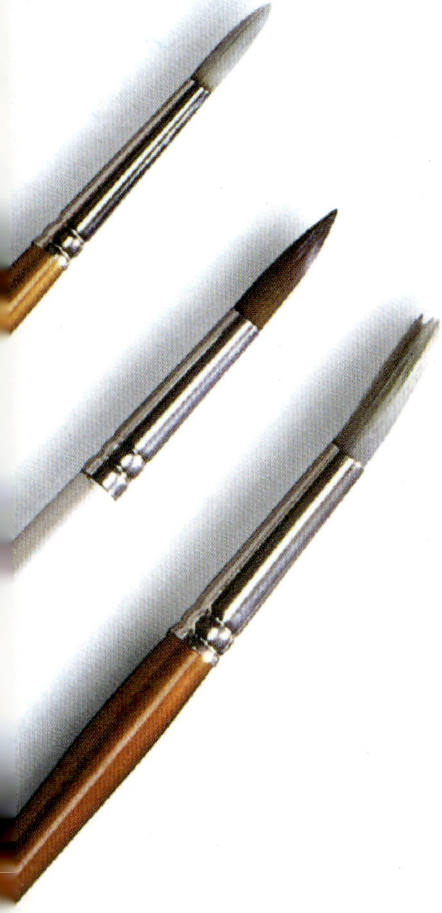

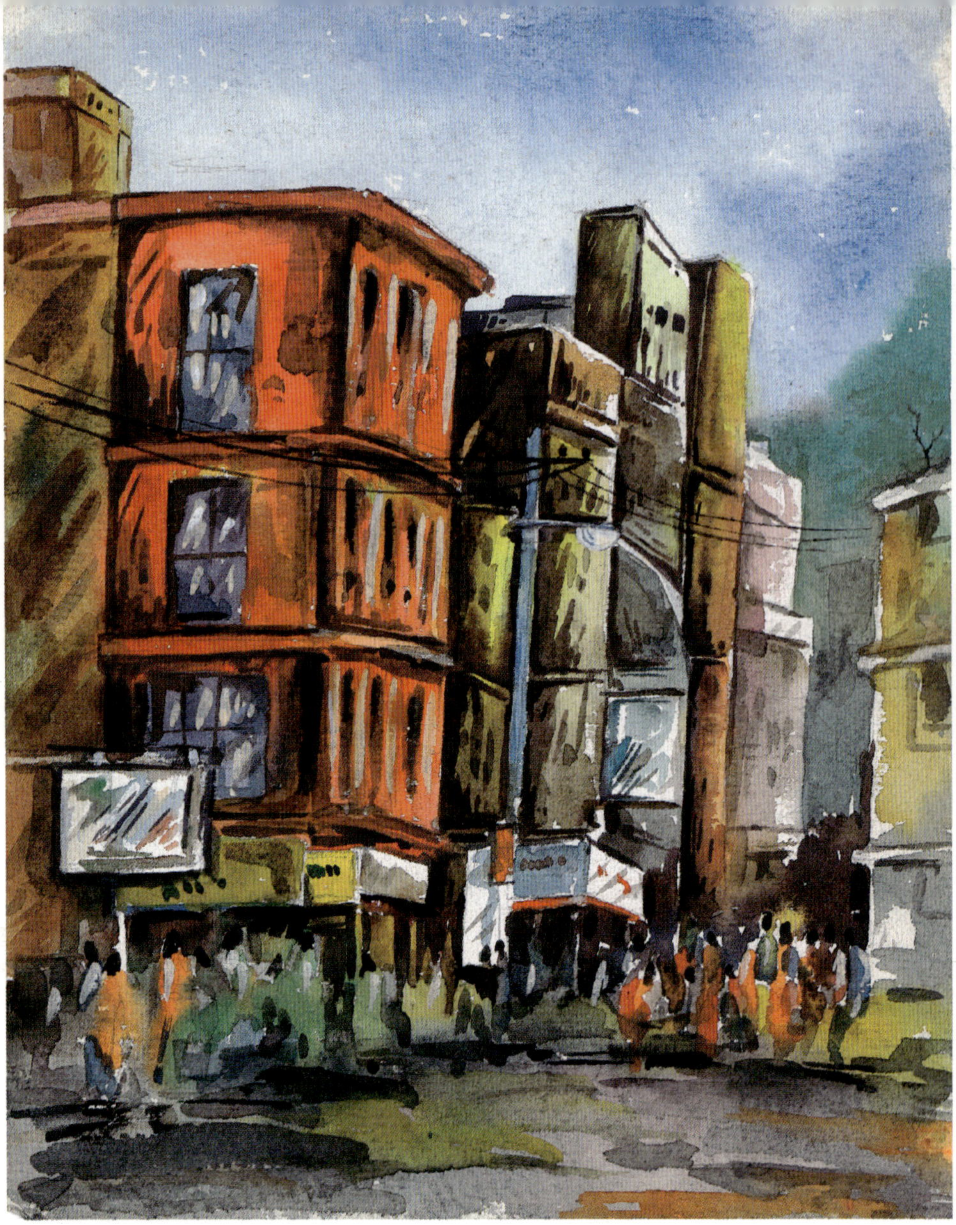

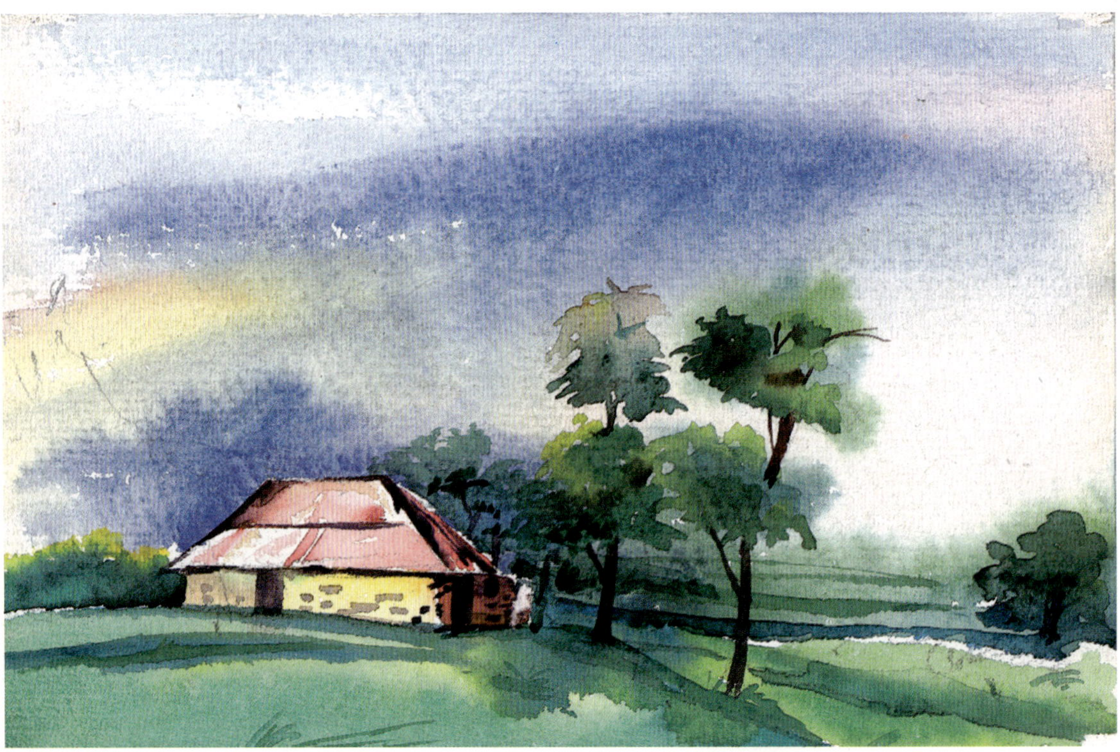

A painting in watercolour is capable of conjuring up your emotions, perhaps because of the freshness and spontaneity of watercolours.

The fluidity of watercolours is what helps the artist to experiment with colours and sometimes achieve interesting effects through hit and trial. For the beginner, this element of uncertainty can deter him from studying the medium. But this unpredictably is what enlarges the scope of the medium.

The secret of success with the medium is to work boldly and with confidence. Watercolours being a transparent medium, you cannot correct a colour scheme that has gone wrong — the advantage you have with oil paints. However, in spite of this disadvantage, some of the best paintings are a combination of accident and design.

The transparency, glow and depth of the watercolour medium are what make it the most unmatched medium.

Once you learn to master the medium, you can relax. Then the medium will do the trick.

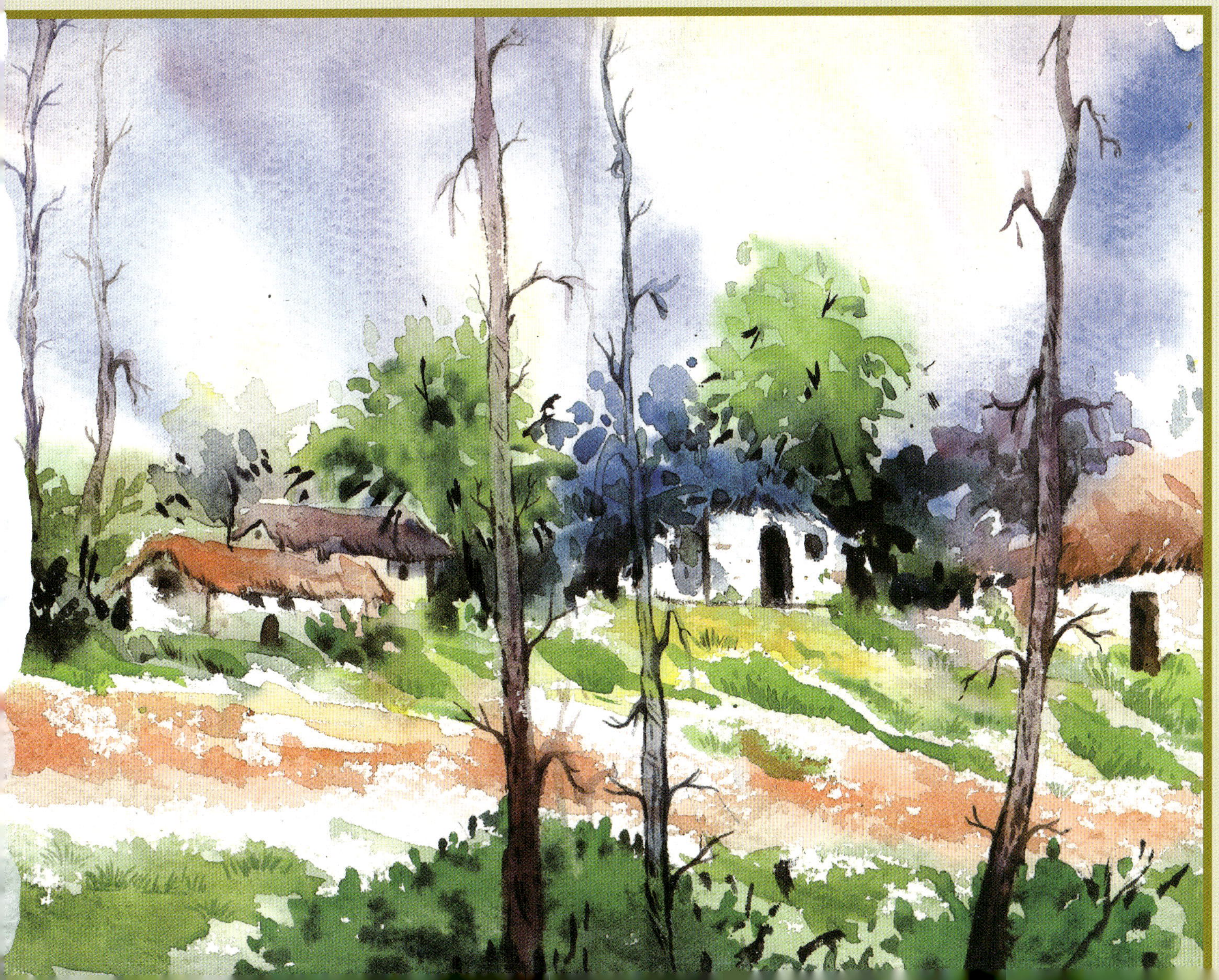

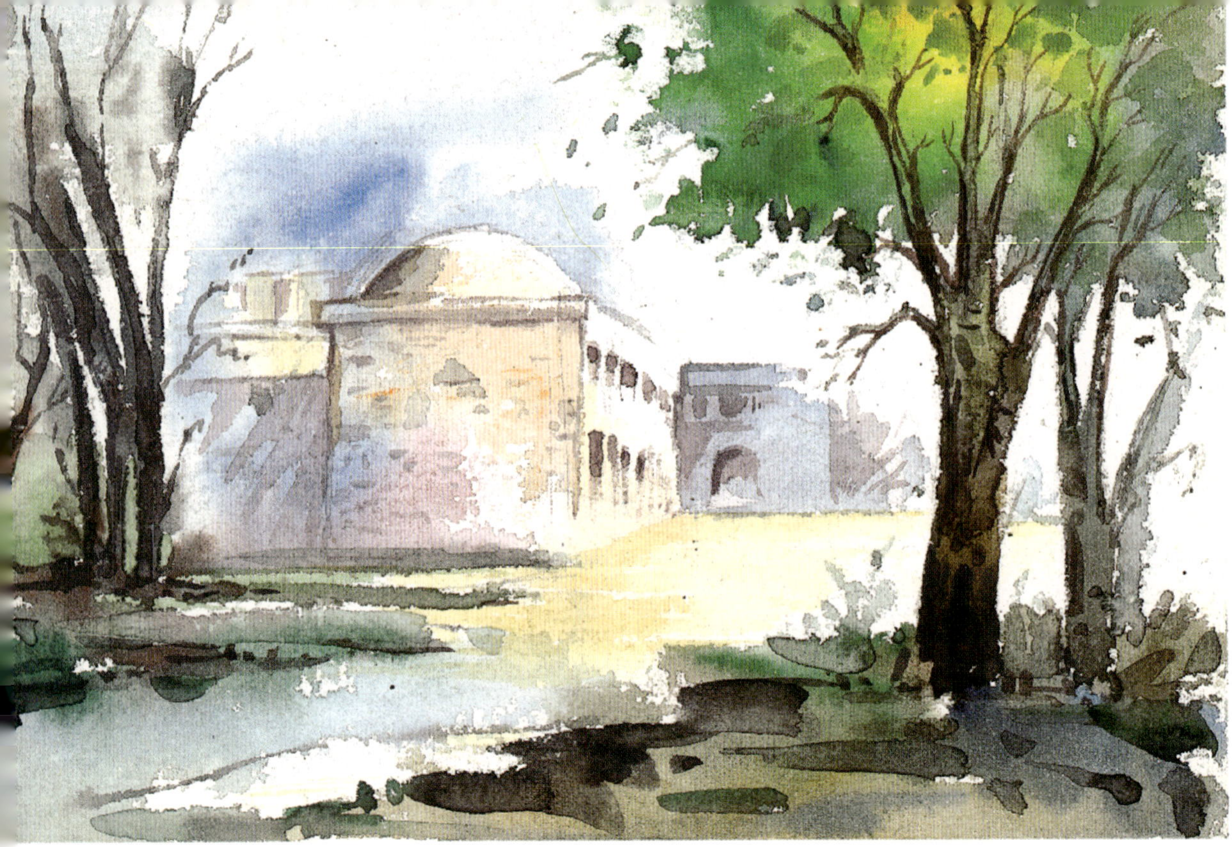

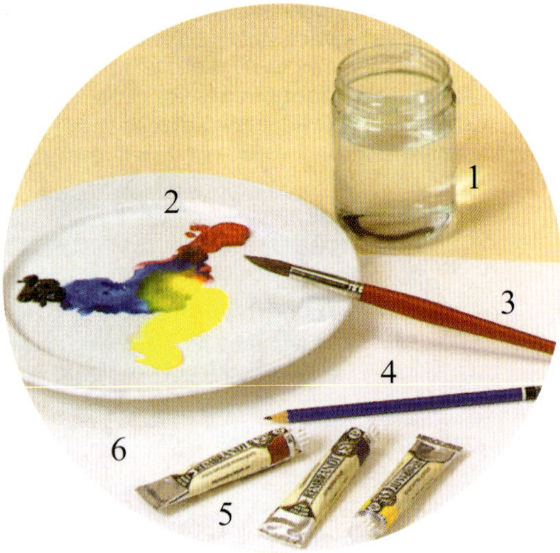

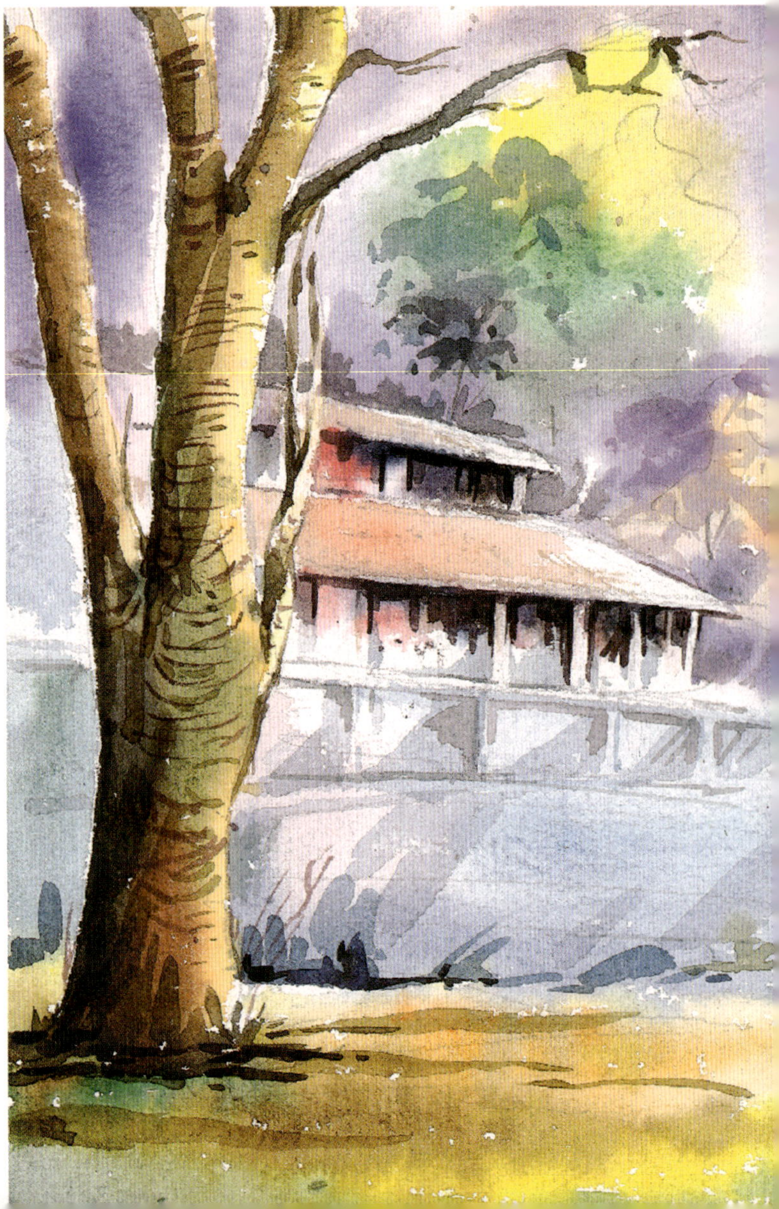

Materials

1. Water Jar
2. Plate
3. Brushes
4. Pencil
5. Tube Colours
6. Paper

The Outdoors

Most artists use photo references when painting landscapes. But photographs cannot capture every colour that the eye can perceive. The feeling and emotions that are evoked when you see beautiful scenery around you should be evoked when the onlooker sees your painting. Then how do you capture the feeling?

When painting outdoors, you should draw only the main elements. Sketch only the main shapes and remove all the unnecessary information. Translate your impression on the paper rather than the details of the landscape.

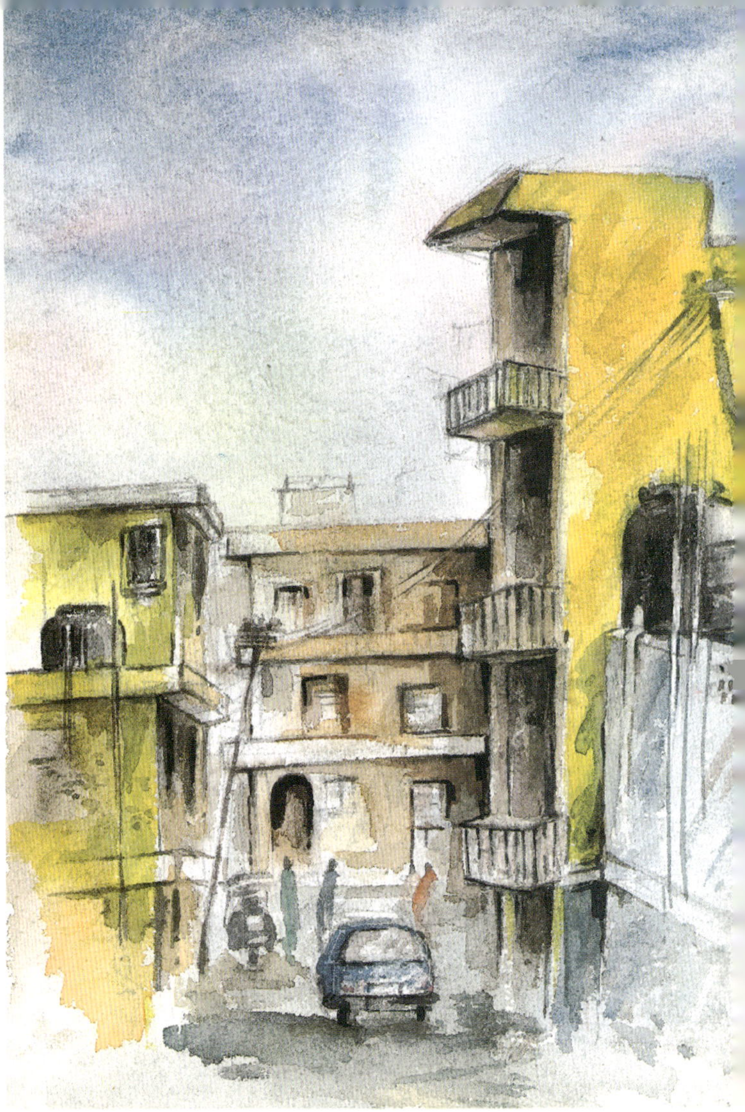

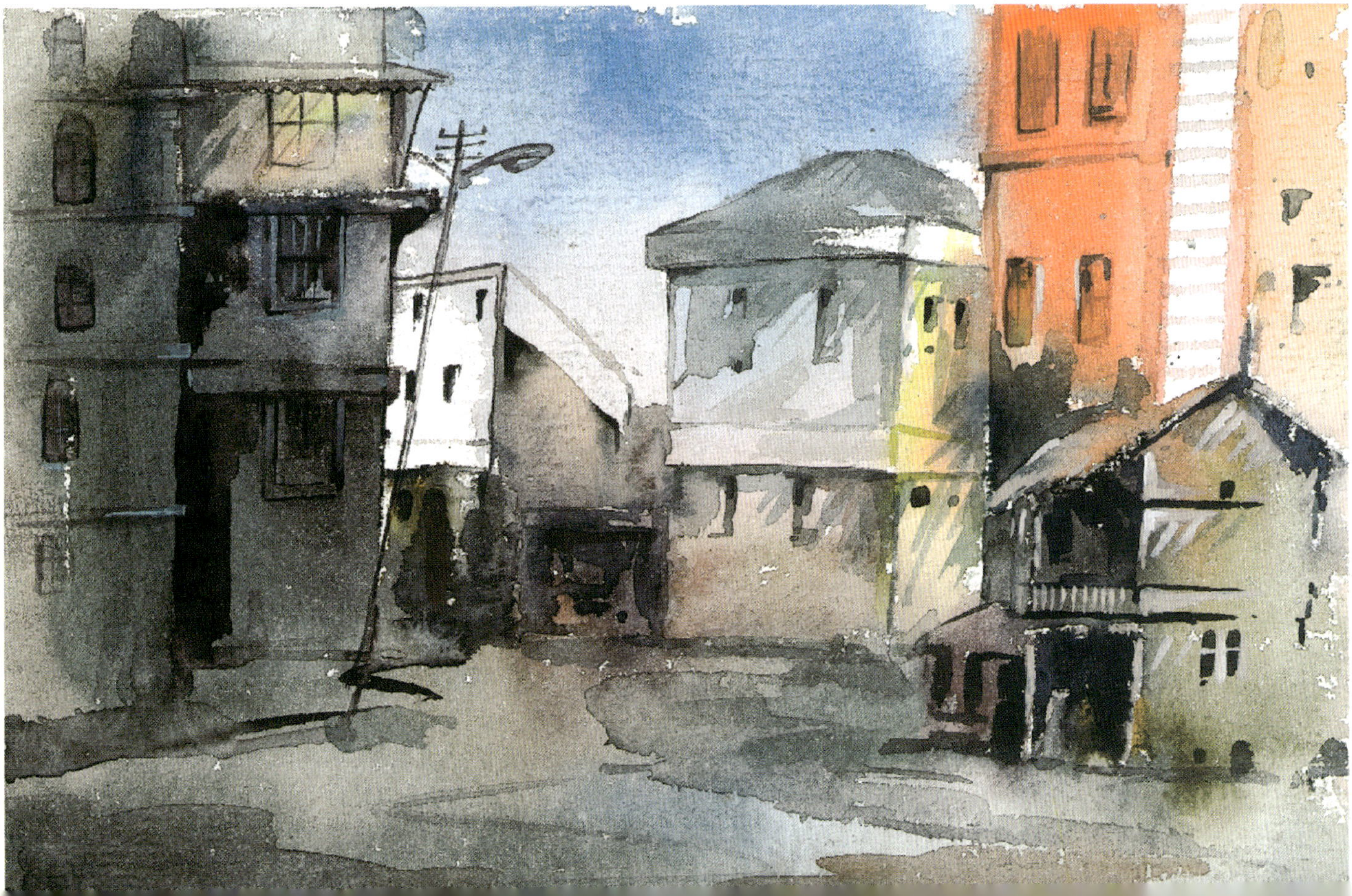

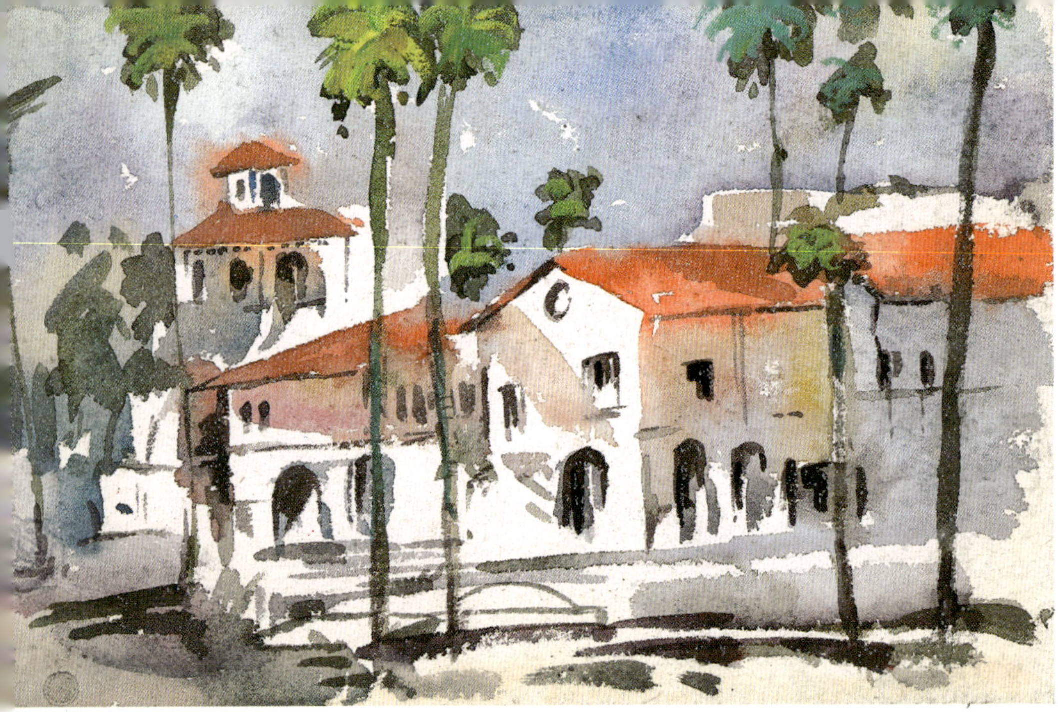

Composition

When elements in a picture are kept separately, their shapes also remain unrelated. If we move the objects in such a way that their planes cross and overlap, this symmetric layout relates the forms to one on other. This 'binds' it and makes the composition interesting. It is the specific arrangement of components or shapes in the picture, considering their interrelationship it is finally arranging the elements in a particular way that adds that touch of beauty to a picture. Paintings are our medium to achieve a dialogue with the onlooker. Therefore, the composition should be in tune with our feelings and emotions. It reflects our experience on viewing a scene.

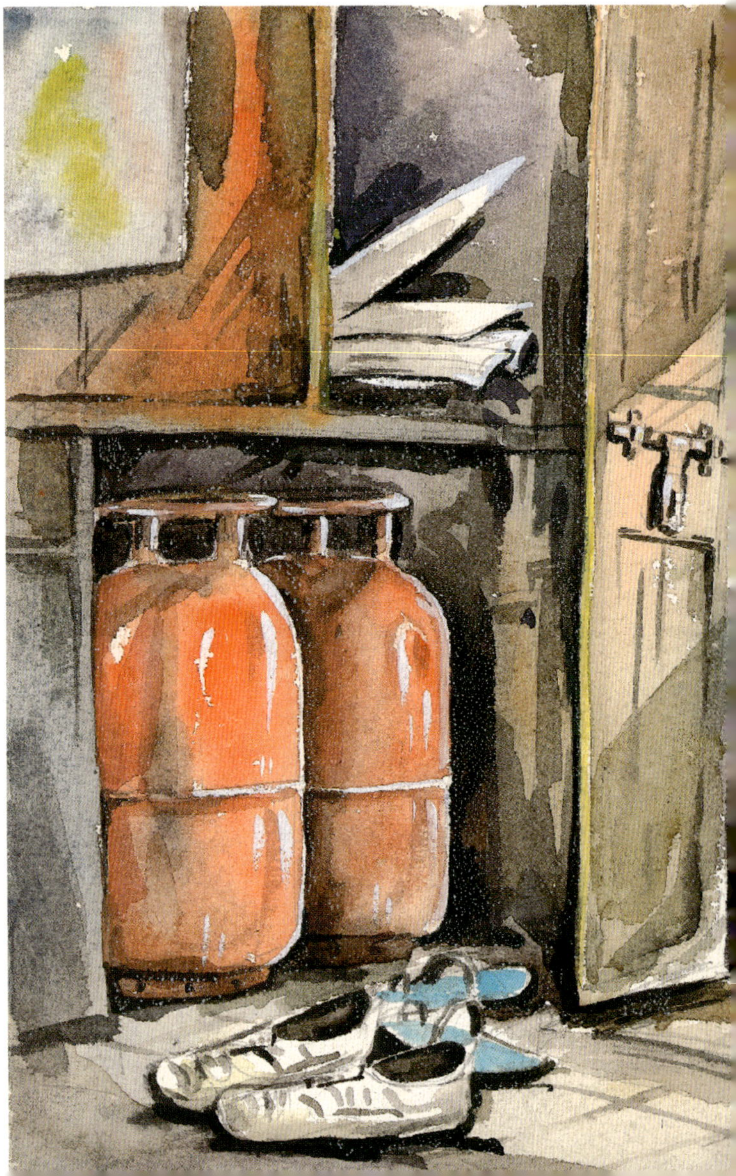

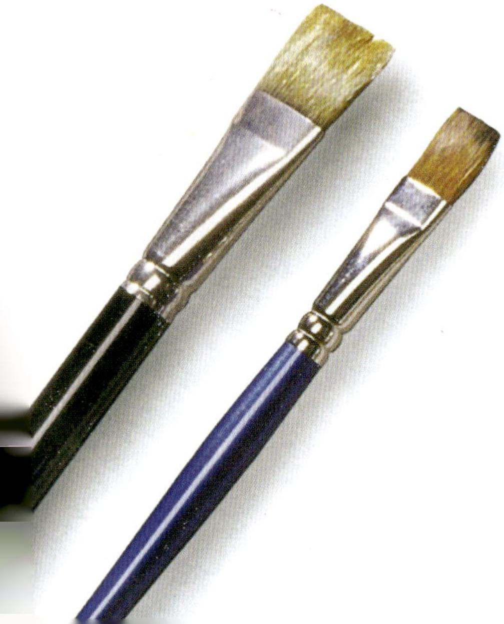

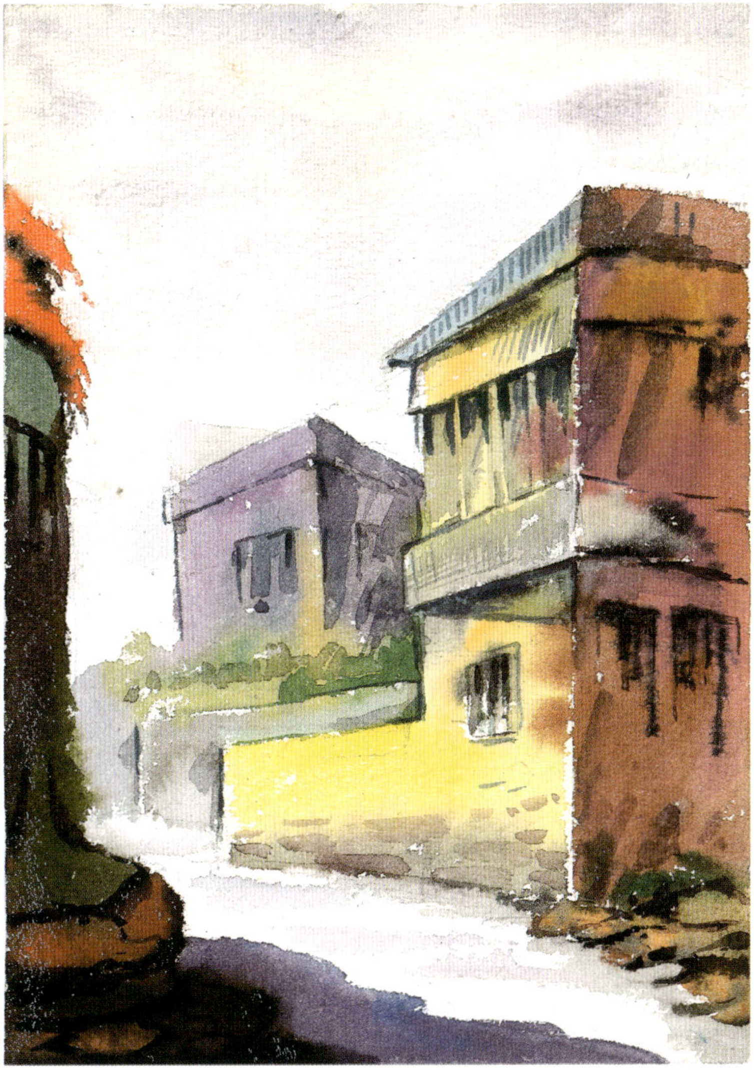

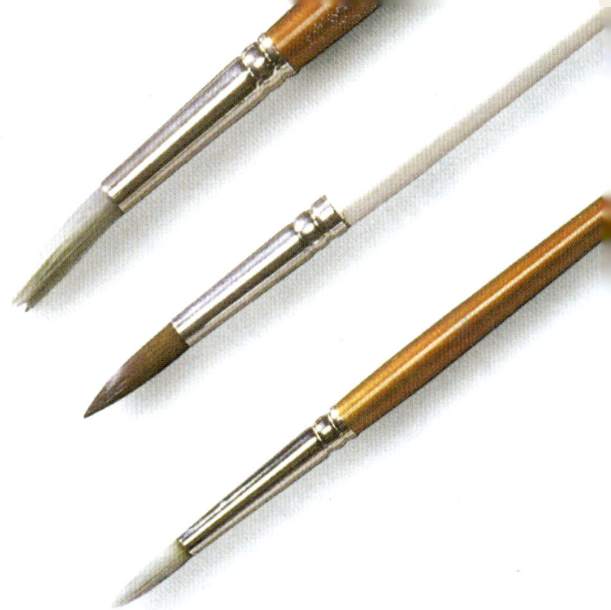

Painting on the Spot

We should observe the spot quietly and soak ourselves in the beauty of the scene, finalise a picture spot and just be comfortable.

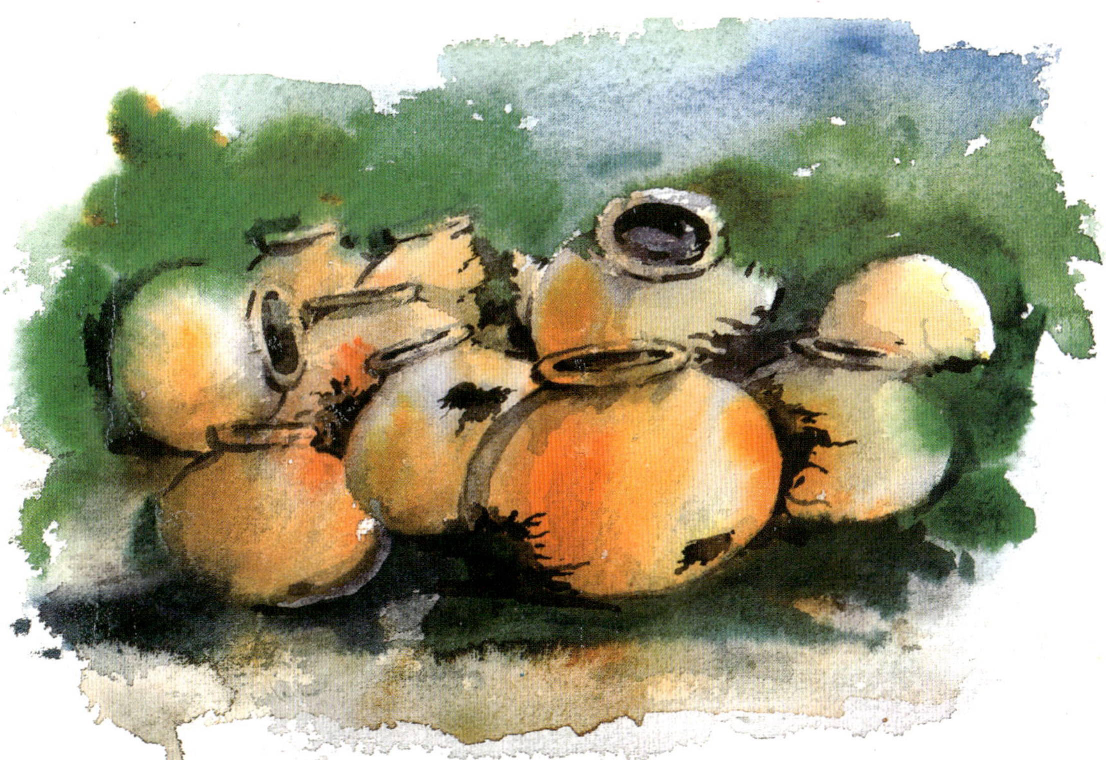

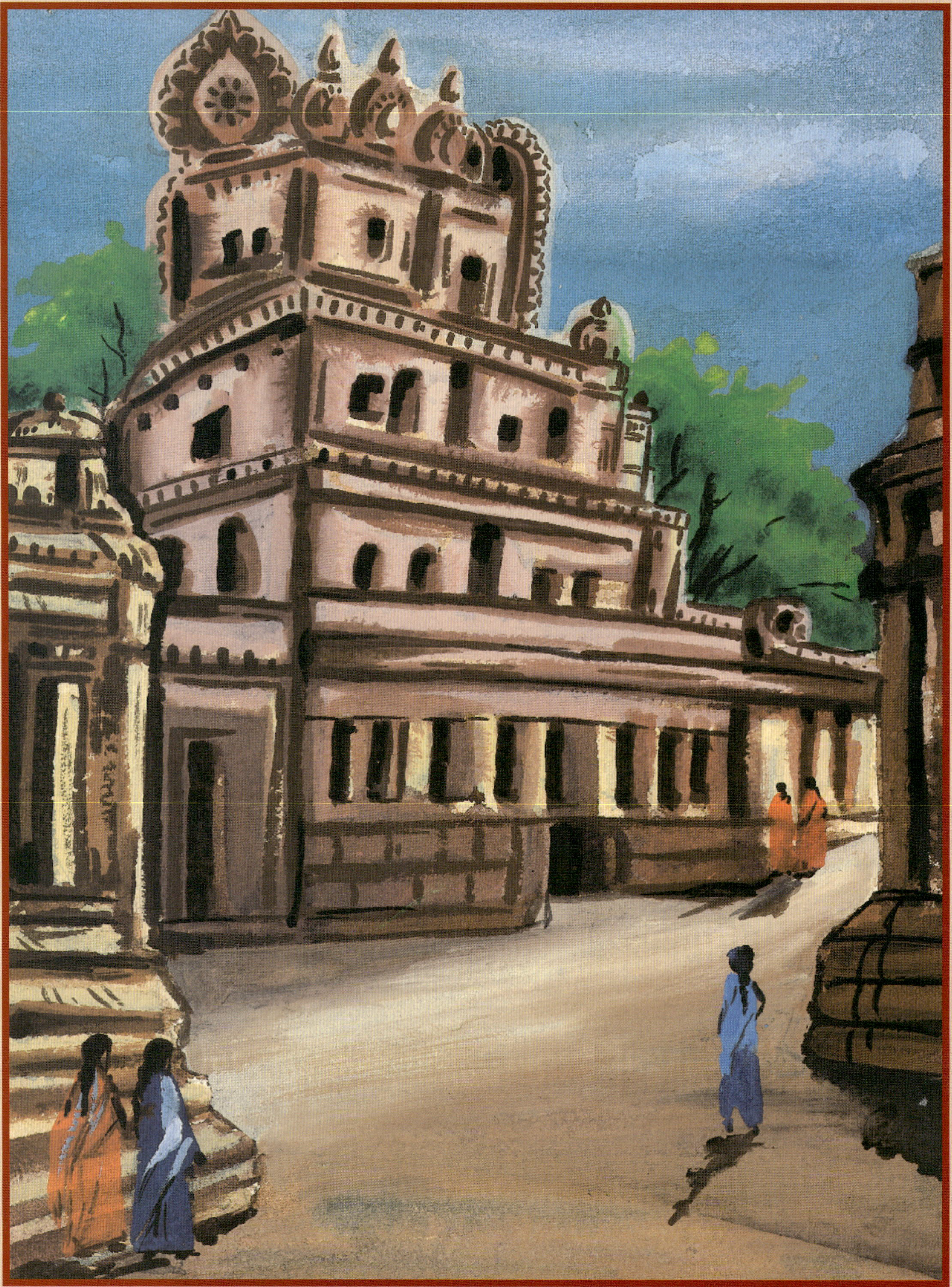

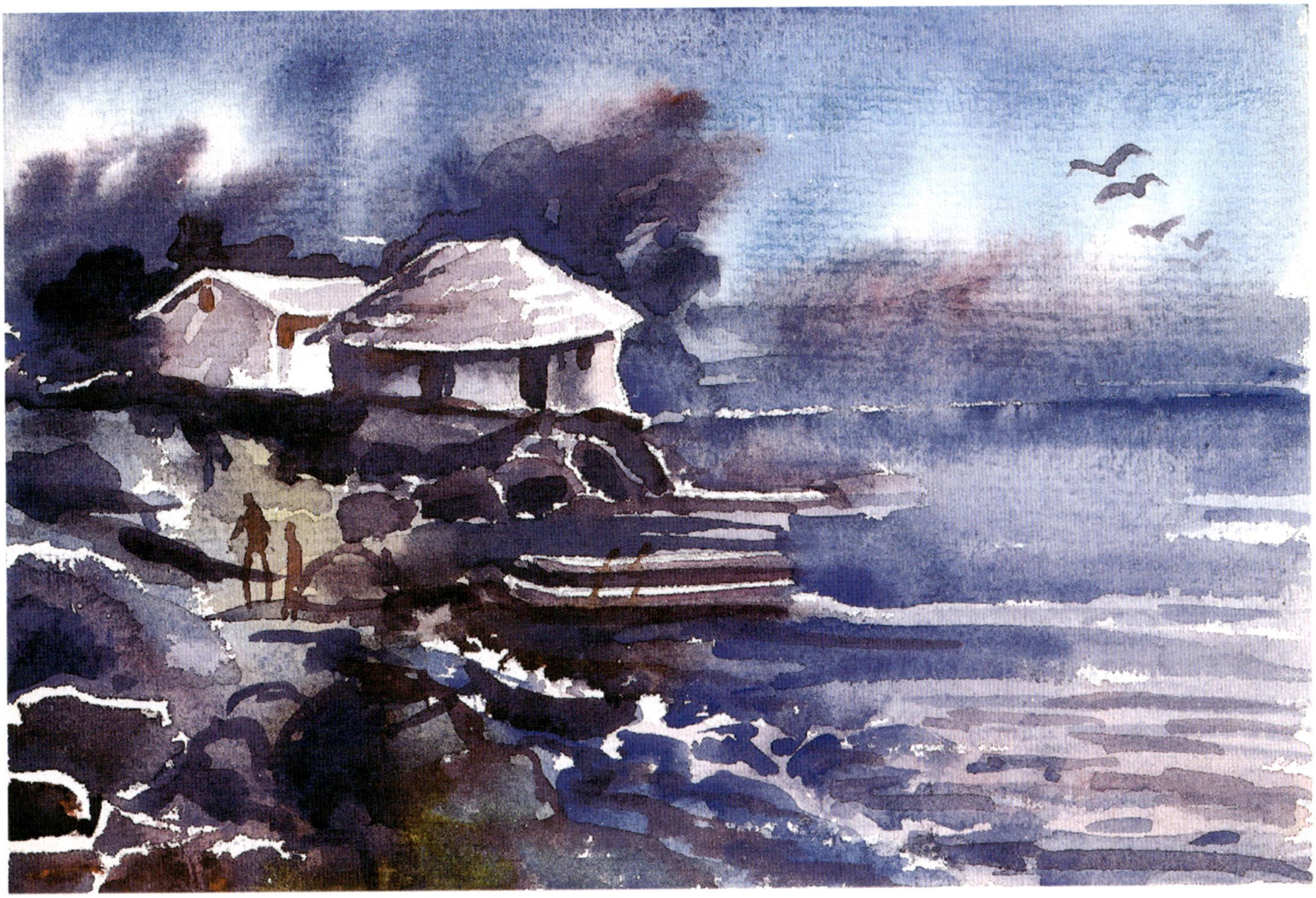

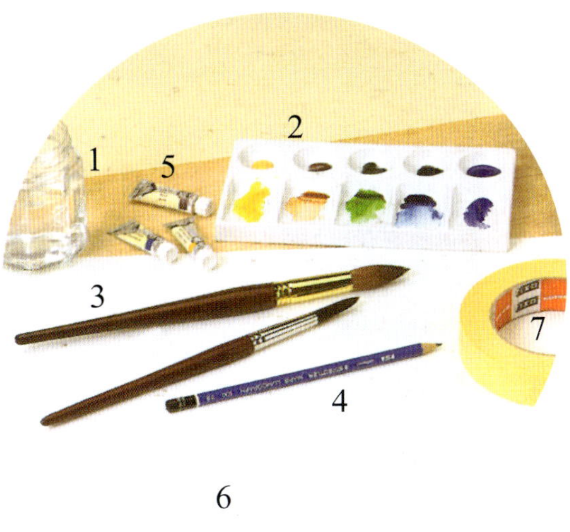

Materials

1. Water Jar
2. Colour Plate
3. Brushes
4. Pencil
5. Tube Colours
6. Paper
7. Tape

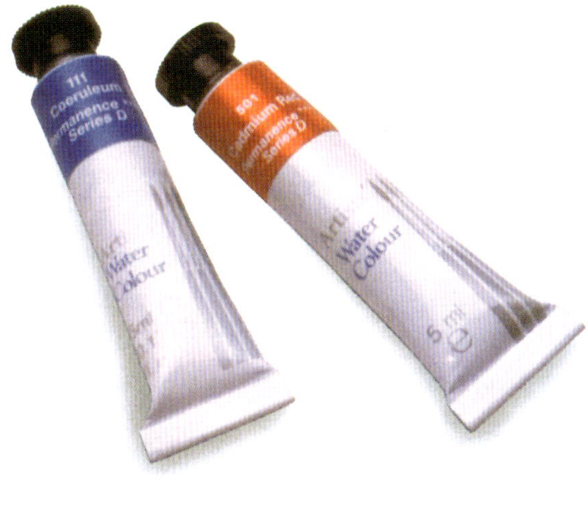

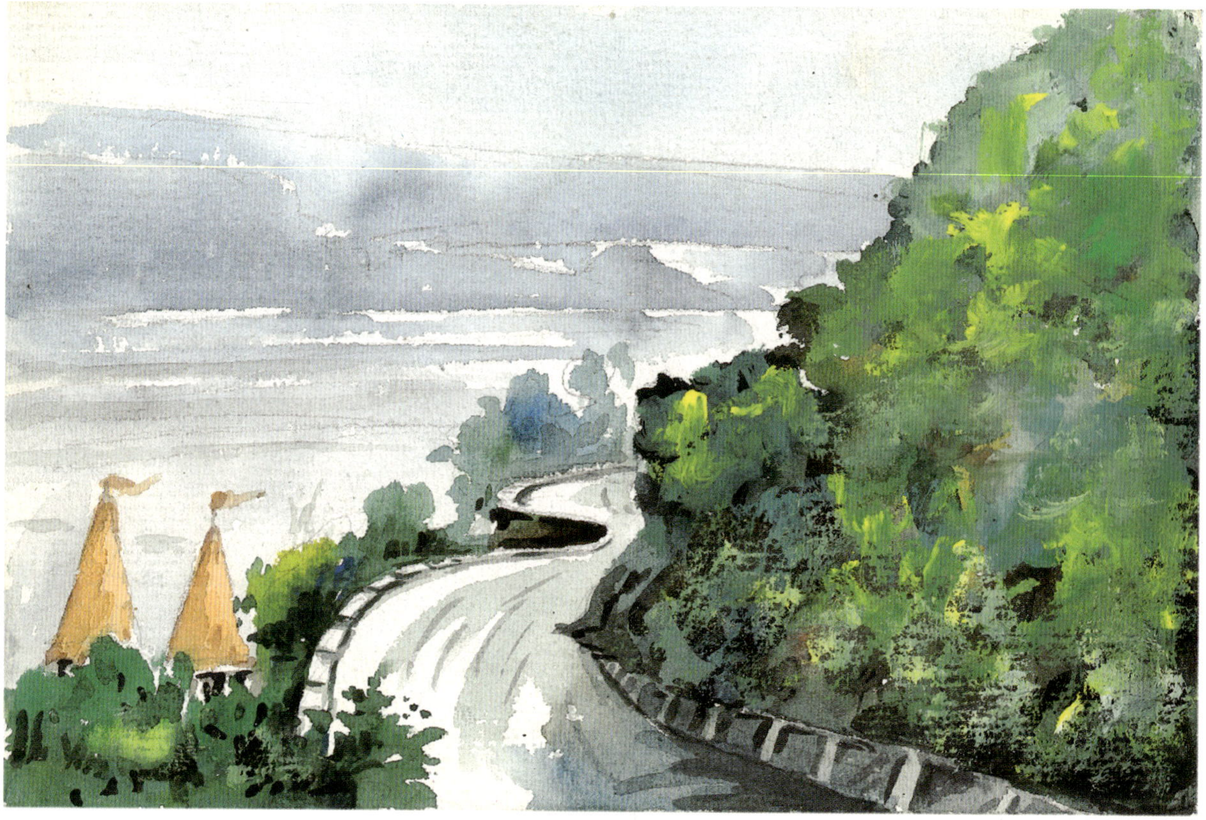

Isn't the magic of the cascading waters of the waterfall along the boulders recreated on paper? The artist used light and dark shades of Burnt Sienna to highlight the boulders, but the artist has not defined the edges, he has applied a light tone of Cobalt Blue with dry brush to depict the waterfall.

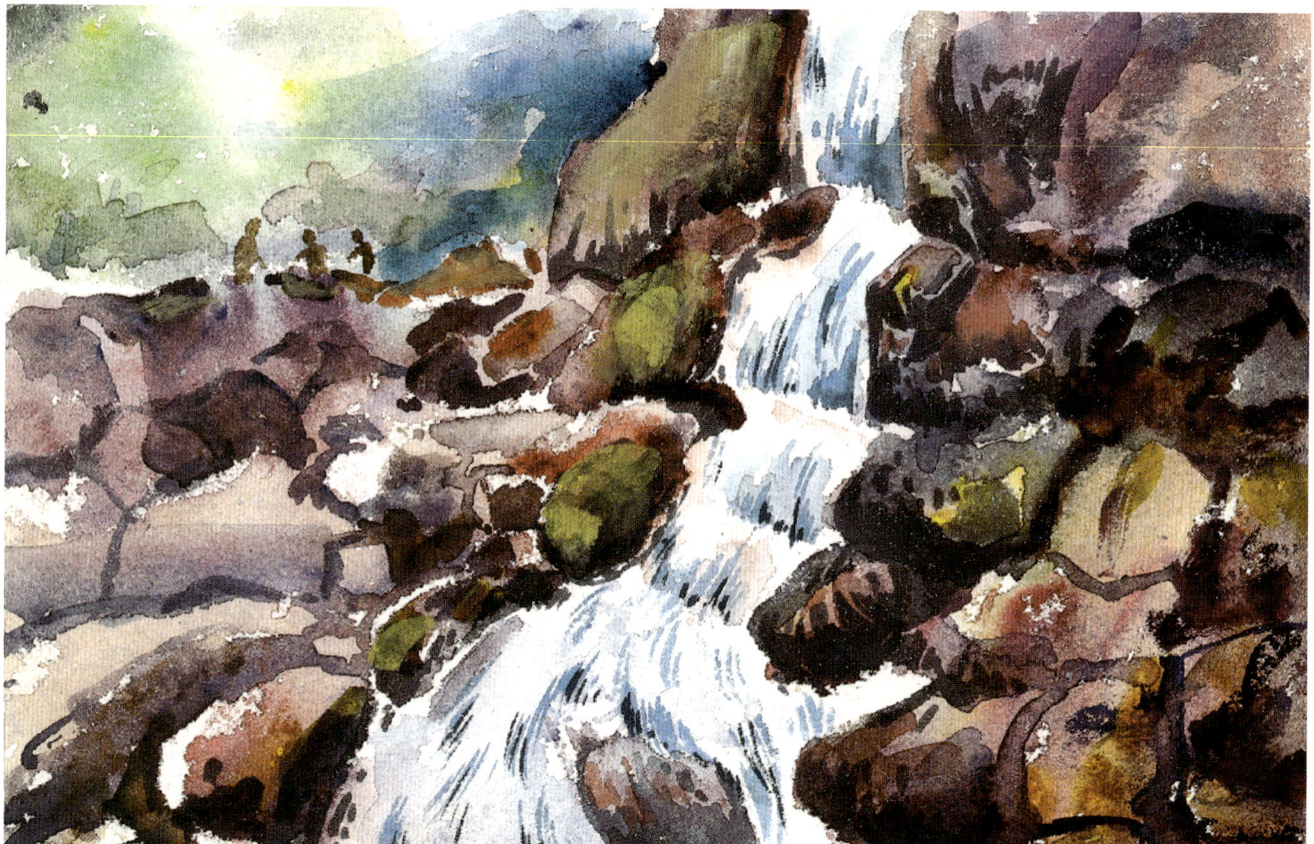

Painting Flowers

The transparent property of watercolours makes it the ideal medium for capturing the beauty and delicate nature of petals and flowers on paper. Flowers can be the centre of interest of a painting or part of a bouquet or a vase. But every flower has a characteristic arrangement of petals and leaves on the stems. You must learn to pick up the differences and the similarities among flowers. With practice, you will be able to master the technique of painting flowers.

You begin every painting with a basic sketch of the object. While proposing to paint flowers, you do the same. You begin with the sketch of the flower you have in mind or in front of you and then block in the dark and light areas with colour.

The artist will take up a few flower subjects and dwell upon the different techniques he adopts while painting them.

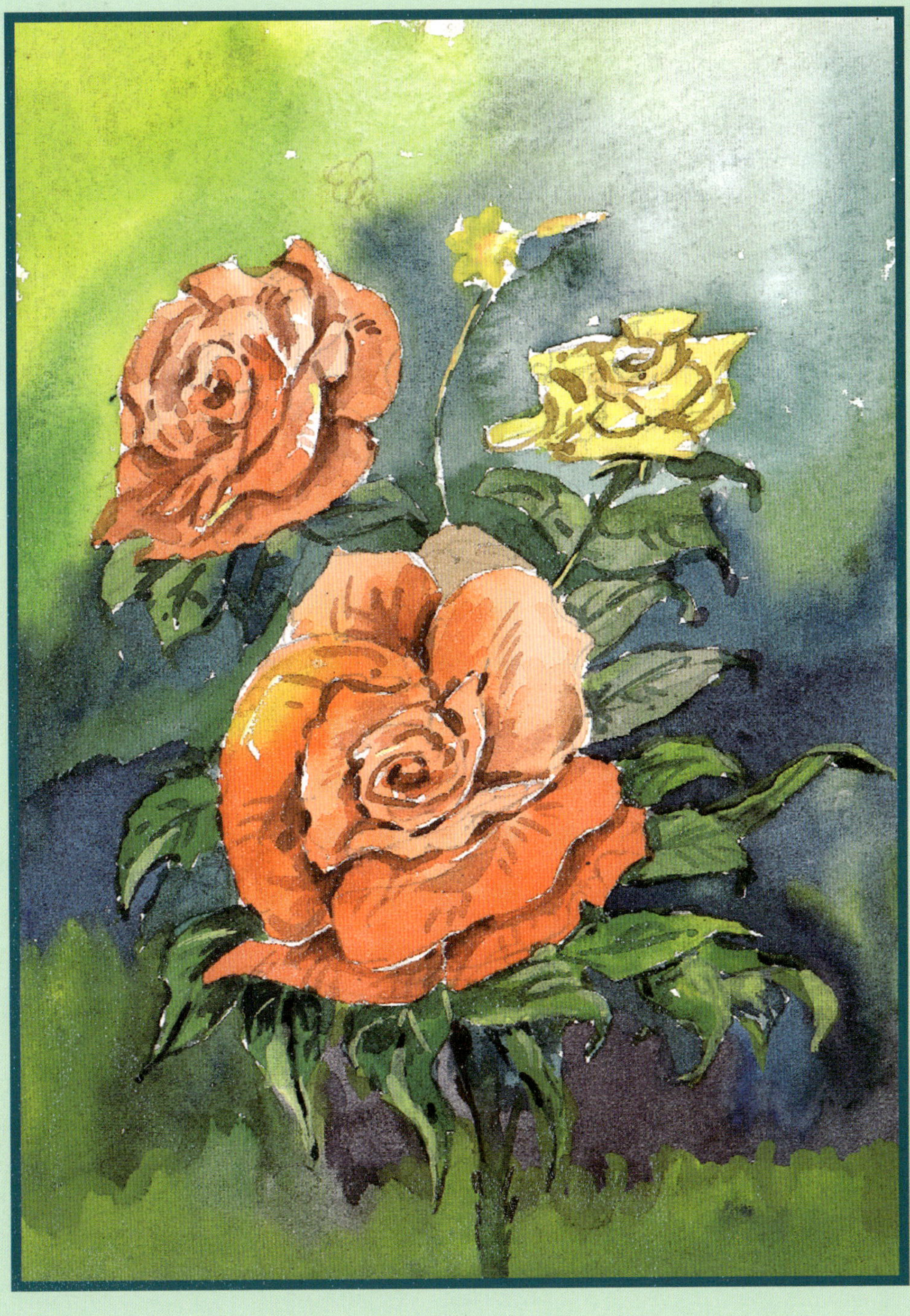

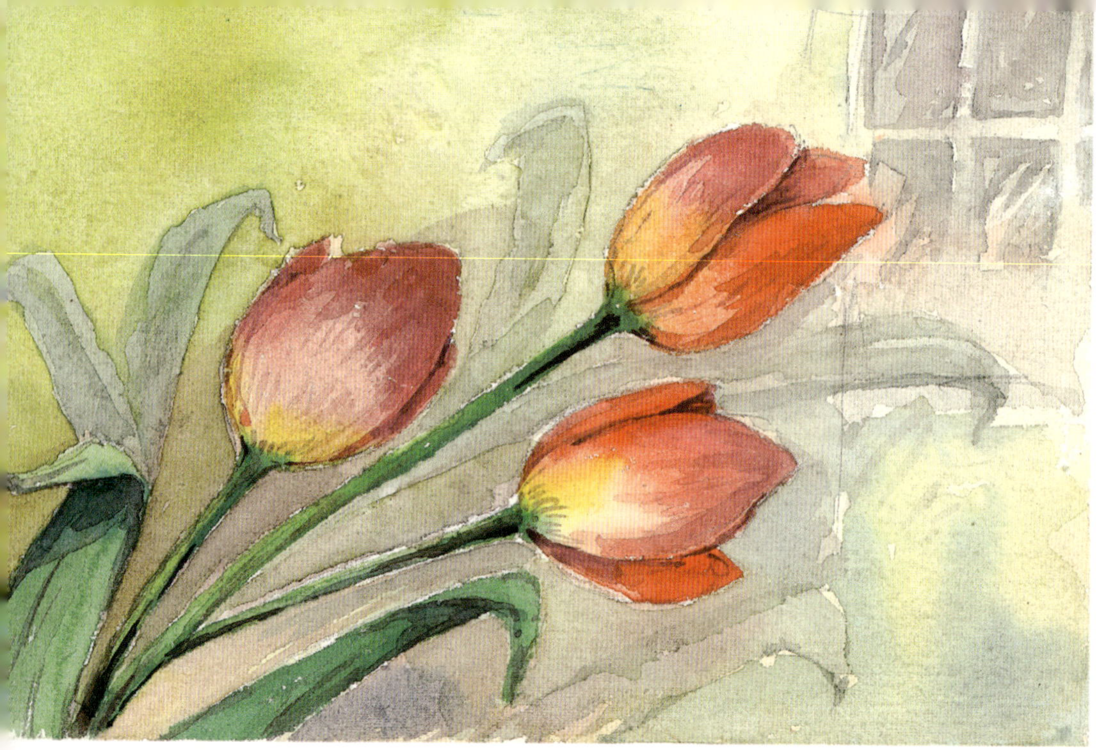

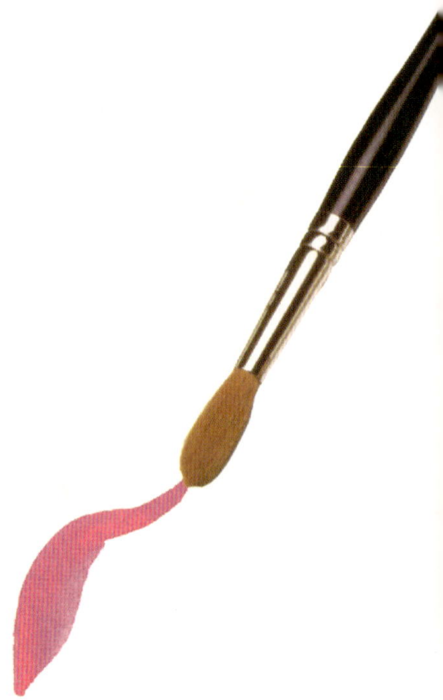

Rose is one of the most difficult flowers to draw. You should observe how the petals fold and overlap. Not only the flower, you should also observe the way the buds and leaves are arranged on the stem. Though the stem is not usually visible, you must know where the flowers are anchored.

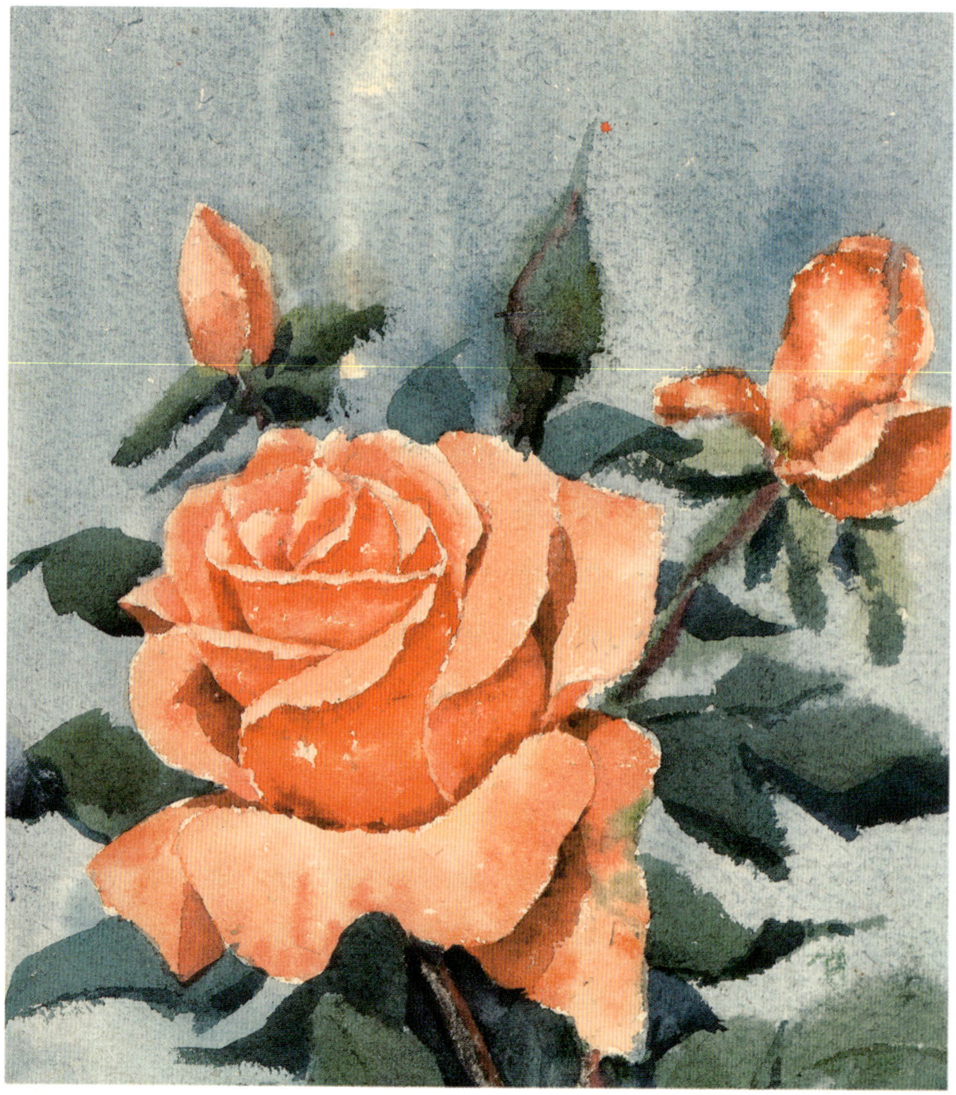

Rendering the Stem

The stem of a rose has simple leaves and many thorns. Here the artist has done it in three tones. For the dark tone, he has used Sap Green, Ultramarine Blue and Crimson. For the middle tone, he has used Sap Green and for the light, light Cadmium Yellow has been applied.

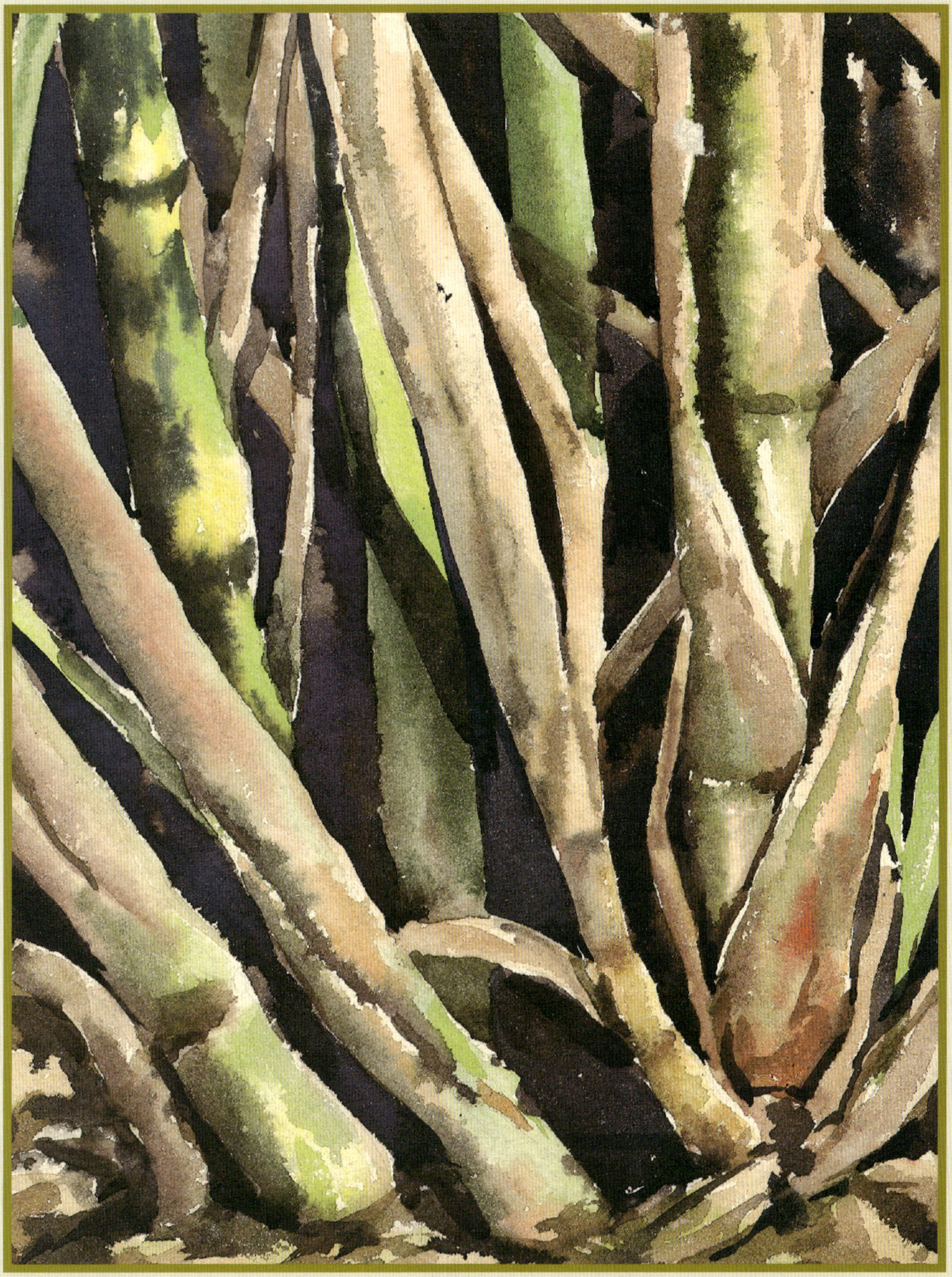

Artist's Tip

To produce the effect of light shining on, work wet-in-wet allowing one colour to spread into another, so that there are no hard edges.

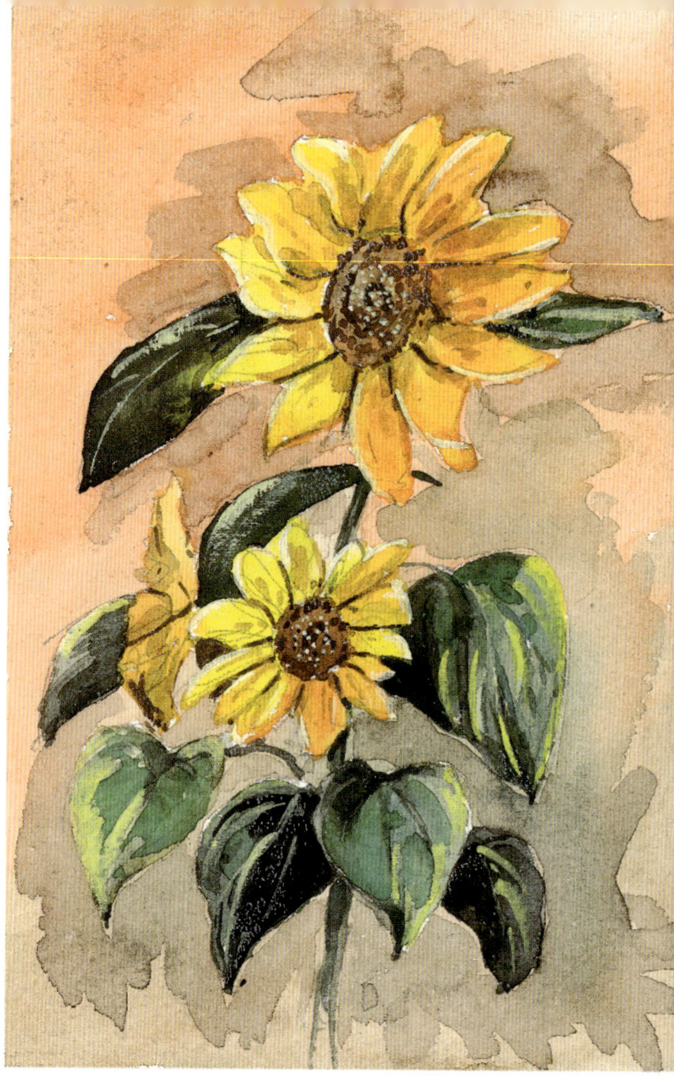

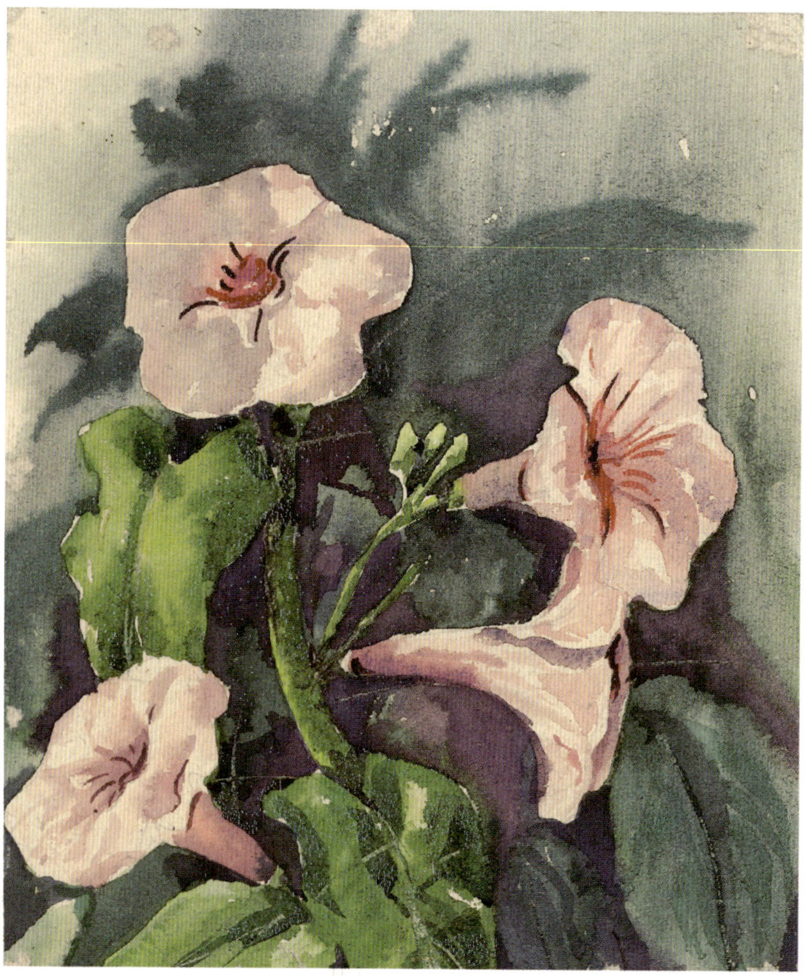

The Petunias

Petunias are bell-shaped flowers. So the petals are usually painted in the light value. Being bell-shaped, the centre of the flower is shown in a dark tone. Apart from the flowers you will also have to take care of the leaves because only then can you capture the effect.

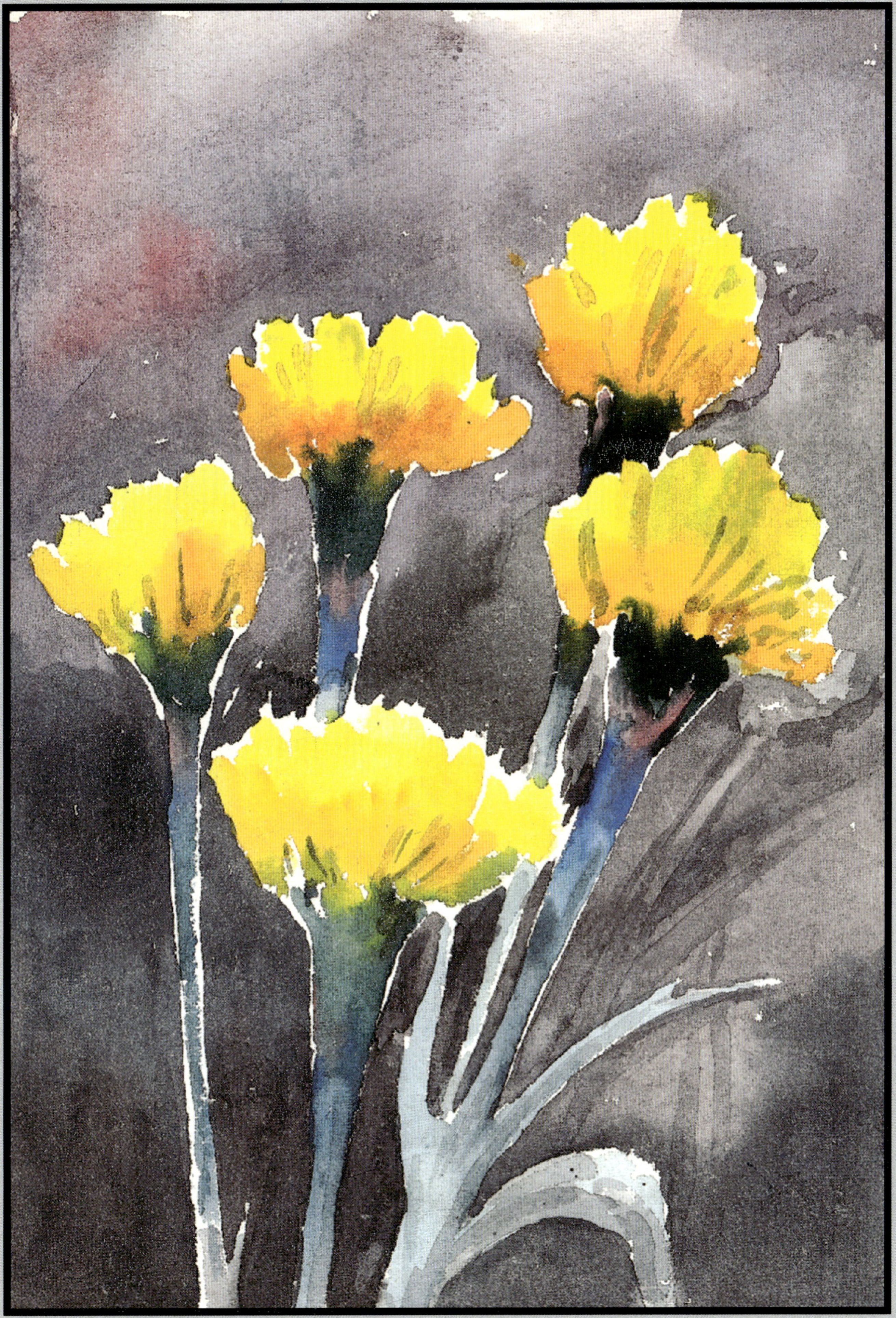

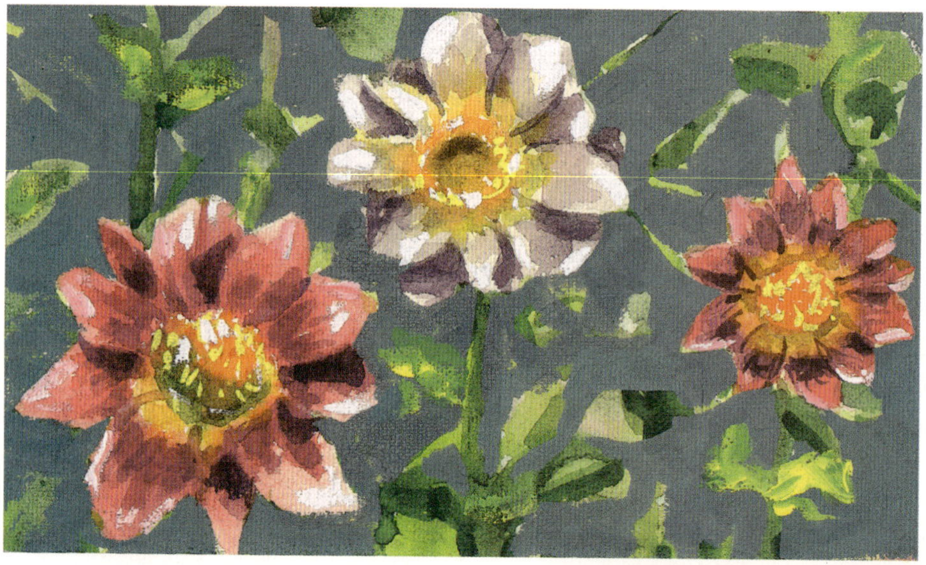

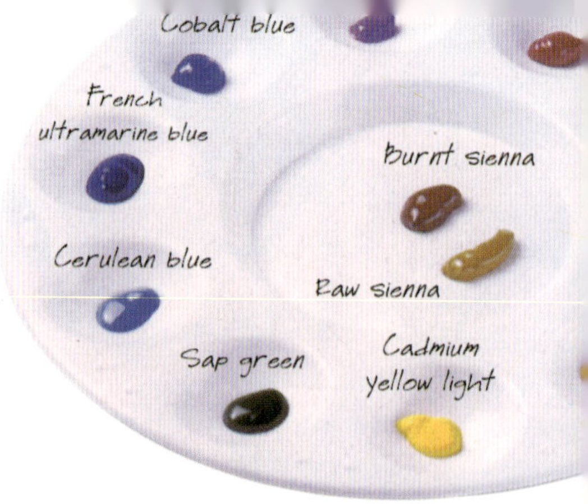
Cobalt blue
French ultramarine blue
Burnt sienna
Cerulean blue
Raw sienna
Sap green
Cadmium yellow light

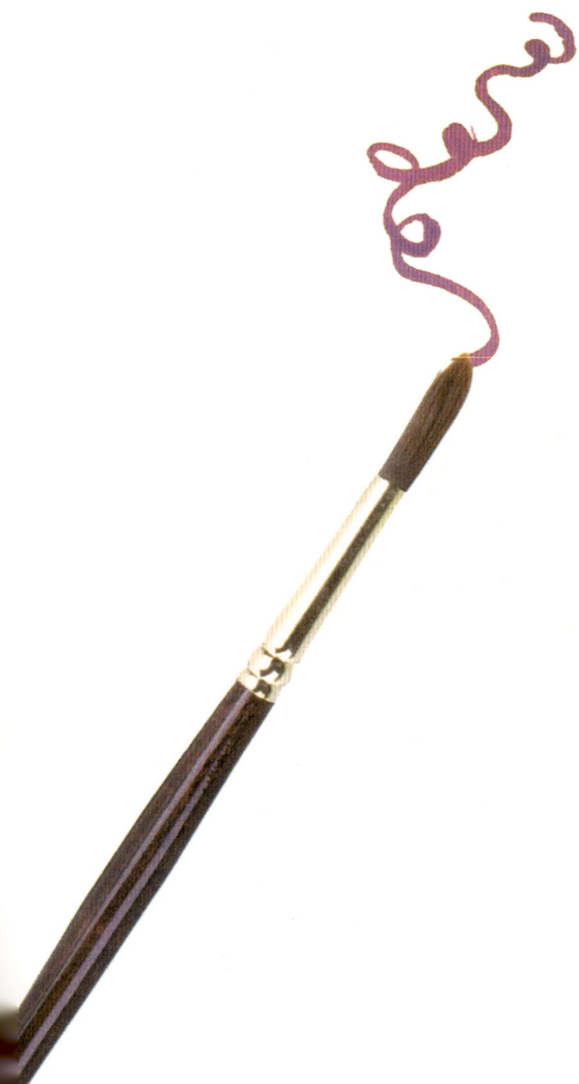

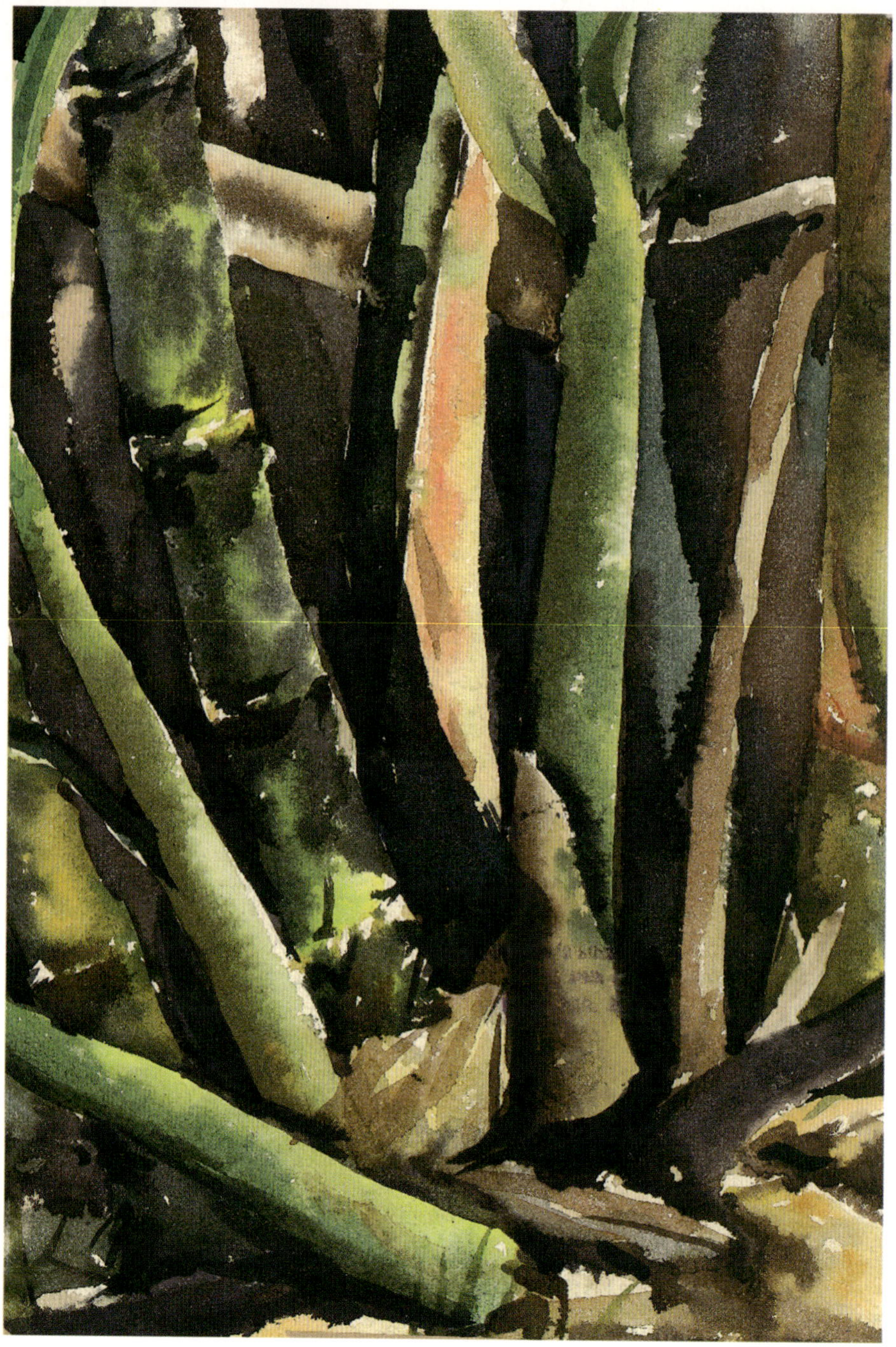

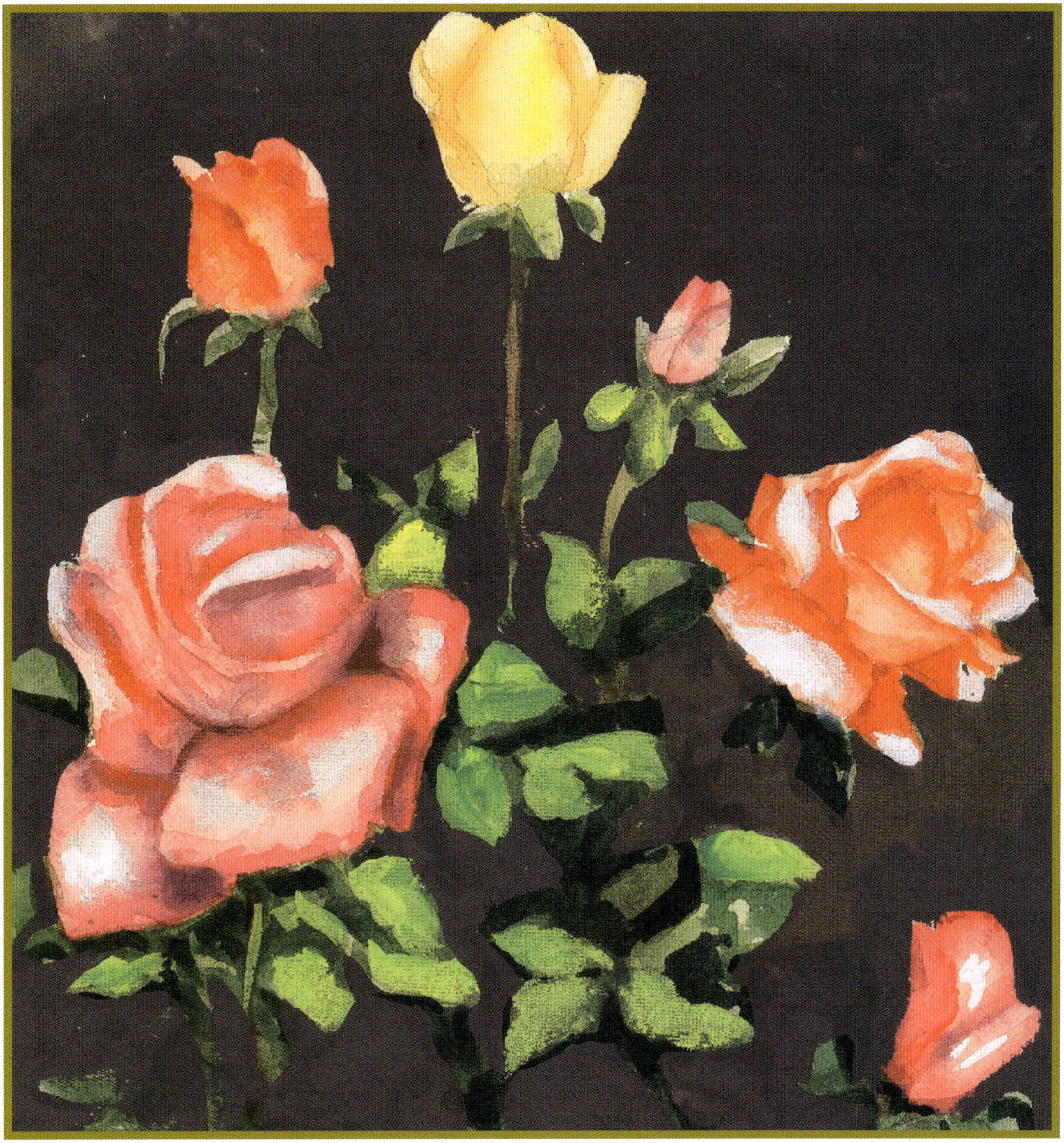

Rendering the Rosebud

Rose is a delicate flower. Even the rosebud and the stems need to be drawn well to capture the delicacy of the flower in a painting. Rosebuds have a distinctive tip. The bud is at the end of a long stem and is enclosed within the sepals. Like the petals, you have to colour the sepals separately, allowing each section to dry before painting the next.

Here the artist has shown roses in their various stages of bloom. Notice the way in which he has used light and dark shades of Crimson to highlight the bud. For the rose on the extreme right, he has used Yellow Ochre for the flower and Permanent Rose to highlight the dark values.

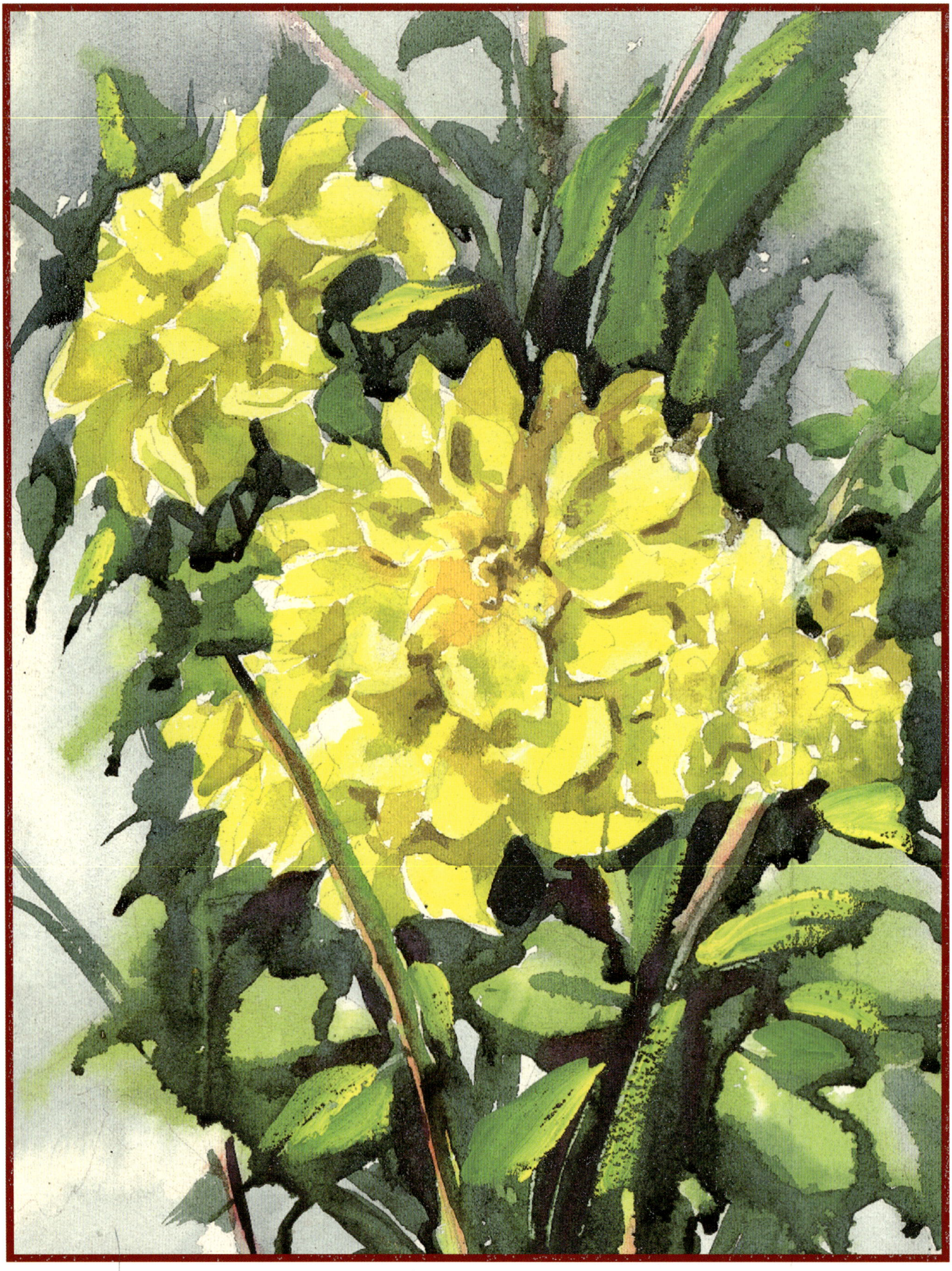

Look as the chrysanthemums! With the minimal of brush strokes, the artist has tried to recreate the beauty of a chrysanthemum in full bloom. After making the basic sketch, he painted the blooms in a light tinge of Yellow Ochre. When it was still wet, he flew a light tone of Cadmium Yellow to indicate the arrangement of the petals in a whorl. Likewise he used light and dark shades of Sap Green to indicate the leaves.

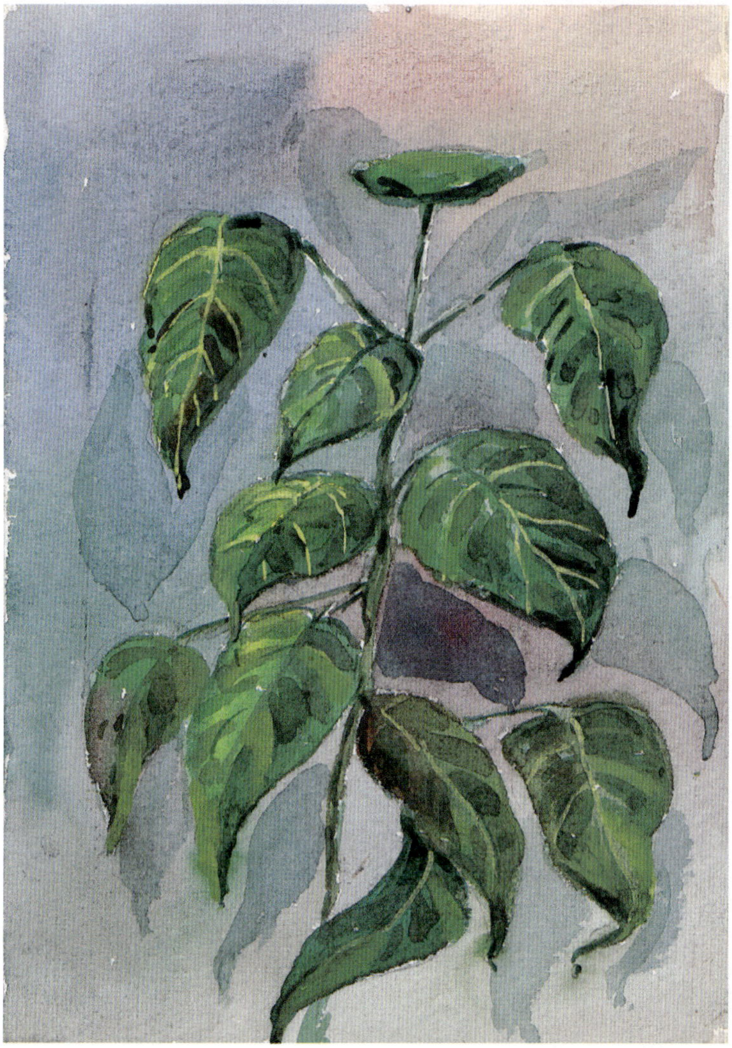

After drawing the sketch, the artist coloured the carnations with Cadmium Yellow and the leaves with Sap Green. Then he has used a mix of Sap Green, Cobalt Blue and Alizarin Crimson along the outline of the carnations and its leaves. Then used a very wet brush and pulled away the colour followed by he covered the flowers with scrap paper. While the background was still moist, he added more colour in the background. When the background dried, I worked on the carnations.

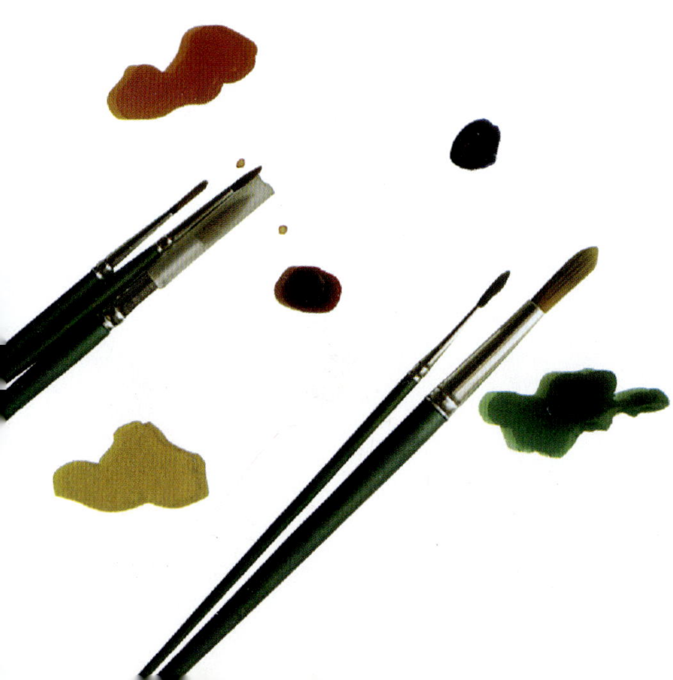

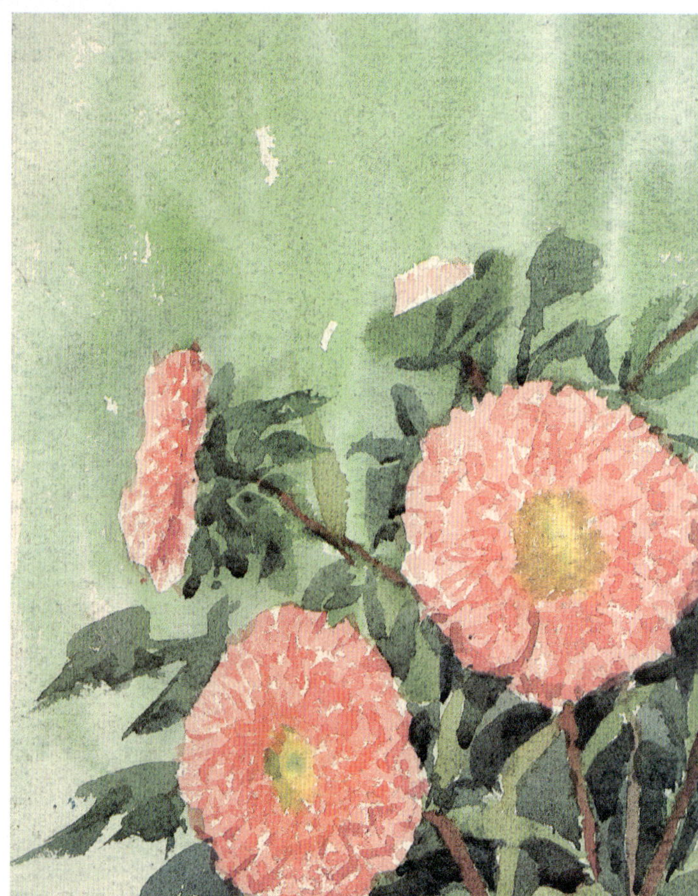

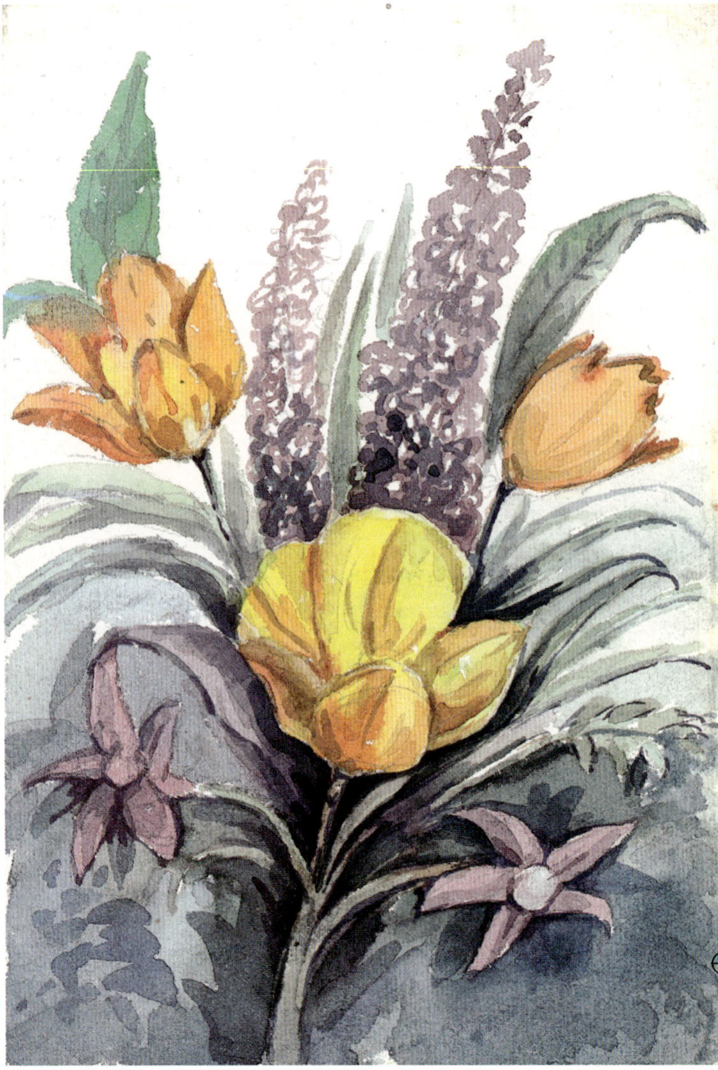

Artist's Tip

If you think you have used more colours than required apply more water and wash out the colour. Then use some crumpled tissue to dry the area.

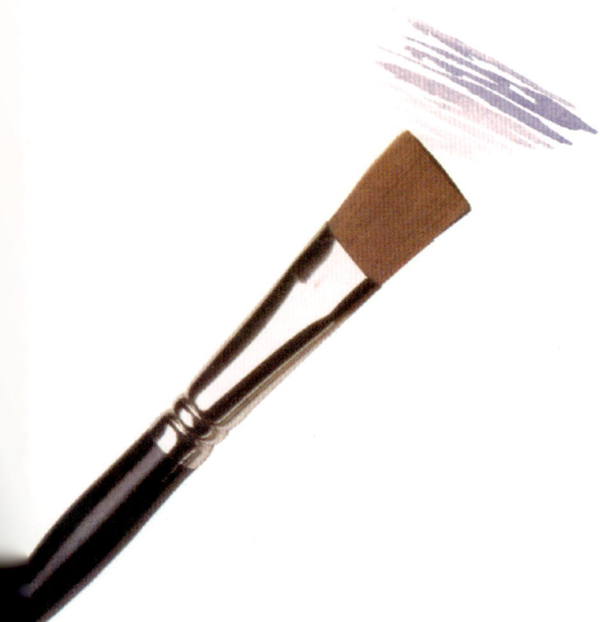

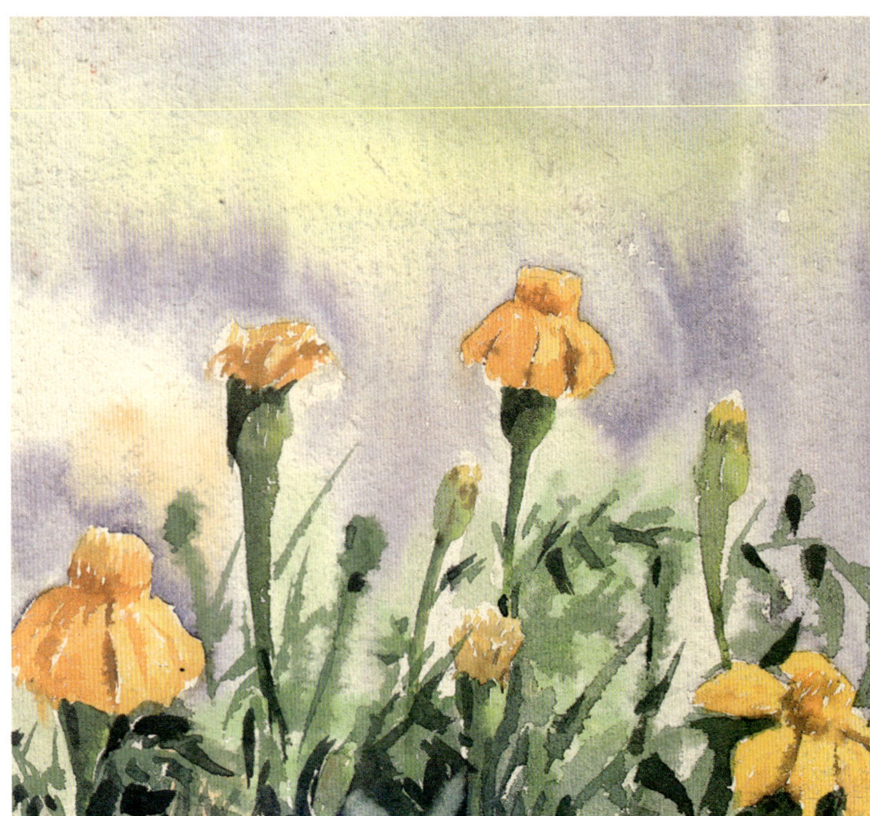

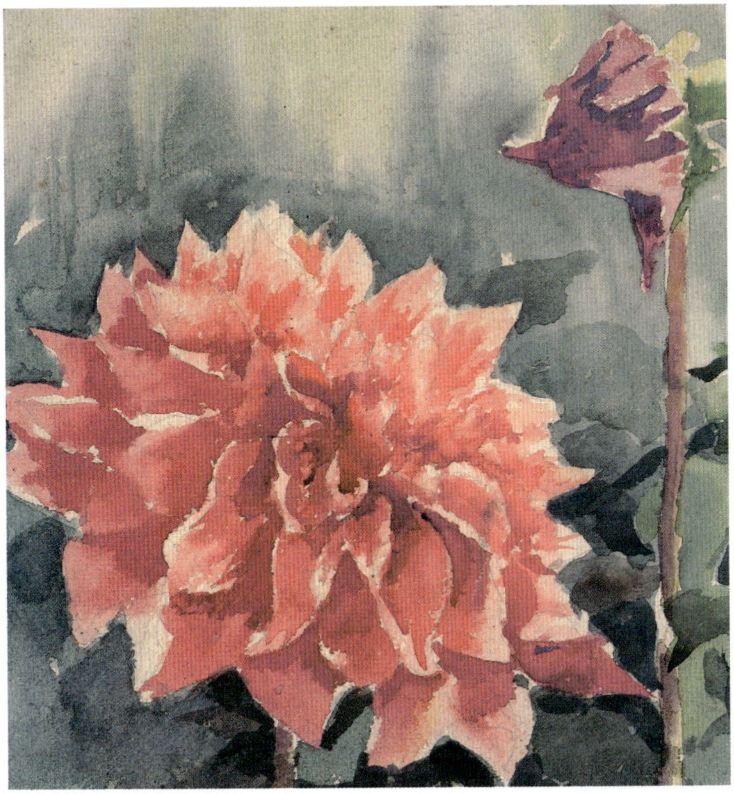

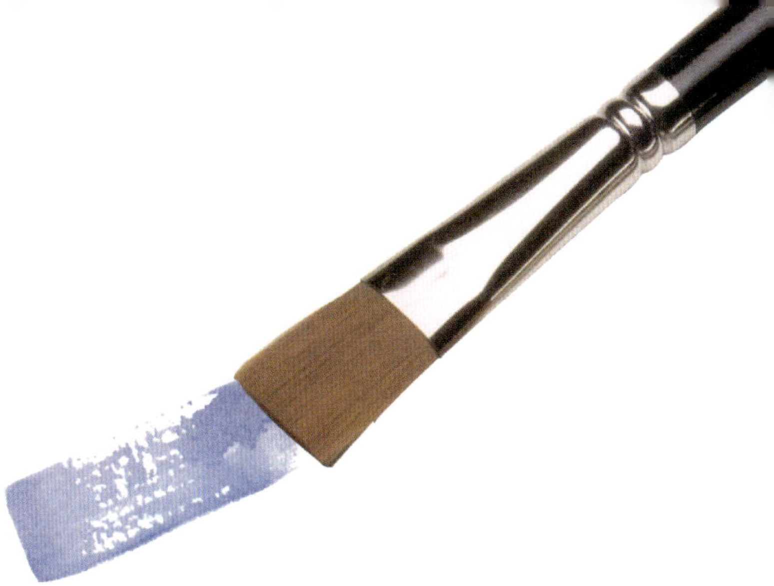

Take your time to study the floral pattern. Then makea sketch. Focus on the basic shape and then define it by adding curves and details.

When you apply colour, work on one petal at a time. Let each area dry before working on the next. After you are through with the rose, you have to highlight the dark and light values to create the shapes of the petals. The petals are arranged in a whorl. Light falls on the tips of the petals and you highlight them with the light values of the previously used colour. And you use dark values where the petals are attached to the centre.

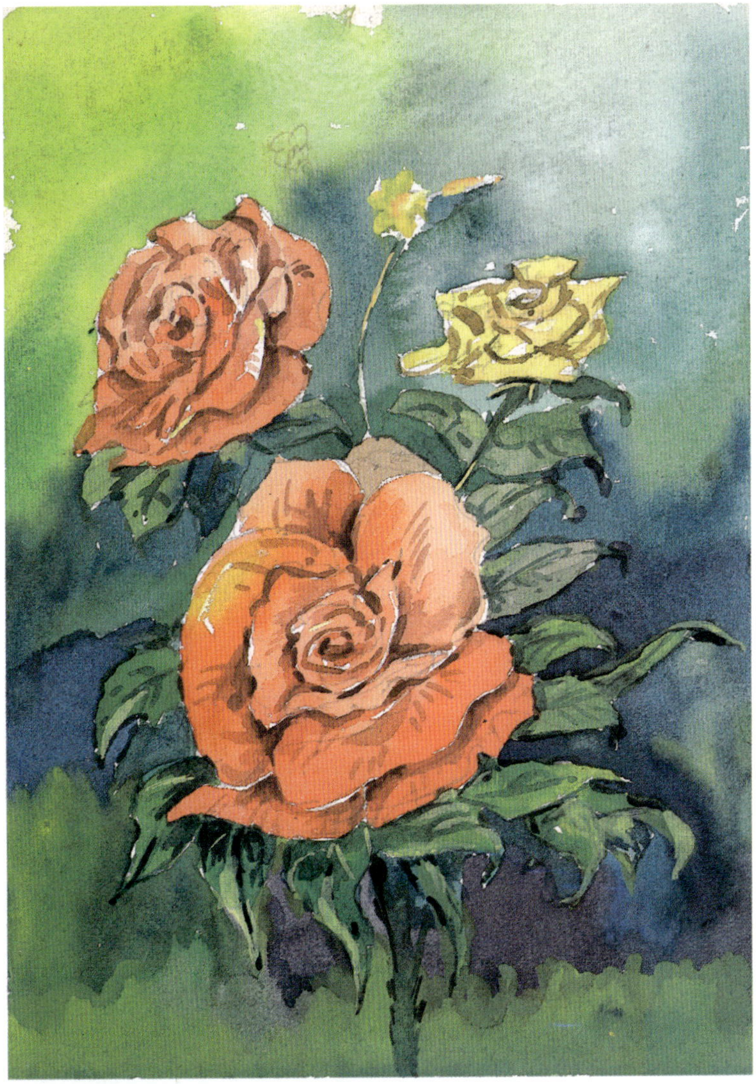

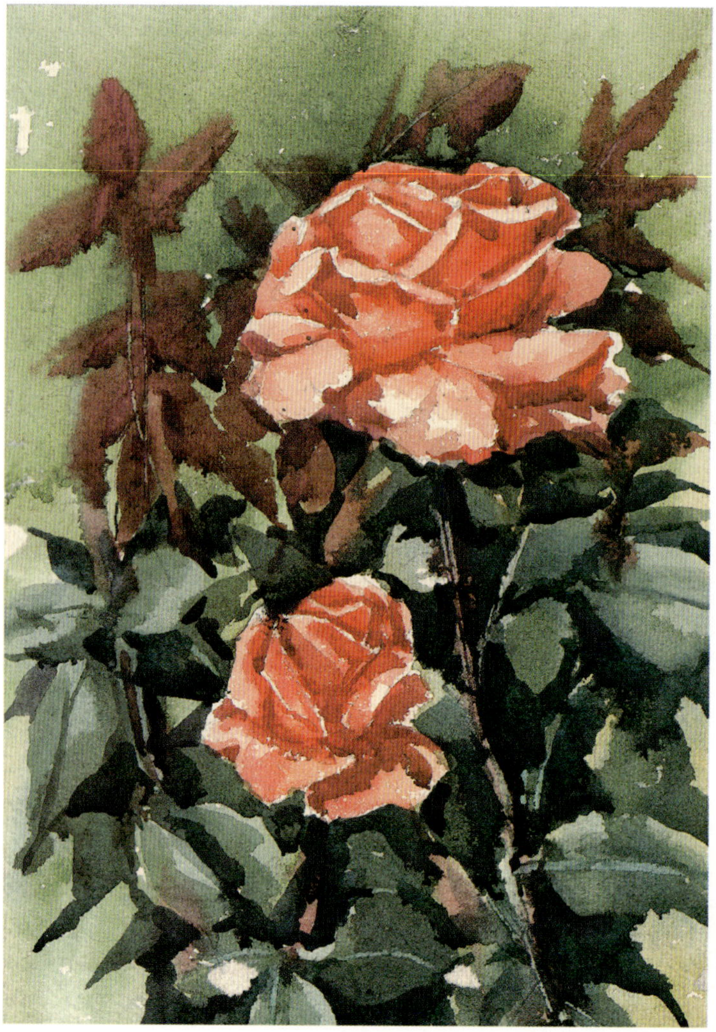

Another wet-in-wet wash with roses. The clever play with colours in the background has helped me highlight the flowers in the foreground.

Contrasting Backgrounds

Not many of us can believe that watercolours can be bold. But watercolours can be used to your advantage by contrasting light values against a dark one. It helps you create a dramatic effect and the creation, really excites the onlooker.

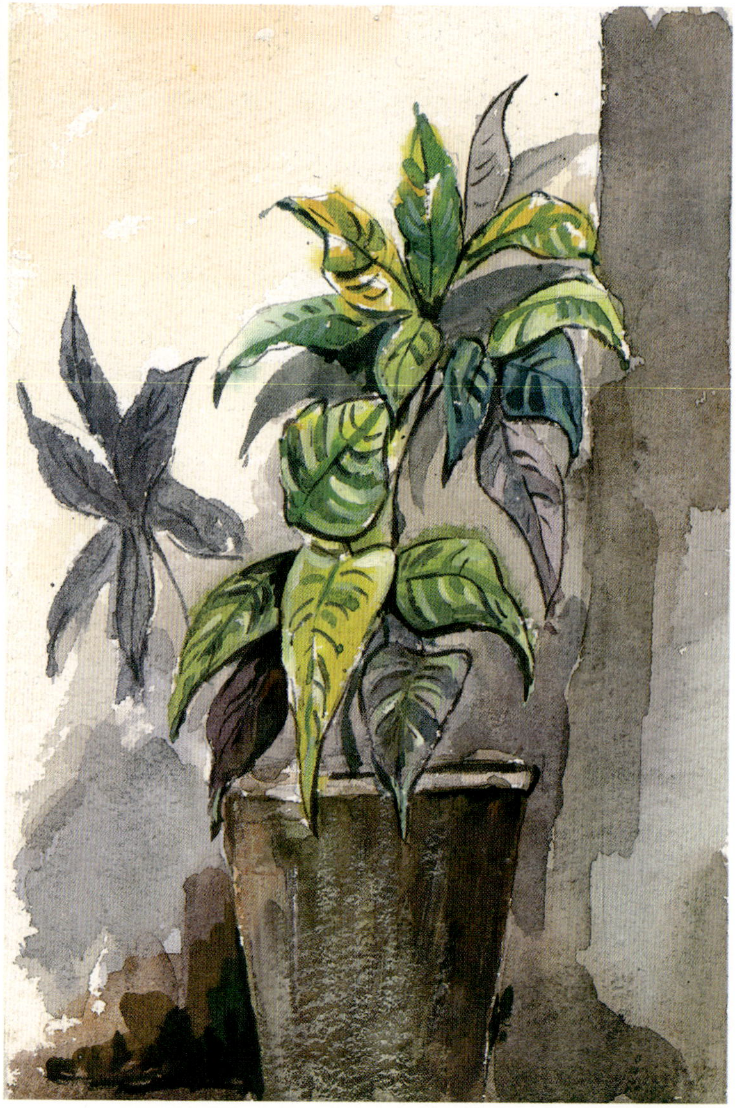

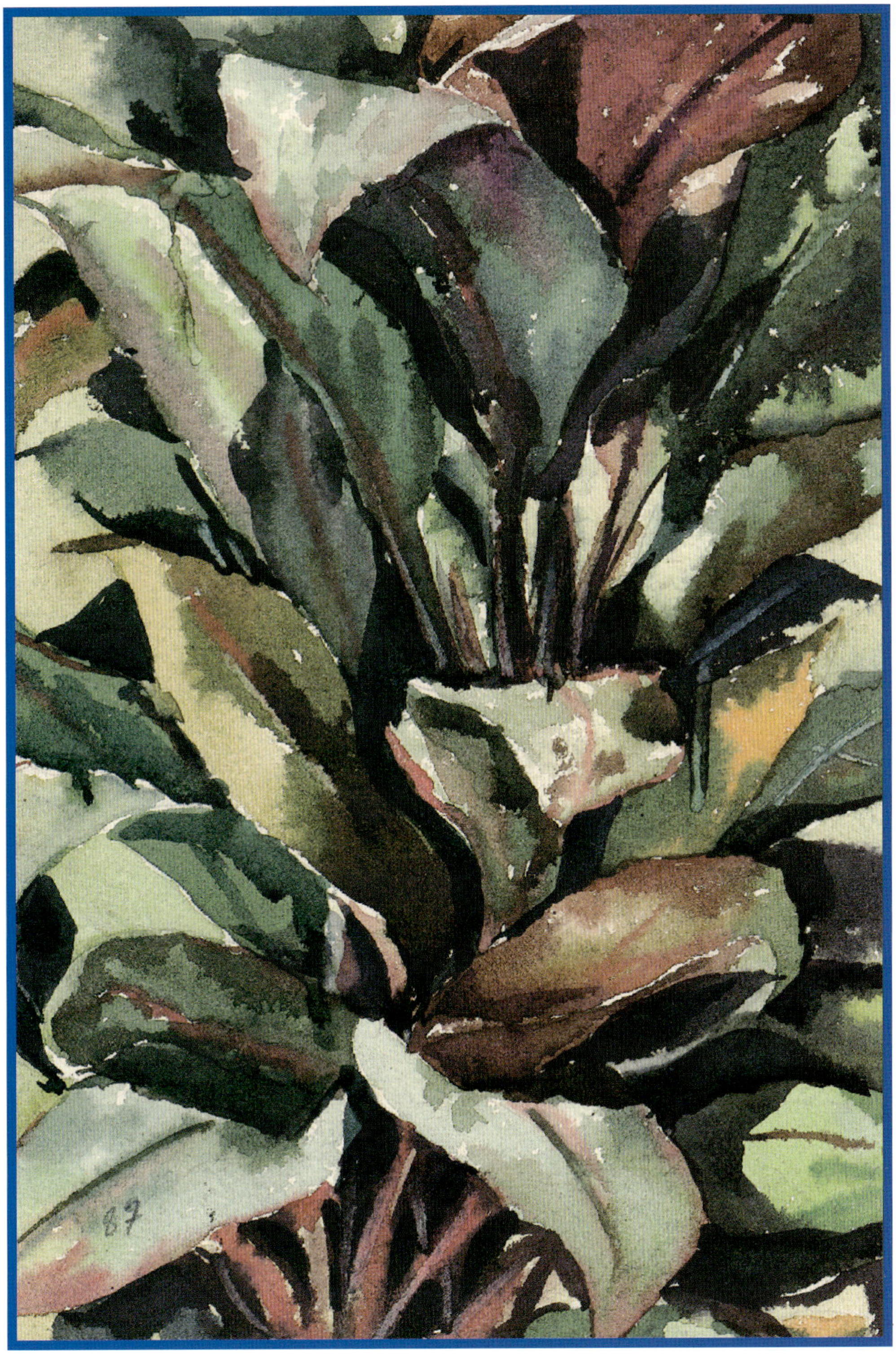

Artist's Tip

Apply thin, transparent washes. This creates the illusion of light reflecting off the white paper and up through the colours.

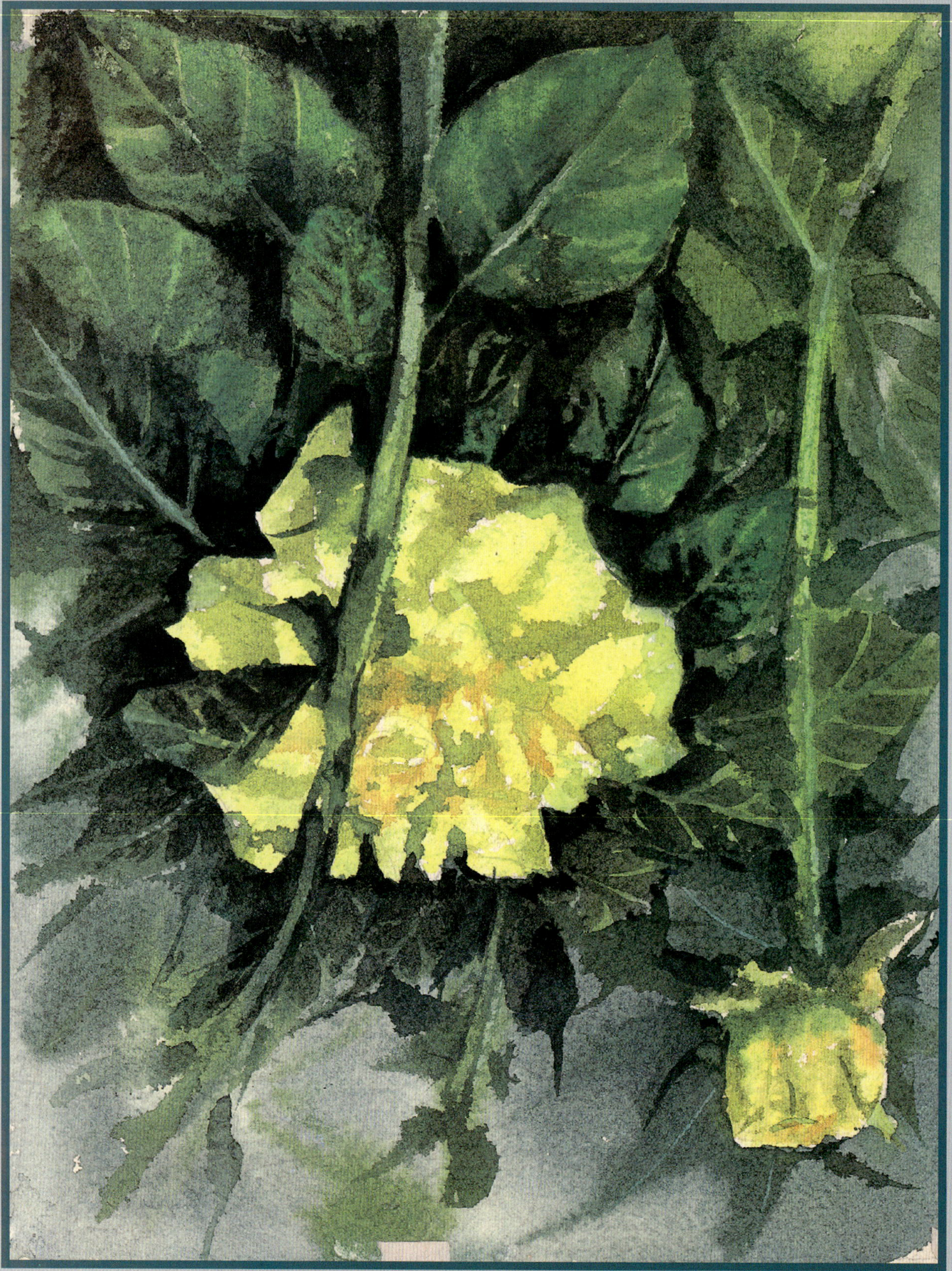

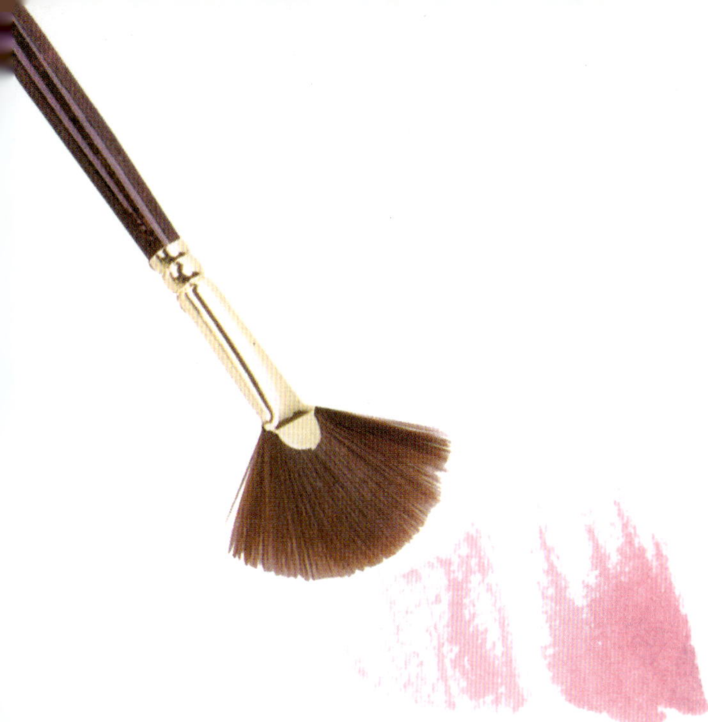

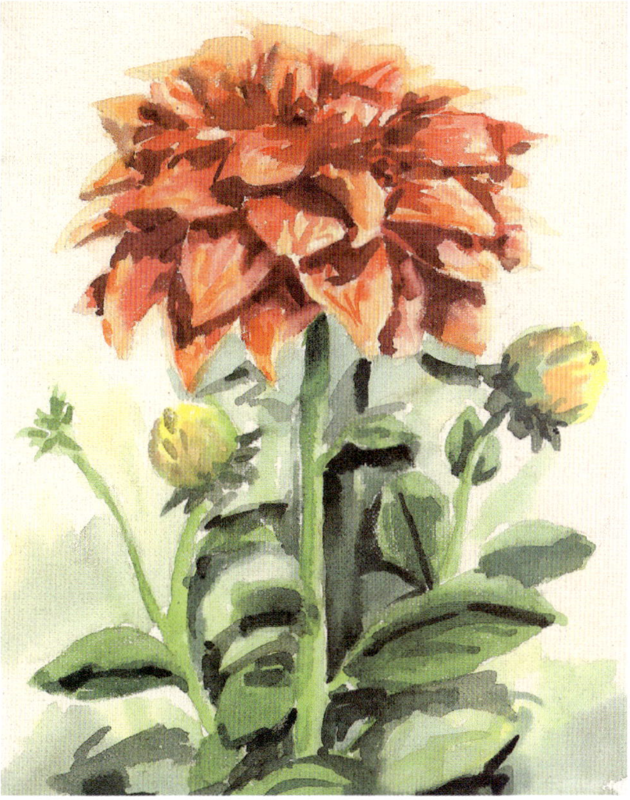

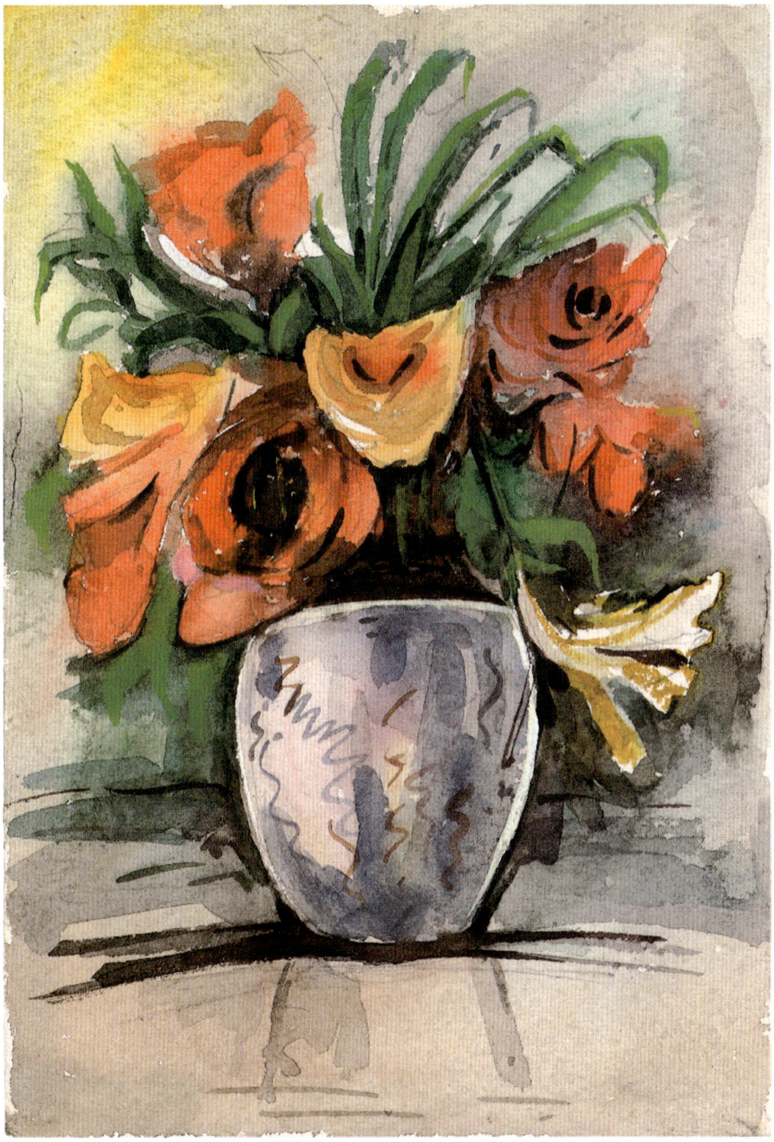

Flowers in a Vase

When you paint a vase of flowers, arrange the flowers in a natural and simple way. Allow them to overlap over each other. Let them stand at different heights. Arrange them the way you will find them in your garden, some flowers turned towards you, some away from you and others in the profile. Rather than having a multicolour arrangement, use harmoniously coloured flowers.

To give the impression that some flowers are nearer than others, towards the back, emphasise the ones near the front with crisp edges. The edges of the flowers at the back should be defined with muted colours and soft edges. To create the illusion of originality, let the petals of one flower overlap the other.

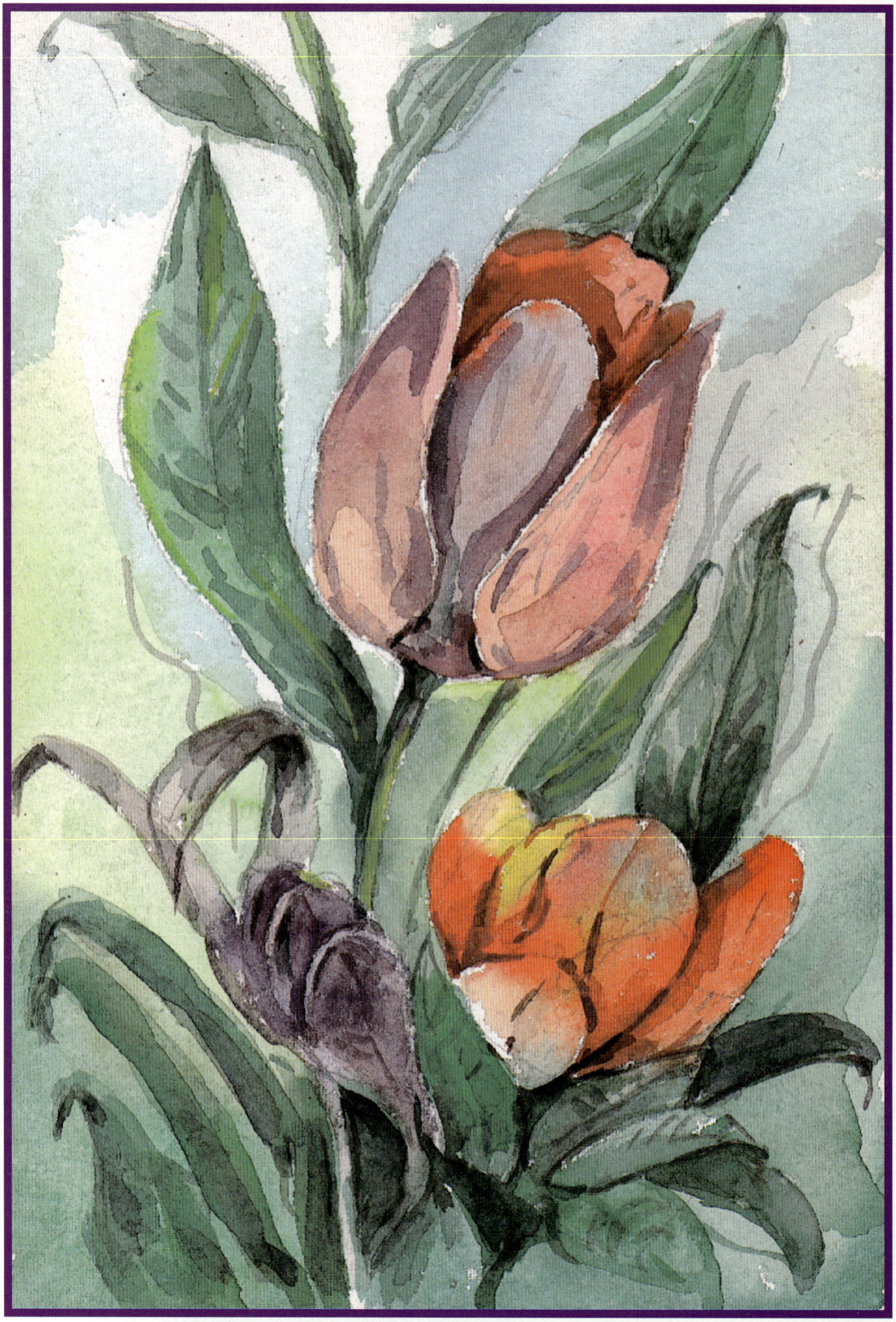

Helpful Hint

If you appear to have used too much colour, simply apply more water, wash the colour out and then dab off the excess with a piece of crumpled tissue.

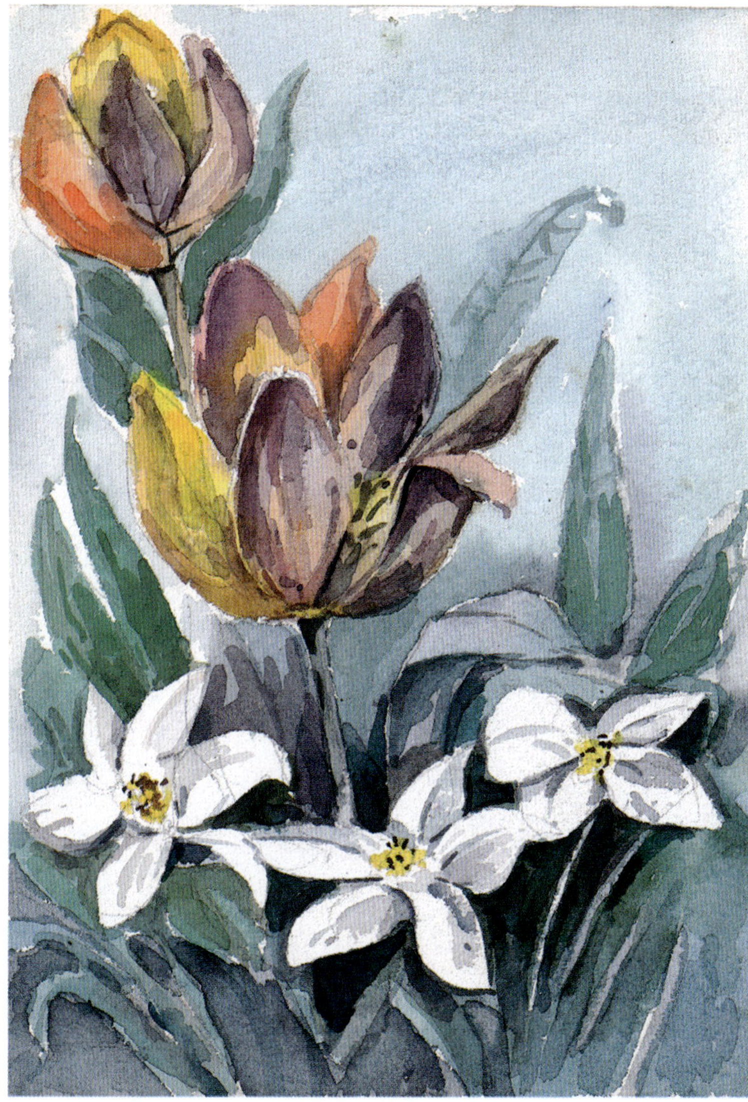

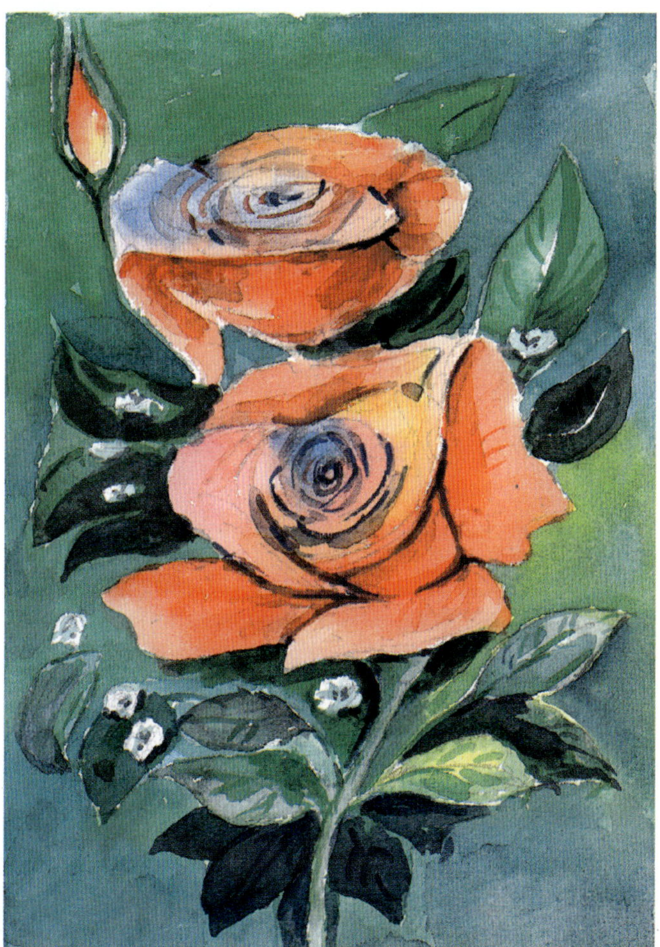

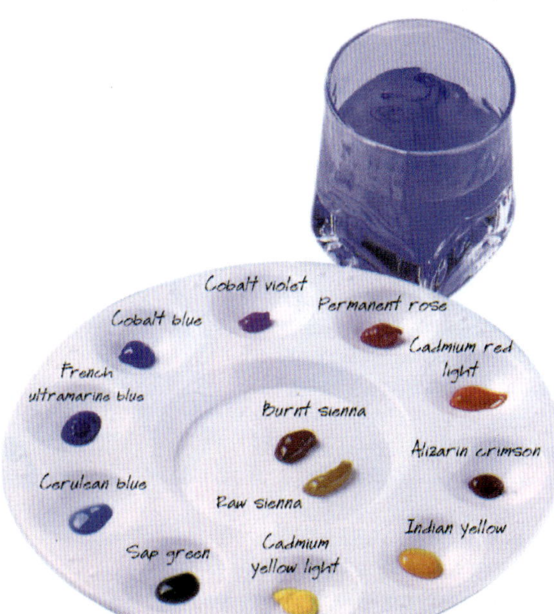

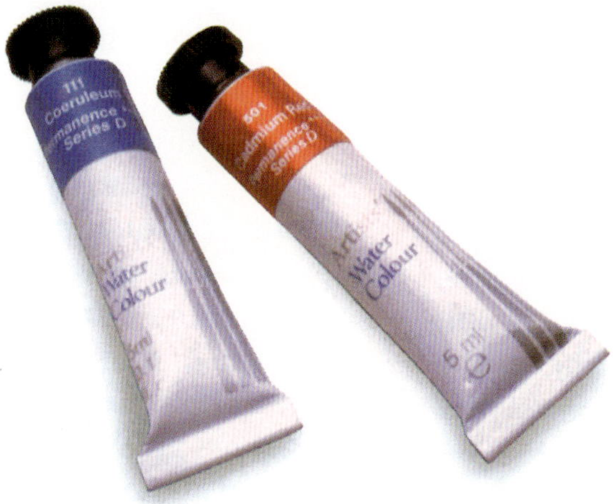
Water Colour
Water Colour

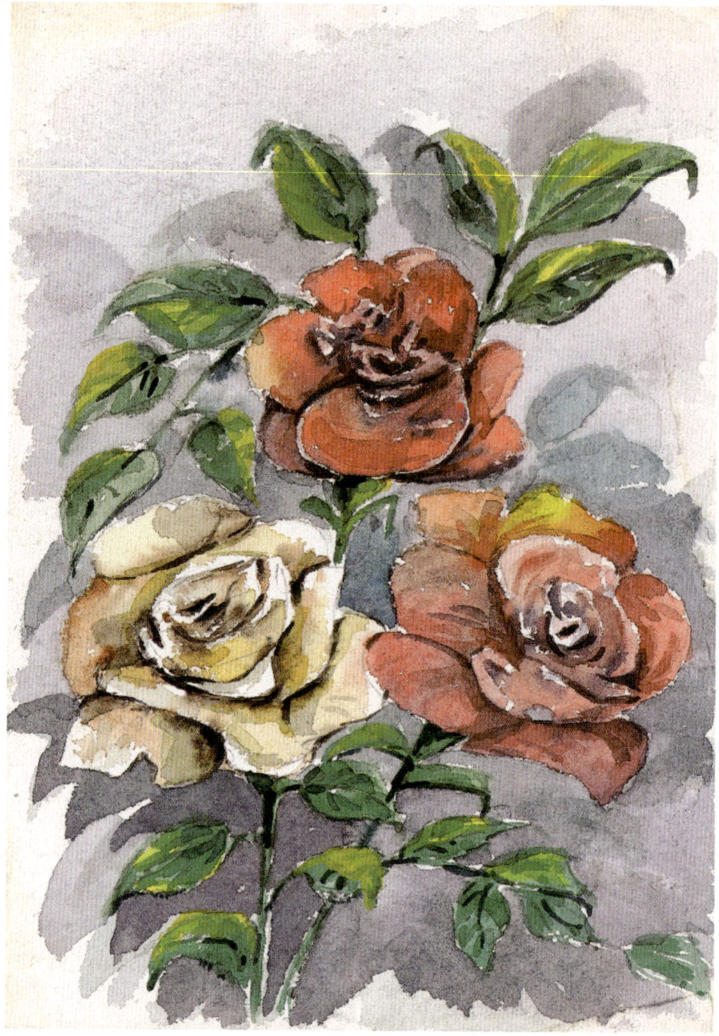

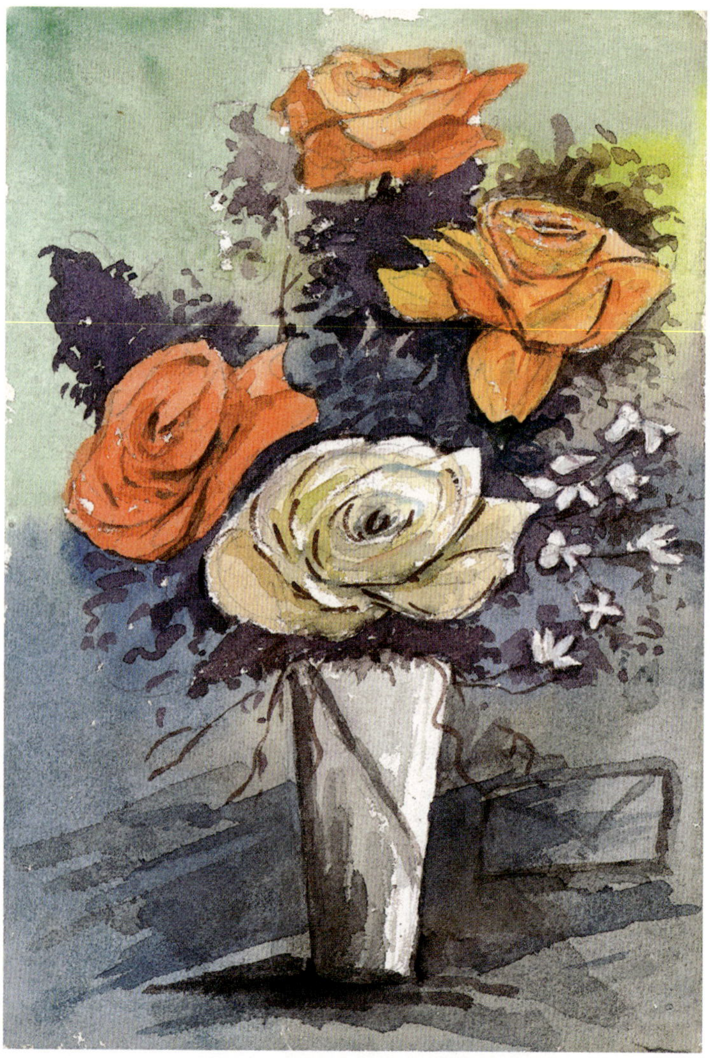

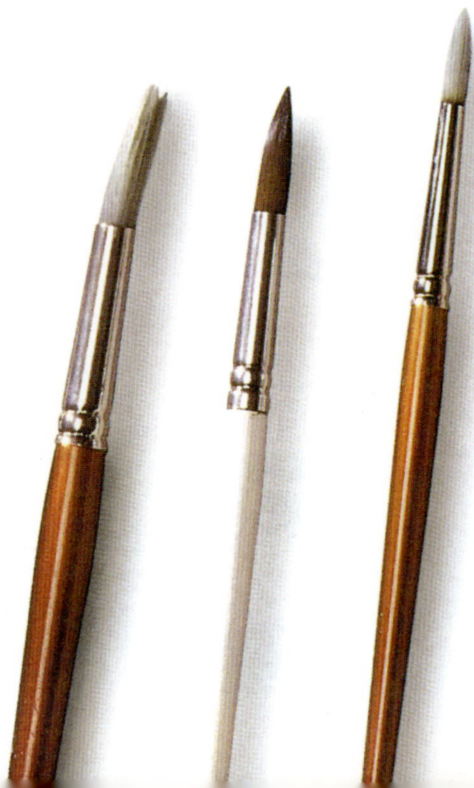

Still Life

Painting a Still Life

Your model for a still life can be just anything. Classical elements were fruits in a bowl, flowers in a vase or apples. But that's not all. You can compose your still life with numerous elements like pottery, crockery or any of the everyday objects that you see around you, anything that it inanimate—lifeless.

To prepare an effective still life, your painting should have some kind of theme. Either you choose objects that are related by type or collection of desk items, flowers in a vase among others.

The advantages of doing a still life are many. You have complete control of the subject. In fact, it is you who choose the subject. You can arrange your subject the way you want to and light it the way you want to. An advantage of doing still life over landscape is that you need not worry about the changing colours and work fast to capture it on paper. When doing a portrait, you have to bear with the whims and fancies of the model, but your model for still life won't fidget and won't need a break.

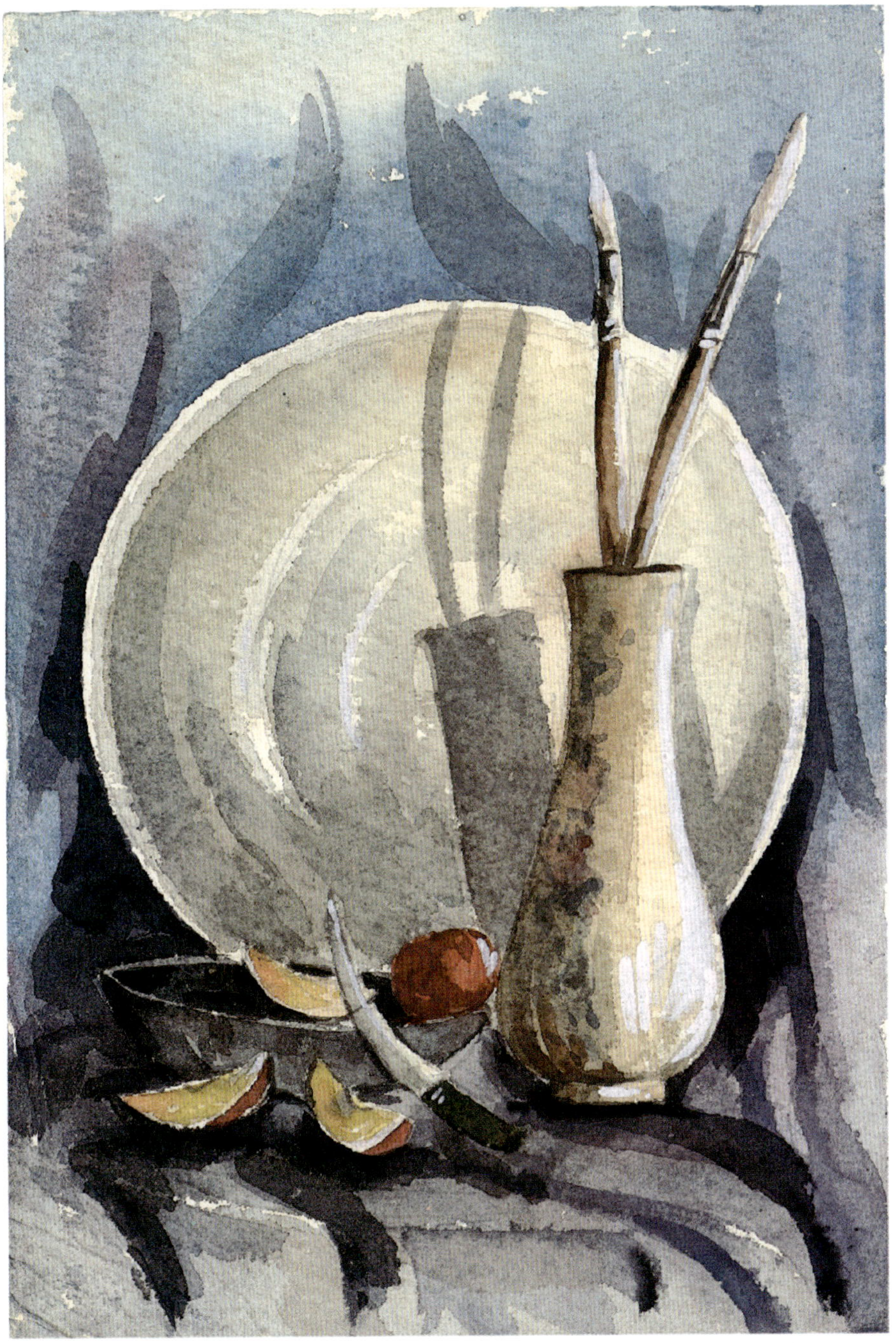

Setting up a Still Life

You must know how to add life to your still life. The objects should appear realistic and playing with light and shadow will help you create depth. Your painting should be able to draw the attention of the onlooker and direct his eye from object to object.

This can be done by the use of diagonal lines because they help to lead the eye around the painting. Horizontal lines tend to lead the eye out of the painting. Then you can arrange them on different planes, so that you are able to capture a good balance of the elements of different shapes and sizes.

Do's and Don'ts while Doing a Still Life

Don'ts

Do not crowd. When you place things too close together you are not able to capture the correct composition. The space around the objects also forms part of the painting. When you group things close together, you spoil the harmony of the things. Do not place the objects too for off. If you place the objects away from each other, the composition of your painting breaks down. When things are spaced out, the eye does not flow naturally from one object to another. The flow is broken because of the space.

Do's

Choosing the right light source is important for bringing out the depth of the painting. This is because light defines the forms by creating highlights and shadows. After you have placed the objects for the still life and chosen the light source, stand back and observe the whole.

A harmonious and balanced composition of the objects for still life is required to add life to your painting. An ideal layout would be without too much bunching or dispersion.

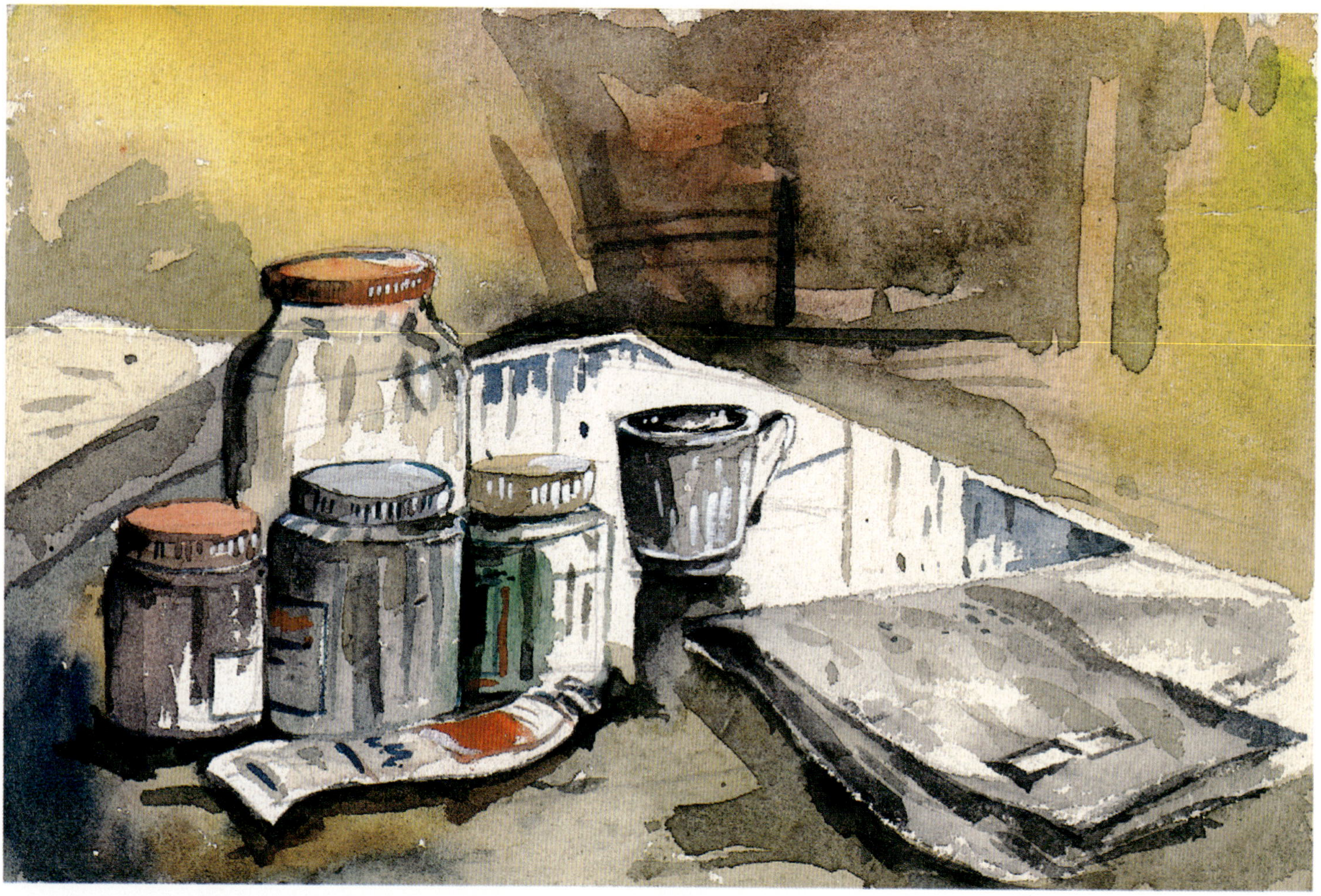

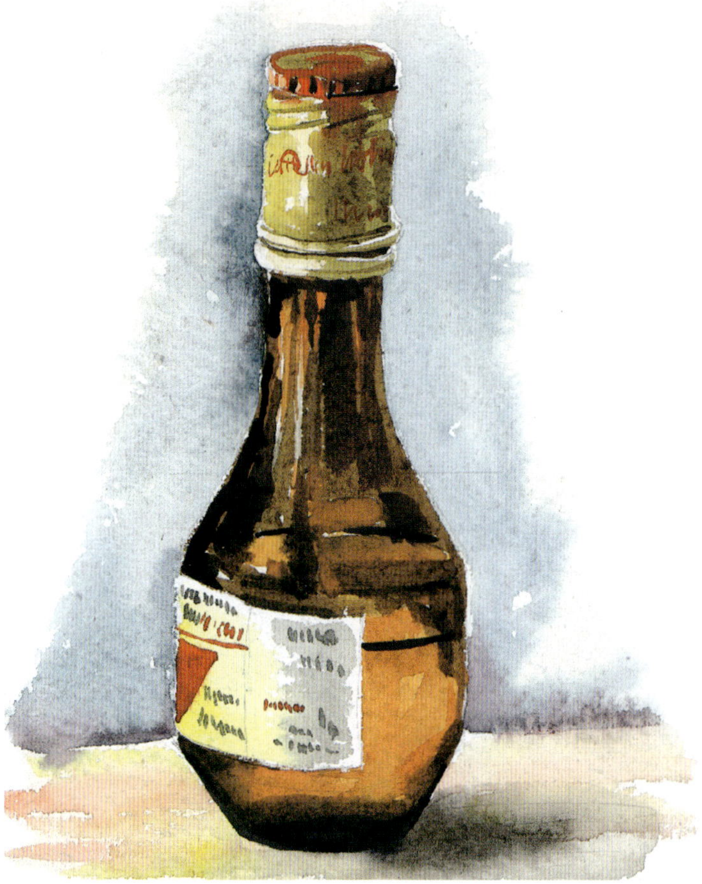

When you are starting out with still life you can just use one object. The artist has used this bottle. To make it appear real, he has tried to make the glass look fragile. The side towards light reflects the light that falls on it, while that in the shade is dark. You already know that in a watercolour painting, you begin working from lighter shade to a darker shade.

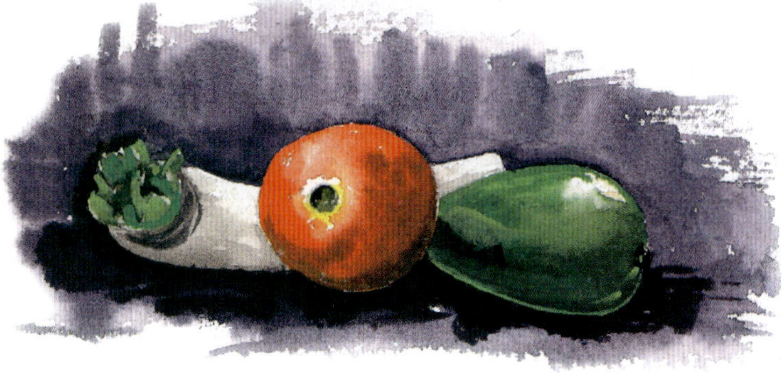

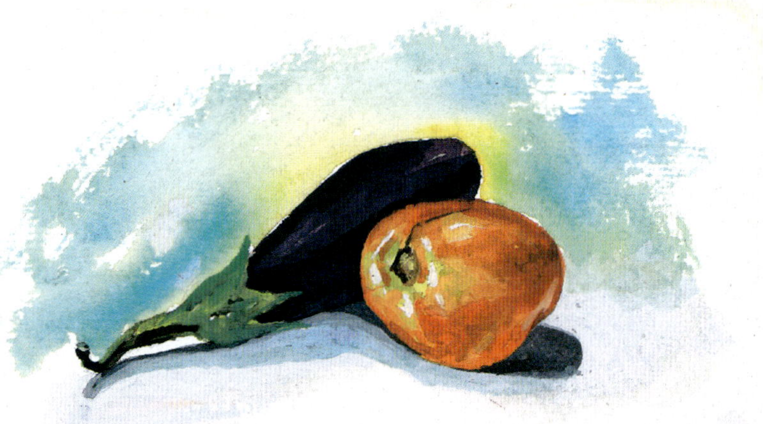

Drawing vegetables and fruits are fun. You have to ensure that you draw them in the right proportion to each other. To give a sense of depth to the picture, he has played with tones and colours in the potato. This makes it appear that it is forward.

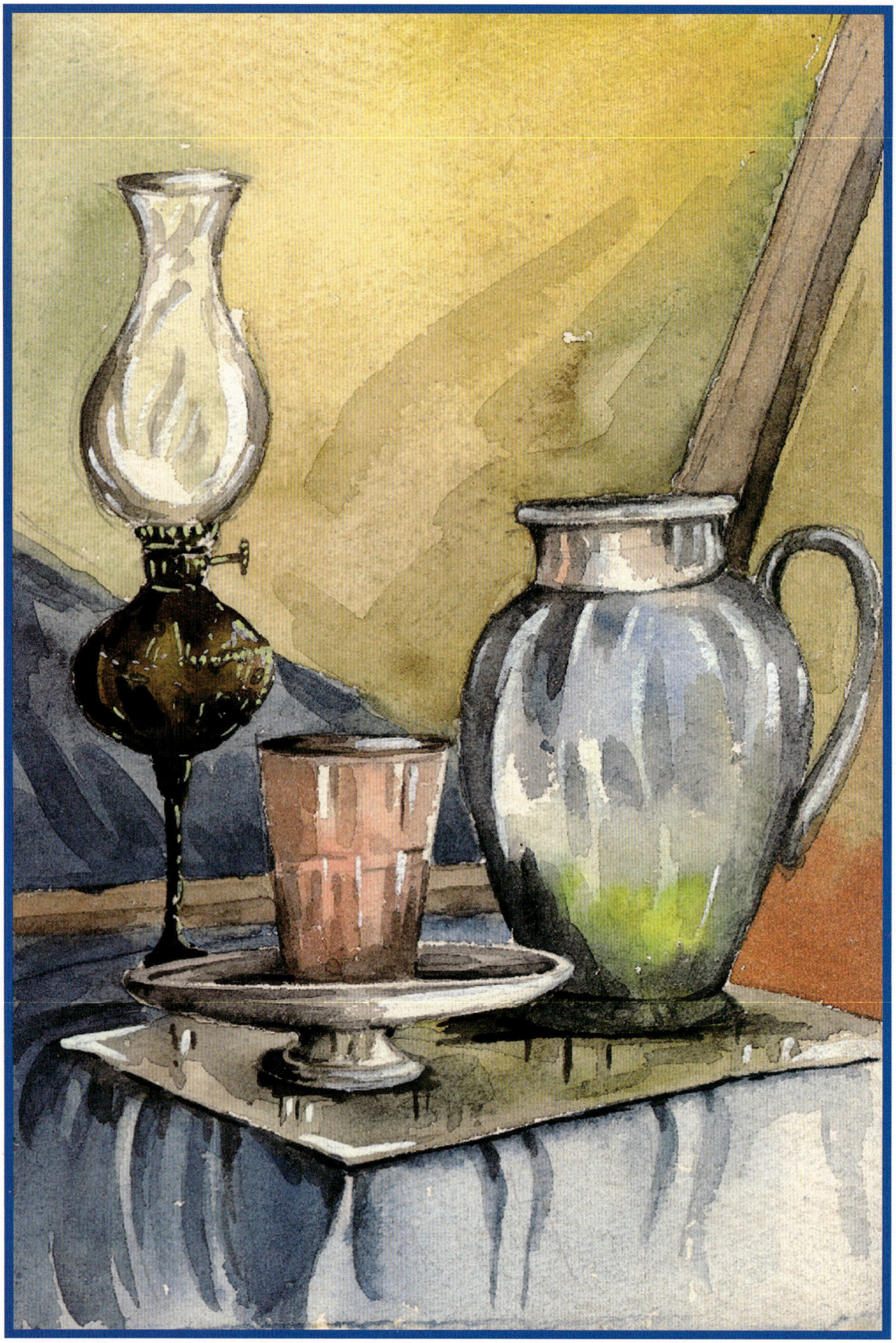

In this painting, you will find it difficult to judge the source of light. When you see the jug, you feel the light source is on the left. But then, the tumbler is not lit up and it is in the dark. The objects are also cluttered.

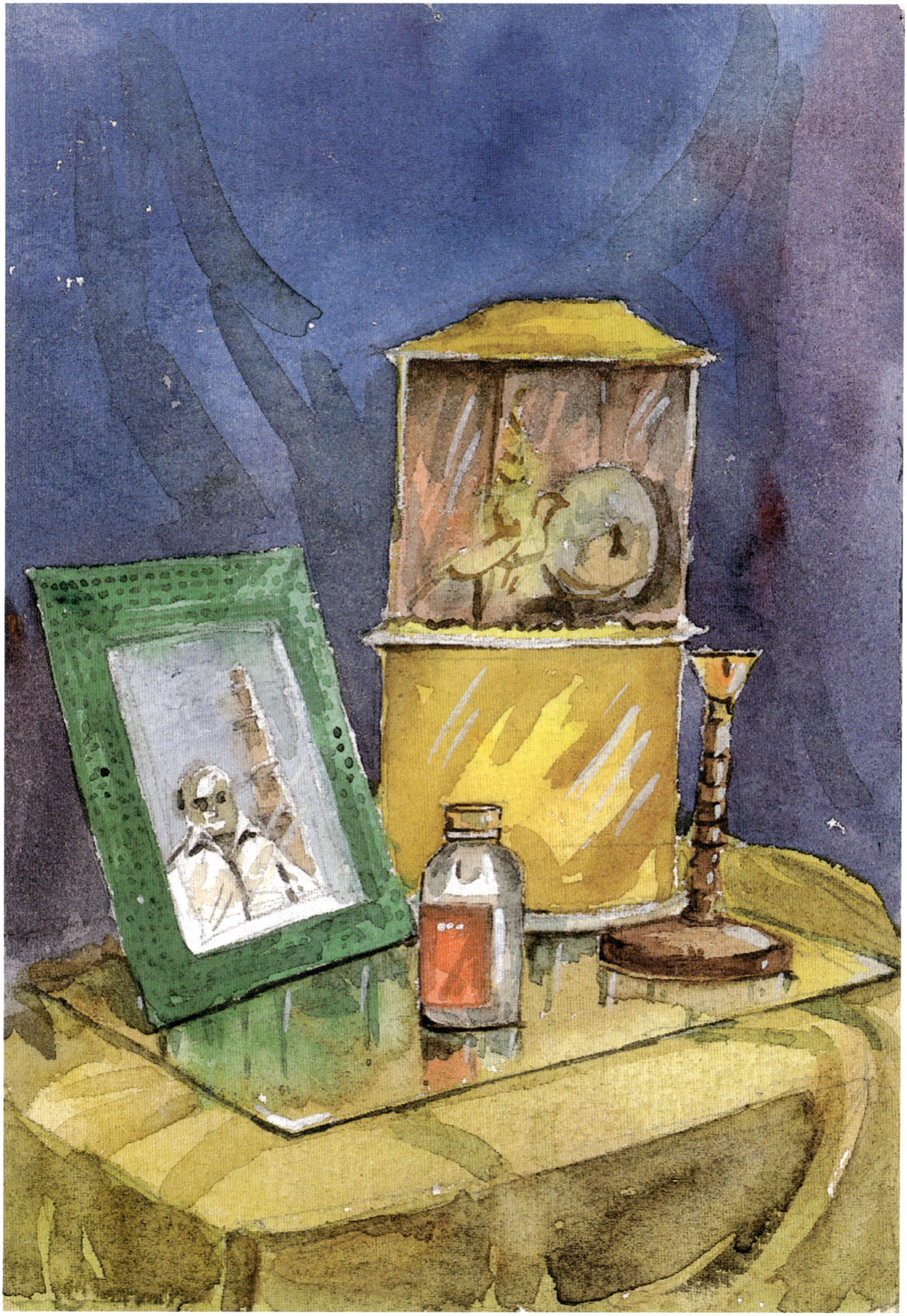

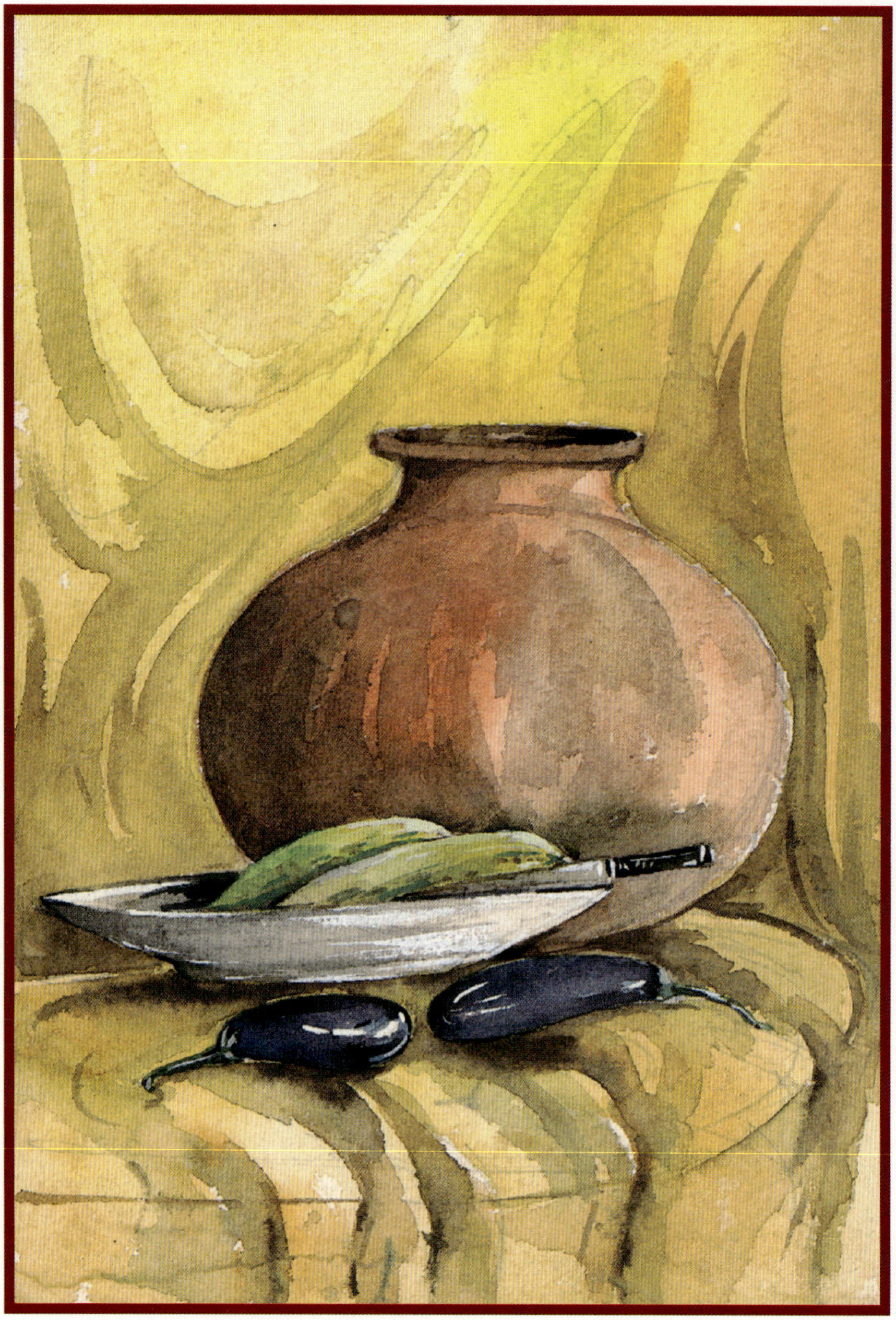

Still Life

Still life is traditionally the pictorial genre that generates most interest. It can be practised from the moment you start with watercolours.

When preparing the still life, some key points have to be borne in mind, like the composition of the grouping of the elements of the still life is fundamental question that has to be considered whenever two or more object are in use. The situation of the different elements as well as the relationships is established according to the distances between subjects.

It is possible to find subject for a still life anywhere, it is just a question of looking around to realise that the majority of objects that surround us can be subject. Up until now we have seen numerous still life's with classic elements, such as, bottle, flower pot, apple, pencil box, even the most everyday object can be used as a model worthy of being painted.

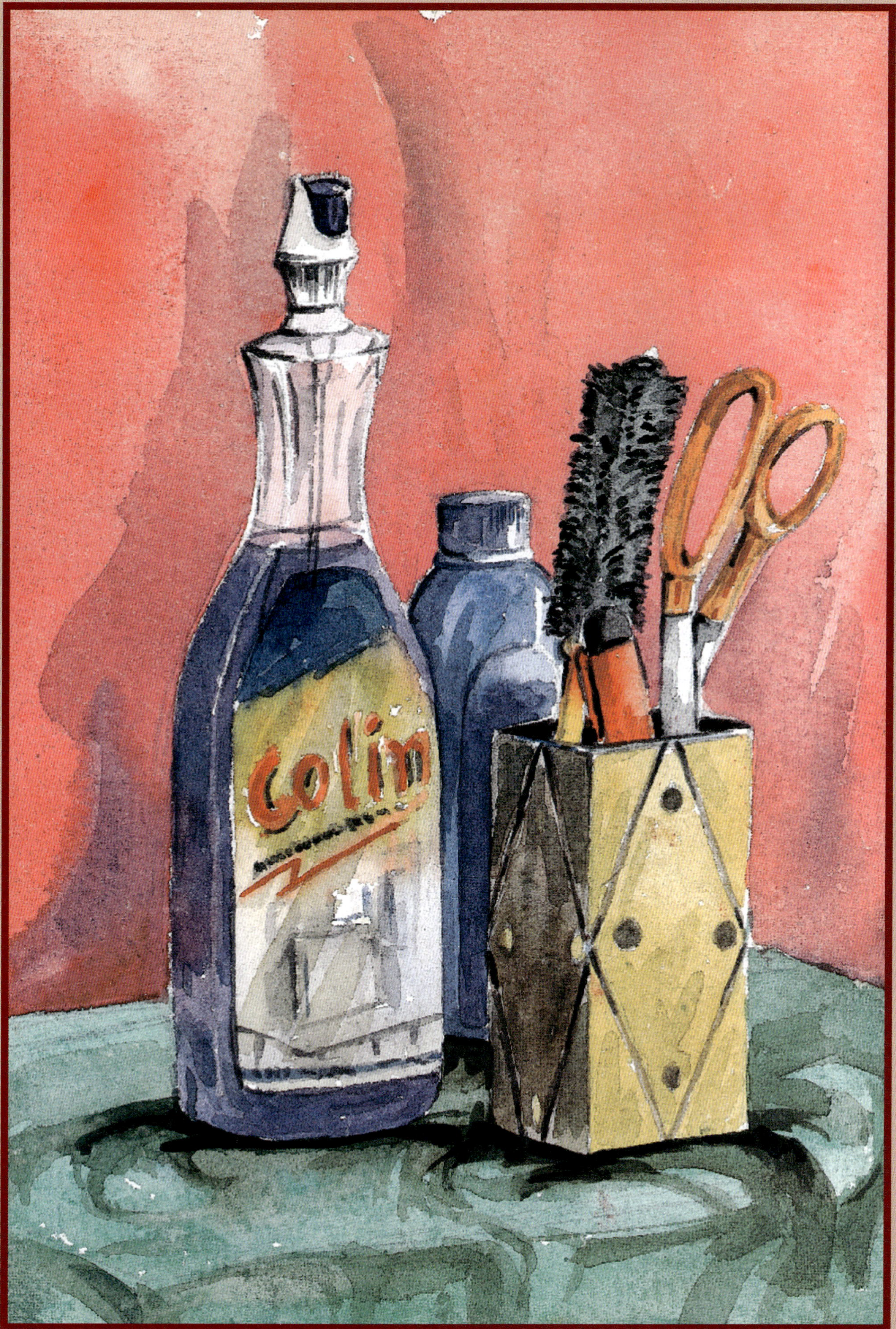
Colin

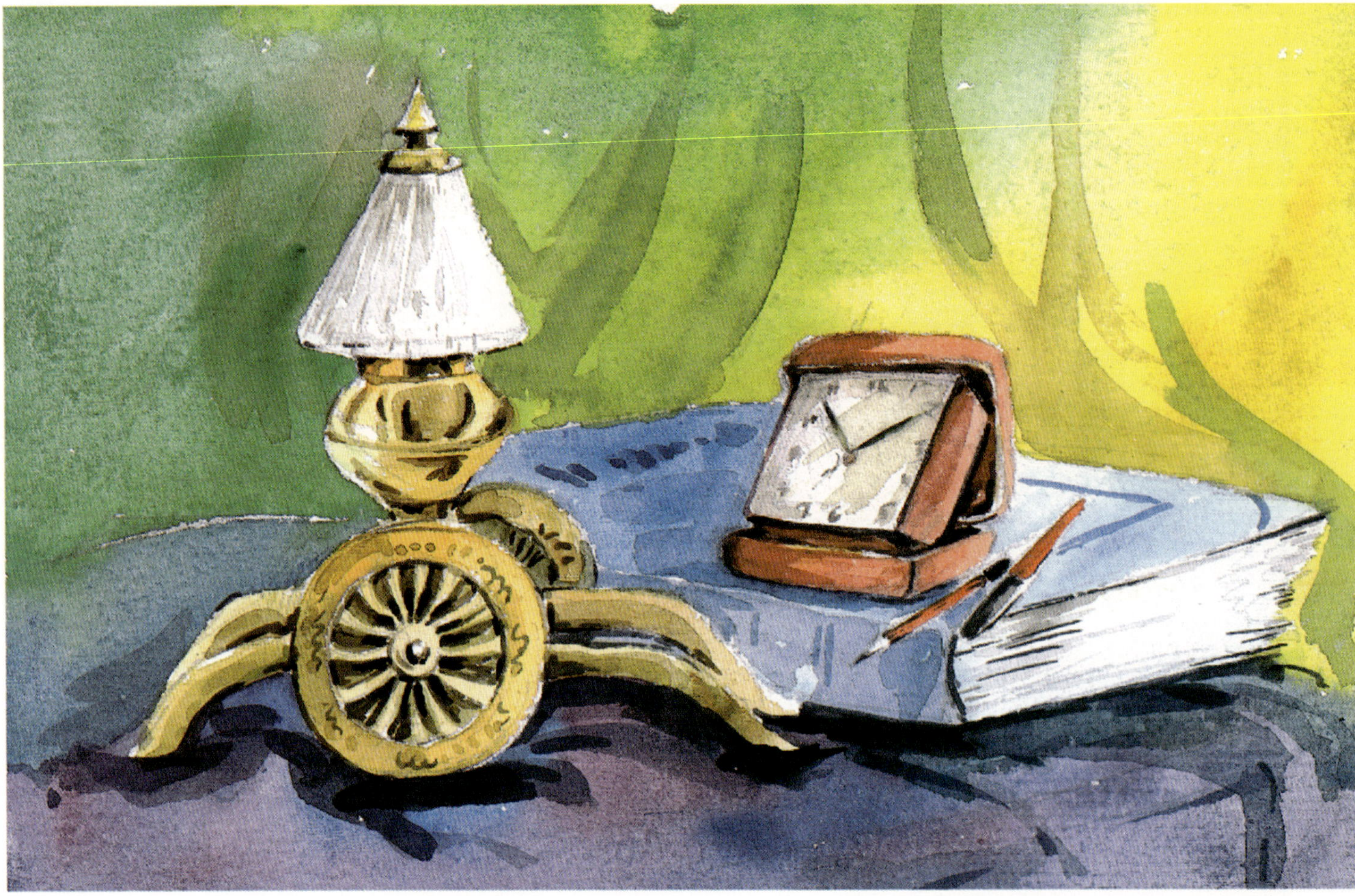

A timepiece, a table lamp and a book are ideal objects for still life. These are the objects that are kept near the bedpost.

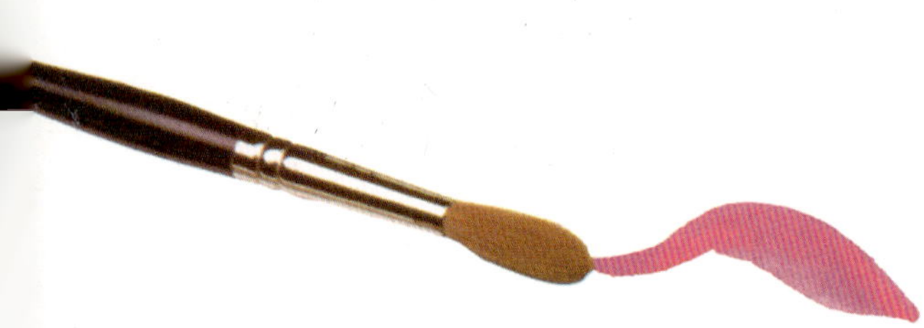

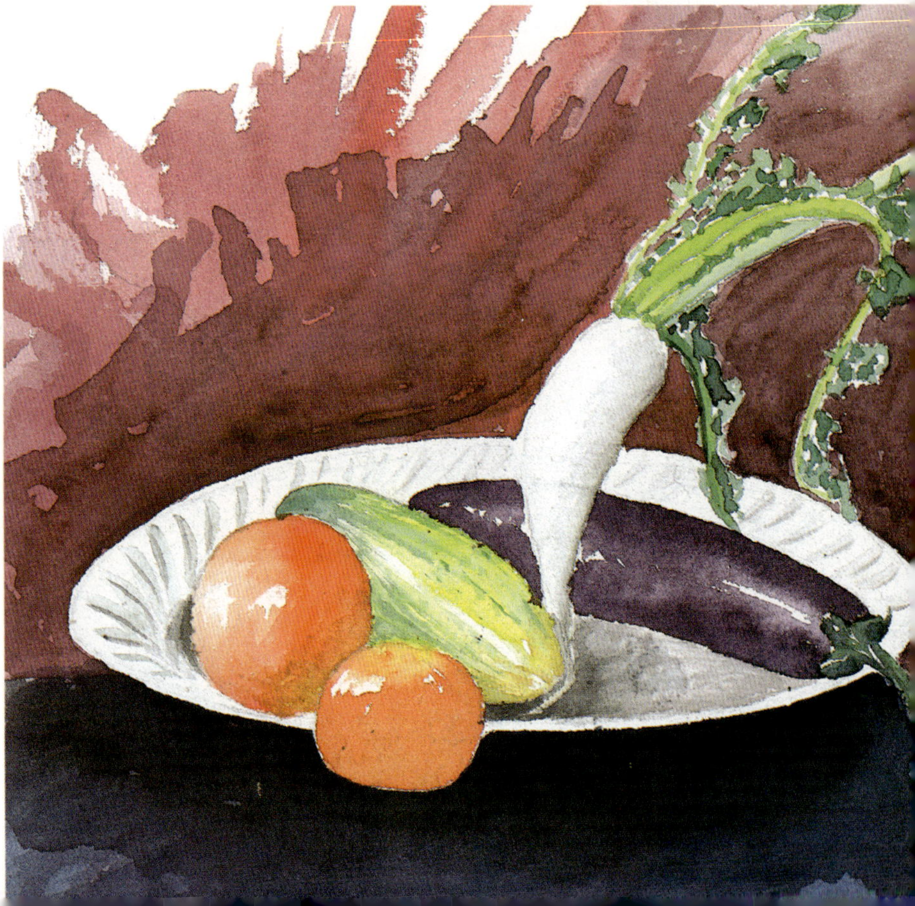

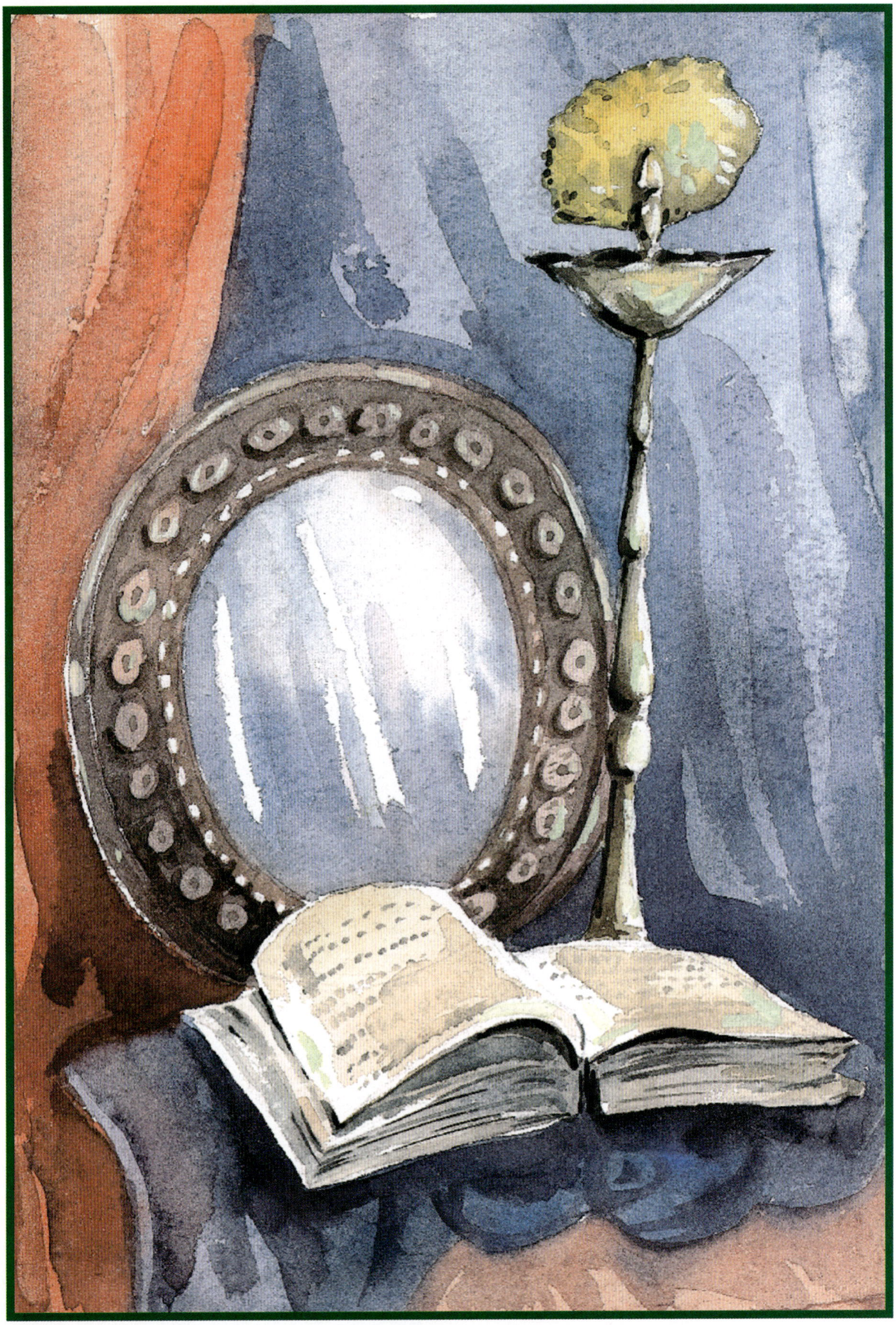

The objects in the painting are hurdled so close that the onlooker would try to seek relief somewhere else. The painting has been kept at eye level which does not lend any depth to the painting.

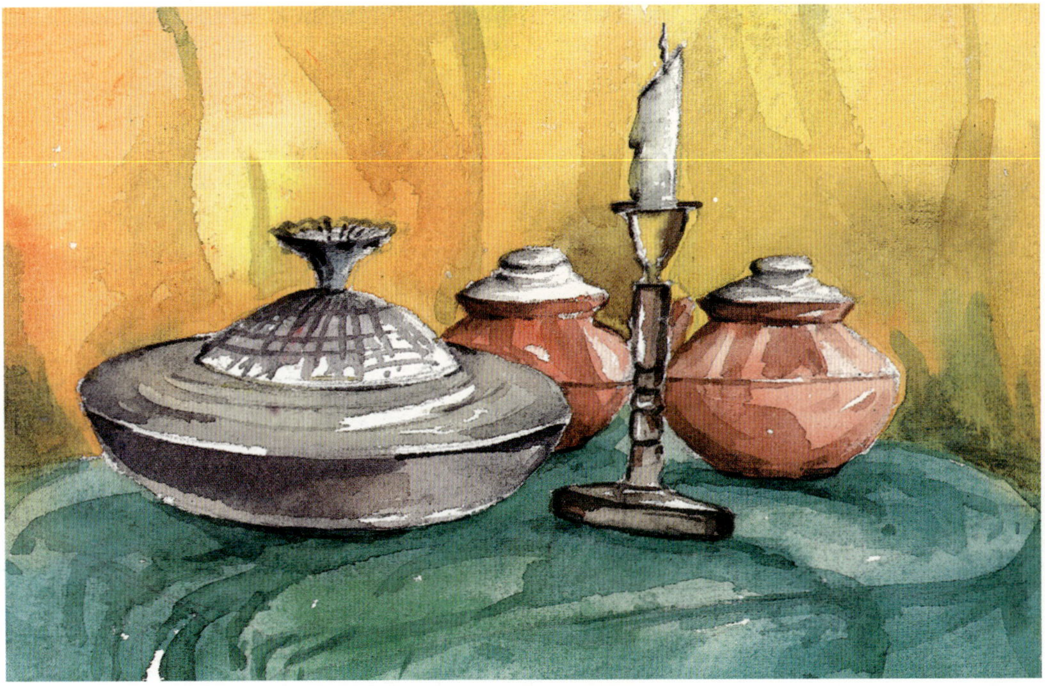

Helpful Hint

To give a sense of depth to the picture, use slightly stronger tones and colours for the objects at the front of the still life group, to bring them forward.

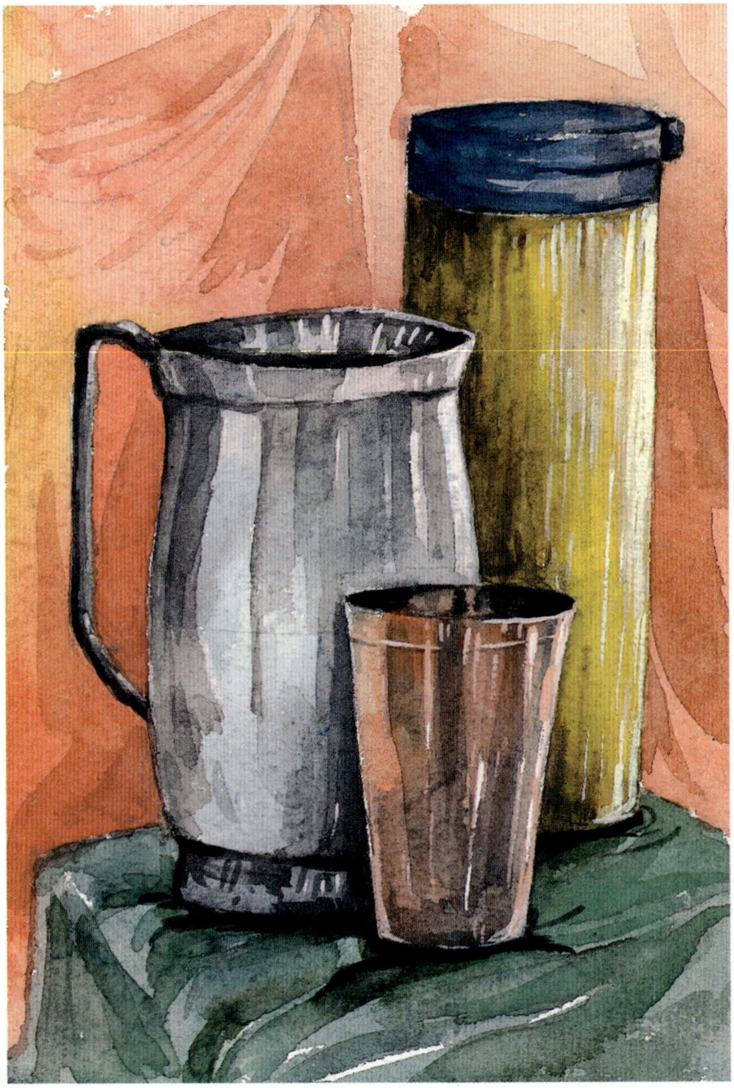

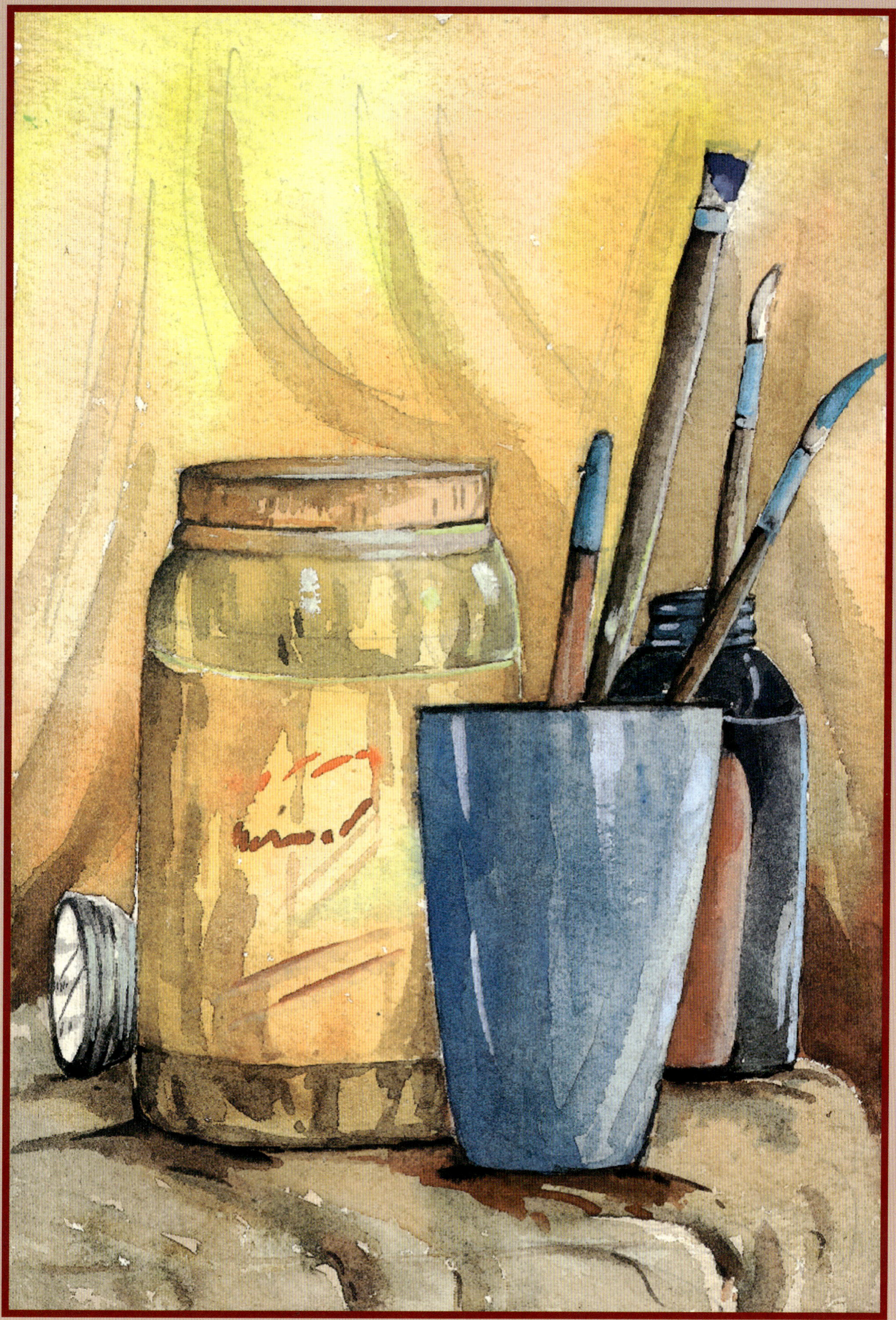

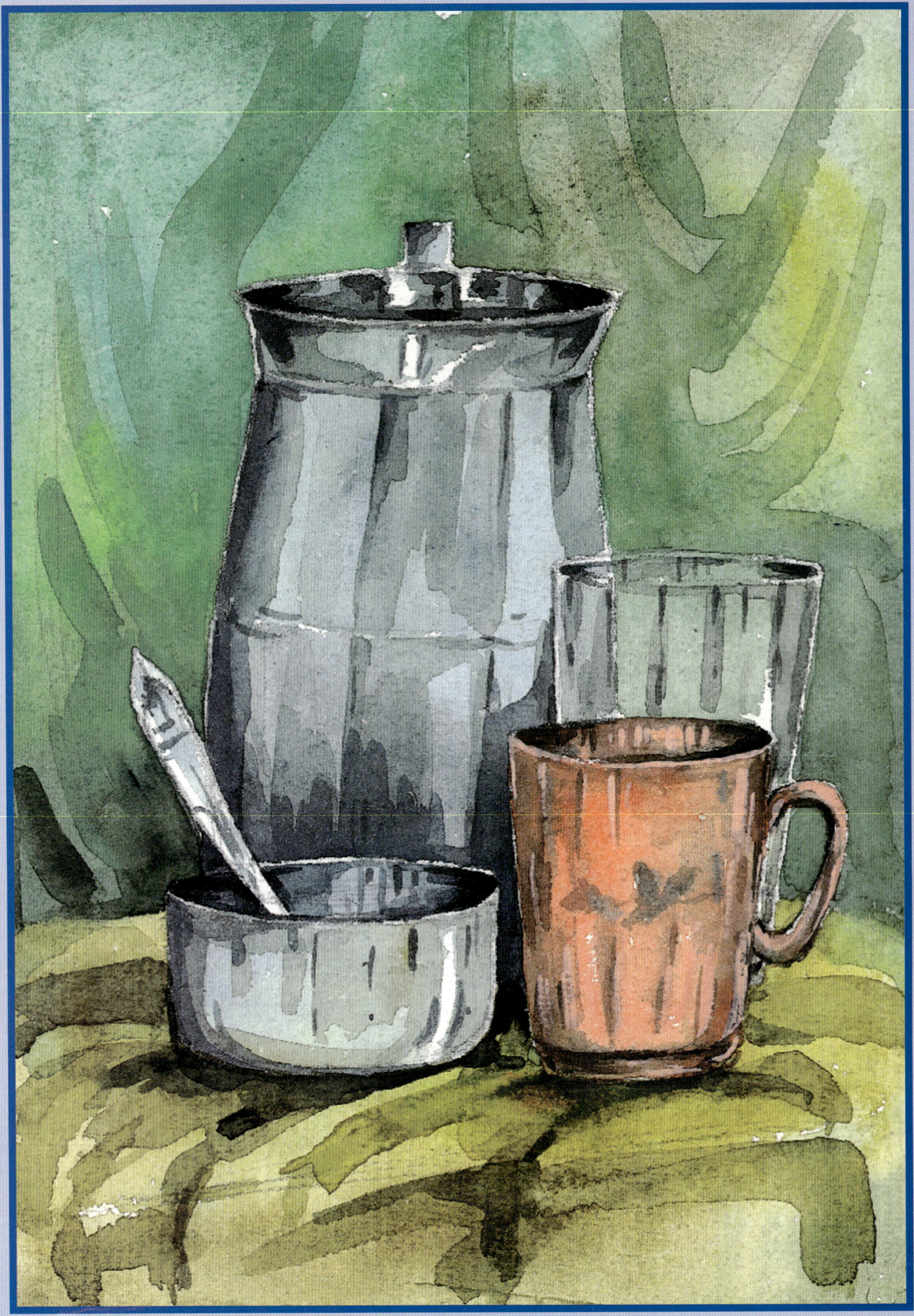

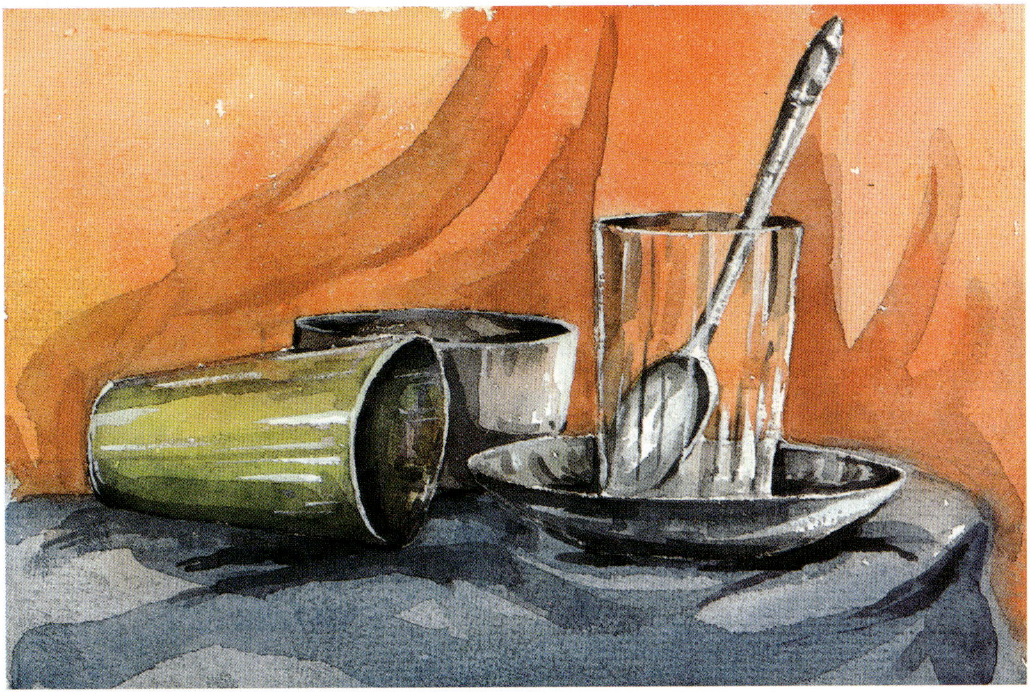

Helpful Hint

When you're waiting for washes to dry, use the back of your hand to test for dryness. It is a more sensitive receptor than the figures and won't leave grease marks on the paper.

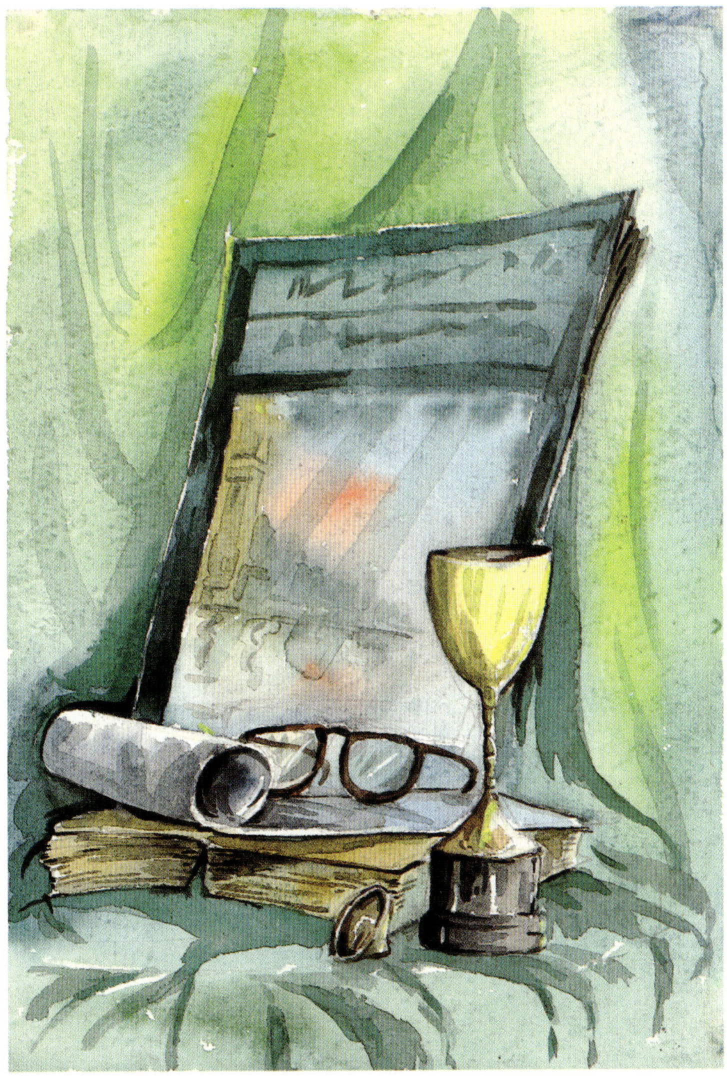

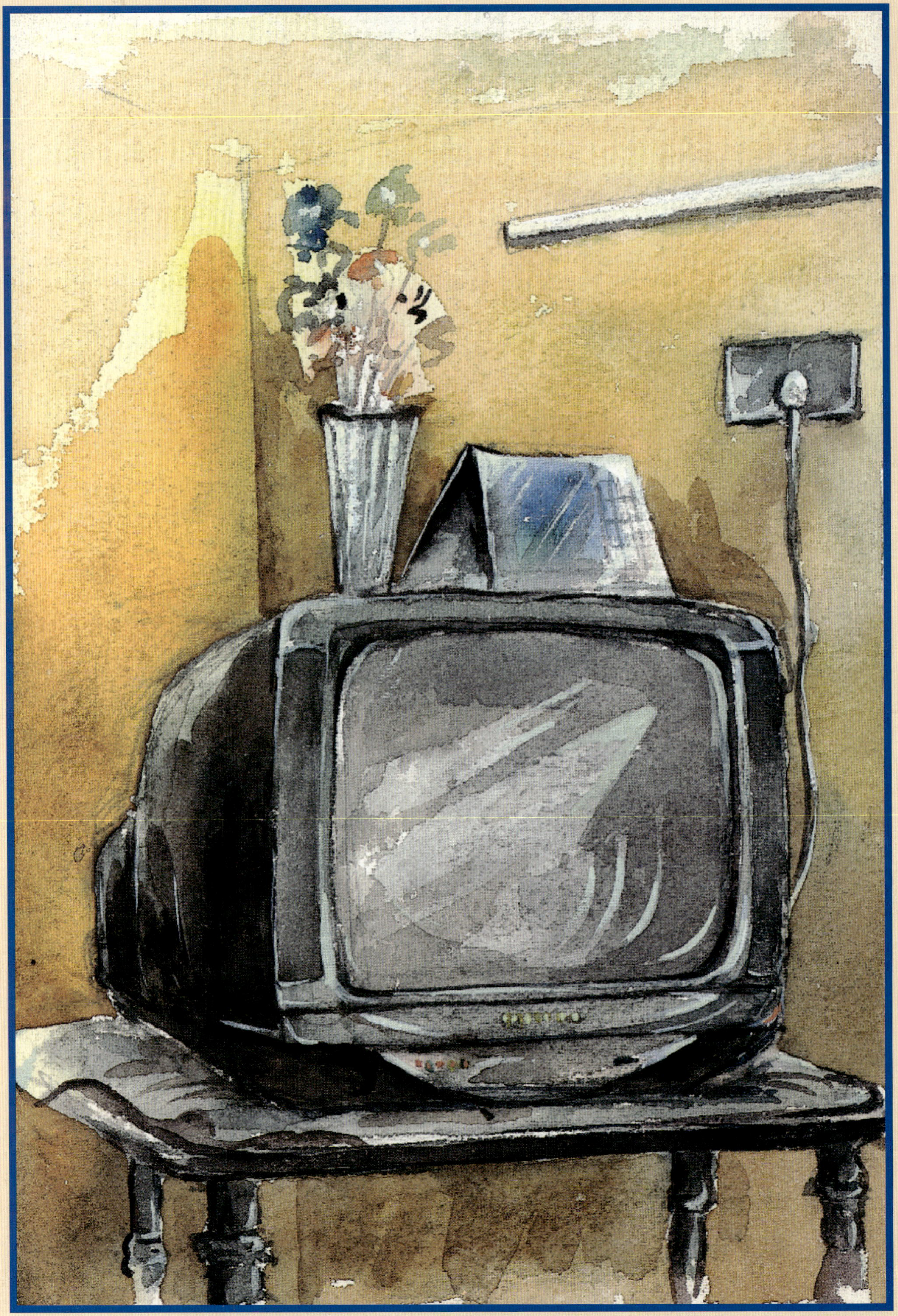

Portraits

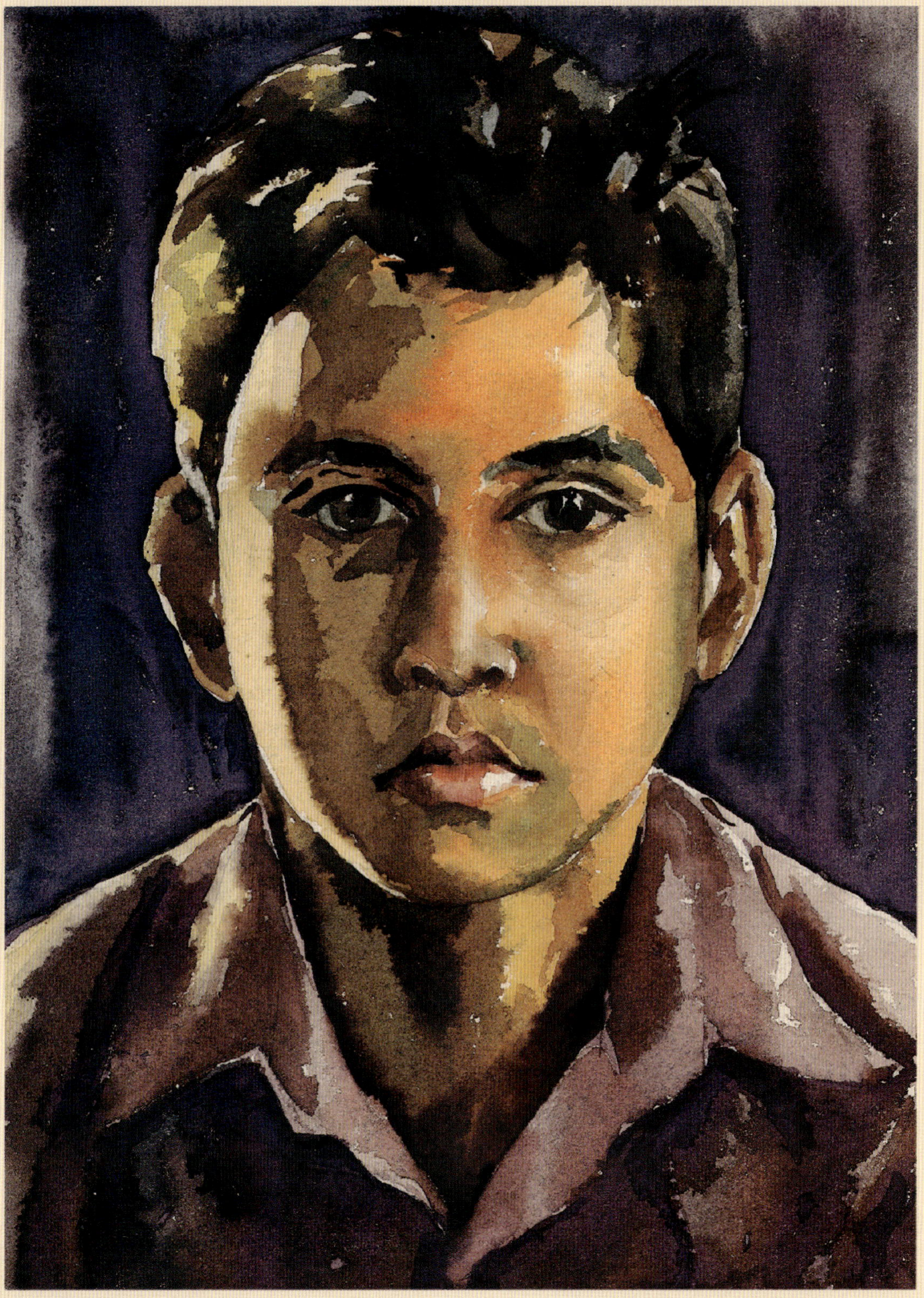

Highlights and Shadows

To make a proper study of the human face, you have to first find out the amount and source of light. The highlights of the skin depend on its tension and the amount of light that falls on it. When you study the human face, you will know that some portion of the skin like that on the nose and forehead is smooth and slightly greasy than the other parts. The highlights of the skin are first established on the portrait and then when the paint dries out, the shadow tones are established.

To proceed with a portrait, the drawing must be as perfect as possible. The knowledge of proportion is a must. Also mark out the areas that are to be highlighted and those that will be in the shadow.

The portrait is of a young boy. The artist has painted the background with a dark tone to put the face into context. When it was dry he applied a transparent layer of sienna on the face. Then he waited to let it dry completely. When totally dried, he applied the middle tone on the face, carrying little to blend it with the previous tone. When the middle tone dried, he used a wet brush to blend the two tones.

Then he applied the dark tone where the artist wanted to show the shadow. After this dried out, he swept a wet brush over it to define the sharp contrasts with a soft profile.

Finally, the artist did the hair and the shirt to complete the painting. But he has used highlights on them too. This lends authenticity to the painting.

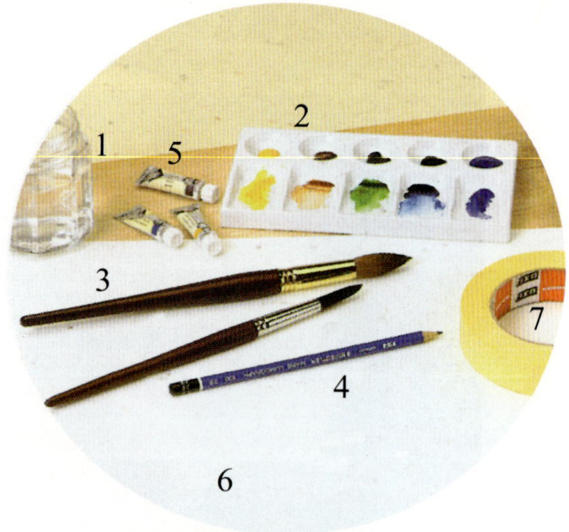

Materials
1. Water Jar
2. Colour Plate
3. Brushes
4. Pencil
5. Tube Colours
6. Paper

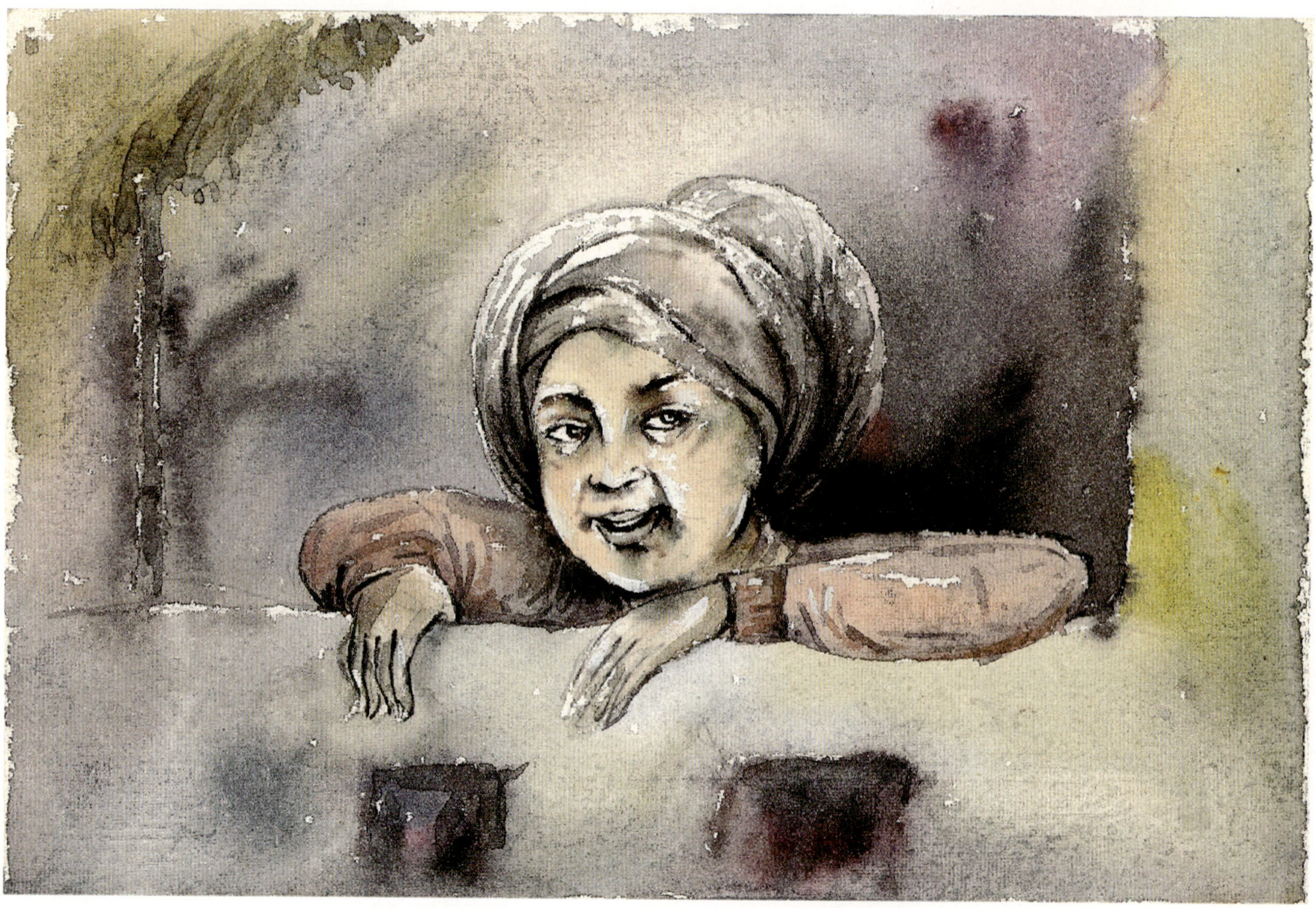

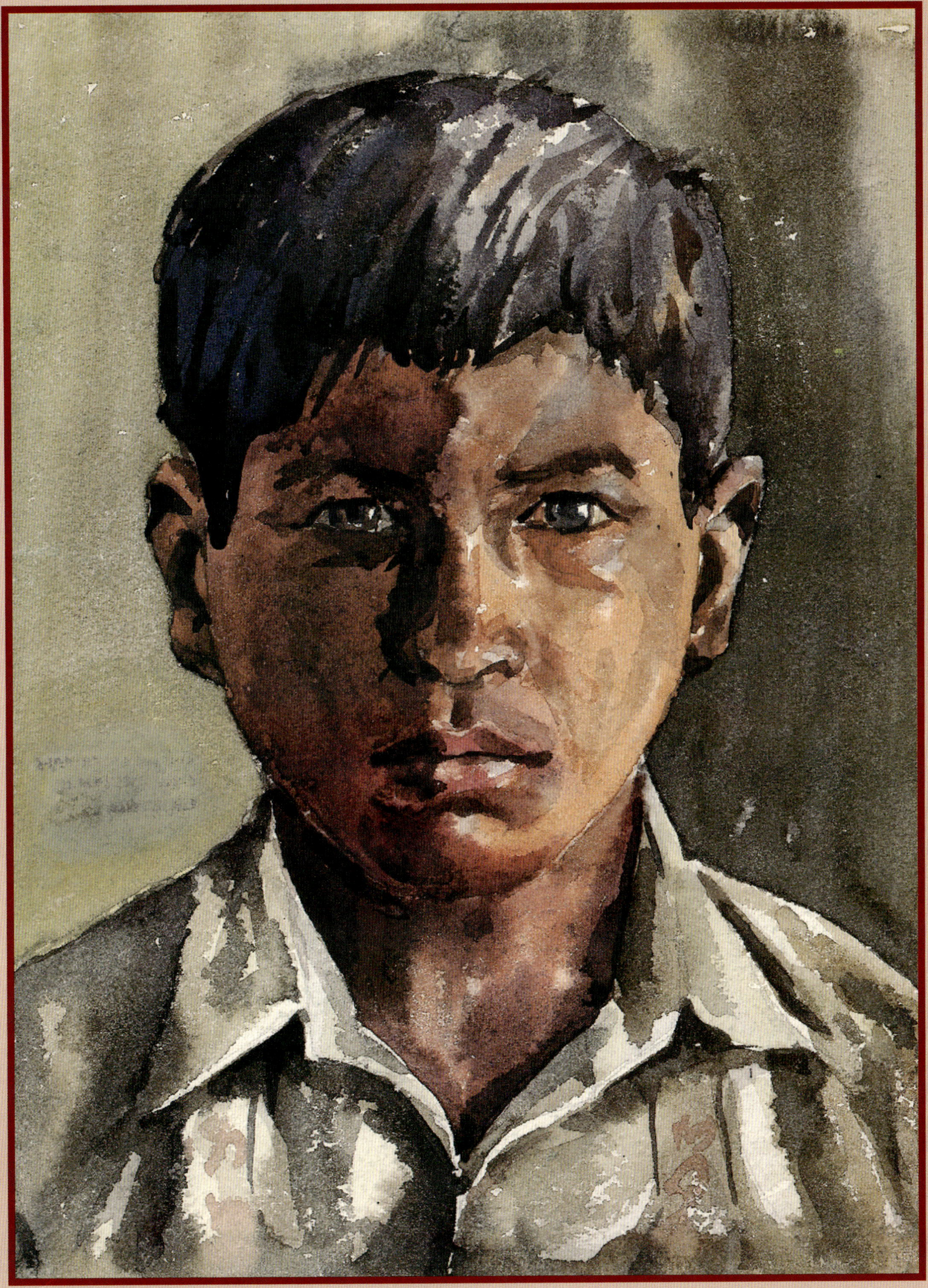

This is the portrait of an old person with a turban. Notice how the artist could manage highlights and shadows even on the turban. He has used Orange mixed with a little Burnt Sienna to show the wrinkled areas on the face and forehead. The beard is first done with a shade of very light grey and then given a darker tone of grey at some places.

The artist used Raw Sienna, Burnt Sienna and Black for the irises of the eyes. Whenever you make the human eye, remember to show the thickness of the eyelids and the pink in the inner corner of the eye.

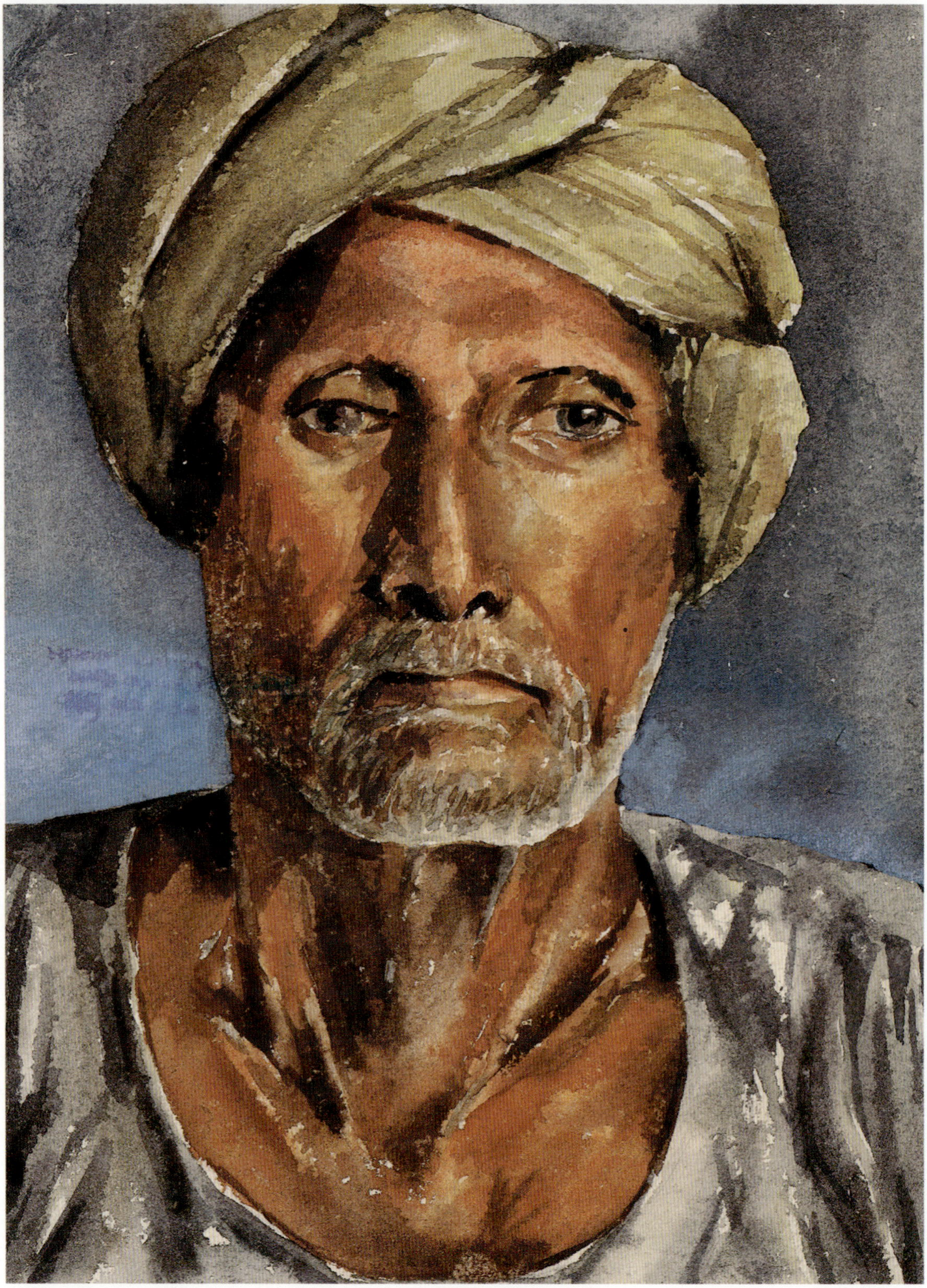

You can master the art of making portraits if you know how to capture the different colours, tones and reflections of the skin. A young skin reflects light uniformly, while an old skin does not. The texture of the older skin intensifies and the features of the face are shadowed by wrinkles.

Carnation, Carmine Yellow and Ochre are the colours of the skin.

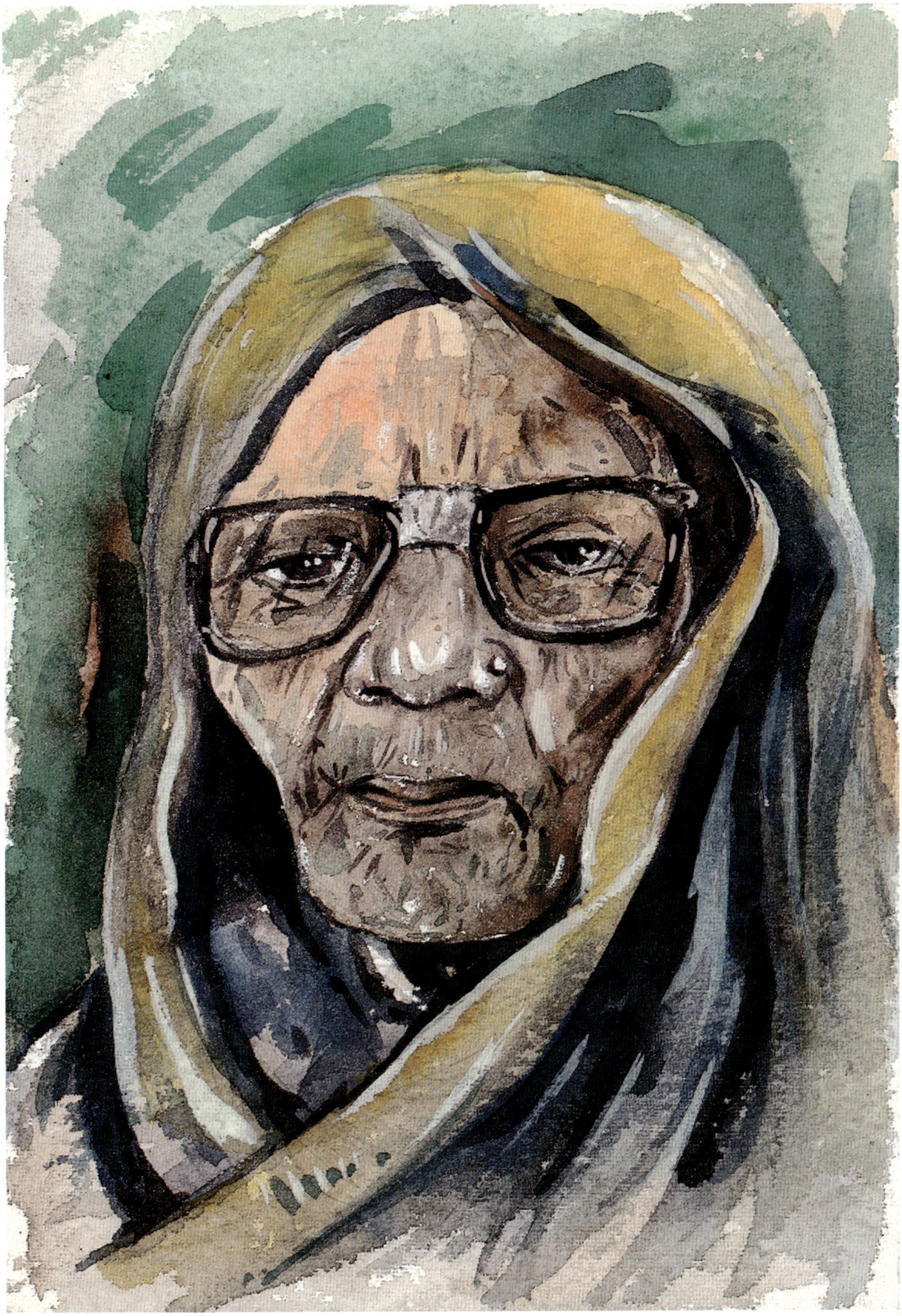

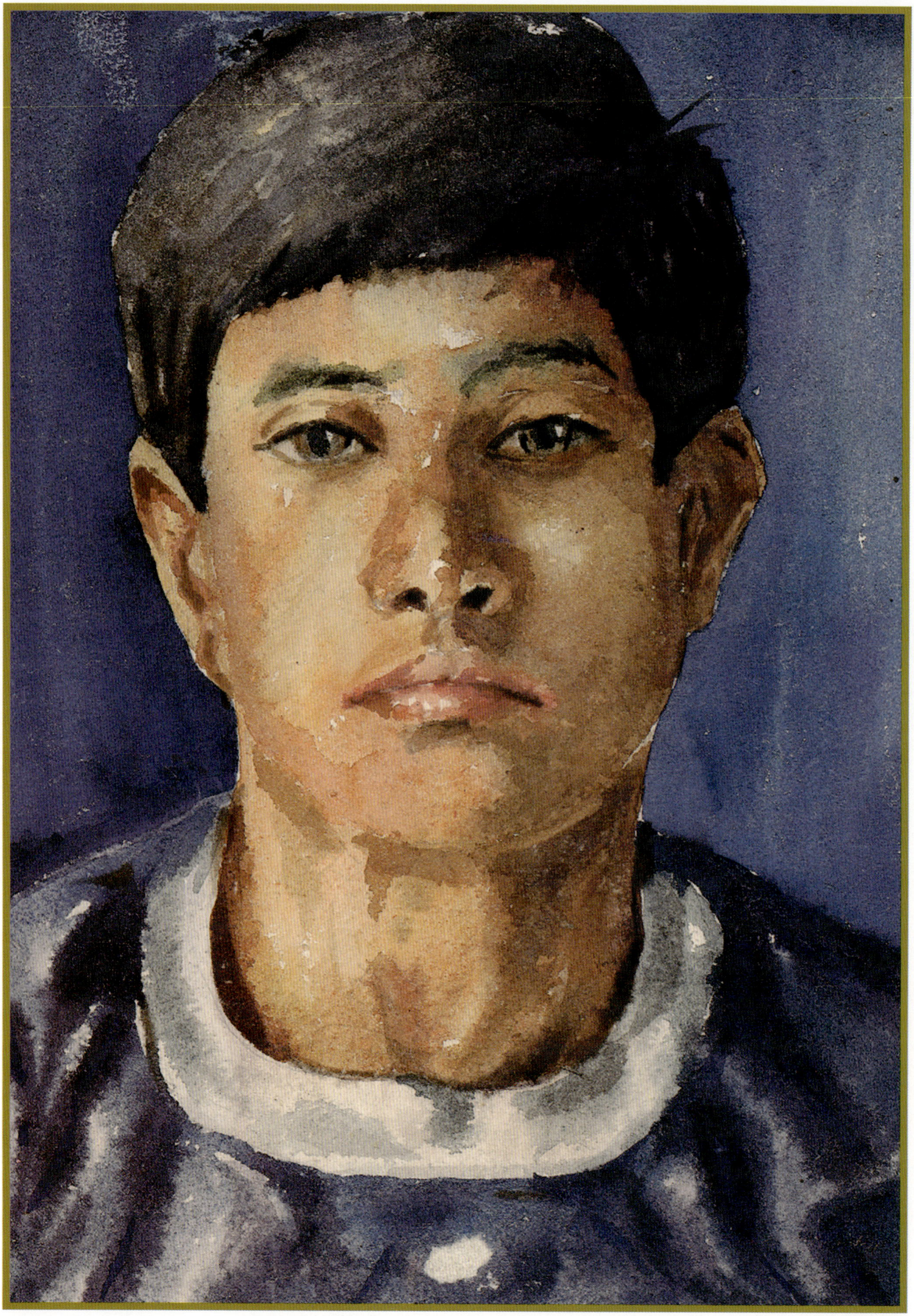

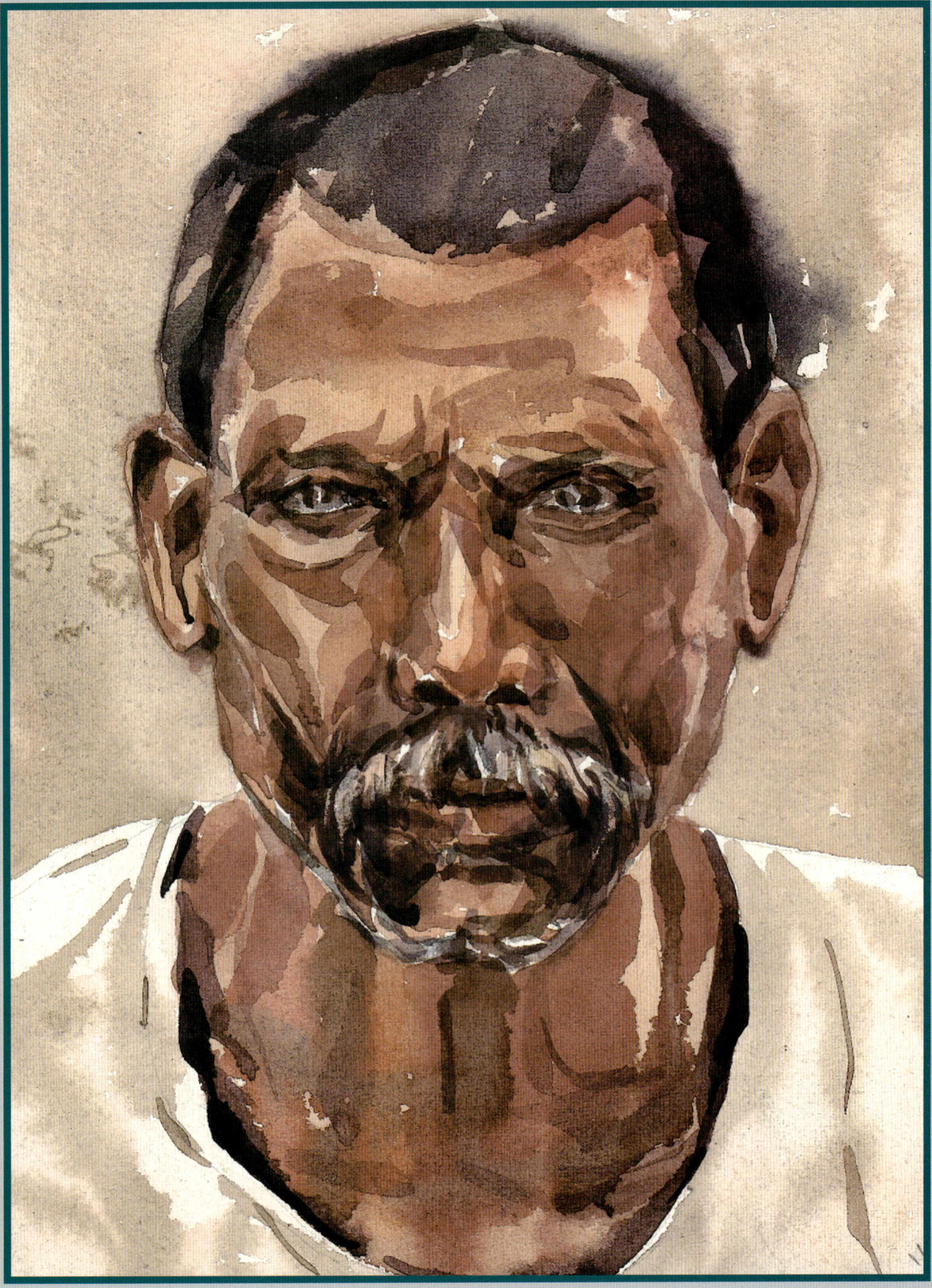

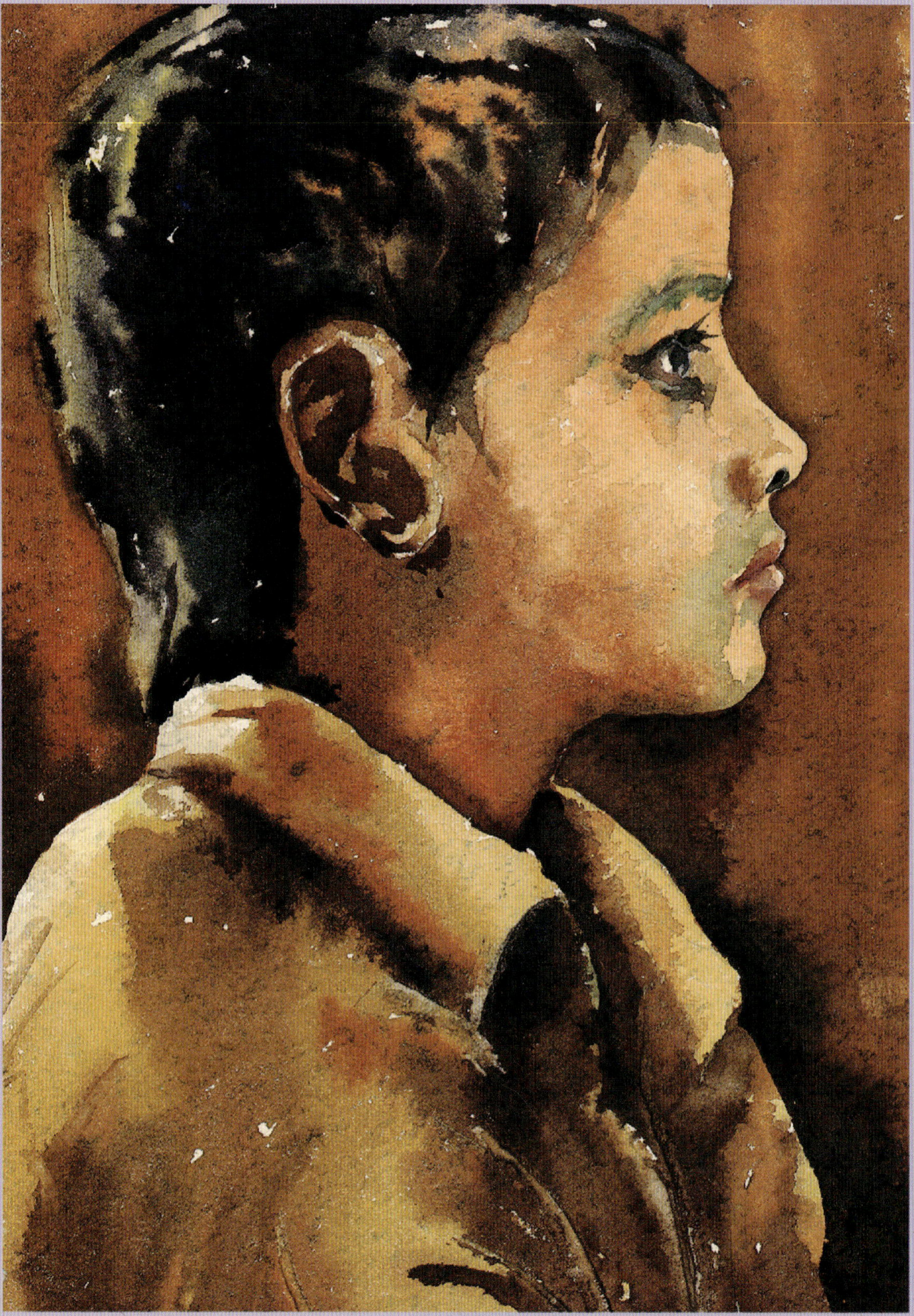

A portrait done in the profile. The artist has used a contrasting dark background to highlight the profile. All the light falls on the face of the boy. Only part of the collar is lit up. Rest of the portion is just partly lit up. He has used a wet wash of Burnt Sienna on the whole portrait of the boy. While still wet, he used a darker tone of the previously applied colour around the neck, temple, nose and side of the lips. Then he applied a dark tone of the same colour around the collar, ear, under the eye and nose. he used three shades of Cobalt Blue for the shirt and Black for the hair. When it dried out completely, he did Burnt Umber in the background to highlight the portrait.

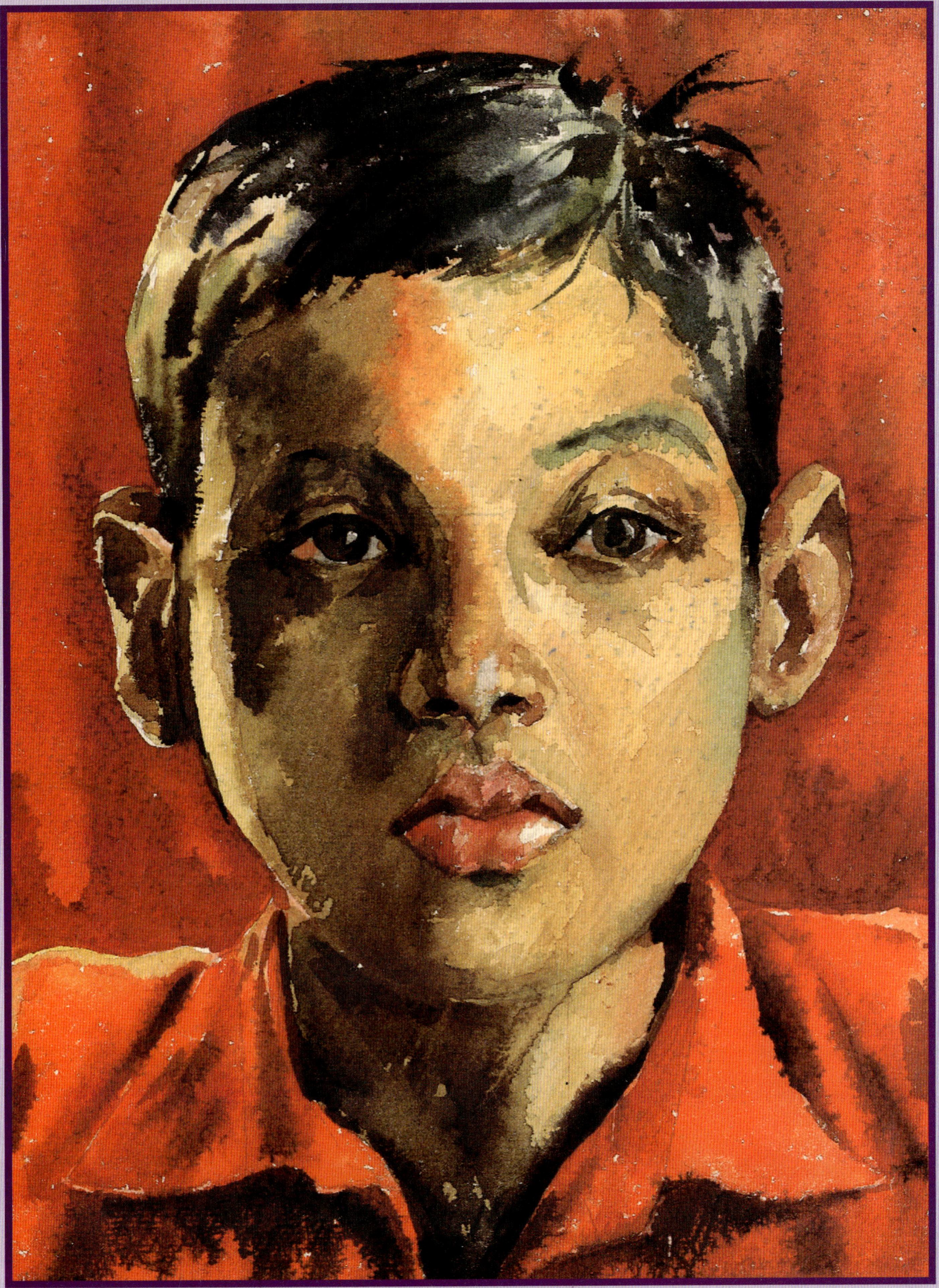

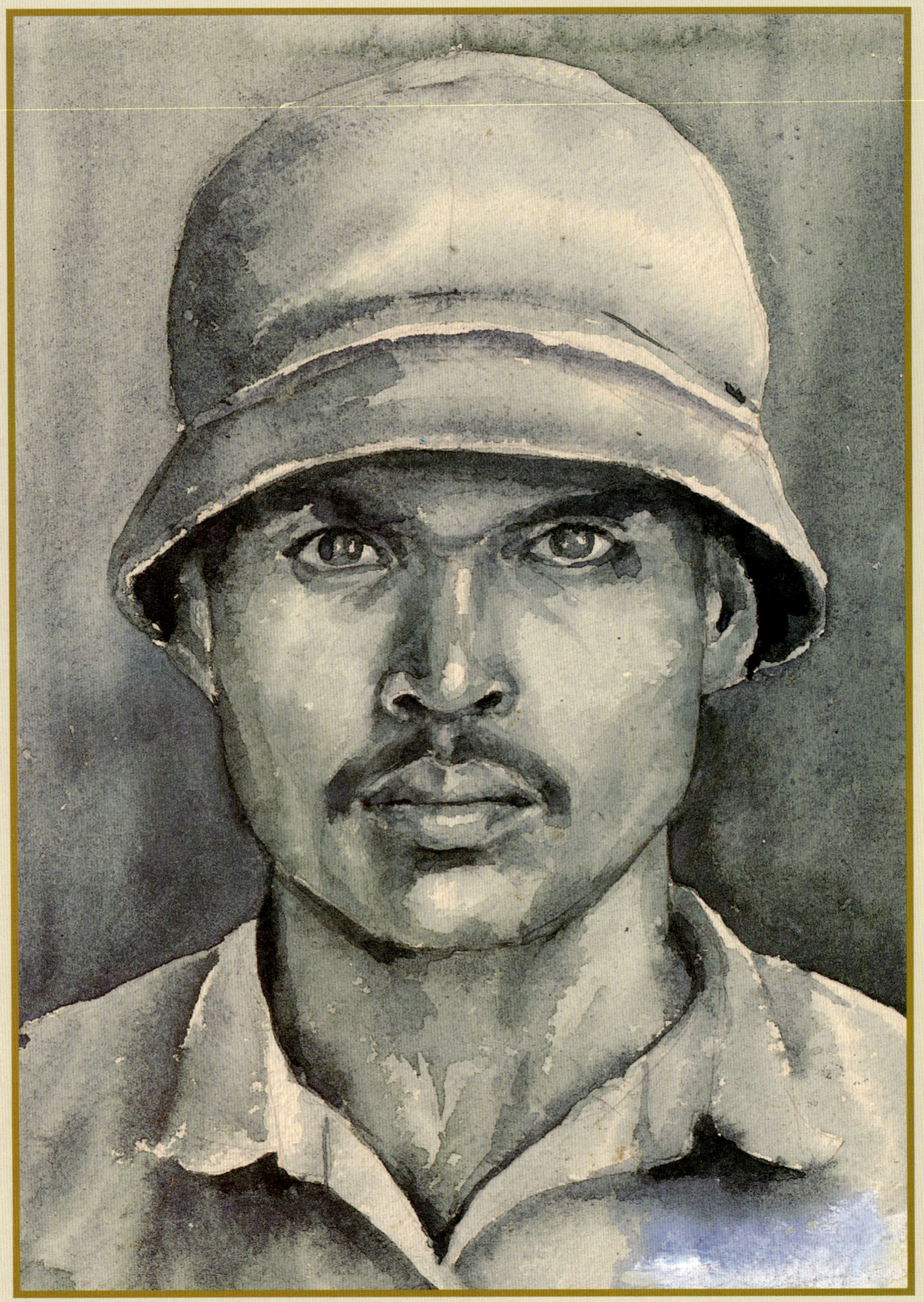

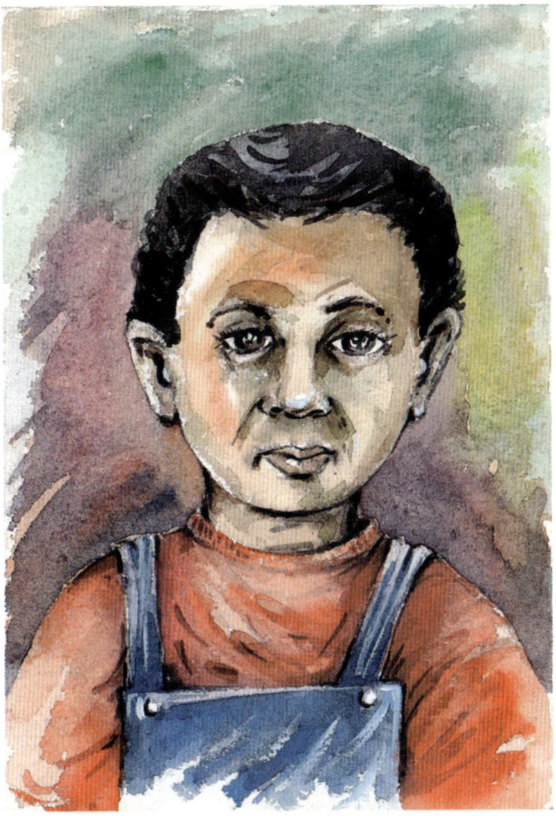

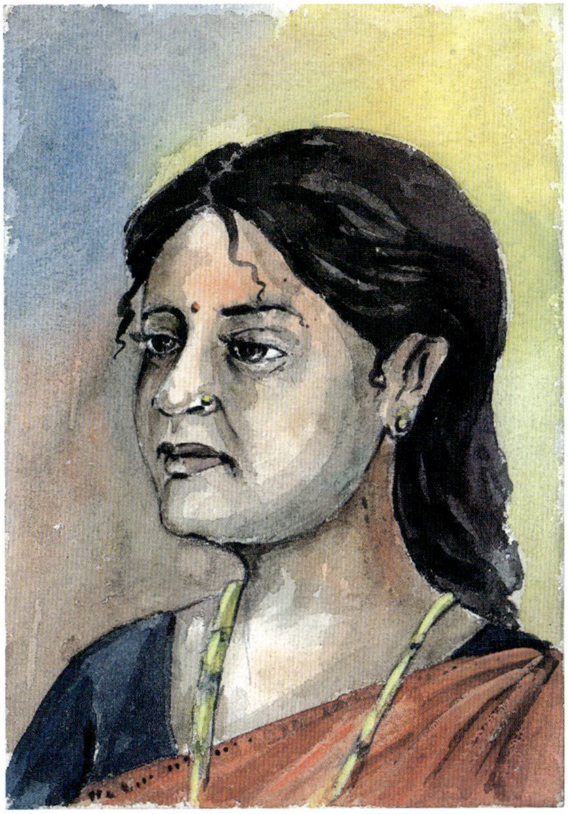

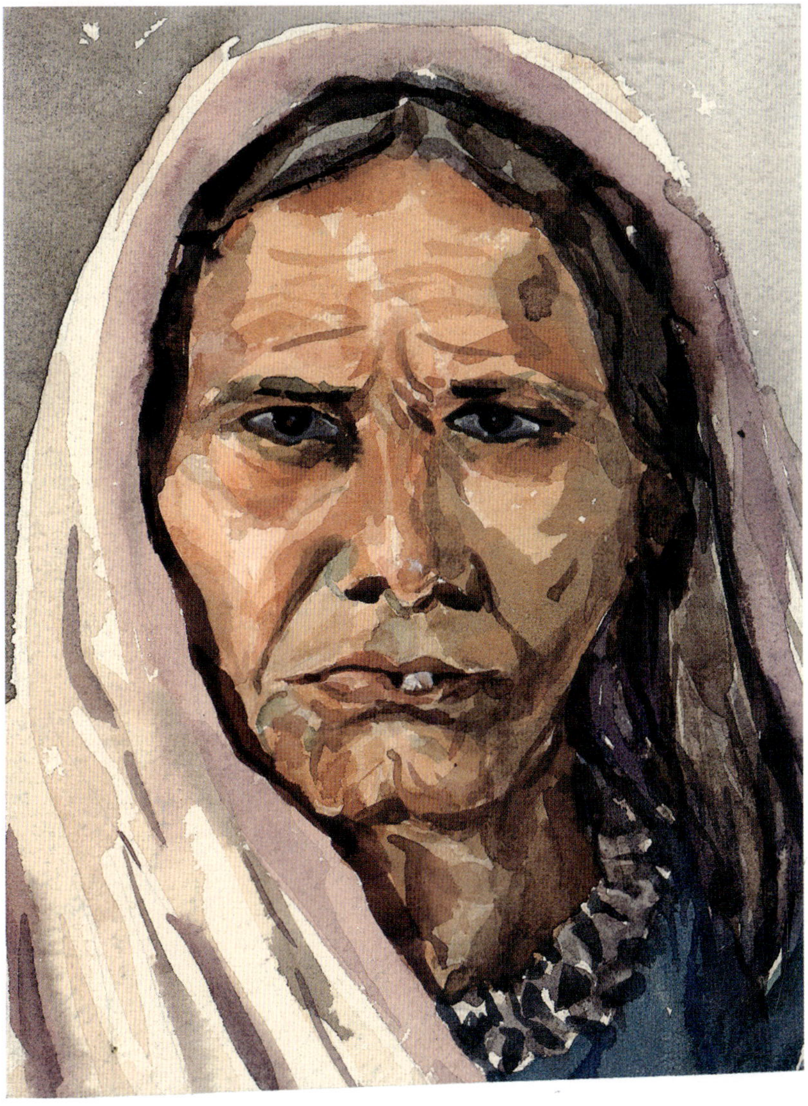

The portrait of an old lady is again a study of highlights and shadows. After making the initial sketch, the artist spent a great effort in doing it well. He defined the features sharply, also the wrinkles and the light and dark zones with neat lines. He used shades of Orange, Ochre and Sienna to depict the highlights and shadows of the face and neck. He used Payne's Grey for the hair. See how the wrinkles of the forehead, face, under the eyes and chin have been captured. They have been done with fine brush strokes.

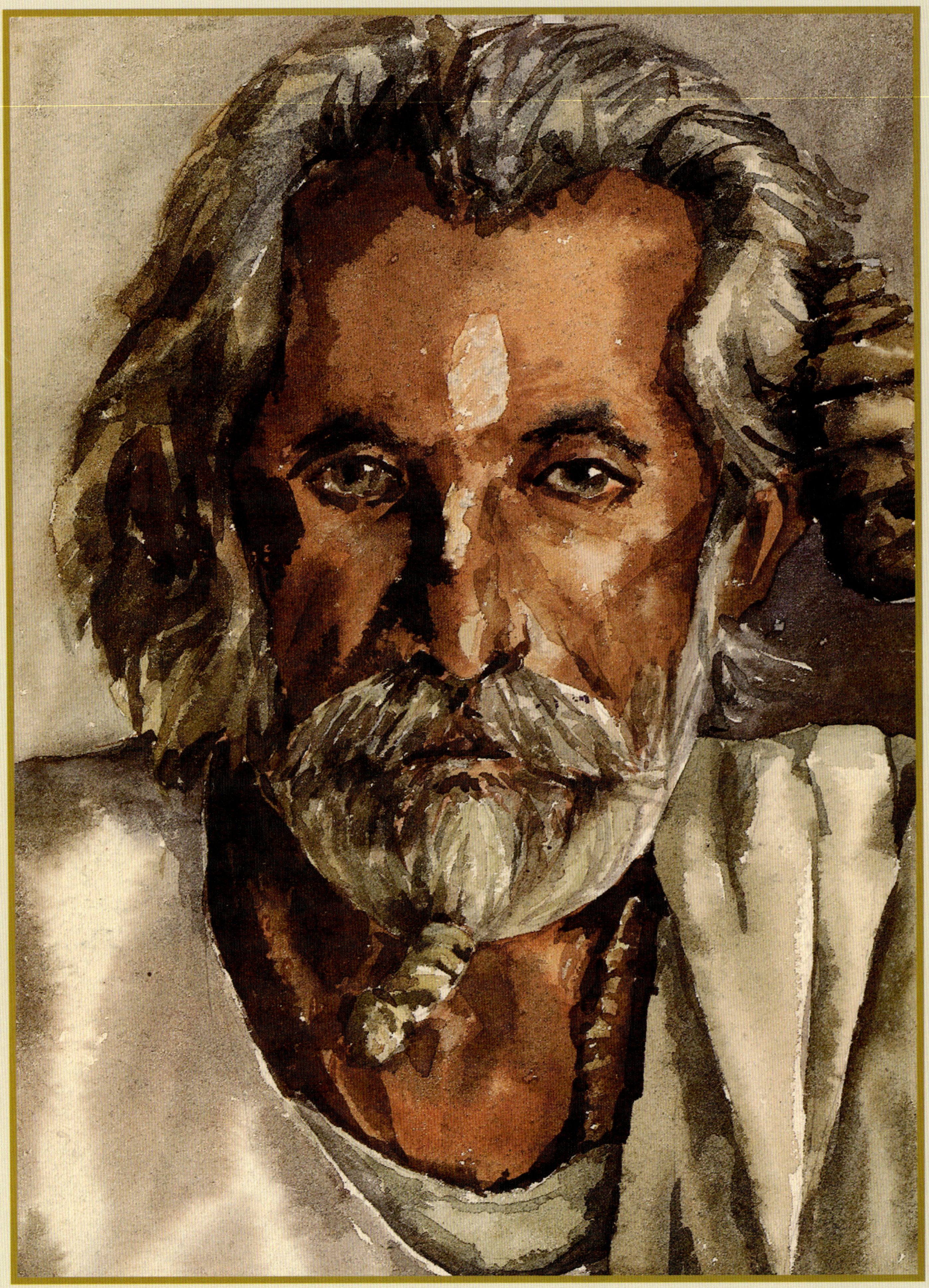

Here is the portrait of a blind man using light, medium and dark shades of Brown. It has been highlighted that the wrinkles with dark shades of Burnt Umber.

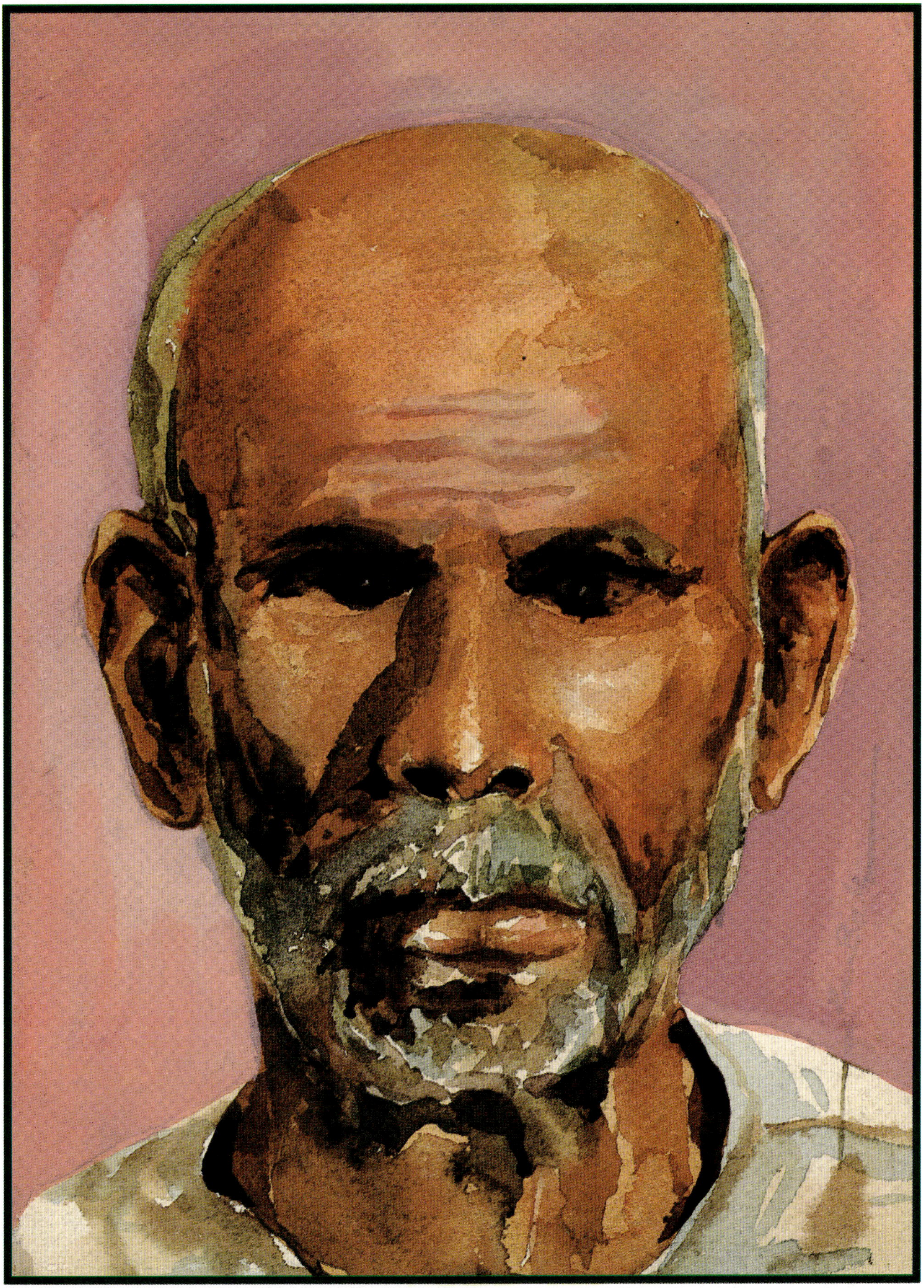

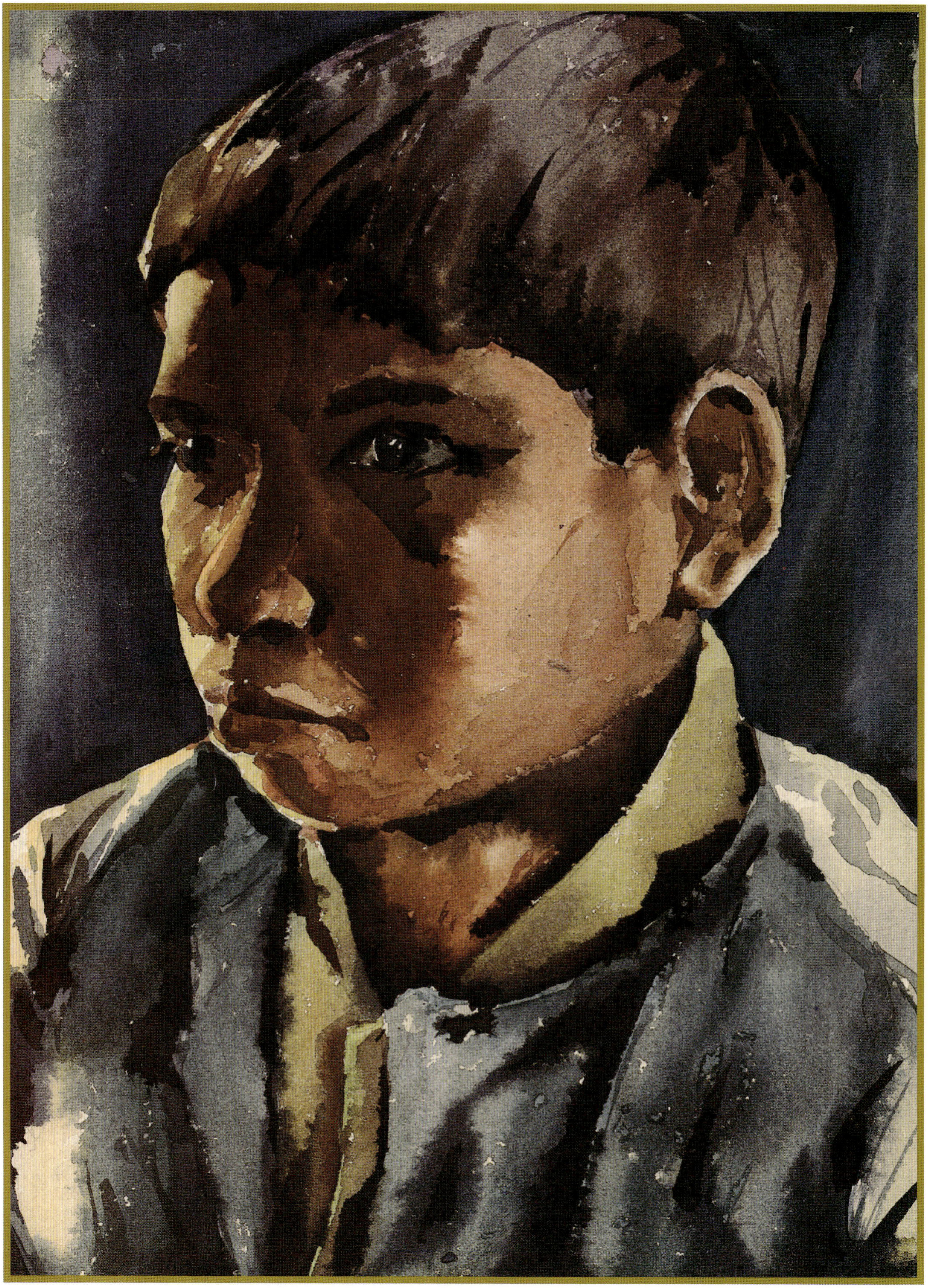

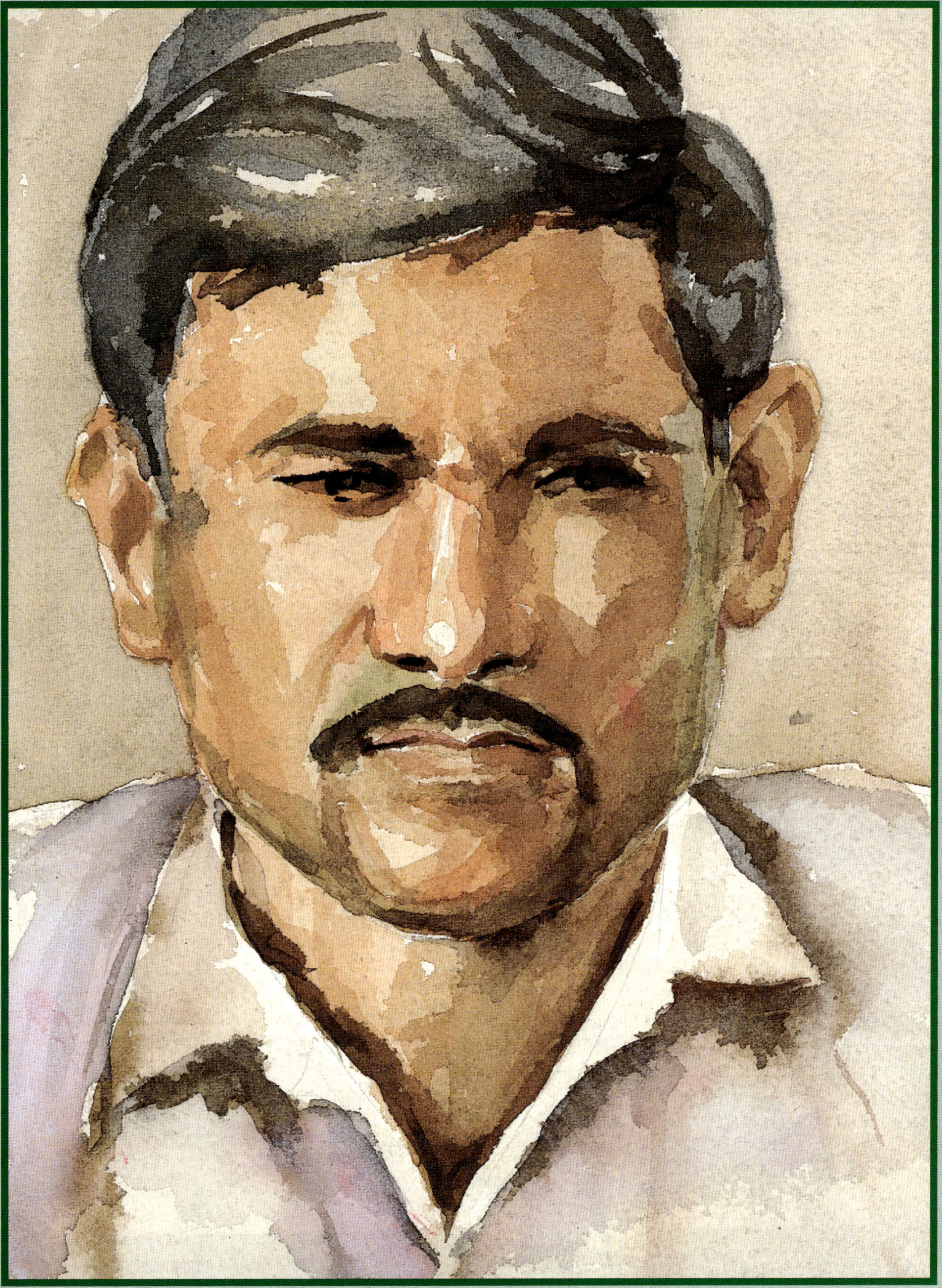

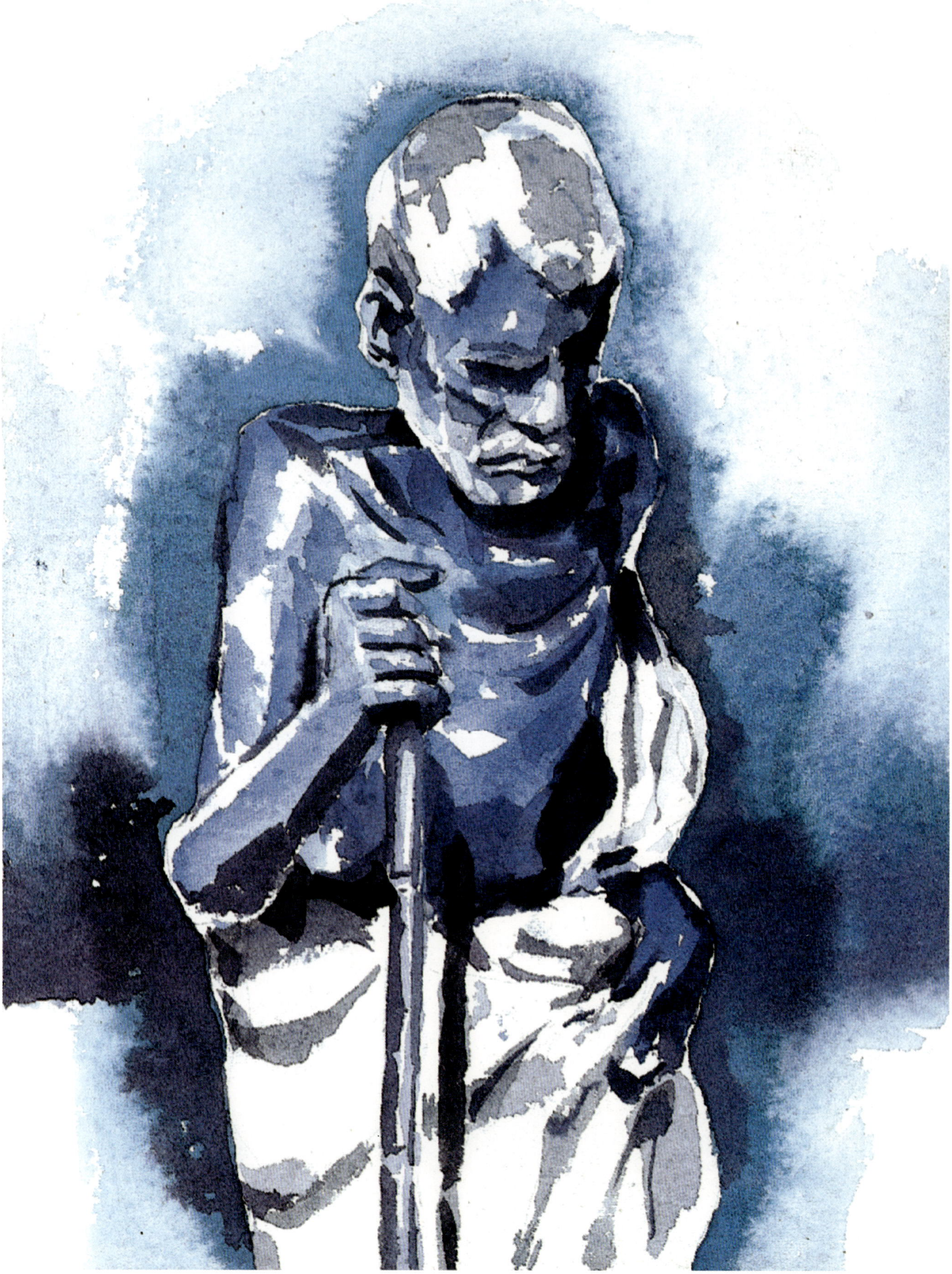

Figures

Figure sketching and painting must be planned in detail. The initial sketch is the most elementary part of any painting. And before sketching, you have to make an indepth study of the human form. The figure is divided on the basis of the several axes on which it moves. These axes are shown by the lines of the shoulders the spinal cord and the hips.

Line 1 is used to indicate the position of the shoulders. Line 2, which is the form of a vertical line, shows the spinal cord. Line 3 is a horizontal line like the one used to indicate the shoulders. Line 3 is the hip line. Now try to build the human form with the help of these guide lines. You may need some time and a lot of practice before you are able to master the human figure. Set the axes of the shoulders and of the hip, then the spinal column. From the shoulders and from the hipline, draw the arms and legs.

The basic drawing should be drawn as correctly as possible. Like other themes, figures are also represented with light and shadows. The light areas are outlined by the shadow. This effect produces value of the figure. The most luminous parts are marked out with the help of darker tones. When the painting is partly dry, medium tones are used to pull some of the darker tones towards the lighter ones. In this way the three tones of colour are blended. To give the contrast to the shape of the body, the artist painted the background in a dark colour. As soon as the painting dried off, he was able to lend it volume.

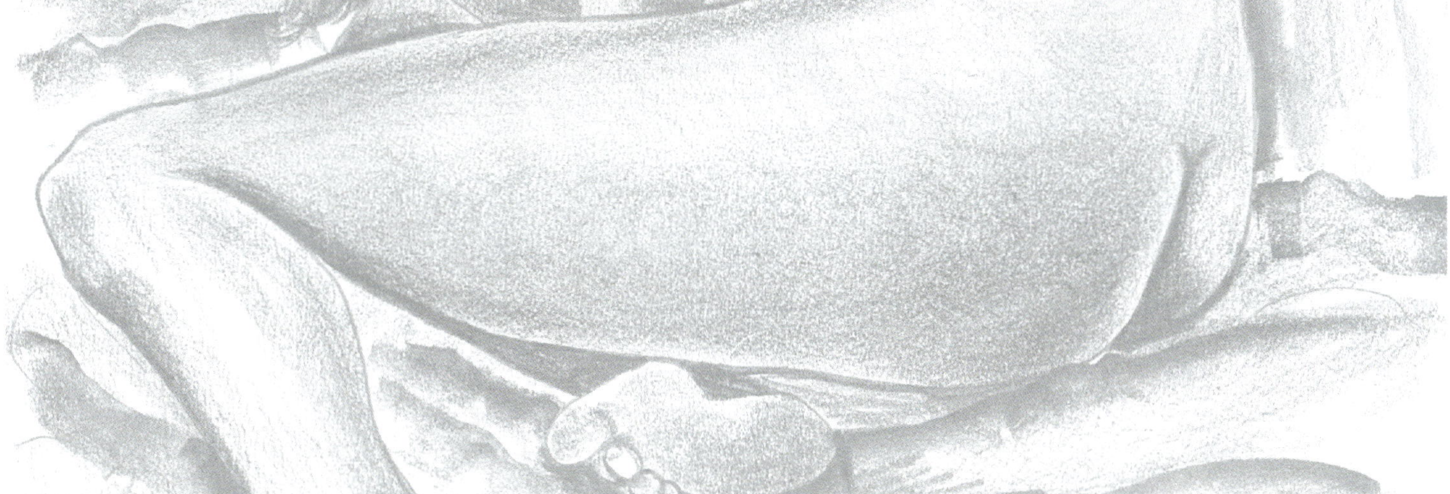

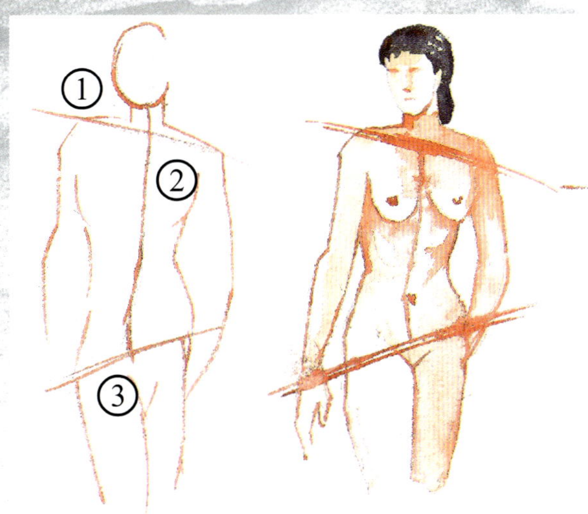

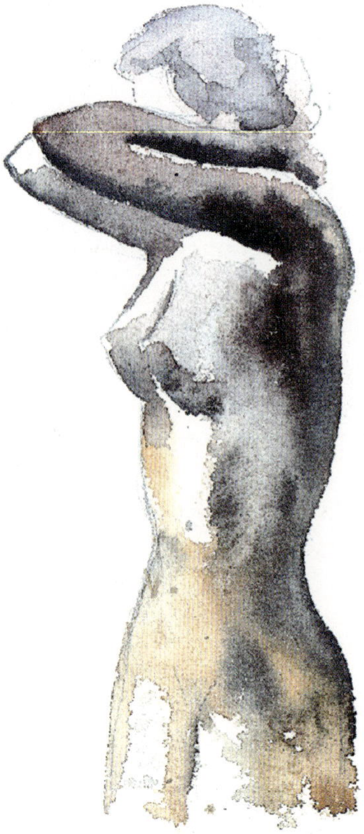

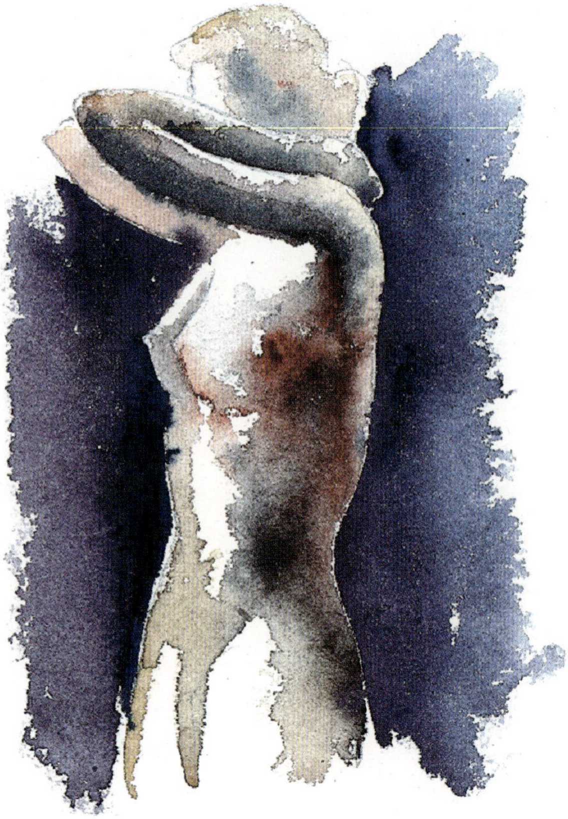

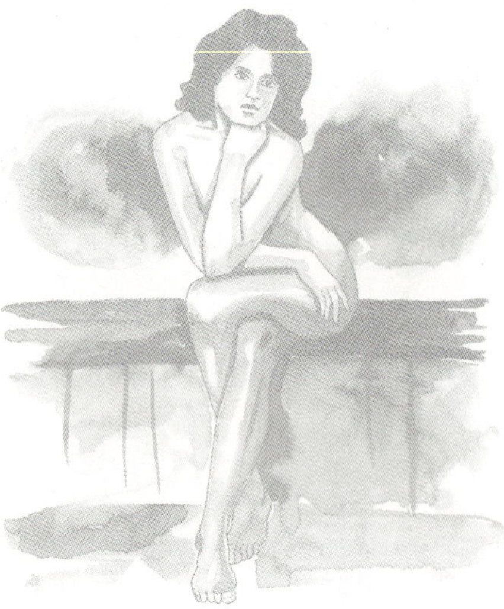

Helpful Hint

Always have two jars of water when working in watercolour. One of the jars of clean water for loading brushes and wetting the paper and one for rinsing the brushes while you work.

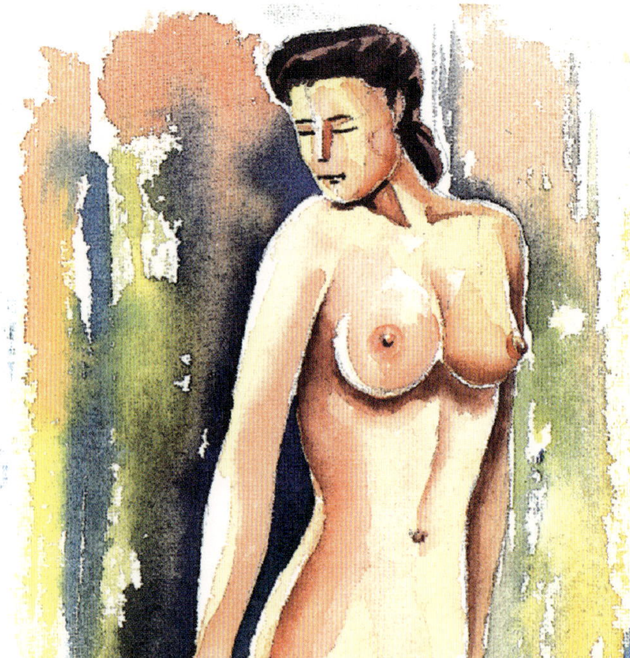

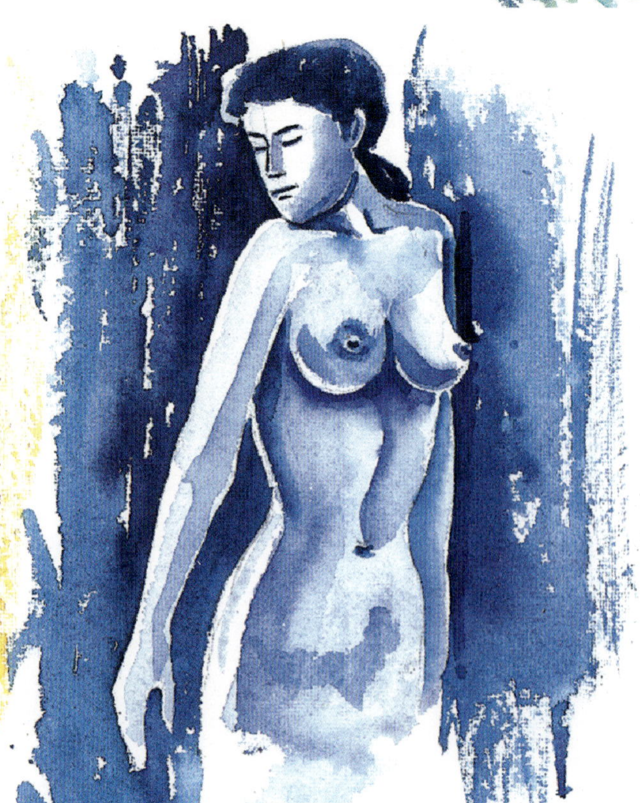

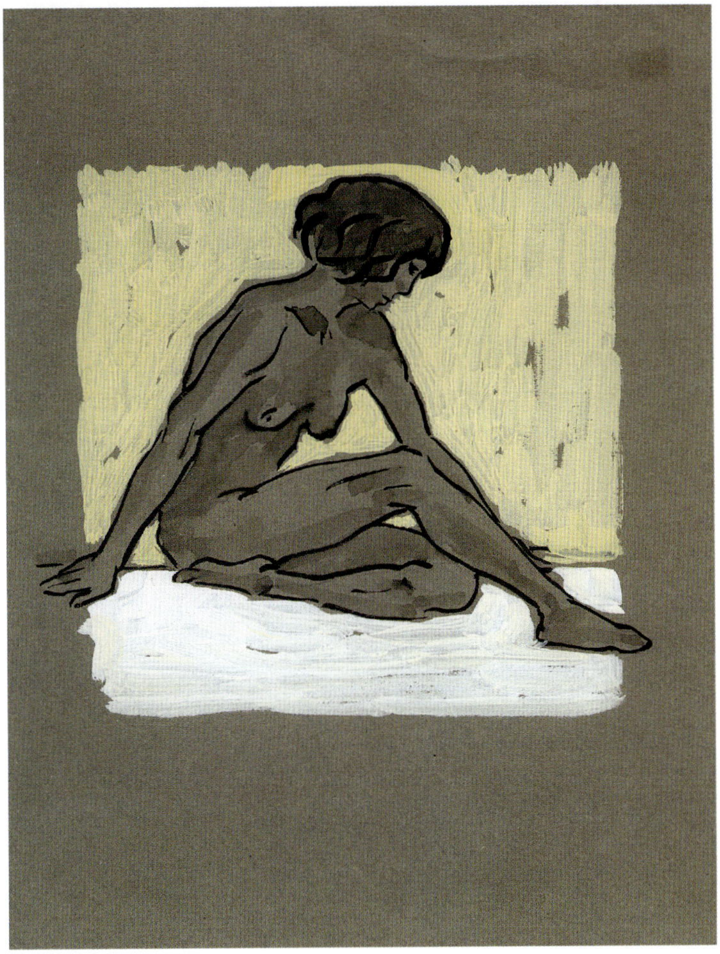

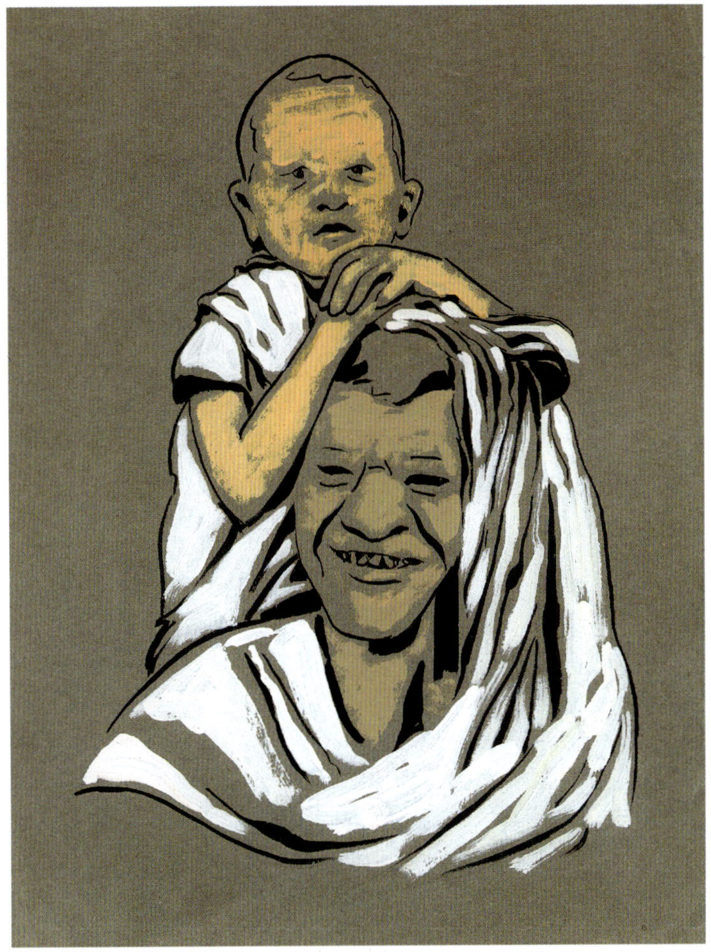

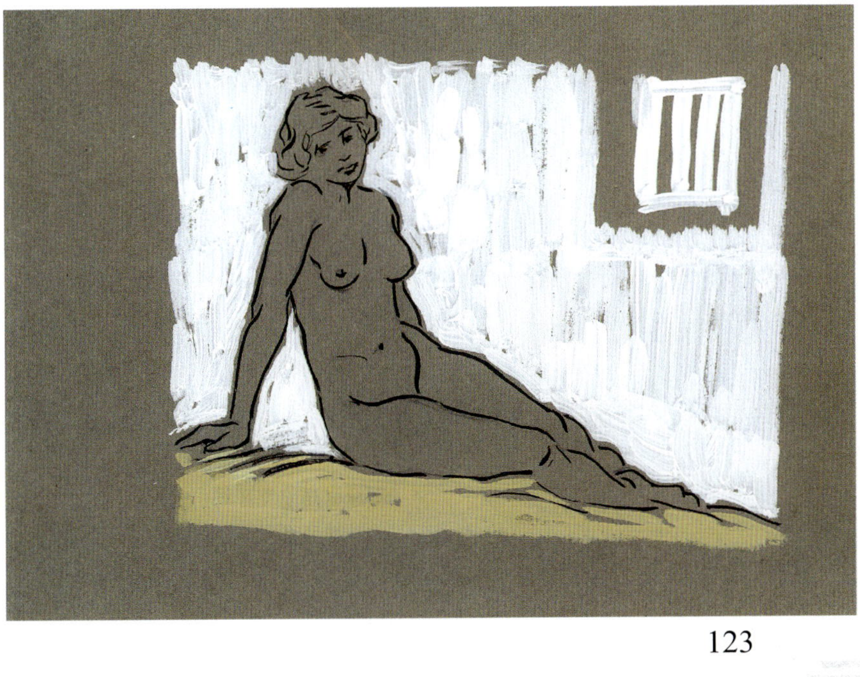

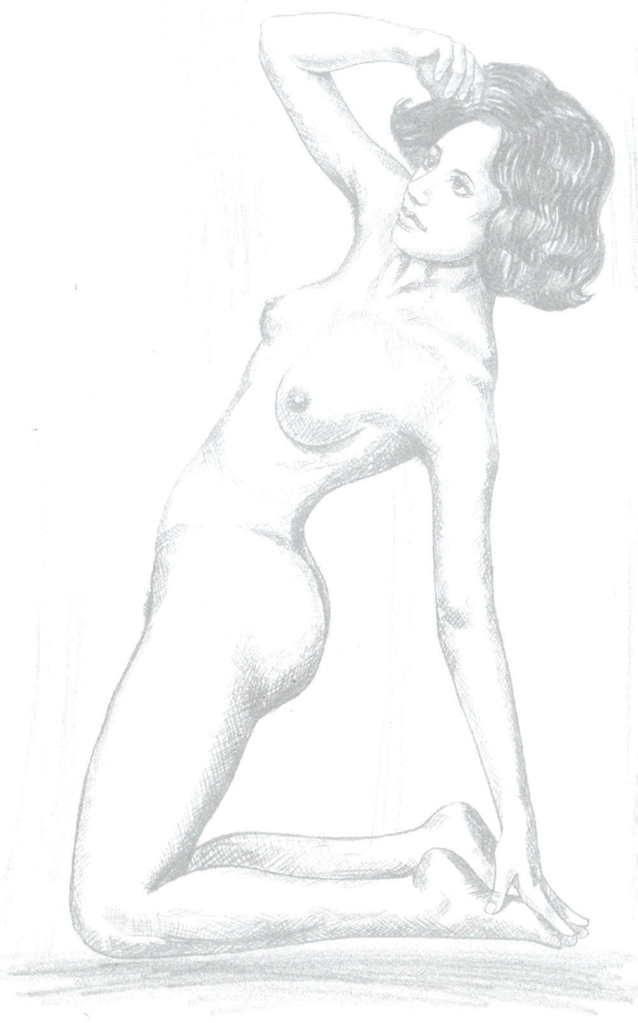

Painting Animals

Necessary practice is required for painting animals with colour. The first thing that an artist must work on before painting an animal is to study its body structure. Anatomical study is a must and you cannot jump this stage.

The structure of every animal can be translated in geometric shapes. Once the basic shape is made, it is easy to draw the animal by dividing it to show where the legs start. This helps to get the proportions of the animal right. In the preparatory stage, these lines help you in understanding the shape, however, complicated it may be.

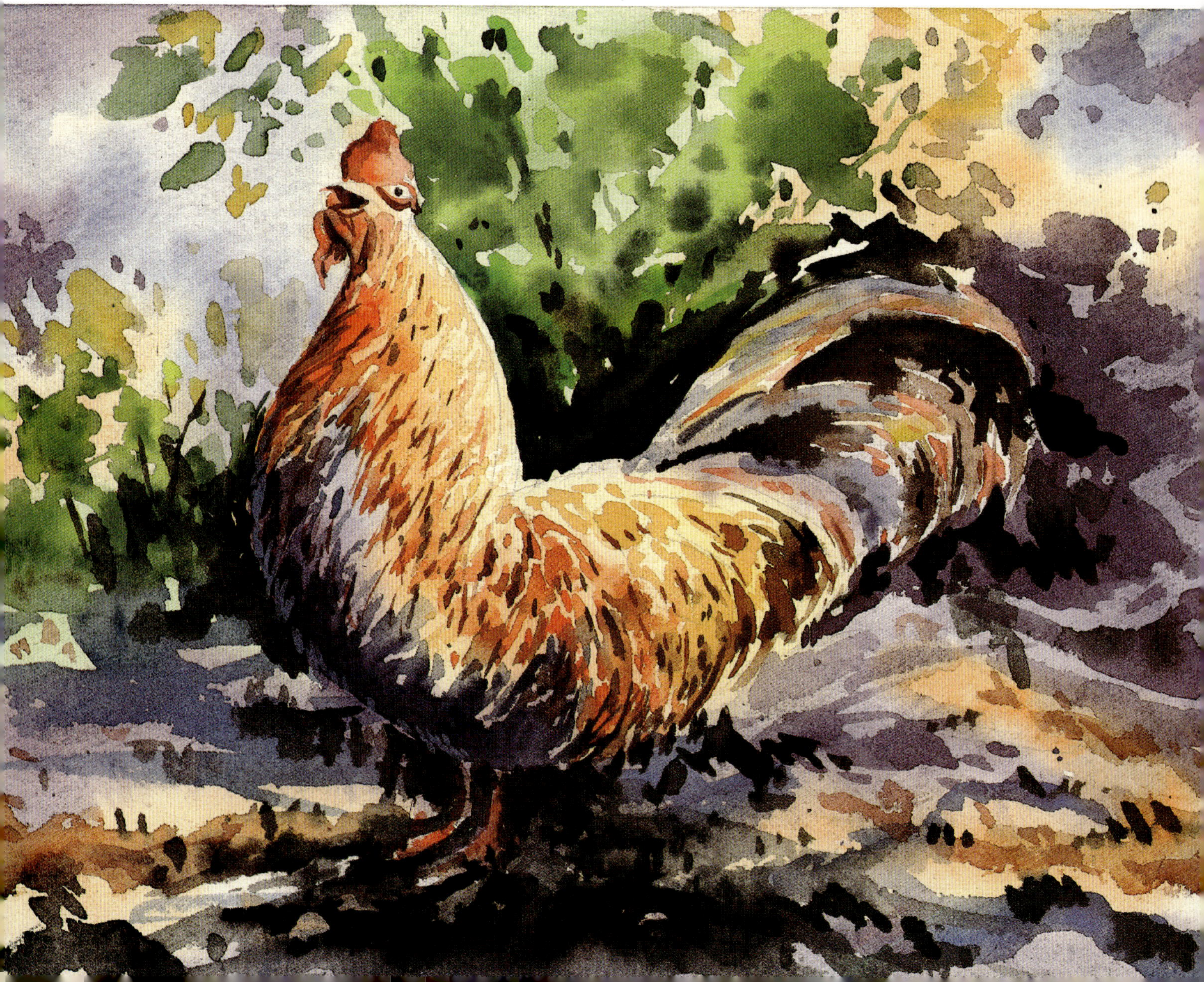

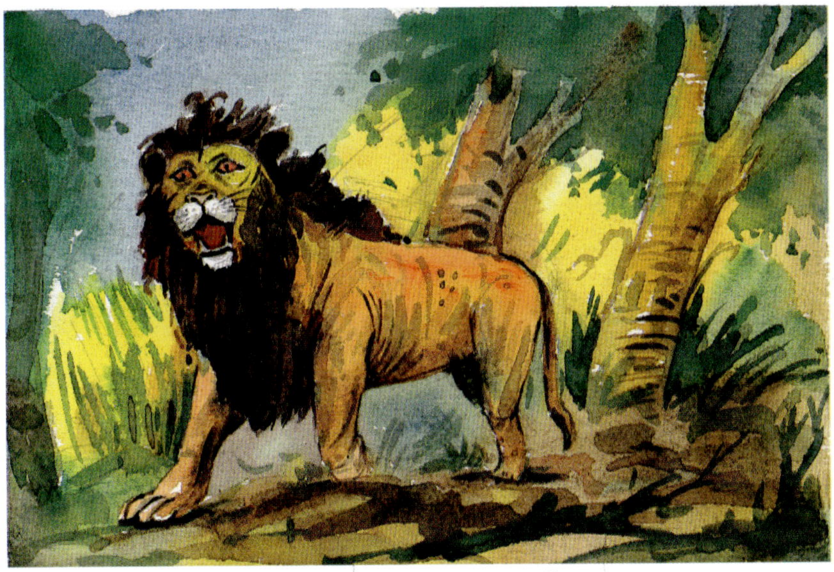

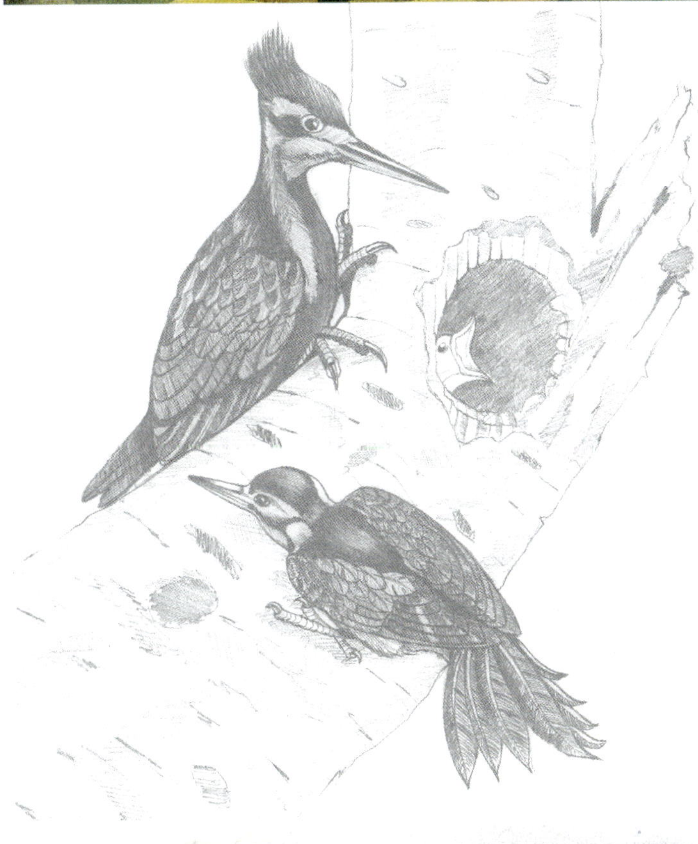

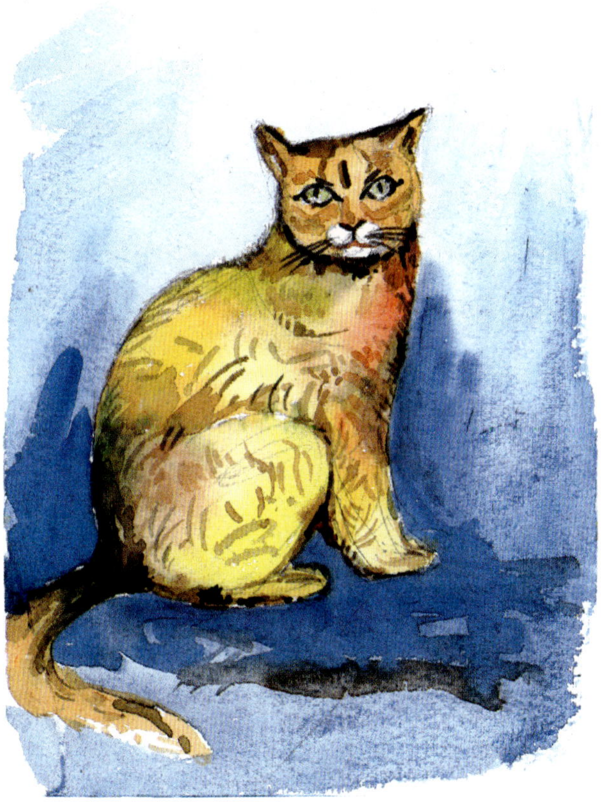

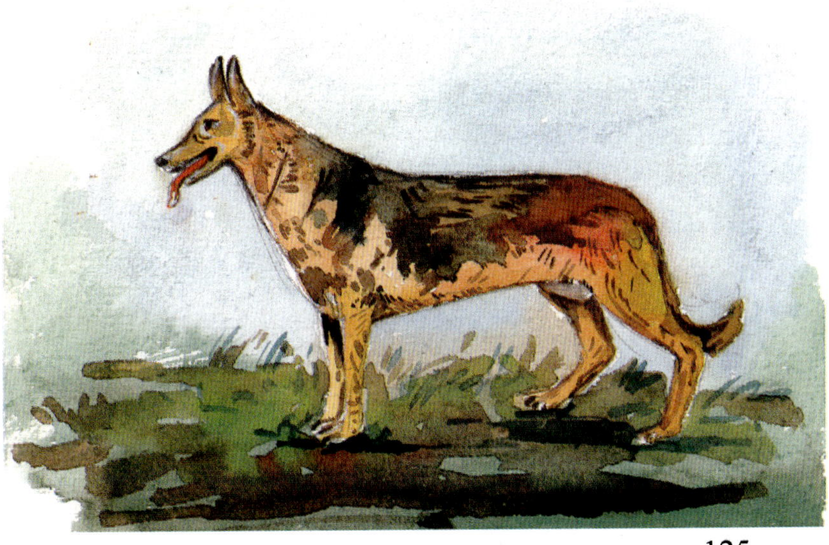

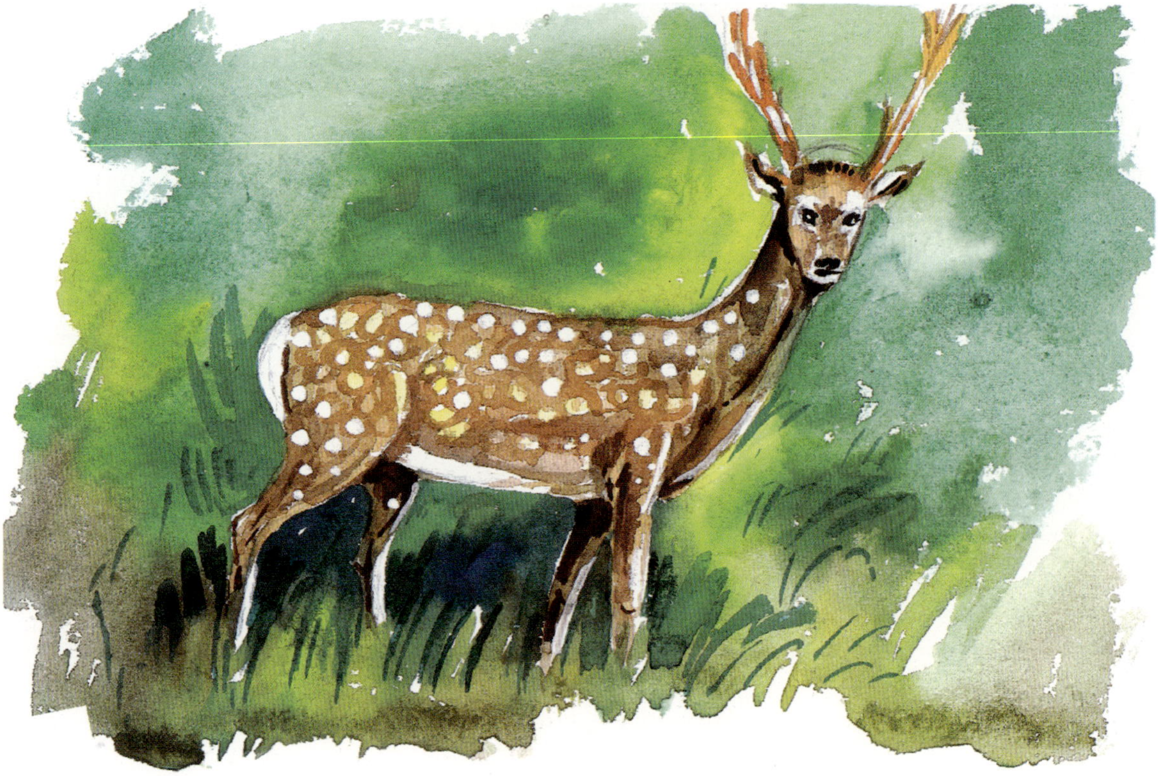

Helpful Hint

Always let one wash dry before painting over it. If you are impatient and attempt to paint on to a damp wash, you may create streaks and runs that ruin the effect of smooth, clean water.

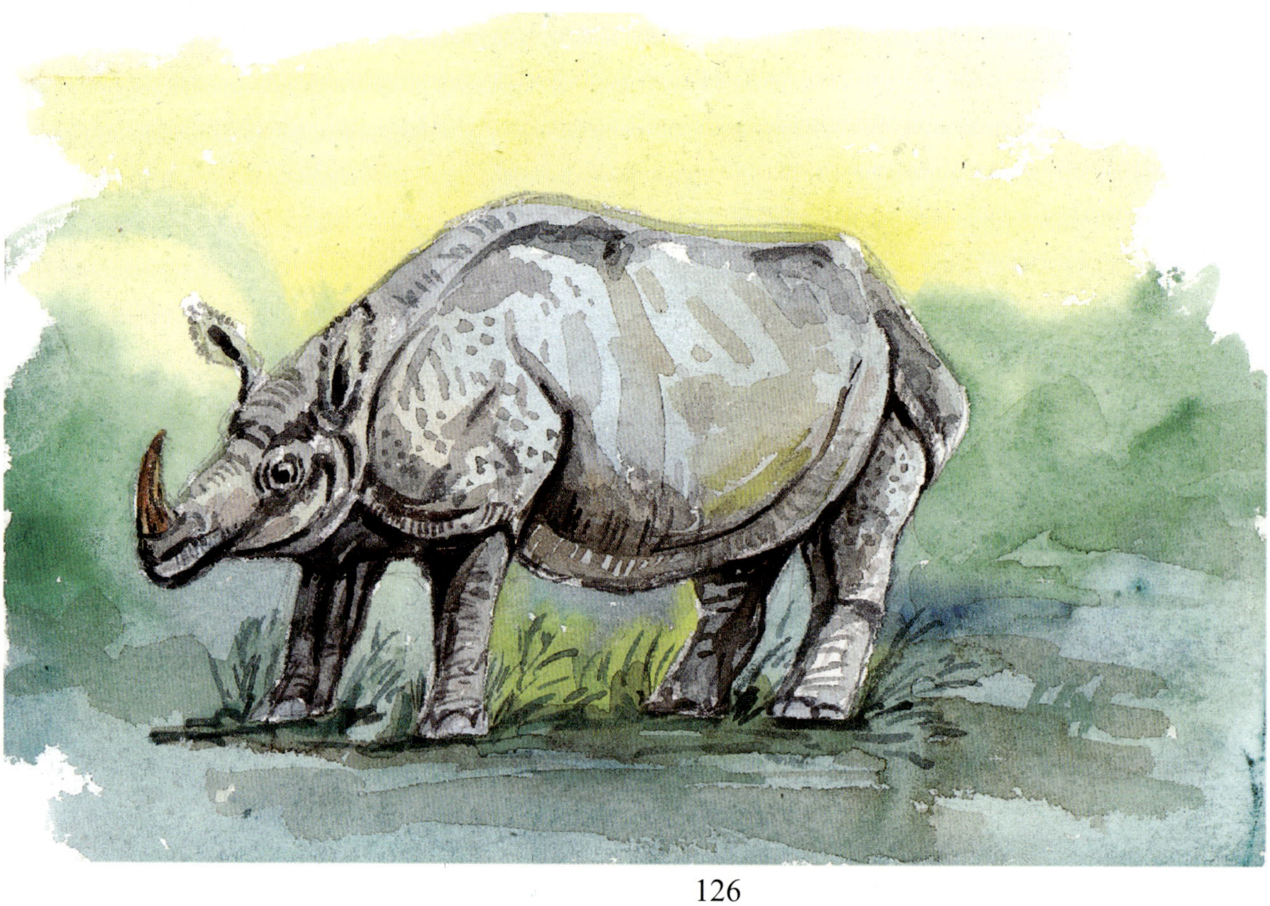

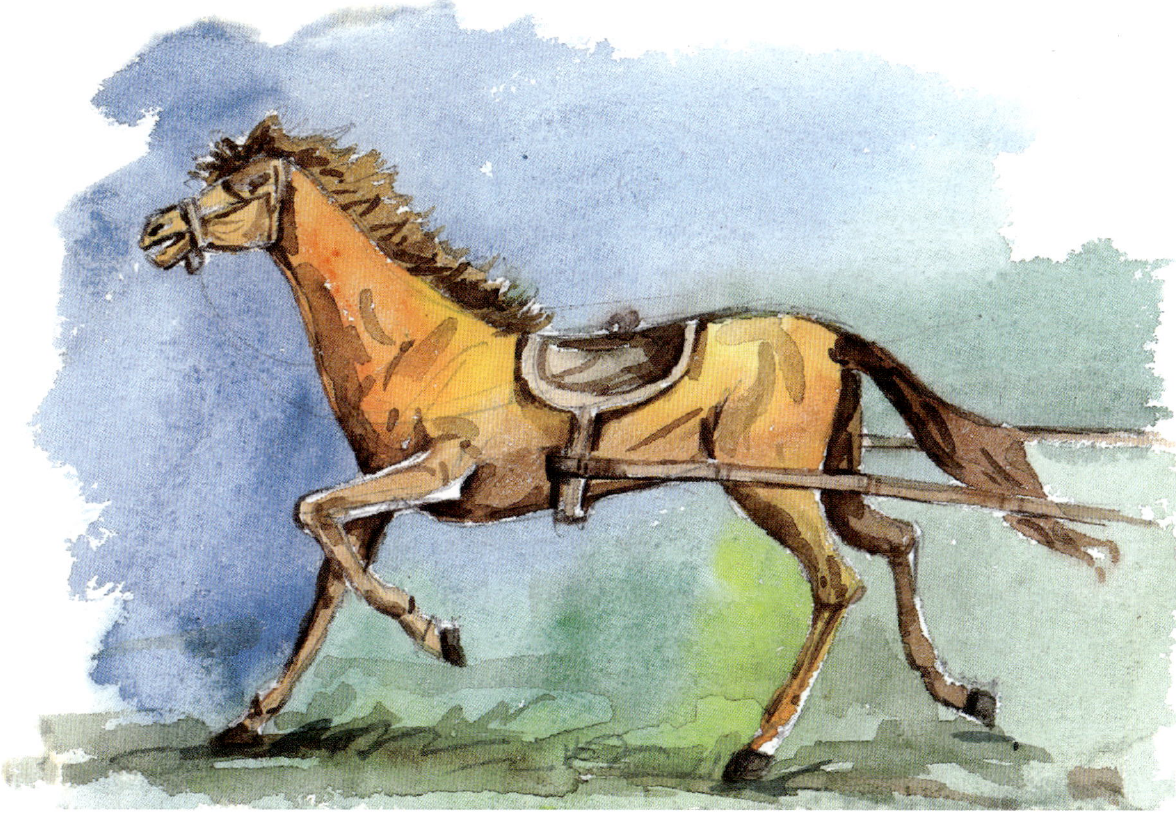

The artist has made the basic shape of the horse. Having done so, he drawn the lines of its form. This then helped to get the proportion of its body right. Proportions, measurements, shadows and highlights must be studied before painting.

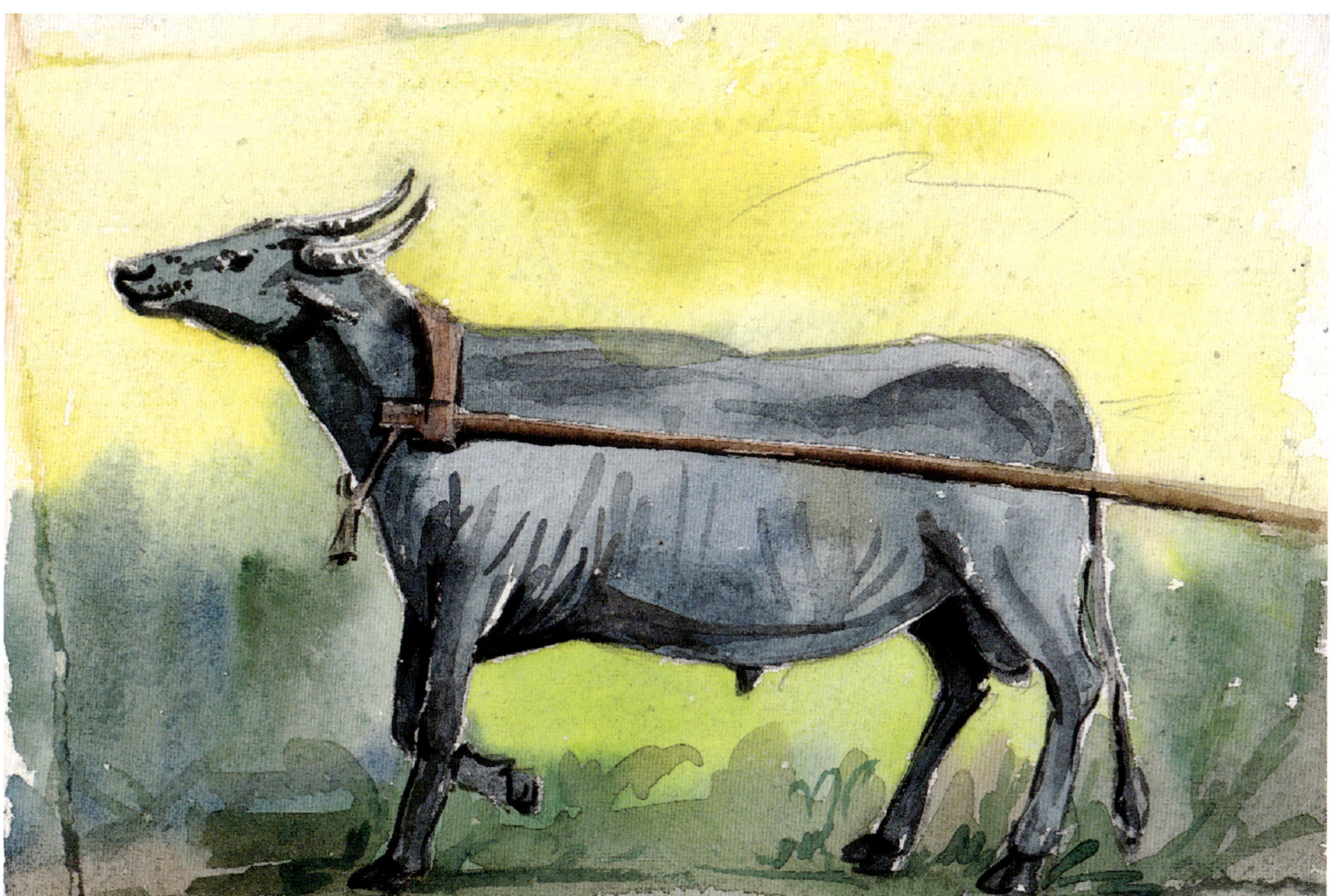

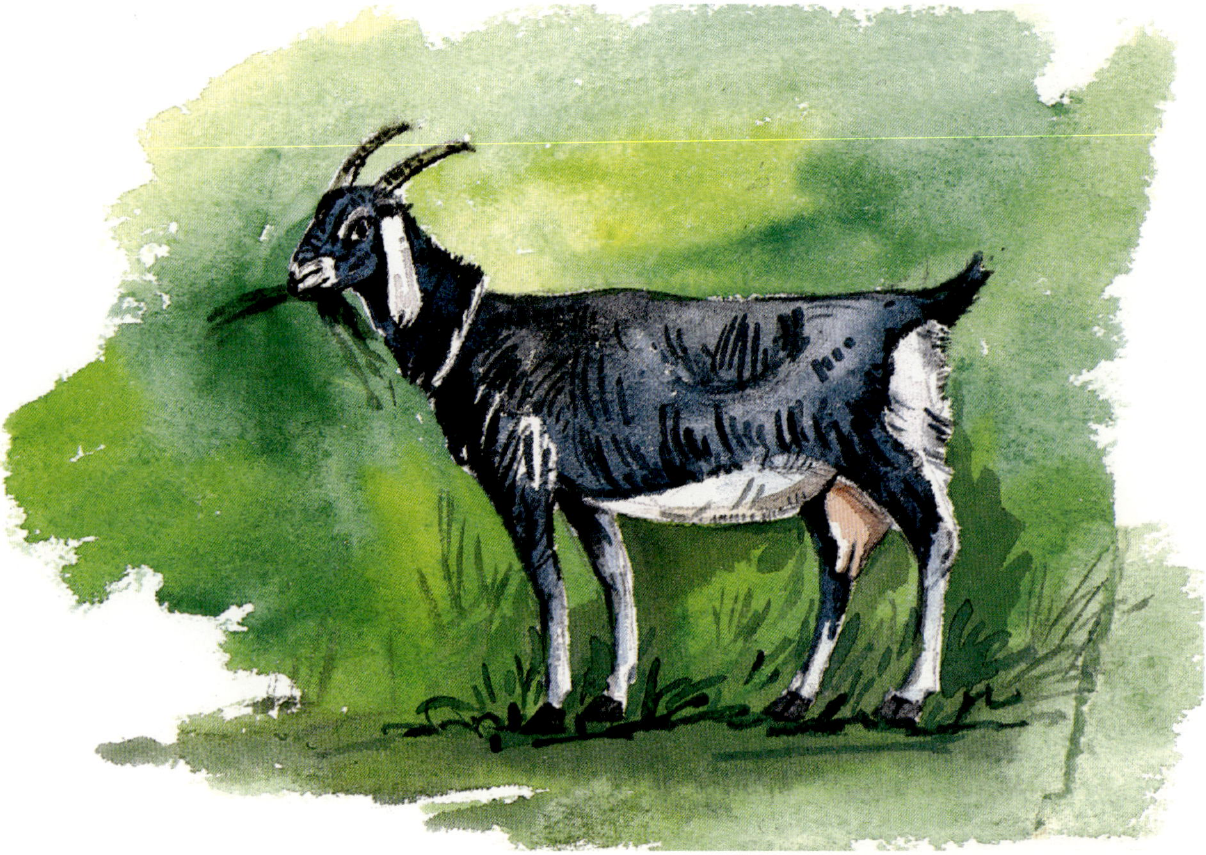

Animals

Animals possess their own specific qualities which arouse our interest and invite us to capture them in drawing. The first thing is the study of its anatomy, proportion, peculiarities, shape, and delicacy, massiveness, power, colour and structure of skin or coat, action and functions of the body in movement.

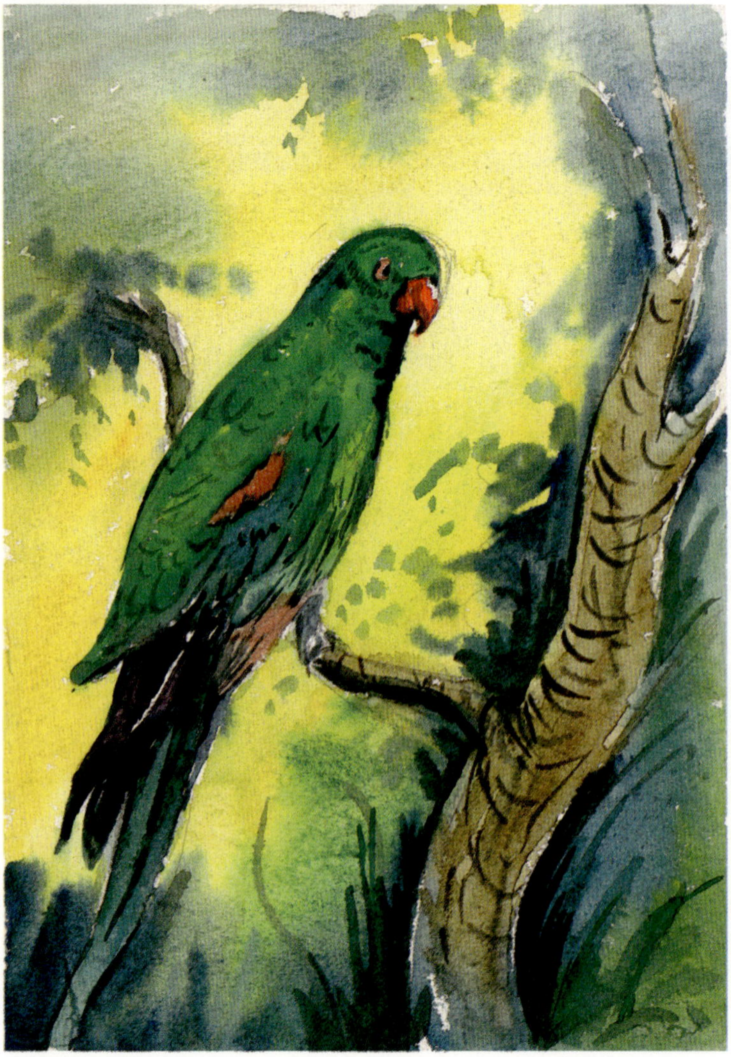

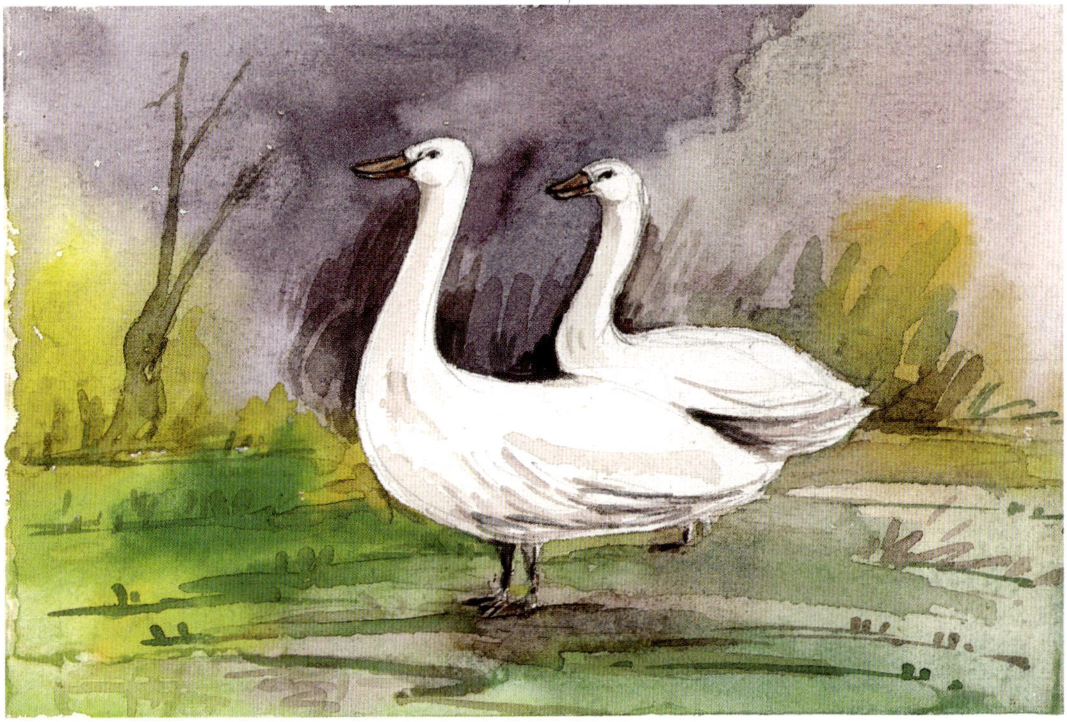

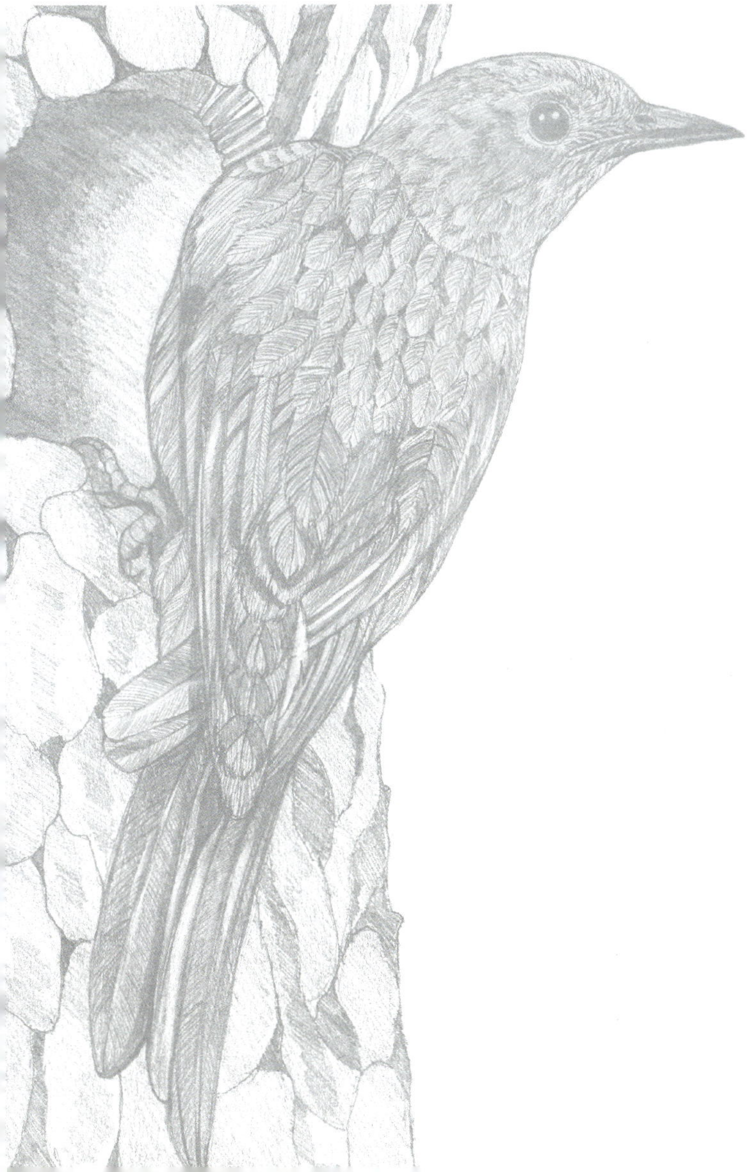

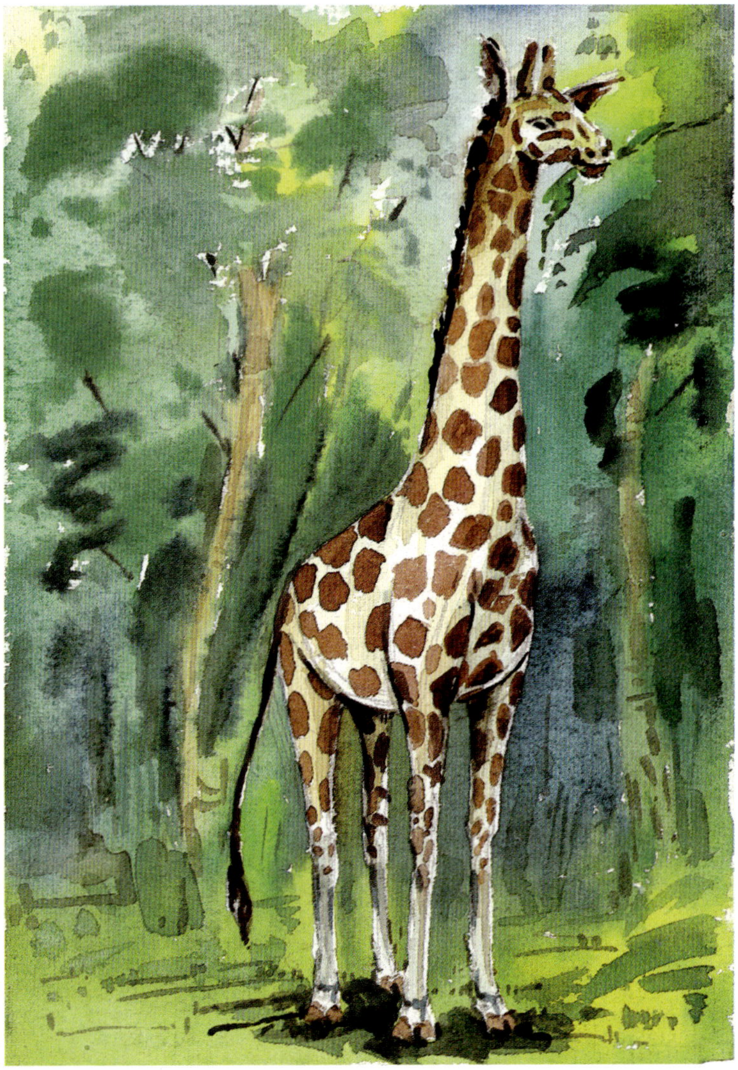

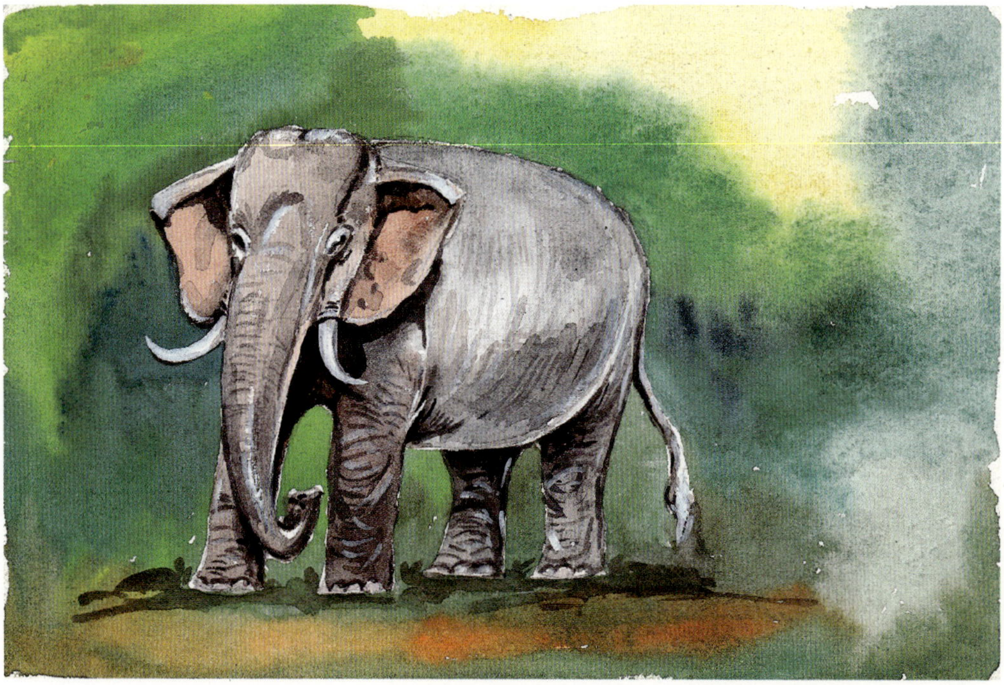

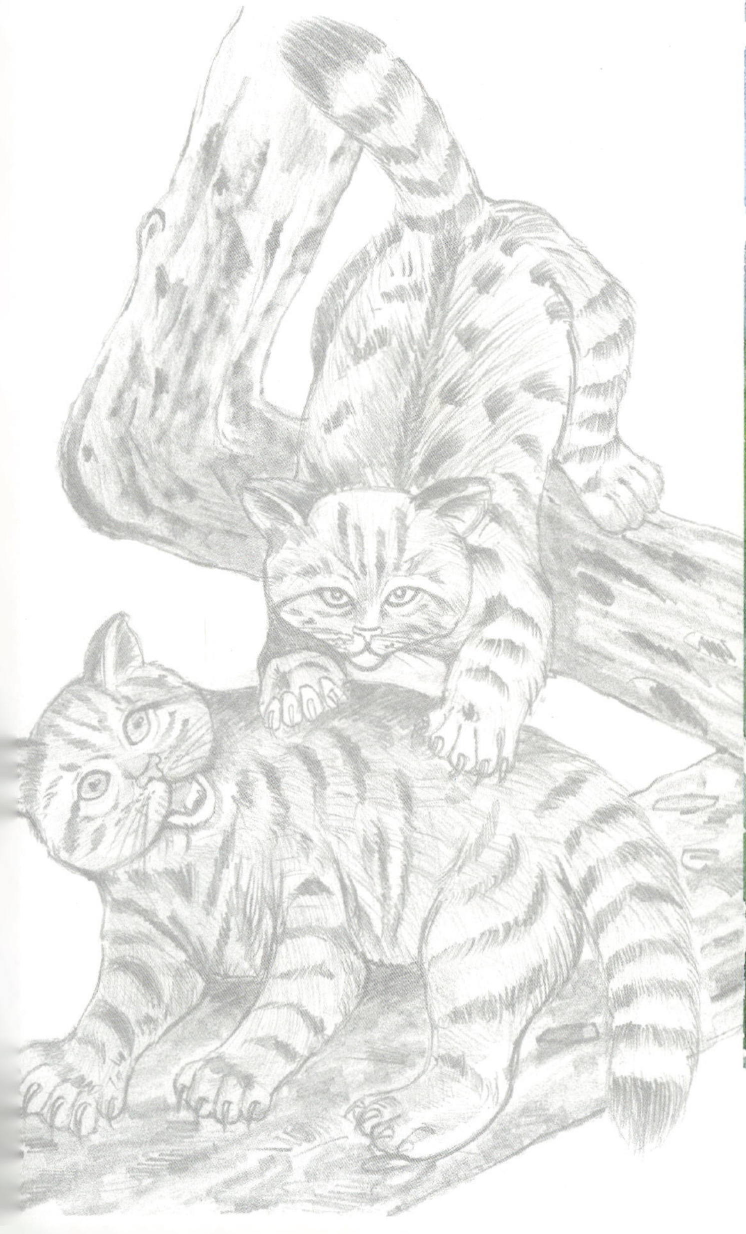

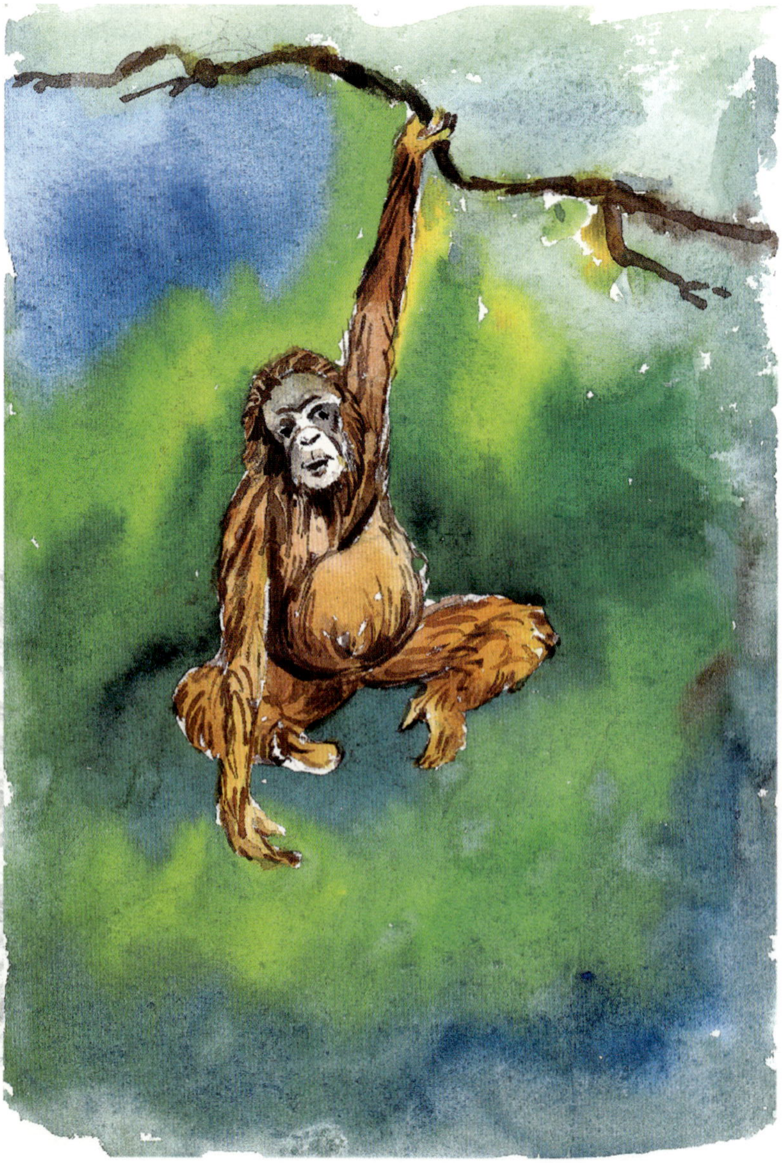

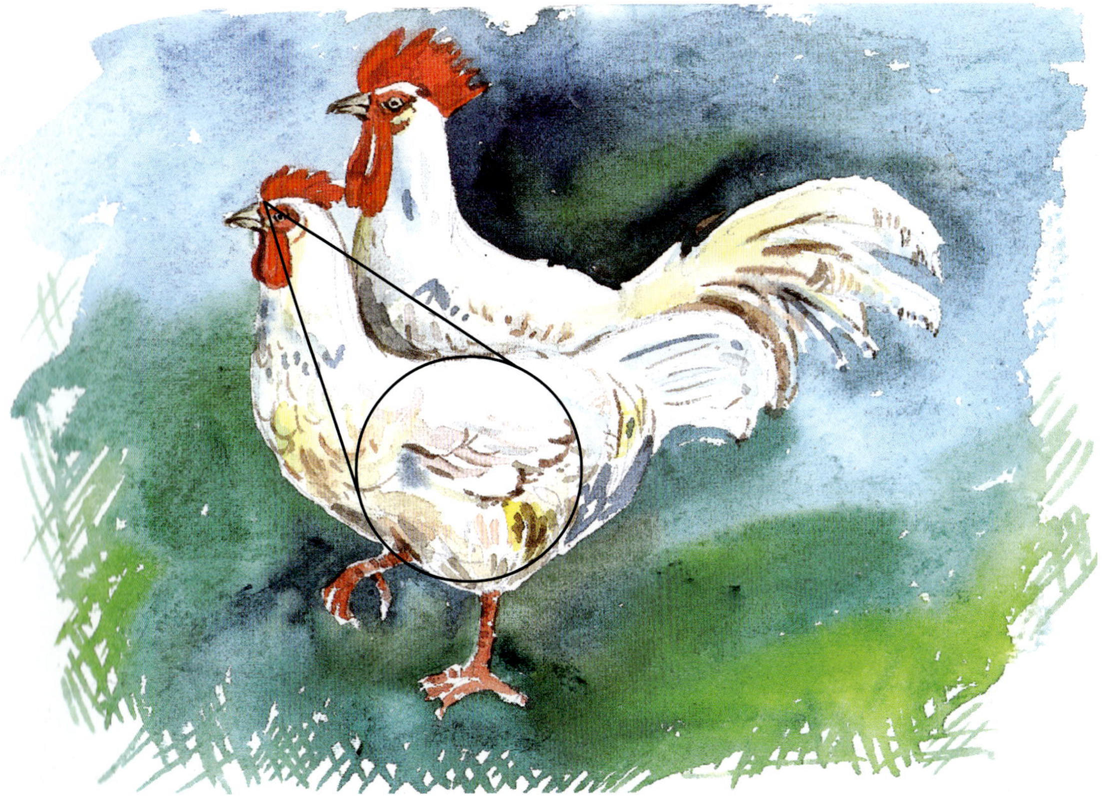

Observe this drawing. The circle describes the body and the triangle for the neck and head. No matter what the pose of the cock this geometric shape will describe it. Once the drawing is complete, the painting process is begun with. The comb is painted with red.

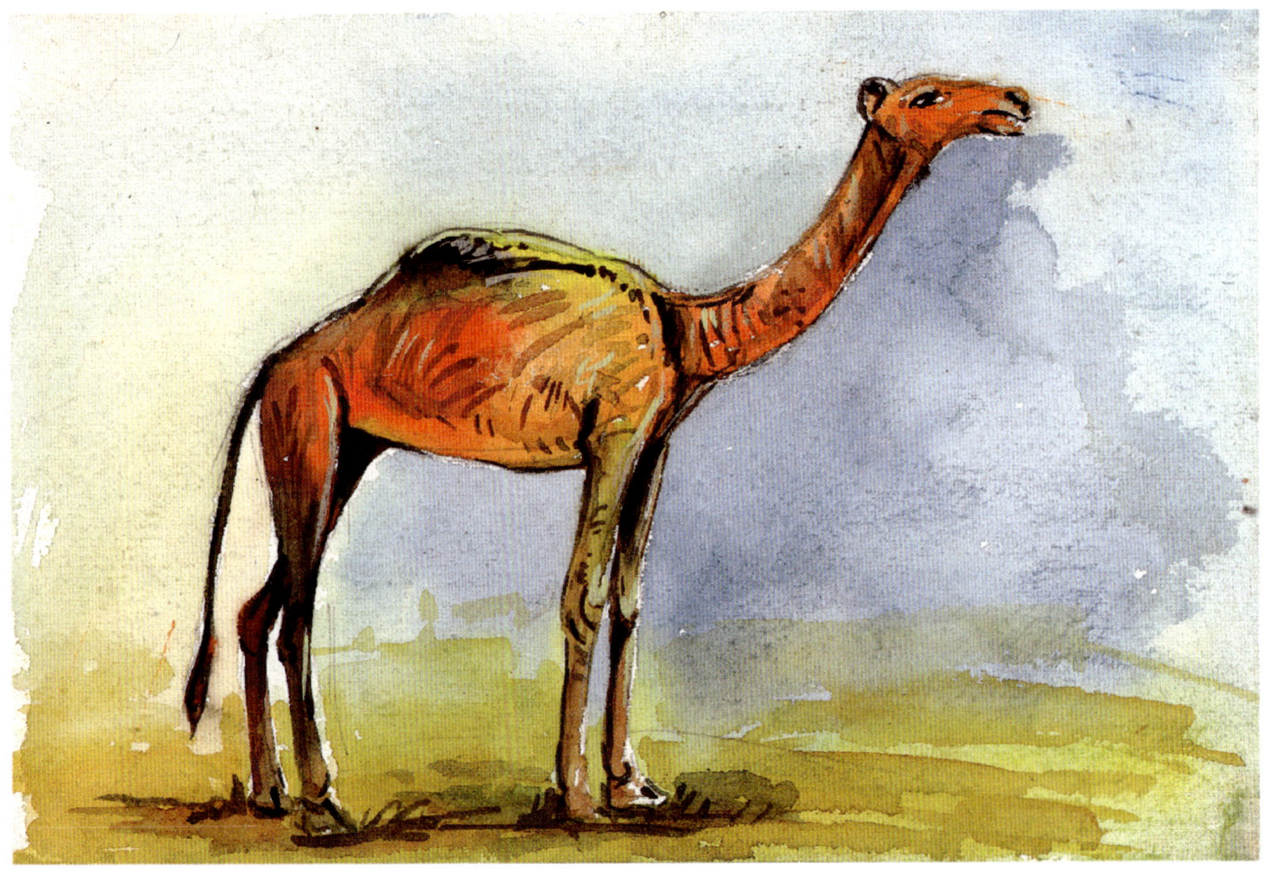

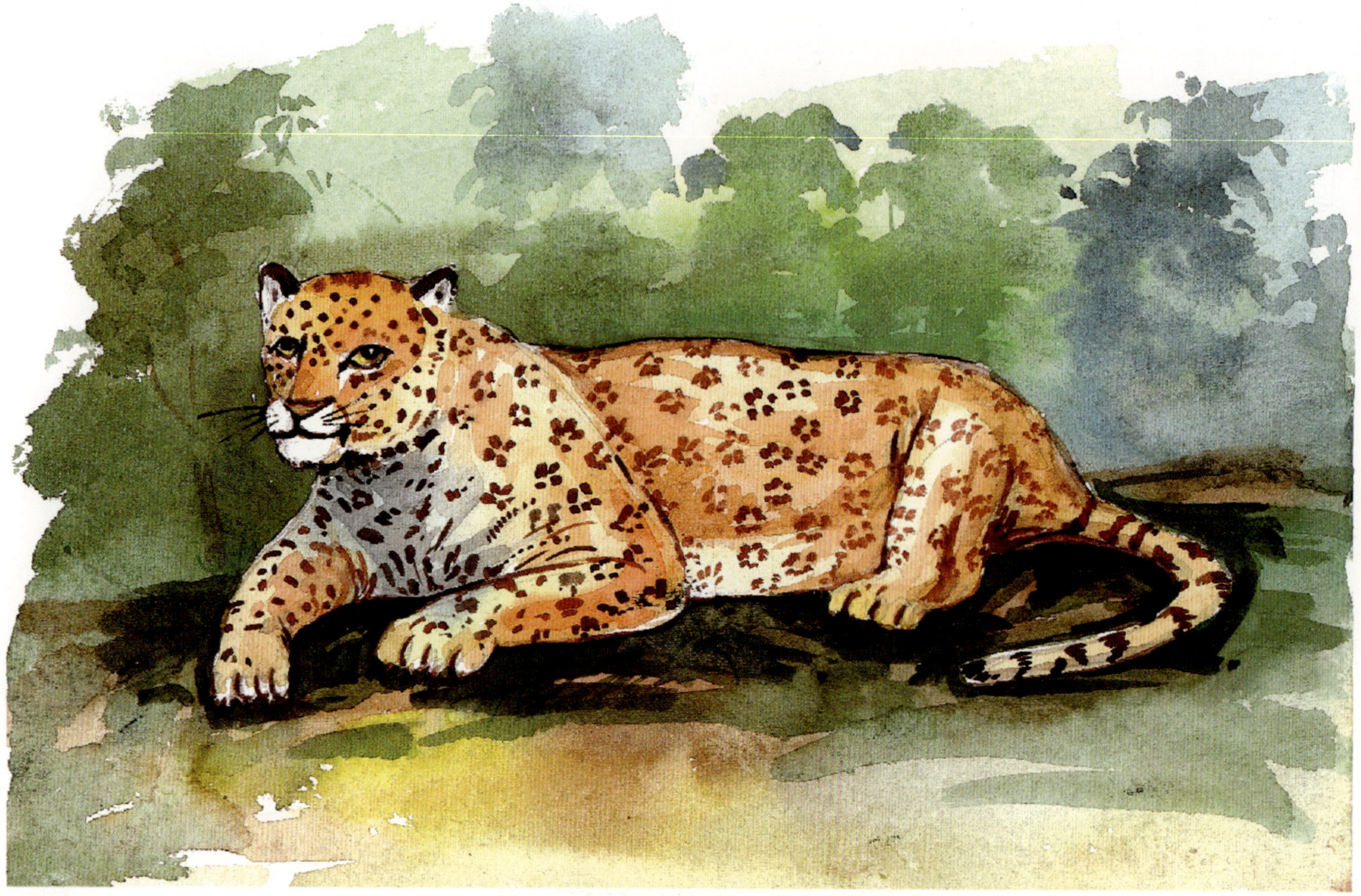

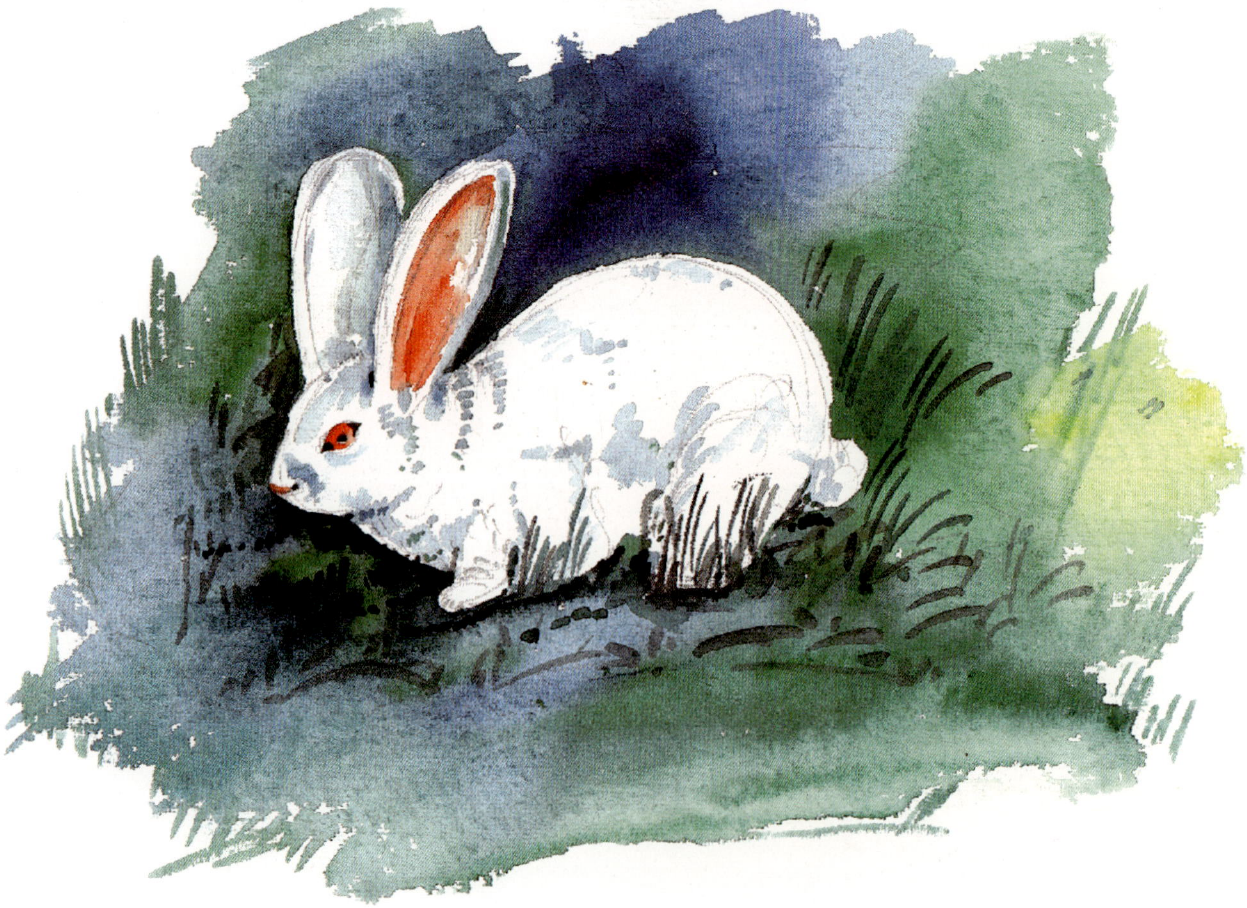

